3—

WHO KILLED CBS?

PETER J. BOYER

WHO KILLED CBS ?

**The Undoing of
America's Number One
News Network**

Random House/New York

For My Family
Kari Granville Boyer
Samuel and Eleanor Jane
and
My Mother and Father

Library of Congress Cataloging-in-Publication Data

Boyer, Peter J.
Who killed CBS?

Includes index.
1. Columbia Broadcasting System, inc.
2. Broadcasting—United States. I. Title.
HE8689.8.B69 1988 384.54'55'0973 87-42650
ISBN 0-394-56034-5

Manufactured in the United States of America
98765432
First Edition

Acknowledgments

I SHOULD FIRST express my gratitude to my editor at Random House, Rebecca Saletan, who suggested this book and who subsequently managed to maintain her humor and patience, even when both must have been sorely tested.

This book means to tell the story of a great American institution during a time of dire change, roughly 1980 to the present (the post-Cronkite era). Telling that story requires an understanding of what CBS News had been—its history and its place in our history. A number of books were helpful in that regard, but I found to be of particular value Ann Sperber's monumental biography of Edward R. Murrow, *Murrow: His Life and Times;* David Halberstam's *The Powers That Be;* Barbara Matusow's *The Evening Stars;* and, especially, Gary Paul Gates's spirited history of CBS News, *Air Time.*

The television press played an increasingly important role at CBS News in this period, and I relied upon hundreds of newspaper and magazine articles, both for an account of events and for a reading of the emerging doctrine of the new CBS News, often dispensed as subtext in the press. Particularly valuable were Cheryl Lavin's lengthy 1983 profile of Van Sauter in the *Chicago Tribune,* and Ron Rosenbaum's article in the November 1982 issue of *Esquire,* which captured first and best what the new age at CBS News was all about—the triumph of "moments."

However, the greater part of the material for this book by far was drawn from hundreds of hours of individual interviews with the people of CBS News, present and past. I would like to acknowledge Dan Rather and Van Sauter, each of whom had reason to be cautious about this project, but who nonetheless cooperated with remarkable openness. Howard Stringer, the current president of CBS News, and Richard Leibner, a major player in this drama, also gave generously of their time. Special thanks should also go to Dick Salant, Sandy Socolow, Bud Benjamin, Bill Leonard, Robert Chandler, Walter Cronkite, and Ernie Leiser, all of whom kindly indulged endless follow-up calls.

The scores of other men and women who shared their memories and anecdotes with me, some of whose input is apparent in the text and others of whom would prefer not to be publicly acknowledged, were no less valuable, and my gratitude to them is no less deeply felt.

I also thank Joel Heller, who was determinedly invaluable as a source but whose generous technical help—his fluency in the mysterious tongue of XyWrite—is greatly appreciated.

Most important, I'd like to thank my wife, Kari Granville Boyer, a fine editor, whose help and encouragement were essential.

WHO KILLED CBS?

Prelude

ONE OCTOBER DAY IN 1985 the generations of CBS News came together in church, St. Bartholomew's on Park Avenue, to hear prayers and lamentations for the dead. There was rancor in the crowded sanctuary.

The occasion was a memorial service for Charles Collingwood, one of the icons of CBS News, who had died a week earlier after a terrible struggle with cancer. As the strains of a Bach prelude faded into the high spaces of the old church, Dan Rather stepped up to the pulpit and beseeched his brethren to be of good cheer. "Charles would have wanted it that way," he said. But even as he spoke, Rather well knew that CBS News had become a bitterly divided place, electric with intrigue and ill will. Two of the people in the crowd before him, colleagues, had approached him that very morning, asking the anchorman to use his influence to keep Edward M. Joyce, the president of CBS News, away from the memorial service. (Rather refused, but the request was natural enough; Rather himself was feuding with Joyce, as everyone in the organization knew.)

But Rather, who is given to the romance of things, had wanted the occasion to be remembered as a great moment in the history of CBS News, and months later, even after the feelings and forces so evident that day had played themselves out, in some cases to disastrous effect, Rather still held to the belief that it had been a great day for CBS. And in some ways it was.

CBS News alone in broadcasting would even pretend to such an event, which more resembled a state funeral than a journalist's memorial. There were the lords of broadcasting, including William S. Paley, the founder of CBS and the patron of broadcast news, and the rank of Collingwood contemporaries, the totems of their times—Eric Sevareid, Walter Cronkite, Richard C. Hottelet, Theodore H. ("Teddy") White. There was no spare room in the 1,200-seat sanctuary. One member of the church, a friend of Collingwood's, told Sevareid that she'd never seen so many people attend an afternoon service; St. Bartholomew's had seen nothing like it since Herbert Hoover had lain in state there.

Collingwood was, in a way, the personification of the CBS legend—suave, handsome, daring, and more talented than someone with such portions of those other qualities had a right to be. The "Duke" his friends called him, one of "Murrow's boys," that extraordinary collection of journalists assembled by Edward R. Murrow, the patron saint of CBS News, in World War II Europe. Collingwood was a Rhodes scholar who left Oxford for the romance of reporting just as the biggest story of the century was unfolding and, as fate had it, just as CBS was inventing a new journalism—that of the airwaves. Collingwood reported from Rheims; he was on the scene when British and American troops invaded North Africa; he was there, on Omaha Beach, at D day, and reported the signing of the armistice. Collingwood and the others of Murrow's boys—Sevareid, Hottelet, Howard K. Smith, William Shirer, Bob Trout, Larry LeSueur—were an uncommonly gifted lot, in the way that founding generations are. They were scholarly, urbane, stylish, and they all were brilliant reporters. They legitimized broadcast journalism with their skill and their daring—Murrow's harrowing accounts of the London blitz, heart-stopping reports of night raids over Berlin, Collingwood struggling with a wet and bulky recorder in the fury of Omaha Beach—and then, through their passion and the manifest power of their medium, they elevated their craft to a level above the rest, creating tradition as they went.

"It was a marvelous way to begin a career," Sevareid would say, remembering that time. "We became household words, far too young and undeserving, but that was the nature of it. There had never been anything like it before; this was the first truly new form of journalism created since block print had come along." It was a time, Paul White (then the director of news, based in New York) used to say, of "a fine, careless rapture."

In the CBS legend Murrow's boys had done nothing less than invent broadcast journalism. And the legend was not far from the truth. When the end of the war came, the CBS team, euphoric, gathered at the bar of the Hôtel Scribe in Paris and vowed, as Murrow put it, to "go back and show what we can do in peace." So they did, pushing, reluctantly at first, into the new medium, television, and attracting a new generation of broadcast journalists drawn by the glow of the CBS News cachet. Long after Murrow was gone and CBS News had become a profit center in cutthroat competition for ratings, to work at CBS News still meant, by some wishful extension, to be one of Murrow's boys. They were the best.

So a gathering such as the Collingwood memorial took on the aspects of ritual peculiar to CBS, a reaffirmation of the faith, with all the elements of the great moment that Rather sought.

But there was an edge to the occasion that day, something quite apart from the grieving for Collingwood, a kind of seething that was almost palpable; a trace of it worked its way into the service.

Morley Safer, who, like Rather, had been taken under Collingwood's wing during a tour of duty in the London bureau—given advice on everything from attire to writing and broadcasting technique, and generally polished up by the older correspondent—was sitting in the front with the other speakers that day and didn't feel it at first. Then, up on the platform and speaking of Collingwood, he looked out at the congregation and saw the full sweep of CBS News, 1,000 faces, most of which he knew. He looked down at the row of executives and saw Mr. Paley, the founder, who had decreed that there would be a CBS News and had put it into a kind of gilded cage, where it could thrive apart from the rest of the corporation; in the same row sat Thomas H. Wyman, the chairman of CBS and the new generation of management, who had come to CBS from the Pillsbury Company. Things were not the same under Wyman, not at all, and Safer thought, seeing Wyman sitting in this gathering of CBS News people, judging just from the look on his face, "He probably has only the dimmest idea who Collingwood was and only the dimmest interest in this assembly of people." Paley had known Collingwood well, but to Wyman, Safer thought, this was probably just an interruption in an otherwise busy day. Still looking at the executives, he added to his talk, "It was Murrow and Charles and a few others who made the mere *business* enterprise of CBS into a proud and vital moving part of the American democracy!" And he felt that he had made a necessary point.

Then Rather, pausing before introducing the next speaker, said something that struck some as strangely two-sided: "If you wanted to make Charles Collingwood's neck swell"—a favorite down-home Ratherism for "angry"—"one way . . . was to knock CBS in any way, in any way, shape, or form."

Near the back of the church Bill Moyers was getting edgy. All this talk about how great Collingwood was, all this company boosterism! Hadn't this same CBS News abandoned Collingwood's kind of reporting, *serious* reporting? Moyers, who'd lost his producer and prime-time opportunity to a show he considered trivial fluff, *West 57th,* certainly knew about *that.* He suddenly stood up and left the church, muttering to a startled usher, producer Sanford ("Sandy") Socolow, on the way out: "Hypocrites! If he was so great, why didn't they put him on the air?"

Many of Collingwood's friends at CBS, including his longtime producer, Les Midgley, would have argued that Collingwood's personal problems had hindered his later career, that the company had been, in fact, quite generous toward him. But Collingwood was almost beside the point; to oppose was the point.

Charles Kuralt, the gentle, poetic Carolinian, an unlikely rabble-rouser, was the final speaker that day, chosen for his ability to capture the mood of a place or a time or a man with poignancy and heart. And he did just that, though it was not what the planners of the program had expected. Kuralt mentioned the unmentionable, that the sainted Murrow himself had become embittered over his treatment at CBS, and he recollected a conversation between Murrow and Collingwood that fitted perfectly with the dark, angry mood of the day. "He remembered, he told me once, that Murrow had told him that this is a business, after all, and people can be discarded in it," Kuralt said. "And something like that happened to him in his professional life. There came those years when Charles was the most honored of all of us, and the most respected, and not on the air very much. He accepted that puzzling turn of events with great dignity, as he accepted everything in his life, but not with much happiness."

And so it ended. The Reverend Bruce W. Forbes, surely meaning no irony, offered St. Francis's prayer for peace: "Lord, make us instruments of your peace. Where there is hatred, let us sow love; where there is injury, pardon; where there is discord, union. . . ."

Rather thanked Reverend Forbes, paid his respects to Collingwood's family, and left the church. As he descended the steps into the sunlight of that bright October day, something startling happened, something, Rather recalled, "almost surreal." A colleague came to his side and, indicating Ed Joyce, said, "Can you imagine CBS News being led by the likes of that?" Rather didn't know what to say. He continued down the steps, and a second colleague, a distinguished older CBS News correspondent, approached Rather and fairly hissed, "If you don't do anything else, get rid of that son of a bitch!"

Rather turned up Park Avenue and walked the several blocks back to the CBS Broadcast Center on West Fifty-seventh Street, but for many of the rest, the ritual spilled over into the Century Club on Forty-third Street. The elegant and exclusive old lair, with its polished wood and creaky floors and literary air, its Winslow Homers on the walls (accepted long ago in lieu of membership dues from the artist), was perfect for a Collingwood wake. Nearly every afternoon at one-thirty, Collingwood had crossed the narrow passageway to the bar, where he'd order a Century martini (dry, served in a silver cup) and pack one of his Oval cigarettes and survey the outer rooms for suitable conversation. That afternoon the entire Billiard Room downstairs at the Century was given over to the Collingwood affair, and there, beneath a Homer etching called *The Lifeline*, the generations of CBS News drank and reminisced and bemoaned the passing of a better day.

In that airless basement room, on that uncommonly warm autumn day, it was not long—just a couple of drinks' worth of time—before the veiled antipathies of St. Bartholomew's Church grew less mute, the angry talk more reckless. Producers, correspondents, former CBS executives from an earlier time— the old guard—openly denounced the turn that the news division had taken in recent years, a turn away from the serious work that had made a career at CBS News, *their* careers, a special calling. Unspared in the excoriation was Ed Joyce, who, as president of the news division, happened to be the official host of the event (having not only approved it but signed the check paying for it—"a delicious irony," he later said). Fearing a scene, Joyce's deputy, Howard Stringer, warned his boss that the mood was ugly, but the warning wasn't necessary; Joyce had heard much of it.

But Joyce wasn't the only cause of the smoldering discontents that day, or even the principal cause; he was, in the view of most there, merely "a little clerk," as the old guard producer Ernest ("Ernie") Leiser put it, an agent for the true source of discord, who at that moment was happily oblivious of the antagonism at the Century. Van Gordon Sauter had gone fishing.

As president of CBS News for two and a half years, Sauter had turned the institution upside down, rejecting as old-fashioned, elitist, and simply irrelevant the very styles and philosophies that many thought had set CBS apart in broadcasting. He had conducted purges and forced exiles (deliberately keeping the former anchorman Cronkite off the *Evening News,* for example, because he saw him as a disruptive force) and had brought to CBS News values that many believed were more appropriate to entertainment than to the high and holy calling of Murrow and Collingwood. If those at the Collingwood gathering that day were the old CBS, the *true* CBS, then Sauter was the new; and the new, it seemed, was there to stay. Sauter was now ensconced at Black Rock, CBS's corporate headquarters, where, as an executive vice-president of the company, he was still in charge of CBS News. What's more, he'd left behind as news president his former assistant and best friend in the company, Ed Joyce.

"We weren't at Charlie Collingwood's funeral," said Don Hewitt, the *60 Minutes* producer; "we were all at our own funeral." Few among the old guard would have argued. They believed that CBS News as they'd known it had died in the last four years, poisoned by Van Gordon Sauter. Now they'd buried it. Cronkite said he realized that day that "the past wasn't prologue any longer," that the great Murrow continuum "had really come to a terminal point." The infidels, Joyce and Sauter, were inside the cathedral; corruption was complete; it could get no worse. But of course, it did.

Eighteen months later Joyce was gone, Sauter was gone, and CBS News was a brokenhearted and defeated institution. Its troubles had become a public diversion, the stuff of party chatter, network news reports, and Johnny Carson monologue jokes. There were budget cutbacks that made what had come before seem trifling; not just "fat" anymore but news-gathering capability was sliced away. The daily operating philosophy in the newsroom was a notion called "intelligent risk," a euphemism for the practice of guessing each morning which stories CBS News could *not* cover that day without too much embarrassment and thereby save money. CBS News had no correspondent covering the Supreme Court beat and no one in Central America, and it showed. Dan Rather was to sign his name to an article in the *New York Times* warning of a fall "from Murrow to mediocrity." Walter Cronkite, less publicly, was to try to get his corporate boss, a man named Laurence A. Tisch, to sign an oath essentially promising not to eviscerate CBS News utterly. And Tisch refused to sign.

The fall of CBS News is partly a story of shifts in the large forces beyond it: the economy; the political climate; technology. But more than anything else it is simply a story of human conflict, of the meeting of a man and his moment, Van Gordon Sauter at CBS News, and the ruinous developments that resulted. Sauter was president of CBS News for a relatively brief time, for a two-year period beginning in early 1982 and again for nine months of 1986. It was time enough to cause divisions that would never repair, setting off an inner savagery of warring egos and clashing values that ultimately brought the place to grief.

Sauter left CBS after an eighteen-year career, driven out by the institution, convinced that the place had brought its grief upon itself, that CBS News was damaged by the knaves inside it, phony pietists and millionaire journalists who used the lamp of Murrow to count their money by. The view on the other side was that Sauter had been a tragic figure, so well endowed and so ill disposed that he used CBS News to advance himself, crushing it under the weight of his ambitions.

Neither view was completely wrong.

Chapter

RICHARD SALANT WAS NOT above begging, and considering the circumstances, begging seemed entirely the appropriate course. It was 1976, the bicentennial year, and Walter Cronkite had come to Salant, then president of CBS News, with a proposal. The daily grind was getting to him, Cronkite said. After nineteen years of anchoring the *CBS Evening News,* he wanted to talk about getting out. Just the thought of it made Salant ache. He was sixty-two years old, less than three years from retirement. He'd been president of CBS News since 1961 (except for a two-year interruption), and in that time the organization had become, above all, an ordered place. It didn't take a Harvard lawyer (which Salant happened to be) to figure out that the departure of Cronkite would bring disorder. He begged.

"Walter, for God's sake, I have to go before you do," Salant said, appealing to the slight difference in age, less than three years, between himself and his famous anchorman. *"You* have to retire *me.* We've worked together, we've been good, do me one favor—hold off, let me stick this on my successor."

Salant guessed, correctly, that Cronkite was willing to be stalled, and although the anchorman did bring up the subject again with Salant, he didn't press it. Thus was Salant able to end his career as he had hoped—with Cronkite in his anchor chair and CBS News riding high.

The looming inevitability of life without Cronkite was an appropriate source of anxiety at CBS News, but in a subtler way the end of the Salant era was as traumatic and, in the long run, as damaging to the organization. Although it may not have been obvious at any given moment of his long tenure, Salant had been a brilliant president of CBS News.

When Salant was appointed to the position in 1961, television news was still in its gawky youth. With its awkward equipment and relative immobility, the enterprise shone brightly at the national political conventions every four years, but it was nothing near the daily national informing force that it was to become. The three nightly newscasts were only fifteen minutes long, and most Americans still received most of their news from their local newspapers. As for CBS, it had not yet been able to transfer the utter preeminence of its Murrow radio years to television; in convention coverage and in the nightly newscasts, increasingly the focus of television news operations, CBS lagged behind NBC, with its anchor team of Chet Huntley and David Brinkley, true news personalities who fitted the medium neatly.

The CBS News that Salant was handed in 1961 had an annual budget of $20 million and a full-time staff of 469 people. By 1979, when he left, the CBS News budget was nearly $90 million and the organization employed 1,000 people. In Salant's time Walter Cronkite became the anchor of the *CBS Evening News,* the broadcast expanded to thirty minutes, *60 Minutes* was created, and CBS came to dominate television news the way it had once dominated radio. But those things might have happened under another executive. Dick Salant's contribution to a CBS News that was defining itself in the unfolding television age was something infinitely more valuable: He gave it character.

Salant's success did not reflect a journalistic talent or television skills, of which he had none. He was a lawyer who loathed lawyering and had come to CBS in 1952 as a corporate vice-president, brought into the company by CBS President Frank Stanton. By credential, therefore, he was truly a company man, and when he was made president of CBS News in 1961, the move was met with a good deal of apprehension among the news staff. In news, he was a curious package, bespectacled and patrician, someone who seemed to have been born in a suit. "Everybody thought it was an awful idea," recalled Ernie Leiser, who was a CBS correspondent at the time. "He was a lawyer; he was an outsider; he was a Stanton protégé." Three strikes, it seemed, but Salant quickly showed that he was something else, too: He was a thoroughgoing news convert. He may have been born into CBS a company man, but in news he became a zealot, more Catholic than the pope.

Perhaps because he had been a company man, Salant possessed an understanding, surpassing that of any who came before him or after, of the peculiar place that news held within the corporate empire. The relationship of news to the company was at once antagonistic and dependent, pampered and perilous. It was a contradiction, an enigma, a quirk. CBS wasn't in the news business, Salant knew; it was in the broadcasting business. Its chief purpose was to lure mass audiences to its air and to sell them to advertisers for unspeakable amounts of money. And news didn't do that.

But Salant also knew CBS history—knew that both the pragmatic desire to keep the government off its back and the individual psychologies of both Paley and Stanton, the man who helped build CBS, had made the news department a favored child. True, Paley had through the years meddled with and fretted over and generally tormented his news department, including the sainted Murrow—*especially* the sainted Murrow. But there was no denying the other side of Paley, the Paley who fostered a news organization with standards and ambitions that far exceeded the imperatives of the commercial broadcasting industry he was helping build. Salant was lastingly impressed with the fact that when the young Paley was building CBS, he chose as his number one assistant not a salesman or a showman, but a former night editor of the *New York Times,* a cheerless man named Edward Klauber, who imposed upon the unformed enterprise of radio public affairs a discipline and a standard no less demanding than those of the *Times* itself. Paley's hiring of Ed Klauber back in 1930 was, for the benefit of an informed public, not to mention the developing craft of broadcast journalism, a fortunate thing; he laid the foundation upon which Murrow and Sevareid and the others would build an institution that was, simply put, worlds better than it had to be.

Equipped with this understanding and driven by a convert's zeal, Salant quickly won over any doubters in news. Where there might have been a certain air of noblesse oblige in Paley's and Stanton's support, Salant genuinely loved the news, loved being near it. (Years later, long after his retirement from CBS, he sat in the den of his New Canaan, Connecticut, house, watching Cable News Network by the hour.) Acutely aware that he was of another culture, that he wasn't actually a journalist, he shied from the daily mix of the news process. But like a good line officer, he saw his first duty as being to the people below him, rather than to those above him, and he earned the respect of the troops in the field. In 1973, when Paley, yielding to Nixon White House pressure, issued an edict forbidding CBS correspondents from performing "instant analysis" following presidential speeches and press conferences, a group of correspondents, led by Roger Mudd, sent an angry letter of protest to CBS management. It was a gutsy move for the journalists (and risky enough to keep the White House correspondent, Dan Rather, from putting his name to it), but they were eased when Salant let them know that their protest had his support.

Again, Salant stood firm behind Rather after the newsman's famous confrontation with Richard Nixon in 1974. (Hounded by Watergate, the president, noting the boos and applause greeting his nemesis at a press conference, looked down and asked, "Are you running for something?" Rather snapped, "No, sir, Mr. President, are you?") When some CBS affiliates wanted Rather punished, removed from his beat, Salant reassured Rather that he was his man at the White House and would remain so, and he told the affiliates the same.

Salant viewed the tension between the news division and the company as not only inevitable but necessary and healthy, so much so that he dedicatedly endeavored to exacerbate it. He saw himself as CBS's own Oliver Twist, picking the fat pockets of the network for the money and airtime that Paley's various executives (who came and went) were so loath to part with. He became the master of the wheedle, a true artist, begging, pleading, cajoling, ever making his case on behalf of news. His medium was the memorandum; he was the Vesuvius of memos, which his lawyerly mind preferred because memos (with lots of names copied in) "put everybody on the record." He wrote memos of varying tones, carrying different degrees of urgency, sometimes polite, then humorous, then desperate, then angry; there were memos asking for airtime, or for more documentaries, or for a weekly piece of prime time, or, that accomplished, for a *better* piece of prime time. One week, he sent Robert D. ("Bob") Wood, the president of the CBS Network for a time, a memo simply noting: "You've had no memos from me this week."

Salant was, despite his patrician demeanor, a cunning and game politician. On those occasions when wheedling alone didn't bend a stubborn network type, he reverted to a back-channel ploy, calling his old friend and mentor Frank Stanton, advising him that he might keep an eye out for this or that worthy project, which, by the way, he was having a little trouble getting on the air. And Stanton would make a call, inquiring about the worthy project, and lo, the thing was done. "You have to be a somewhat devious politician," Salant later said. "You have to play games, and time it right, and not be too shrill sometimes, and very shrill other times. You have to play by instinct." *Play.* Well, it was rather a game, Salant thought, all the back and forth with Black Rock, and he relished it. Jack Schneider, another of the Black Rock executives with whom Salant had parried, could still get exercised over the subject of the news budget years after his CBS career had ended. "You don't want to create spoiled children; you don't want to say, 'Anytime you want money, just come and ask.' It's not very good," he said, as if he had half thought another of those damned memos from Salant might hit the desk at any moment. "There had to be restraints." One year, 1975, the restraint was a Schneider directive that CBS News couldn't lose more than $30 million. Thirty million dollars in the red! The executives of other divisions within CBS, whose own jobs were never more secure than the current bottom line, deeply resented the favored child. "They all thought we were a bunch of spoiled brats," Salant recalled with a little glee, "and we were."

But Salant knew that was the way it had to be, that there was a reason that in the CBS annual report CBS News was listed ahead of all the rest of the operations, which followed in alphabetical order. CBS News is what gave the company its real worth. Salant knew that, and he exploited it. That was his genius.

If corporate politics was a game to Salant, the news itself was serious business. In Salant's time television passed newspapers as the principal source of news for most Americans. It became the great information source for the mass society, a mass society that had been created, in fact, by television. There was no *USA Today* then, no national newspapers, no Cable News Network, no satellite-fed supply services enabling local stations to give comprehensive world news reports. There was only network television, and CBS News was its leader. That realization was an awesome weight, even a bit scary, and it made Salant and his executive staff all the more determined that CBS News would embody the most demanding possible journalistic ethic, articulated in a series of memorandums and policy statements that, published together and distributed as the CBS News Standards handbook (bound in loose-leaf notebooks to allow for additions—and there were always additions), institutionalized at CBS News in the television age a remarkably serious, even elitist journalistic attitude.

There were rules against putting music (for filmmakers a valuable tool for pacing and punctuation) in a CBS News report, rules against yielding to television's need for "picture" by recreating any part of a story for clarification—rules, in short, guarding against all the natural seductions that the medium presented. If the policies were severe "perhaps to the point of eccentricity," Salant said in his introductory memo to the standards book, it was with reason: All of television's efforts, high and low, tumble into the American living room from the same tube, with no physical dividing line between the *Evening News* and *The Beverly Hillbillies*. Television journalists, therefore, had to make the distinction themselves, in their work. "This may make us a little less interesting to some," said Salant, "but that is the price we pay for dealing with fact and truth." Several years after Salant's retirement a young CBS producer, who'd been a teenager when the standards were drawn and who'd been reared, professionally, outside the CBS culture, remarked with amazement and a little annoyance, "It's against the rules here to be interesting!" It was almost true. The overriding attitude (and the seat of the elitism) was that CBS News would give viewers what they needed, not what they wanted. "It is my strong feeling," Salant said in his memo, "that our news judgments must turn on the best professional judgments that we can come to on what is important, rather than what is merely interesting." To be "merely interesting," he made clear, was the lowly aim of the rest of television, of prime time, where "it is entirely proper to give most of the people what most of them want most of the time. But we in broadcast journalism cannot, should not, and will not base our judgments on what we think the viewers and listeners are 'most interested' in. . . ." And that is why, on the night in 1977 that Elvis Presley died, the story was not the lead item on Cronkite's *Evening News* (nor, needless to say, was there a thirty-minute news special on Presley from CBS News that night). More routinely the attitude was displayed nightly in the heavy domination of each newscast by the Washington bureau. In one memorable Cronkite broadcast, every story but one emanated from Washington, and the single exception was a Watergate-related piece that happened to take place in New York.

It helped, in all this, to have Cronkite. It was not coincidental that the values embedded in the institution under Salant were also Cronkite's values, the values of a Murrow-era newsman trained in the straight-ahead style of a wire service. But Cronkite's greater contribution was simply in being Cronkite. He became the man from whom America had decided it wanted to get its news, and that was that. His unassailable credibility was important, but his unassailable ratings were what made everything else possible. Cronkite's phenomenal success with viewers, beginning when his ratings passed NBC's *Huntley-Brinkley Report* in 1967 and growing through the seventies, was a shield against the harsh outside, behind which Salant and his organization were free to set their high tone, to shape the CBS News of the television age into a certain kind of place.

Cronkite's popularity was a liberating force, imbuing a generation of CBS News with a sense of entitlement, a sense that theirs was indeed a special calling, immune to such crass considerations, for example, as ratings. "We didn't have to worry about ratings then" is the echo of nearly every news staffer asked in a later day what the Cronkite era was like. They exaggerated, of course, but only a little. In Cronkite's time, Tuesday was just a day of the week, not the Sabbath that it was to become, the day when the A. C. Nielsen Company released the national ratings, the sacred numbers that network newsrooms would seek for validation. Cronkite's huge ratings lead was, for CBS News, a license to believe, to accept blithely that doing first-rate *New York Times*-level journalism and *winning* at it were the CBS News birthright. It was part of what looked to the competition like a maddening arrogance, evidenced perfectly in the notion of the *Evening News* as America's "broadcast of record," as the *New York Times* was America's paper of record. It was, of course, a preposterous conceit, as no broadcast, least of all one lasting only twenty-two minutes, is much of a record of anything;

broadcasts inform, or arouse, or stupefy, or divert for a brief space in time and then vanish forever. But the ambition was telling. It rarely occurred to CBS newsmen of the Salant-Cronkite era that had their profession taken its natural course, its likelier course, television journalism might more have resembled the hokum newsreels of the movies than the *New York Times,* in the same way that prime time more resembled vaudeville than O'Neill.

But Salant knew all too well the value of having a top-rated evening newscast. When he first came to CBS News, a lawyer out of his element, all seriousness and eagerness to show his merit, he was foolhardy enough to focus attention on CBS's war with NBC's top-rated *Huntley-Brinkley.* CBS had expanded its news operations to accommodate a half-hour *Evening News,* opening bureaus and hiring more staff, and Salant declared that CBS News, with its stronger bench, would prevail over NBC. Of course, NBC responded publicly, and the newspapers had a good time with stories about the competition, which only raised the stakes and caused Mr. Paley to wonder why, by 1964, CBS hadn't yet overtaken NBC as Salant had predicted. Suddenly Salant was out, "promoted" back to the corporation by his friend and mentor Stanton at Paley's command and replaced by Murrow's former producer, Fred Friendly. When, two years later, Friendly self-immolated in a dispute with Black Rock and CBS asked Salant to return to News, he hesitated, still deeply humiliated over having been turned out in the first place. He did go back, but he never underestimated the value of being on top in the nightly news wars.

That is why, when Cronkite came to him in 1976, asking out of the daily grind, Salant begged him to stay. He would let his successor handle that one.

In 1976, no one at CBS News doubted who Salant's successor would be. In the well-ordered way of the place under Salant, CBS News had a strong and distinct operational structure, with a vice-president for "hard news" in charge of the daily broadcasts and the news bureaus and a vice-president for "soft news" overseeing the other areas, such as *60 Minutes* and documentaries. The structure, inherited from Friendly but made truly functional by Salant, reflected Salant's distance from the daily operations. The two vice-presidents actually ran things and at the same time provided to the institution a clear line of succession. The hard-news vice-president was understood by all to be the next in line for the presidency, and beginning in February 1974, that job was held by William Small.

Small had spent his entire career in broadcast management, first in local stations in Chicago and Louisville and then, starting in 1962, as the Washington bureau chief for CBS. A square, compact man, Small was tough-minded, abrasive, an astute assessor of talent, and altogether a brilliant Washington bureau chief. In his tenure, such star correspondents as Dan Rather and Roger Mudd, Marvin Kalb and Daniel Schorr reached their flower; Eric Sevareid found his place as a daily commentator; and correspondents whose names would become familiar— Leslie Stahl, Bob Schieffer, Connie Chung, Fred Graham— were recruited. The CBS News "bench," both a source and a reflection of the organization's strength, resided largely in the Washington bureau and was so overwhelmingly impressive under Small as to be be intimidating. When the *New York Herald Tribune* folded in 1966, Small tried to recruit a *Tribune* man, Douglas Kiker, whose work he admired. He invited Kiker to visit CBS but didn't hear from the journalist until a month later, when he learned Kiker had taken a job with NBC. Small asked why Kiker hadn't given CBS a shot, at least for the chance to drive up his value at NBC, if that was where he wanted to go. "I looked at your staff in Washington," Small recalled Kiker as saying, "and I said, 'If I went to work for them, and the first string was wiped out in an airplane crash, and the second string died of heart failure, I'd still have trouble getting to be first string.' " Under Small, the Washington bureau dominated the *Evening News,* and even into the 1980s Small was regarded by many at CBS News as the best Washington bureau chief the organization ever had.

Small was ambitious, and he had an important ally in Eric Sevareid, who had been in New York anchoring a weekend newscast, out of his milieu, before Small brought him to Washington, where he found new life as a commentator. Small and Sevareid, the "Gray Eminence," became close in Washington, often lunching together, and the younger executive expressed keen interest in Sevareid's work. Sevareid was hugely impressed with Small, so much so that he went to New York to see Paley and told the chairman, "Small is the man for tomorrow for CBS,

he could be the next president of CBS News, and he should be."
Small's work in Washington had impressed Black Rock, and the
Sevareid recommendation clinched it. With his appointment in
1974 as vice-president for hard news, the future was assured,
and the crucial issue of succession was settled. Small would be
the next president of CBS News.

But between Small's designation and his coronation a hitch
developed. The hitch was Bill Small. The magic he had worked
in Washington didn't happen in New York, where all that
seemed to show of his renowned mental toughness was the
abrasiveness. As Bill Leonard, Salant's vice-president for soft
news, succinctly put it, "Small messed up the opportunity. He
surrounded himself with very poor people; he was dictatorial; he
didn't handle things right. He did all the wrong things."

They were little things mostly, annoying things, hardly indictable, but they disturbed the confident and untroubled mood of
the place, and that was dangerous. Small brought to New York
a close circle of Washington aides, his own court, so to speak,
which put a "them" and "us" odor in the air. And from "them"
there soon began to emanate a series of directives on cost controls: Expense reports were sloppy and getting out of hand, too
many people had too many subscriptions to too many periodi-
cals, and something had to be done about all those coffee
machines—was CBS in the broadcasting business or was it a
purveyor of coffee? The rather obvious ploys of a new manager
trying to show a firm hand came across as petty meanness.
Sevareid quickly picked up on the inevitable grumbling ("Bill
was a bear on expense reports," Sevareid recalled sadly) and
had a talk with his protégé. "Bill, this isn't the first place you
should put your attention," he said. "Put your mind on more
important things."

Sevareid wasn't the only heavy hitter beginning to have
doubts about Small. After the crash of two 747s in the Canary
Islands in 1977, one of Small's deputies, mindful of the cost
hold-downs, refused to approve the chartering of a plane to fly
a CBS crew and correspondent to the scene. It was a huge story,
the biggest air disaster in history, the very stuff of TV news. But
the crash closed the islands to commercial traffic, and without
a charter CBS was locked out of the story for two days. CBS was
drummed by the competition, and Cronkite was furious. Small
had acquired a dangerous antagonist.

Word of Small's alienation among the troops began to filter up to Black Rock, and in a meeting between the London bureau and the network president, Jack Schneider, the trickle became a flood. Correspondents Susan Peterson and Jack Lawrence, a highly regarded journalist who had distinguished himself, and CBS, in Vietnam, let loose on Schneider, detailing the complaints against the Small administration that were building in the field. When Small heard of the meeting, Lawrence was reassigned to the States. He refused the invitation and left the network.

None of this was helping Small in what should have been a fairly smooth period of apprenticeship before succeeding Salant, and none of it was so damaging, in the end, as the alienation of the man who had done the most to help him, Eric Sevareid. Sevareid had hoped that Small would grow in the job, that in New York he would become a leader, rather than a mere manager. He imagined, for example, that at the end of each day Small would meet in his office with some of the great editorial minds in New York and analyze the nightly news broadcasts. "But instead," Sevareid said, "he'd sit there with his old cronies." Small was given to letting loose a little at day's end, inviting his close circle into his office for the newscasts, where they'd share a little gossip and a few laughs. Sevareid didn't like it; but Sevareid was in Washington, and besides, Small already had the job. But losing Sevareid proved to be a mistake.

Sevareid, one of the last of Murrow's boys with a vital daily role in the operation, had developed a relationship with Paley that was closer than most in CBS News ever suspected. He didn't lobby Paley often, but when he did, it counted. So, deeply disappointed in Small, he went to the chairman and told him that he'd made a terrible mistake, that Small hadn't grown into the job at all; he'd become a disaster in New York and should never be made president of CBS News. As it happened, that opinion, shared by Cronkite, had already taken root in Black Rock. "Small was okay for hard news, but if you listened to the people who worked for him, you came to the conclusion that you couldn't give Bill the president's job," Schneider said later. "Bill just didn't have the touch to lead people. He was autocratic and very vindictive, and that in itself shows you some personality flaw that disqualifies you from ultimate leadership."

Small, hearing of Sevareid's visit to Paley, went to Washington and confronted Sevareid. They met behind the closed door of

Sevareid's office, but the loud exchange, especially Sevareid's ultimate point, could be heard across the newsroom. "I put you in that job, Bill, and I have told Bill Paley that it was a terrible mistake and that the worst thing that could happen would be for you to be the next president of CBS News."

So Small was out. That resolved one crisis but created a larger one. It was, by now, the spring of 1978, and Salant's retirement was less than a year away. With Small gone, there was no clear successor in place. Bill Leonard, the executive who had been the vice-president for soft news under Salant, had been "retired" to the comfortable post of CBS lobbyist in Washington, and although the man who replaced him, Robert ("Bob") Chandler, embodied the values of both Salant and Leonard, he wasn't well known at Black Rock. Further complicating matters was the changing picture at Black Rock. Gene Jankowski, a salesman who had climbed up through the corporate ranks to the finance department, had replaced Jack Schneider as the president of the CBS Broadcast Group, the corporate stratum that oversaw all broadcast operations, including news. Given the touchy, sometimes explosive relationship between news and the company, Jankowski didn't want to make a decision on the next news president lightly. He was unfamiliar with Chandler and some of the other lower-level candidates at CBS News, and the two obvious choices—Bill Leonard and Burton ("Bud") Benjamin, an esteemed producer who had replaced Small as hard-news vice-president—were nearly as old as Salant. Given those options, Jankowski, as became his wont in the job, chose what he thought was the safest course: He delayed the ultimate decision by asking Bill Leonard to return to New York as the president of CBS News.

Leonard, who was sixty-two, would be an interim president, and he was an obvious choice. Highly regarded by those who worked with him at news, he had been part of Salant's team. What's more, he possessed what Black Rock viewed as the compelling attribute of having been away from CBS News for nearly three years, his experience as the corporate lobbyist in Washington perhaps having softened the contrariness that seemed to be in the oxygen in the news division. In his memoir Leonard told the story of how, when he was taking the corporate job in 1975, his new boss, Kidder Meade, summoned him to the thirty-fifth floor at Black Rock (the executive chambers), and as they sat there talking, Meade's secretary walked in and handed her boss a folded piece of paper. He unfolded it, read its contents, smiled, and pushed the paper across the desk to Leonard. On it was written only "$38\frac{1}{2}$." "That's the price of CBS stock at noon," Meade said to Leonard. "That's the bottom line. You're not in the news business anymore."

Salant always believed that the selection of Leonard was a reaction to him, that after years of wheedling, Black Rock was ready for someone who knew the price of CBS stock at noon—or at least appreciated that someone had to know it. "They were sick and tired of my sixteen years of fighting management," Salant said. That might explain why the handling of the transition from Salant to Leonard was so awkward, almost cruelly inept. One weekend late in the spring of 1978, nine months or so before Salant's retirement date, Jankowski called Salant and said he wanted to drive down to New Canaan from his home in upper Connecticut to discuss the succession. Salant said sure, he'd be there. Jankowski came down and told Salant that the next president of CBS News would be Bill Leonard, Salant's old friend and assistant. That was just fine with Salant. Jankowski said that Leonard would be given a title of some sort and would be coming to New York to help out during Salant's final months. But what Jankowski didn't tell Salant was what he'd told Leonard weeks earlier, in a meeting in Athens: that Leonard was to assume daily command as soon as he got to New York. That was the version that was leaked to Les Brown, the television writer for the *New York Times.* When Brown called Salant for a quote, Salant said no, he was still in charge and would be until his retirement, in the spring of next year. So Brown wrote his story, which made it obvious that Salant, the Harvard lawyer, just didn't *get* it. Salant recalled that Jankowski's top aide, a man named Gene Mater, read the *Times* story, and called Salant, and gave him hell. "What do you mean? Bill's going to run that division!" Salant was deeply wounded, and though he hated leaving CBS News, his last months there were painful and unhappy.

For Leonard's part, he was happy to be back at news and ready to give it his best shot. He even had a specific agenda for his presidency, a list of just what he wanted to accomplish while leading CBS News into the future. He would finally expand the *CBS Evening News* to a full hour, he'd make a daily morning show that could compete with *Today* on NBC and *Good Morning America* on ABC, and he had this idea for a new Sunday show, a leisurely morning program designed for people who don't think there's anything worth watching on TV. And if he had the time, he would put together his own line of succession. It would be a brief tenure, Leonard thought, but if he could accomplish those things—and he saw no reason why he couldn't—he could make it count, he could make an imprint. It was, as it turned out, a terribly innocent view.

Chapter

2

VAN GORDON SAUTER CAME to CBS because in early 1968 a somewhat desperate news manager at the CBS radio station in Chicago was looking for another Edward R. Murrow. In what would
become for Sauter an eighteen-year career at CBS, it was the last
time that anyone confused him with Murrow.

But to John Callaway, the news director at WBBM radio,
Sauter was an important find, and hiring him for WBBM was the
crowning moment in what had been, for Callaway, the most
challenging and difficult assignment in his career. Weeks earlier
CBS management had dropped into his lap what he privately
referred to as his "mission impossible": WBBM was going to
reinvent itself, dropping its talk format to become an all-news
station. This was going to be accomplished, Callaway was told,
in the space of about six weeks, and he, Callaway, was going to
be point man. The switch was Mr. Paley's idea, and Mr. Paley
was in a hurry. The year before, the CBS flagship station in New
York, WCBS, had been converted to a news format, but it was
beaten to the punch by station WINS. Now there were rumors
that the Westinghouse station in Chicago, WIND, was going all
news, and Paley was determined that WBBM get there first.

At the time WBBM's news department was a comfortable
operation of moderate size, small enough to allow Callaway to
squeeze in his administrative chores without giving up on-air

reporting. Now he had to build a staff that could put news on the air nearly twenty-four hours a day (blessedly the all-night *Musi- Till Dawn* show would stay on the air in the early stages of the transition). It was an awesome, intimidating assignment, and there was really no blueprint to study for guidance since the conversion to news of WCBS, being right there in New York and connected to the network and its huge news staff, was a different case altogether. But one thing Callaway knew was that he needed people, lots of them, and WBBM pursued people with the determination of a conscription gang. To say that the station went on a hiring spree would be to understate the case wildly, as can be verified by the experience of a young man from Alton, Illinois, named Lane Venardos, who happened to be in Chicago at the time on a shopping trip with his wife. Venardos was the operations manager of a radio station in Alton, and he hated shopping, so while his wife was off perusing the emporiums of Michigan Avenue, Venardos thought he'd take a tour of the big CBS radio station, WBBM. He asked the lobby receptionist if the station conducted tours. "Do you want a tour or a job?" she asked. Just a tour of the place, thank you, Venardos said, and the next thing he knew, he was in the grasp of Dick Etter, Callaway's assistant, who conducted a rush tour of the station and then got to the real point, which was: Would Venardos like to come work for WBBM? So that afternoon, when Venardos met his wife with her packages, he had a little surprise for her: They were moving to Chicago, where Venardos now had a job as a newswriter, at top union scale.

Callaway stocked WBBM with writers, producers, reporters, and anchors, thirty or so in just a few weeks, until there was just one job unfilled, a special job that would be, if Callaway could find the right person, the best job in American radio. Callaway had plenty of people to cover Chicago's fires and alderman races. Now he wanted someone to be WBBM's star, a national correspondent who would roam the country and send back radio portraits that would distinguish the new all-news station. He wanted a writer, someone with—as Callaway put it—"a deep sensibility." And then one of Callaway's staffers said he knew someone who just might fit the bill, a reporter for the *Chicago Daily News* who'd done some interesting work. Maybe Callaway had heard of him: Van Gordon Sauter. Heard of him! Van G. Sauter was a by-line that Callaway had made a point of following, a new name that stood out even in a town filled with star newspapermen. Callaway had admired Sauter's stories on race relations, stories of style and feeling, but he wondered if he could interest Sauter in the job—Chicago was a newspaper town. He called him, and Sauter said sure, he'd like to try an audition.

A few days later Sauter came for his audition, and Callaway knew in an instant that he'd found his man. He was attractive as hell, Callaway thought, a Hemingway type, with his full beard and casual dress; if he had been invented for the role, Van Sauter couldn't have better suited Callaway's expectations. The two talked for a while in a sound studio, Callaway asking questions, Sauter answering, a tape rolling. It wasn't that Sauter said anything especially memorable, anything that would stay with Callaway when he remembered the meeting in later years, but it was the way he said it. It wasn't just talk, really; it was more like word sculpture, deft little phrasings that came effortlessly and just sort of hung there, as if to be admired. And Callaway admired. True, he couldn't be sure how well Sauter would read radio copy, but he wasn't after a studio slick anyway; he wanted a Murrow sort, someone who could really get in touch with a story. He offered Sauter the job. For some reason, Callaway never was quite sure why, Sauter was available and willing to leave his job at the *News*. A few weeks later Sauter began his career in broadcasting, starting with the best job in American radio.

Sauter was already thirty-two years old, which gave him a late start in broadcasting, but behind him he had a newspaper career that was, in its time and place, genuinely legendary. It was legendary not because he was so great a newspaperman (although he was quite good) but because legend building was what Sauter did. *That* was his career; the newspaper work was part of the overall creation, in the way that acting skill is a component, by no means the defining one, in the composition of a movie star. People recalling Sauter at the places he'd worked would remember pieces of the legend first, an anecdote or an impression or an incident, and then offer the journalism he'd done as verification of the legend. It wasn't to belittle the journalism—he was an able and stylish reporter—but at the other, the mythmaking, he was quite brilliant.

Kurt Luedtke, who became a famous Oscar-winning screenwriter, was a new assistant city editor at the *Detroit Free Press* in 1965. The Sauter legend was one of the first things he heard about, how this guy Sauter had somehow talked the *Free Press,* which had never before had a foreign correspondent, into sending him to Vietnam. One day Luedtke was waiting for an elevator outside the newsroom; it arrived, the doors parted, and Luedtke's jaw dropped. Out stepped this person, large and imposing, who looked like Hemingway in a thick black mustache, and he was dressed in full combat fatigues, right down to the boots, as if the jungles of Vietnam had just delivered him forth into the number three elevator at the *Detroit Free Press.* "Hi, brother!" said this creature, breezing by Luedtke and into the city room, down the length of which he promenaded in his combat outfit, "Hi, brother!" all the way. Van Sauter was back from the war.

As is the case with many people who achieve notoriety, what Sauter became was in some part a reaction to what he had been, an average kid in one of the most average places in America, the aptly named Middletown, Ohio. He was born Freeman Van Gordon Sauter at the peak of the Depression, 1935, to a family that began breaking up almost as soon as he arrived. His father, Freeman Sauter, was a fireman, the son of a fireman, and intensely Roman Catholic; his mother, Cornelia Banker, was from a family that was intensely Protestant and slightly anti-Catholic; and the difference was a source of serious friction, exacerbated when Freeman's drinking became a problem. So, before the youngster ever knew his father, he was gone; Sauter's parents divorced when he was two, and young Van (the first name seemed to vanish with his father) was raised in his mother's home by her parents and her sisters, Van's adoring aunts.

Middletown was not unpleasant, nor was it particularly exciting, a small town set down upon verdant farmland, its center force being the great steel mill of the Armco Corporation, where at night the pig iron was poured and the sky lit up in violent shades of red. It was a town steeped in the midwestern ethic, where everyone knew his roots and expectations, and those of everyone else, too. When Sauter was very young, Cornelia Sauter went to work, selling hats in a local department store, and sometimes left Middletown for brief stretches to work in the big stores in Chicago. Sauter grew up an only child in a household of hovering females, and although the Banker family was not desperately poor, it had very spare means. It was, for a bright, imaginative boy, the sort of life that lent itself to the improvements of mythmaking.

In high school Sauter was acutely aware that many of his friends lived in nicer sections of town than he did, that they had cars or access to cars, which he didn't, and that they were comfortable in certain social circumstances that were to him quite foreign. These were the friends he cultivated, the sons and daughters of Middletown's professional class, the children of Armco engineers, and he came to take on airs of sophistication that were not at all grounded in his experience.

He became a fervent reader of *Time* magazine, with its worldly prose (or so it seemed by the light of a bedroom lamp in Middletown, Ohio), and one day he came across a new word —*chic*— that he could hardly wait to employ in the company of his tony friends. The next day he and four or five of his group were cruising in a car, Sauter just bursting to impress them, and as they passed an establishment in current favor, he dropped his voice and said, with casual aplomb, "Yeah, that place is really *chick*!" The mispronunciation (of a word that had never been uttered in the Sauter household, a word that had no reason to exist in its vocabulary) brought gales of laughter and ridicule, and it was quite a traumatic moment for young Van Sauter. He realized right there that his friends had something he didn't have, something he wanted, and that he would have to scramble like a son of a bitch to cover some ground. People who knew Sauter in later years would be struck by his uncommon gift with language, his way of speaking in perfectly formed phrases, as if each word had been carefully weighed and measured in advance, as of course, was exactly the case.

The Banker family was not well educated—only one of Sauter's aunts had attended college—but it valued learning (Grandfather Banker had served as head of the school board for a time), and it was always hoped that Sauter would attend college. He had neither the wherewithal nor the academic standing for an Ivy League school, which wouldn't have occurred to the family in any case. He was accepted to Ohio University, a few hours away in Athens, which seemed about right, and Cornelia Sauter took a loan from Household Finance to pay tuition. He had no particular aim in life, but because one of his aunts had married a man who worked at a bank in New York, which seemed a possibility, he entered the business school at Ohio U. He proceeded to flunk statistics and accounting and was floundering when he came upon the School of Communications, a haven, Sauter later said, for "artsy-craftsy people who were curious and sort of lazy and unfocused and undisciplined." That is to say, Sauter fit right in, and thrived.

He began to think of himself as a writer, took to smoking a pipe, and became a columnist for the school paper. Then he and two friends published a humor magazine, which Sauter edited, and by graduation he'd come as close as he would to deciding upon a vocation: He would try advertising, which was, in the late 1950s, a hot profession. He sent job applications to ad agencies around the country and was stunned and delighted when one of the largest agencies in the country, McCann-Erickson in New York, offered him a place in its executive-training program, apparently on the strength of his work on the humor magazine.

In New York he rented a one-room walk-up a block from the agency, thereby maximizing the recovery time following misspent nights, of which there were many. The training program class seemed to be populated by two sorts, the M.B.A.'s and the creatives, into which category Sauter classified himself. He saw at close hand that advertising could be a lucrative and possibly interesting way to make a living, but it wasn't nearly as glamorous as he'd imagined. And there was something else about it: It was so *anonymous*.

He'd taken to reading the *New York Post,* which was then a solid and lively newspaper, and he envied the people whose by-lines he'd followed through escapades ranging from serial murders to encounters with the literary lions of the moment. It also happened that young Sauter was developing a potent strain of hedonism, a characteristic to which he would surrender completely in the coming years. Suddenly Madison Avenue didn't seem the appropriate arena for a would-be writer inclined toward untethered self-indulgence; the unstructured and free-wheeling world of daily journalism, on the other hand, did. So he packed it in and enrolled in the Graduate School of Journalism at the University of Missouri, where he would learn how to be a reporter and refine the craft of being Van Sauter.

At Missouri he met a young man named Ron Martin (who was one day to become editor of *USA Today*), and they became fast friends, haunting the college-town pubs of Columbia, Missouri, drinking and talking late into the night. They'd talk of writing, mostly, intoxicated by the enthusiasms of young men in love with the idea of writing, and Martin regarded his friend with something approaching awe. Sauter seemed so sure, so bright, so knowing, and how he could talk! As for himself, Martin was contentedly bound for a life in newspapering, but Sauter could become a famous novelist, Martin was certain of it. Even after Sauter got married, to Pat Allen, a girl from the personnel department at McCann-Erickson, the two men's late-night sessions continued (a token of Sauter's view of domestic life), and they remained close friends through the years.

After Missouri, Martin landed a job at the *Detroit Free Press,* which was building a remarkably strong staff of first-rate reporters and editors in the 1960s, and Sauter went to the *New Bedford* (Massachusetts) *Standard-Times.* The two kept in touch, and Martin soon got a letter from his old friend, describing, in Sauter's fetching way, his setup in the romantic little New England coastal village. He'd smoke his pipe and walk his dog along the quaint old streets facing Buzzards Bay, he wrote, and think writerly thoughts. "That impostor," thought Martin, who was learning at first hand that real-life newspapering for a novice was high on sweat and low on glamour, but when he visited Sauter, he found that, even with a child and a weekly income of only eighty-five dollars, Sauter had in fact managed the dreamy circumstance he'd described. The Sauters lived in Mattapoisett, on Cannon Street, a cobblestoned affair named after a leading builder of whaling vessels in the nineteenth century. Not only that, Martin found, but they lived in Cannon's very house, which was quaintness itself, with a master bedroom built to resemble the captain's suite on a whaler. And there was, indeed, a dog.

At the *Standard-Times,* Sauter worked hard for low pay, and in turn, he learned how to be a newspaperman. Along the way, of course, he worked on the legend. There was the time a wrestling bear came to town and Sauter, well lubed, talked the bear's trainer into taking a walk to the *Standard-Times,* where the animal proceeded to chase a maintenance man up a ladder and onto a chandelier, to which he clung desperately until the bear was safely evicted.

But for an ambitious reporter, a place like New Bedford is good for only a couple of years, and in 1963 Sauter began casting about for a new job. He called his pal Ron Martin, by then an assistant city editor at the *Free Press,* and Martin got Sauter an interview for the job of chief of the Gastonia, North Carolina, bureau of Knight Newspapers, the chain that owned the *Free Press.* Sauter went down to North Carolina, cruised Gastonia with the outgoing bureau chief, waited in the car while the outgoing bureau chief stopped to take photos of some kids sliding down a hill on some tires, and concluded that Gastonia bureau chief was not at all what he wanted to be. Then Martin arranged an interview with Derrick Daniels, a *Free Press* editor, who gave Sauter a job in Detroit.

In Detroit, Sauter cooked, almost from the moment he arrived. After the John Kennedy assassination Sauter, who'd been to the Kennedy Hyannis Port compound for the *Standard-Times,* wrote a sidebar about it, giving the *Free Press* a valuable close-up touch to its coverage. And a month later he scored on a story that was, in all its aspects, vintage Sauter.

Sauter saw a wire story reporting that Dinah Washington, the great, troubled jazz and blues singer, had died of a drug overdose in Chicago. Sauter, still a new kid in the city room, convinced his editors that the Washington death was a great story, a chance to plug the *Free Press* into the then-developing awareness of black America. Besides, he argued, there was a local angle: Washington was married to Dick ("Night Train") Lane, the star halfback for the Detroit Lions. The desk consented. Sauter left the building for a time and returned that afternoon to write a story that dazzled his editors, weaving bits of biography and knowing assessments of Washington's music into a moving and eloquent obituary. "That impressed people around there, that this guy could do a piece of writing like that on deadline," Ron Martin recalled.

But what made the story truly memorable to several of Sauter's colleagues was the stack of Dinah Washington records that somebody later brought to the newsroom. Several key passages of biographical material and critical comment in the album jacket notes were underlined. Sauter's obit was retrieved and compared. The parallels were remarkable.

Nevertheless, the obit had shown ingenuity and the ability to recognize a potential story from the barest signs. Like most ambitious reporters, Sauter loathed routine stories, fires and United Way functions; unlike most reporters, however, he consistently came up with compelling alternatives.

When Sauter came to Detroit, the mainstream press largely ignored black America or, more accurately, just didn't notice it. But Sauter sensed that black America was about to impose itself upon the national consciousness, ready or not. Not that Sauter was an "issues" journalist in the usual sense, seeking to inform policy debate. His particular talent was in feeling the undulations of mass culture that would ultimately be abstracted into issues. Racial relations were to become a literally burning issue in Detroit by 1967, but Sauter's first handle on race, typically, was his discovery (at least it was a discovery for the *Free Press*) of a small Detroit music company called Motown. The black music idiom, like black anger, was just about to spill into the American mainstream, and Motown would be its vehicle. Sauter wrote stories about Motown when it was still a place where secretaries dropped their notepads and stepped into the recording studio to sing background. He so ingratiated himself at the company that he was asked to go on a European tour with its top acts, an invitation he accepted, taking a two-month leave from the paper. He got on a plane at the Detroit airport with the Supremes, "Little Stevie" Wonder, the Four Tops, Smokey Robinson and the Miracles, and Martha and the Vandellas, forty-one people in all. Sauter and Little Stevie Wonder's tutor were the only whites. In England he went shopping with the Supremes and helped carry forty-two pairs of shoes back to the hotel; he toured castles with Martha and the Vandellas after Berry Gordy, the Motown impresario, asked him to show the ladies some culture.

Sauter had made of himself the house expert on black culture, and that proved to be a valuable credential as the sixties unfolded.

In 1964 the Student Nonviolent Coordinating Committee and the Congress of Racial Equality coordinated young people from the North into bands of freedom riders who were to go south to confront segregation. Sauter covered the training sessions at Antioch College, where the kids were taught how to tuck themselves against the blows of police sticks. That summer, "Freedom Summer," he went to Mississippi to cover the confrontations there, reporting, among other things, the search for the three young civil rights workers who were murdered in Neshoba County. "What he had," said Neal Shine, one of Sauter's editors at the time, "was a journalistic prescience, a knowing of what journalistic trends were going to develop."

He came to be regarded as *the* writer at the *Free Press,* "the star writer," as Luedtke put it. Sauter was called "Bear," not at all the nickname he would have chosen but nonetheless descriptive of the huge presence he exerted in the newsroom. He created a star role, cast himself in the part, and then played it to the hilt. He played Van Sauter brilliantly, and what an impression he made. Bill Serrin, who later became a *New York Times* correspondent and a book author, was a reporter for the *Saginaw* (Michigan) *News* when he first saw Sauter. He was covering a demonstration against Saginaw realtors when a black sedan pulled up. Out slid this bear of a guy, thick black mustache, sucking a pipe, notebook casually stashed in his coat pocket, and acting for all the world as if he owned the story. Strictly big-league, Serrin thought, and when he came to the *Free Press,* he said to himself, "If I can just hang out with guys like Sauter, I'll be a pro." But Serrin saw that there were no guys like Sauter, only Sauter. "He was just *the* person at the *Free Press.*"

Style was all. It was what mattered above all else. The congenital shabbiness of newsrooms and of the people in them (in which regard the *Free Press* was a showcase example) was no more acceptable to Sauter than covering four-alarm fires, and he simply rejected it. While the *Free Press* working area was a model of Newsroom Dreary, bashed metal desks on linoleum floors, the "Sauter corner" was an island of style. He furnished it with an oriental rug, an end table with a lamp, and a huge oak rolltop desk upon which was perched his stand-up telephone. His dress and speech, the books he read, and the music he listened to were always ahead of the trends, and in the mid-1960s anticipating trends was a quality of transcendent worth. His colleagues recalled that he had a saying he casually dropped into conversations: "Form without substance, style without meaning." It seemed deep at the time.

In 1965 the war in Vietnam was definitely a trend. The *Detroit Free Press,* however, had no correspondent in Vietnam, or on any other foreign soil for that matter, and had no particular plans to dispatch one anytime soon. Of course, that meant nothing to Sauter, who convinced his editors that the paper had to have someone on the scene to bring home, in a way that would be meaningful locally, the implications of the escalating war. That someone was Van Sauter, naturally, and so off to war he went.

His stuff appeared under the headline OUR MAN IN VIETNAM, which was just the image Sauter was after. He loved playing the role of war correspondent, the distant adventurer, and if his stories were relatively limited by the local imperative—human-interest features with a Detroit angle—well, he was in Southeast Asia, wasn't he? He played it to the hilt, colleagues recalled, sending back postcards from places like Bangkok with messages such as "The Thai girls have a fine thing involving ice they know how to do." When he'd call the paper to check in, someone in the newsroom would cry out, with slight sarcasm, "Saigon calling!" and at the end of the call Sauter often rang off with the portentous declaration "I'll be outta pocket for a few days. Heading up-country." There was, of course, a certain amount of envy in the newsroom, and there was a great deal of satisfaction when an issue of *Editor & Publisher,* the newspaper trade magazine, ran a feature story on the Da Nang press center, describing what amounted to a relatively comfortable setup. It was basically a motel (said to be the former site of a house of pleasure catering to French officers during the Indochina War) managed by the U.S. Marine Corps, with a restaurant, occasional movies, and a most accommodating bar. A photograph ran with the story, and there, in the center of the picture, was Our Man in Vietnam, smiling broadly and clutching a can of beer. The photo was promptly posted in the *Free Press* newsroom, under the headline VAN SAUTER, UP-COUNTRY.

Among his colleagues in Detroit, Sauter was a star, but he was not mistaken for a serious journalist. Kurt Luedtke remembered that Sauter had a profound distaste for asking questions that might reveal his own ignorance, which is part of the trade craft of the working journalist. "And it hurt him reportorially because when he was involved in a news situation," said Luedtke, "he was much more comfortable watching and commenting on it than in going to someone and saying, 'Well, how does the Michigan Democratic party work anyway?' He was just so uncomfortable with that part."

When Sauter went south, he wrote great evocative pieces on the overturning of buses carrying freedom riders or of a black congregation singing "We Shall Overcome" as it stood watching its church burn to the ground. But he always worked the surface, never trying to get below to the root causes, never seeking to explain. In Vietnam he wrote wonderful personal portraits of scenes he'd witnessed, such as the poignantly awkward act of soldiers lifting body bags out of a marine helicopter.

But interpretive stories, pieces probing the larger issues of Vietnam, Sauter left to others. In a sense, two of the great stories of the 1960s, race and Vietnam, stories that Sauter recognized early, became for him great canvases upon which to display his personal art.

"He wasn't the world's greatest reporter," Neal Shine recalled. "He could write the hell out of the story, but there was not a lot of depth in it. He was not interested in asking a lot of solid questions. Sometimes he'd do a story without a quote in it. You'd say, 'Shit, Van, did you call these guys?' And he'd say, 'Hell, I don't need to call them.' He was a great scene setter, but he was not the kind of guy who liked to spend a lot of time digging for information. He liked to get in and out quickly. He was a very facile writer, a good writer, a wordsmith. And he used his ability as a good writer to write around the gaps in stories."

Of the work of Sauter the War Correspondent, Shine said, "All of it was good, all of it was heart-pulling and touching, but again, it was not dealing with the larger issues. The one thing nobody thought would happen was that Van would win a Pulitzer Prize."

Perhaps for that reason, there wasn't a lot of resentment toward Sauter during his glory times at the *Free Press*. When he made his triumphal march through the newsroom upon his return from Vietnam, wearing his battle fatigues, there were a few erasers and crumpled wads of copy paper tossed at him, but overall, the Sauter act played to an appreciative audience. And why not? He *was* big-league, and his presence was uplifting. Although he took himself very seriously, he never seemed to; that was part of his charm. "He had this marvelous personal style that was terribly attractive and was just very impressive," Kurt Luedtke recalled. Neal Shine, who remained at the *Free Press* and became its city editor, said of Sauter, "For some reason, he was not resented. He was very well liked by the staff, a very genial guy. There are people who have come through my life as a reporter who were roundly hated by the staff for working deals for themselves, cutting deals for the good assignments. Van did that and nobody said, 'Why not me?' "

At home, however, Sauter was not nearly so successful. He had two children now, but husband-father was not a part of the Sauter routine that received much effort. He became a self-described "roué" and earnestly tried to live up to the description. Nights were late, and alternatives to the domestic norm vigorously pursued. It was a life-style that may not have been invented for the sake of the legend, but it did fit nicely.

By the time he returned from Vietnam, having had a good run at the *Free Press,* Sauter was looking for a new stage, and he decided to write a column. It would be a city column, a sort of "critic-at-large" affair, and the paper, which had learned to go along with him, said yes. It was to run every Sunday, two columns wide on the front page of the feature section. The trouble was, Sauter hadn't the faintest idea how to write a column. Shine, by then the city editor, made a couple of suggestions, which were good for a couple of Sundays, but then Sauter ran dry. Just before deadline on his third or fourth column he called Shine and said he just couldn't do it. "Your ass, you can't do it!" came the response, but no, Sauter really couldn't come up with a column. The Sunday editor made up the page without the Sauter column, and did so every Sunday thereafter. Sauter soon left the *Free Press.*

That brought him to Chicago, to a new town and a new stage, the *Chicago Daily News.* He was hired by the city editor, a man named Jim McCartney, who'd had good luck with past recruits from the *Free Press.* Chicago was a four-paper town then, very competitive, and as in Detroit, Sauter quickly impressed all with his style. "He was an extremely talented, clever, and imaginative writer and a good reporter," McCartney said later. "He was a good story maker. He had a tendency to be a little less careful with the facts than might have been. . . ."

The *News* had a good record on race stories, and Sauter's credentials made him a natural on the beat. He covered Martin Luther King in the South, and when the tensions bubbled over into the urban battlefields of the North, Sauter covered that, too. When Detroit erupted into race riots in the summer of 1967, there was no doubt that Sauter was the man to send. It proved to be a most revealing episode.

He breezed into the *Free Press* city room as if he'd never left, made his way to an empty desk, and yelled, "Get me the dupes from the lead riot story!" He scooped up the copy, pounded out 1,200 words, and dispatched it to Chicago. After things had calmed down, he stopped by Kurt Luedtke's desk and told him about something that should be looked into. He'd been out to the Algiers Motel, he said, where three young black "snipers" had been shot and killed by police. He'd been in the room and seen the bodies, and there was something fishy about it. The "snipers" were supposed to have been shot through the window of the room; but their brains were splattered across the floor and up one of the walls (Sauter still had his descriptive flair), and it didn't take a forensic scientist to figure out that they'd been shot at close range. Then he left town.

Luedtke passed the tip to City Editor Shine, who put an industrious reporter named Barbara Stanton on the story, and Stanton returned from the scene convinced that there was a big story out at the Algiers Motel. The *Free Press* hired a ballistics specialist and a pathologist and, on the day of the youths' funeral, had private autopsies conducted. The conclusion was that the youths had been shot at close range by police rifles. The paper ran with the story, some cops were indicted, and the *Detroit Free Press* won the Pulitzer Prize for its riot coverage. Shine puzzled for years over the fact that Sauter had tipped the *Free Press* to the story. "It speaks to his unwillingness to do anything except hit-and-run. Van was the first guy to smell it, but instead of saying, 'Holy shit, I'm working this, I'm calling Chicago and blowing the lid off of it,' instead of that, he told us. He just didn't have the inclination. It was not the kind of coverage he cared about."

In Chicago the Sauter legend flourished, and he earned a place on the wall of Billy Goat's saloon, the newspaper hangout that enshrined local legends. Billy Goat's, in fact, became his home away from home, or rather, home became his home away from Billy Goat's. He intensified his efforts in the role of debauchee, boozing and womanizing with vigor, occasionally disappearing for days at a time. "The paper was very tolerant," he said later, but the life was beginning to get a little seedy. His marriage broke up, he lived in a hotel, and some of his nights were ending in blackouts. He began thinking about another tour of Vietnam, just to get away, and the paper agreed to send him; but there were delays. Then came the flameout.

As the legend came to be written—the legend as told by Van Sauter to writers of newspaper and magazine profiles—Sauter left newspapering for broadcasting when he quit the *Daily News* in a pique of anger over an ethical issue. It was April 1968. Sauter had been been in Memphis covering Dr. King, and he called the desk in Chicago to say there was nothing happening,

he was coming home, and he left. It happened to be the day that
King was shot outside his motel room, and that night riots
erupted in the streets of Chicago. Sauter was called in to work,
and there were some good stories; in the aftermath he was
assigned to write a piece examining how the Chicago Bar Association had functioned in a mass-arrest environment. It had functioned poorly, Sauter concluded, and he wrote a story reflecting
his view. But someone high up in the paper had ties to the head
of the Chicago bar, and McCartney ordered the story changed.
Sauter, furious, refused, and, the legend holds, with fourteen
dollars in his pocket and unlimited credit at Billy Goat's, he
walked out of the newsroom for good.

It was a lovely denouement, one that McCartney saw in print
over and over in the coming years. When asked about it long
after, he was unreserved in his comment: "That's bullshit."
There had, in fact, been a newsroom scene, and Sauter's story
had been ordered cut. McCartney didn't like it either. "But
Sauter didn't quit in anger, he didn't quit over that incident,"
McCartney said. "He got another job offer, with WBBM radio,
which he said would pay him more money." The *Daily News* was
paying Sauter $225 a week; WBBM was offering $400 to start.
McCartney tried to talk Sauter out of it, told him he was crazy
to go into the "electronic media" (an epithet in a print man's
vocabulary). As McCartney and Roy Fisher, then editor of the
Daily News, remember it, Sauter came to Fisher with heavy heart
and sadly explained that his marriage was on the rocks, his
personal life was a mess, he'd gotten this other offer for a lot
more money, and though he didn't really want to leave the *Daily
News,* he felt that he had to.

In fact, Sauter had toyed with the idea of broadcasting before,
despite professing the newspaperman's standard-issue disdain
for broadcast reporters as being overpaid and underskilled. If
those dolts could do it, he could, too, and probably better. It
happened that the Field family, which owned the *Daily News,* also
owned a local television station, and its news department stationed a camera and a producer in the paper's lobby, so that
reporters could stop as they left work and read the day's big
stories into the camera. It was a kind of joke among the *Daily
News* staff; but Sauter absolutely ate it up, not least because of
the thirty-dollar fee it paid, and he was always trying to get his
stories on that newscast. The segment was produced by a fellow

named Jon Ward, until Ward quit to go to work at WBBM radio. It was Ward who became Sauter's connection to WBBM when the station was gearing up for its switch to the all-news format. With his life in a mess and the recent newsroom blowup as a prod, Sauter decided that if somebody were going to be over-paid, it might just as well be he. He quit the paper and went to work in broadcasting.

Over at WBBM, of course, John Callaway knew nothing of all this; he only knew that he'd found his Murrow.

Chapter

IT WAS A COMICAL scene and slightly absurd, and if the mood hadn't been so tense and the stakes so high, those involved might have even gotten a laugh out of it. As it was, the two CBS News executives and the studio production team assigned to special duty that memorable weekend patiently watched and waited and tried to get through. It was Saturday, March 7, 1981, the dawn of life after Walter Cronkite, and Dan Rather, who had been given the astonishing sum of $22 million to sit in Cronkite's chair, didn't want to sit in Cronkite's chair.

The night before, Cronkite had anchored his final *CBS Evening News* broadcast after a nineteen-year run, a time in which he had acquired a place in the national myth that ranked somewhere above most presidents. And now Dan Rather had the weekend to make the broadcast his.

Rather was to make his historic debut on Monday, so on Saturday he came to the CBS Broadcast Center on Manhattan's West Fifty-seventh Street, where he met Sanford Socolow, the executive producer of the *Evening News,* and Burton Benjamin, the vice-president in charge of the broadcast, for a series of run-throughs to get ready for the big event. Socolow and Benjamin, whose nicknames, Sandy and Bud, respectively, bespoke their geniality, were eager to do what they could to make Rather comfortable. They lit up the Cronkite studio—a slightly cramped newsroom set—manned the cameras with a crew, loaded the TelePrompTer with the script from Cronkite's last broadcast, and went through all the motions of preparing to put a broadcast on the air. Rather, in coat and tie, had makeup applied and his hair patted and combed into place and went to Cronkite's desk to read the news. But he wouldn't sit down.

"I'd like to try this standing up," he said. Socolow and Benjamin, who between them had fifty years' experience in putting news programs on the air for CBS, though it was a nutty idea— an anchorman standing to deliver the news!—but they were there to make Rather comfortable, and Rather didn't feel comfortable sitting in Cronkite's chair. So he tried reading the news standing up, and when that wasn't quite right, a barstool was appropriated from somewhere, and Rather tried that a couple of times. Then he thought he should try making an "entrance," and he sort of strolled over to the anchor desk, and that wasn't quite right either. They went through it all over and over, standing and sitting and strolling, again and again.

In the background, in between takes, carpenters worked on making Cronkite's office into Rather's office, putting in wood paneling where a glass partition had been, and changing the background of the world map that was the *Evening News* backdrop from beige to blue. It was a minor change, hardly noticeable, really—and that was precisely its significance. CBS was trying to manage what one magazine writer called a "death-of-God" transition, from Cronkite to Rather, from myth to man, by the application of a coat of blue paint. In every other aspect—in its producers, its writers, its studio set (the "Cronkite newsroom" it was called), in its look, feel, and philosophy—the *CBS Evening News* would remain exactly as it had been with Walter Cronkite—except, of course, it would be without Cronkite. It was a telling and ultimately costly display of the institution's certainty (or arrogance) and of its remarkable innocence about the world that had meanwhile evolved outside the sheltering arms of Cronkite and Salant.

Early in the yearlong interval between Rather's selection and his ascension there had been some talk of devising a plan for the post-Cronkite age. A sort of committee had even been formed, and Don Hewitt, the resident genius who had produced the *Evening News* before Cronkite, a fifteen-minute nightly whirl with Douglas Edwards, was even brought in from *60 Minutes* to offer his ideas. Hewitt came up with a few notions, including the idea of putting a huge graphic on the screen that would have dwarfed Rather; but he dropped out of the discussion after a while, and the planning committee eventually fizzled out.

Months passed, the date got closer, and by late 1980 Sandy Socolow had started to worry. Socolow, one of Cronkite's closest friends, had been asked to remain as executive producer of the *Evening News* after Cronkite's departure, to ensure a smooth transition. But Socolow thought that there ought to be *some* plan, some preparation for Rather, so he laid out his thoughts in a three-page memo to Bill Leonard. He wanted, in the next few months, to "fold" Rather into the broadcast gradually, having him report some important stories, appearing regularly at the *Evening News* desk with Cronkite, and in the final month or so to coanchor the newscast with Cronkite, to let the folks know that Dan was all right, he was Walter's guy. At a meeting in Leonard's office Socolow outlined his plan to Leonard and his senior staff, Bob Chandler, Bud Benjamin, and Ed Fouhy, the Washington bureau chief who was soon to replace Benjamin as vice-president in charge of hard news. Cronkite and Rather were there, too. They all seemed to agree on Socolow's plan, but the next week Leonard suddenly scotched it.

"They have this research," Leonard told his executives, who knew immediately that "they" meant Black Rock, and the research showed that the best thing was to minimize the change in anchor as much as possible. Cronkite's dominance had been not only a matter of pride, but a matter of dollars, each rating point of his lead over the competition being worth as much as $25 million in advertising revenues. Why emphasize his departure? Socolow, not believing what he'd heard, asked with some sarcasm, "Are you saying that we're gonna sneak Rather over when nobody's watching?" To which Leonard snapped, "Don't give me any bullshit!"

In short, the CBS transition policy amounted to a kind of fantastic bait-and-switch ploy. There had even been raging arguments inside CBS News over whether Cronkite would even acknowledge on the air that he was leaving the broadcast. Cronkite didn't want to say good-bye. It wasn't as if he were *dying*, and besides, he'd been given assurances that he could appear on the *Evening News* whenever he wanted. But Leonard knew that Cronkite's last broadcast would be bigger news than any story it would report. He prevailed upon his anchorman to say a little something, and Cronkite finally agreed. At the end of his last *Evening News* broadcast, on Friday, March 6, 1981, he said that his colleague Dan Rather, a good man, would be on the broadcast come Monday. And he intoned in that voice as familiar as family, "Old anchorman don't go away, they keep coming back for more" (a prospect that made Dan Rather none the more comfortable).

And so Rather, knowing that if failure came, it would be monumental and would have his name on it, wanted to do something that would somehow distinguish his presence from Cronkite's. Because he wanted to make the broadcast his, on Saturday he stood and sat and strolled late into the night, and he was back on Sunday. Finally Monday arrived, and Rather neither sat nor strolled nor stood. He made his debut as the permanent anchor of the *CBS Evening News* in a kind of squat, a contortion that was awkward just to watch, much less to hold while reading the news. It made a painful, pitiable display of Rather's first performance in Cronkite's chair, which would have been terrible enough anyway. He looked as if he were getting ready to run off somewhere, as, in retrospect, might have seemed a good option. And it didn't get much better over the next few weeks, even after Rather had abandoned his squat for a more conventional posture. The transition was a complete disaster.

Although it was not at all what he'd had in mind when he accepted the job, the pursuit, care, and feeding of Dan Rather, anchorman, became Bill Leonard's vocation when he returned to CBS News. It was a mission for which he had neither much appetite nor much aptitude, it turned out, but it was the circumstance that defined his brief time as news president and, ultimately, that ended it.

Leonard had gotten a strong hint of things to come right away. Just a few days after he left the CBS lobbying job and moved to New York in July 1978, when Dick Salant was still technically the president of CBS News, Cronkite walked into Leonard's office and said he wanted off the *Evening News.* Leonard begged him to stay—it had worked for Salant—but Cronkite was determined now, and as the weeks passed, his determination grew more firm. He was tired, he said, but it was more than that: He wanted to go out on top. He was obsessed with the thought, and he wouldn't be moved.

The "Walter problem" nagged at Leonard for weeks, and he sometimes talked about it distractedly to the few colleagues who also knew that Cronkite was determined to leave. But after a time the problem seemed to go away, and one of those at CBS News who'd known about it asked Leonard what was up. "It's taken care of," Leonard said with a smile. "It's amazing what three hundred thousand dollars will do."

Leonard had bought himself some time. He knew that Cronkite was interested in long-term security, not to mention money, and Leonard offered him a package that gave him heaps of both. Cronkite had had, since 1973, what many would consider a "dream" deal with CBS—three months off every year and a salary, $650,000 annually, in the movie star range—but he had been more than worth it. Leonard offered a salary of nearly $1 million a year and a contract that would carry Cronkite well into his seventies. He threw in a number of other perks, including the title of special correspondent, which would exempt Cronkite from prohibitions on product endorsement and other money-making opportunities forbidden to CBS journalists by the CBS News standards (Salant again). Leonard asked only that Cronkite stay put until his retirement time, November 1981, that he cooperate in the transition, and that he not ply his craft on anyone else's air. Cronkite agreed.

Leonard had bought a little time, but just a little; the Cronkite succession would have to be dealt with soon. In the meantime, he was getting an unanticipated and entirely unwelcome initiation into the new world of network news management.

The business had changed since Leonard's days under Salant; it had changed even in the short time, from 1975 to 1978, that he had been away from CBS News as the network's lobbyist in Washington. A new factor had come into play, and it was changing everything: the Arledge factor. ABC, long the third player in the three-network competition in both entertainment and news, had staged a remarkable surge in prime time in the mid-1970s, soaring to first place in the prime-time ratings and reaping, after a history as poor cousin, the attendant riches. Now that it could afford one, ABC wanted a first-rate news department, and it turned to its only proven franchise builder, Roone Arledge, the producer and executive who'd built ABC Sports into the best in the business when the network had precious little else. Arledge became president of ABC News in 1977 and immediately set about the task of building an organization that could compete with CBS and NBC. He went shopping for news talent.

He found a well-stocked market in the corridors of CBS News. The place was so deep in talent, the path to the top so crowded that, pulls of institutional loyalty aside, many were not deaf to the whispers of big money and instant position. One after the other they left, a dozen producers and correspondents, people who'd been the backbone of CBS News, the bench strength, the edge. There were big-name producers like Rick Kaplan and John Armstrong, correspondents such as Barry Serafin, Sylvia Chase, John Lawrence, Hal Walker, and Richard Threlkeld, and a lot of worthy operatives in between.

Artfully working this environment was a man named Richard Leibner, an accountant/talent agent who was becoming easily as great a force in the business of CBS News as any who worked there. Leibner was, he said of himself, "an act": a fast-talking, Brooklyn-accented study in street manners, who spoke the epithets of many tongues, most often the earthiest of Yiddish. But he was as astute as he was unpolished, a sharp negotiator with a scent for opportunity so keen it was maddening to many of the network executives who had to deal with him. He was a wheeler-dealer in a business generally unaccustomed to such maneuvers, and if he was honorable, it made him no less a pain in the ass. That was precisely why more than 100 CBS News employees, from star correspondents to field producers, hired Leibner and his wife, Carole Cooper, as their agents.

At CBS top news talent seemed to be falling out the windows, and Leonard's CBS News had neither the contractual mechanisms (such as the right of first refusal to a competitor's offer) nor the instinct to deal effectively with the new freewheeling marketplace. It was such an unexpected development that CBS News was slow to respond, and when it did, it overresponded. Like a rube tourist in a Turkish bazaar, even the bargains it got weren't bargains. CBS lost people it wanted to keep and paid too much for many people it kept and probably could have afforded to lose. "Every name, we're whipsawing him," recalled Leibner of that golden moment in the agenting business. "And they don't make up their minds, 'This is who we gotta keep, and this is who can go.' And they dissipate gloms of money on people who they shouldn't have." Leibner, merciless, even hired away from CBS one of its bright young negotiators, Stu Witt, who became an agent in Leibner's rapidly expanding agency, N. S. Bienstock, Inc.

At one point Marvin Kalb, a CBS star in the Washington bureau, tried to exploit the situation and made such strong demands (including not only money but a new contract for his brother, Bernard, and guaranteed airtime on the *Evening News*) that Leonard, frustrated and angry, just said the hell with it and let Kalb leave CBS for NBC. Although contract demands had always been private, or were supposed to be, Leonard issued an angry press release saying that giving in to Kalb's demands "would have distorted our news content, tailoring the broadcast to meet a contractual arrangement."

No, this was not what Leonard had had in mind when he took the job. But it was nothing next to the odyssey that was just around the bend.

As it happened, one of Leibner's clients was Dan Rather, then one of the stars of *60 Minutes* and the man Leibner had believed to be the inevitable successor to Walter Cronkite. Leibner's was a minority view, however, and that was the belief underlying a meeting he called in May 1979 with Rather and his wife, Jean, at the Leibners' home in Great Neck, Long Island. The group knew that Roger Mudd had long been, and remained, the favorite to succeed Cronkite and that Rather had some difficulties within the organization. His tumultuous tour of duty at the Nixon White House, when he became the symbol of the friction between the president and the press, convinced many at CBS News that Rather was a self-serving grandstander at best or a political advocate at worst. His journalism aside, many at the organization, and not just the Mudd supporters, believed Rather to be a disingenuous self-promoter and regarded him with some contempt. If the next anchor was to be chosen right then, in May 1979, it would be Mudd, and Rather knew it.

But such odds had always increased Rather's determination. In 1969, for example, Rather had heard that the anchor job on the Sunday *Evening News* was vacant and about to be filled by another CBS correspondent, John Hart.

The weekend anchor job was a plum, a nice showcase for the cadre of up-and-coming newspeople with anchor ambitions, and Rather, then the White House correspondent, was furious that

he'd been passed over, apparently without serious consideration. Hart's CBS career had pretty much tracked Rather's—civil
rights in the South, a tour in Vietnam, Washington—but Rather
had three years' seniority on Hart. Rather marched into the
office of his bureau chief, Bill Small, and demanded an explanation. "Is this true?" Rather asked, and Small, who was one of
Rather's strong supporters, said yes, it was true. "Wait just a
damn minute," Rather said. "If this is some medallion, if this is
some reward for good work, then I'd like to know when I might
get in the fight. You're telling me this is going to happen, and
I'm hearing from everybody that this is one of the ways of rewarding good work, that this is the ladder up." Small again said
yes, that was true; but people got paid to make such decisions,
and in this case the person was Gordon Manning, the vice-
president of news, and Manning's decision was John Hart.
Rather said that he'd just see about that, and he flew to New
York, where he confronted Manning.

Manning, who respected Rather as a reporter but believed his
hard-edged style (*superventilated* was Manning's term for it) was
ill suited for anchor work, told Rather flatly, "Life is selective,
Dan, and I've selected Hart." It was a pretty cold bath, but when
Rather got back to Washington, he went in for one more round
with Small. "You've got trouble with me, beginning now," he
told Small. He reminded Small of all the armpits of the world
that he, Rather, had toured on behalf of CBS News, of all the
Christmases and children's birthdays he'd missed, and now this
was his reward, to be passed over when the goodies were being
handed out. It was angry talk, and it had an effect. A few weeks
later Rather was called to New York, where he was told that he'd
be the temporary Sunday anchor, and after a few weeks he got
the job. Manning still preferred Hart, but he decided that Rather
wouldn't embarrass CBS and that maybe things would be easier
all around if he were given the job. Hart never knew what hit
him.

Ten years later, with the big prize at stake, Rather wasn't
about to let Mudd, favorite or no, stand in his way. He'd run this
race.

Unfortunately for Rather, though, in May 1979 CBS hadn't
yet recognized that there was a race. Mudd's contract wasn't up
until 1980, conveniently coming due just before Cronkite's
planned retirement. Rather's contract, on the other hand, had

more than two years remaining on it. There was, in other words, no routine means of forcing the contest upon Leonard and his management staff, who were taking their sweet time on the succession matter. If things just took their natural course, Leibner thought, if CBS just fell into its next anchor, Mudd would get the job.

Through the summer of 1979 Leibner waited and worried and waited some more. Summer turned to fall, and there was still no sign of development. Then, in October, Rather caught a break. Someone (suspicious eyes would be cast on the Rather-Leibner camp) leaked to the *New York Daily News* a story that Rather had been talking to Arledge and was bound for ABC. Leonard hit the roof. He called Rather into his office and asked him about the story; how could he talk to ABC without giving CBS News a shot, where was his loyalty? Rather denied that he'd done anything. Upset, he called Leibner and relayed the encounter. But Leibner wasn't upset at all, quite the contrary. "We're twenty percent of the way home," he told his client. "We're there." The issue had been forced.

Leonard wasn't anywhere near ready to make a choice yet, but now he was obliged to think about it. And the awful thought suddenly occurred to him that in such a crazy environment he stood to lose both of his top correspondents and heirs apparent. He set out to bind Mudd and Rather to CBS, making luncheon appointments with both men within three days.

Mudd came first. Leonard offered to write him a new contract, with no promises of the anchor chair but lots more money and, of course, a guarantee that he would be at the top of the list when it came time to choose. Mudd, confident in the extreme and apparently believing that CBS would be making a world-class mistake to choose anyone else for the Cronkite job, said no, thanks, this wasn't the time to talk, he'd stick with his present contract and take his chances.

Two days later Leonard met with Rather and Leibner at a restaurant called New York, New York, around the corner from Black Rock. Leibner quickly set the tone, scoring Leonard for even suggesting that Rather would be so dishonorable as to ditch CBS without giving Leonard a chance to negotiate. Rather would, Leibner said, gladly enter a fair and open discussion with CBS. He didn't think anything would come of it, there was big, big money to be had elsewhere, but he would hear what CBS had to say. Through it all, as rehearsed, Rather sat quietly, with stiff upper lip. Then, as coffee was being served, he excused himself and left the restaurant, again as prearranged. Leibner then proceeded to maneuver Leonard into a major tactical error, a concession that Leibner had predicted back in that May meeting would become his ace in the hole in the Rather negotiations.

He told Leonard that there was one condition in Rather's dealings with CBS: that CBS promise in writing to keep Rather on *60 Minutes* no matter what came of the negotiations, until sixty days before his contract expired. Leonard said he'd have to run it by his legal guys, but he saw no problem, he'd send him a letter in a couple of days. Right there at lunch, without leaving the table, Leibner knew that if Rather wanted to stay at CBS, he could and that he could have at least a coanchor arrangement. After lunch Leibner met Rather at their arranged rendezvous, where Rather asked what had happened. "It's seventy percent done," Leibner said. "I'm getting the *Sixty Minutes* letter." As Leibner saw it, CBS had dealt away its leverage—the threat of damaging Rather by keeping him off the air for two years if he went elsewhere. What's more, Leibner could now guarantee both ABC and NBC that the anchorman he was offering them would be delivered fresh from the most popular show on television, where he was seen by fifty million viewers every week.

The next step in Leibner's plan was to separate Rather from Mudd, to make Leonard see that there was too much animosity between them and their supporters for the two to work as an anchor team. Leonard didn't need to be convinced. Mudd had already told him that he wasn't interested in sharing the anchor desk, and that settled that; it would have to be one or the other. The question was which. Leonard put it to a vote of his senior staff—hard-news vice-president Bud Benjamin, Benjamin's deputy, John Lane, soft news vice-president Bob Chandler, and Washington bureau chief Ed Fouhy. Only Bud Benjamin voted for Mudd.

If the vote didn't decide it, what was beginning to happen outside CBS News would. Roone Arledge wanted Dan Rather as the cornerstone of his new ABC News. Bill Small, who'd lost out on his chance to run CBS News and become the new president of NBC News, had the same idea at NBC. There began a dizzying high-stakes chase for Rather that put the price of television news talent into another sphere. Suddenly Roger Mudd became irrelevant. As Leonard later put it, "Roone Arledge and Bill Small came to the conclusion that the person that might turn their news division around was Dan Rather. They didn't come to the conclusion that the person that might turn their news division around was Roger Mudd."

So Rather it was. The only questions left were, Would Rather stay at CBS, and if so, how much would he cost? He would cost a lot. One day, early in the sweepstakes, Leibner returned from a meeting at ABC, where he'd been testing the waters, and said to Rather, "Look, just to give you an idea, if you want to work for one of the other two right now, and if we decide that's the best thing for you to do, I can tell you you will not make less than six million for five years." At the moment Rather was earning $300,000 a year as a correspondent on *60 Minutes.* His agent was telling him his salary would be quadrupled. Rather paused, then said, "If that's true, sign it."

But that was just the beginning. There was lots of dealing yet to come, lots of bumping the ante yet to be done. For a while it seemed certain that Rather was headed for ABC. Arledge and his top aide, David Burke, were ideal suitors, lavish in their admiration, attentive to Rather's concerns. Dan was worried about the lack of depth at ABC News? ABC would hire twenty producers—name them—from CBS. They talked through the night in clandestine meetings conducted in a series of hotel rooms, and Rather was being won. Another factor favored ABC. Rather knew that he would have a tough go of it at CBS, that the disappointed soldiers of the Mudd camp would harbor resentments and that Cronkite people, too, would likely be measuring the new man against the impossible standards of his predecessor. And Leibner was pushing ABC. "There are rocks under the water" he'd say of CBS, and, "The next guy after Cronkite will get his head blown off."

Rather knew all that, but he couldn't quite get himself to leave. Not only did he have a real institutional loyalty, but he genuinely respected the overall strength of the organization and realized it would be tough to have to go up against it. Beyond that, he wasn't sure that fear—fear of the infighting, fear of Cronkite's shadow—was a good basis for decision. So in January 1980, in a meeting with Jean, Richard, and Carole at the Rathers' apartment, he told Leibner that if CBS would get in the ball game in a serious way, if it would come close to the ABC offer, he would stay.

But CBS was nowhere close to the ABC offer, which by then had topped $2 million a year. Leonard was still talking numbers half that amount, and he wasn't budging. He just didn't seem to get it, Leibner thought, or else he wasn't adequately presenting the situation to Black Rock. Didn't CBS know that it could lose Rather? Leibner wanted desperately to get past Leonard, to work over Jankowski himself as only Richard Leibner could. But Jankowski refused to meet with him. Leibner tried calling in a favor and asked Tom Leahy, a network executive with whom he'd had dealings, to arrange a meeting with Jankowski. Nothing doing. Leibner tried one more ploy. There was someone in Chicago who might help, someone he trusted, someone, he thought, who just might convince Jankowski that things were at a critical stage. He called Chicago. The next day Leonard called Leibner and told him he'd get his meeting with Jankowski. Ed Joyce, the general manager of WBBM-TV in Chicago, had come through.

Within days Leonard was back at the table, and now his numbers were in the ball park. A few days later he had a deal. Commencing in 1981, Rather would be anchorman and managing editor of the *CBS Evening News,* and he'd be paid $22 million over ten years for his efforts (the pact actually took effect retroactively, beginning January 1, 1980). It wasn't up to ABC's offer, not quite, but CBS was willing to throw in something else, a "window" at the halfway point that would allow either side to get out of the deal. It seemed a cheap enough concession at the time. Five years later another president of CBS News, Ed Joyce, discovered just how costly a concession it was.

On Valentine's Day 1980, Rather signed his deal with CBS. It was the worst day of Roger Mudd's career. After scheduling a press conference for that afternoon to announce the Rather signing, Leonard flew down to Washington in a CBS jet and gave the news to Mudd personally. He didn't take it well. After Leonard left, Mudd quietly gathered some things and left the bureau, speaking to no one. He later issued a statement, however, that made clear his views: "The management of CBS and CBS News has made its decision on Walter Cronkite's successor according to its current values and standards. From the beginning, I've regarded myself as a news reporter and not as a newsmaker or celebrity." Mudd spent the next eight months off the air, in well-paid exile, before leaving CBS for NBC News. (Leibner, victorious, gloated over Mudd's strategic blunder in refusing to talk about a new contract with Leonard back in October. "Leonard invited him to the ball and he didn't write his name on the dance card. So, when he got the news on Valentine's Day four months later, only one person had put the poker up his ass—himself, the putz.")

Up in New York, though, Dan Rather was nothing but smiles. He met reporters at the CBS press conference and posed for pictures with Walter Cronkite. *Time* magazine was there to do a cover story on the "$8,000,000 Man" (if only it'd known). The story reported that Rather had accepted Leonard's invitation to stay at CBS with the statement "I have decided to make a new covenant of excellence at CBS." The quote was worth a few hoots at the Broadcast Center when someone dug up a copy of Rather's autobiography, *The Camera Never Blinks,* published just three years before, in which he referred to Barbara Walters's 1976 million-dollar-a-year contract from ABC as a "heist." In answer to his own rhetorical question, Is anyone worth $1 million a year? he'd said, "In my own view, no one in this business is, no matter what or how many shows they do, unless they find a cure for cancer on the side." Now Rather was making, even by *Time*'s incorrect estimate, $1.6 million a year. As convenants go, Rather's was an excellent one indeed.

All this left Bill Leonard, who turned sixty-four shortly after Rather's signing, precious little time to think about his own successor and precious little time for the candidates to showcase their abilities. But once Rather had assumed the anchor, in March 1981, Leonard began to put a lineage in place.

First in line was Ed Fouhy, the hard-nosed Boston Irishman brought to New York by Leonard to assume the old Gordon Manning-Bill Small job, vice-president of news, which had been traditionally viewed as the official heir apparent's post. Fouhy was a former wire service reporter whose biggest impact at CBS had probably been in his role as the *Evening News* senior producer in Washington in the early 1970s. It was Fouhy's job to sell Washington stories to New York, a relatively easy chore for him because he had first-rate correspondents and because he truly believed that Washington stories were intrinsically the most important stories. Fouhy was a newsman's newsman, a Salant kind of newsman. In fact, after Salant had retired from CBS in hurt and anger, he had accepted a job at

NBC as vice-chairman in charge of news, and the first thing he had tried to do was to hire Ed Fouhy as NBC News president. Fouhy had declined, and now that decision seemed likely to pay off.

To make room for Fouhy, Leonard moved Bud Benjamin, who was entering his sixties, from the vice-president's job to a new post with the all-purpose title of senior executive producer. John Lane, a former newspaperman who'd worked in the CBS Chicago bureau and then spent most of the 1970s as a senior producer on the Cronkite broadcast, was Fouhy's assistant and another contender. Leonard moved Bob Chandler, his longtime deputy from the Salant days and now the vice-president in charge of all soft news, to an administrative vice-president's position, which also put him directly in the line of succession. Replacing him was Roger Colloff, a young lawyer who'd impressed Leonard on the CBS lobbying staff and who, Leonard thought, would himself be in line for the top job someday.

If the choice had been entirely Leonard's, he would probably have picked Chandler, who had the longest executive experience. But Fouhy and Lane were good men, too, Leonard told Jankowski. All three were cut in the serious and honorable tradition of Dick Salant, and Black Rock would do well in choosing any of them when the time came.

That done, Leonard turned his attentions to other matters, such as the tricky effort to sell CBS affiliates on the idea of an expanded, hourlong *Evening News,* which would be, he thought, his legacy. He'd already started the new *Sunday Morning* show, a literate and artful program produced by Robert ("Shad") Northshield and anchored by Charles Kuralt, and he had in the works a spin-off of *60 Minutes* called *Up to the Minute,* featuring the stars of the popular Sunday-night broadcast. Leonard had about a year remaining in his short reign, and with his hand-picked staff running the daily operation and leaving him free to tend to his pet projects, it seemed that his tenure might turn out a success after all.

But Black Rock's ideal of news management was not Leonard's, and being cut from the Salant mold was not considered a compelling credential. There was a new world to deal with, a high-stakes, highly competitive arena in which the ability to win was the credential that counted most. In that respect Black Rock was not so sure about Leonard's team.

Foremost, there was the Rather problem. Dan Rather had not only not found the cure for cancer in return for $22 million, he had not even found the cure for ratings anemia. He came across as edgy and uncomfortable and, sensing that, was becoming all the more edgy. He simply wasn't very good on the air. Critics were unkind, as might have been predicted, noting, in some cases with apparent glee, that Rather on Cronkite's broadcast looked like a gangly kid in a grown-up's suit.

Worse—much worse—Rather's ratings were falling. He'd inherited a 2.5-point ratings lead from Walter Cronkite (each point representing nearly 800,000 TV households), but through the spring and summer of 1981 that lead was slowly squandered. ABC's *World News Tonight,* with its three-anchor format and a snappy, graphics-enhanced look, was edging inexorably closer to Rather. Everyone at CBS had anticipated some audience loss when Cronkite left, even a lot of audience loss, but when it actually happened, it hit like a blow to the gut. Suddenly the blessed haven that Cronkite had built was gone, and with it, the easy self-assurance that had marked the organization in his time. The place that had once happily ignored ratings was now being defined by the ratings, and the most telling indication of how bad things were, the development that couldn't be ignored, was this: The price of a thirty-second commercial on the *CBS Evening News,* which at the peak of Cronkite's popularity was $40,000, had slipped to $30,000, the same rate charged by the competition.

Rather was miserable and frustrated. Why didn't somebody do something, anything, to help him? It seemed to him that the organization was almost pulling against him, wanting him to fail. As Rather slowly sank, the sense of vindication emanating from the sizable Mudd camp was almost palpable. Even some of the CBS News executives, the people who were supposed to be helping Rather, seemed to be undermining him. Years later Rather recalled with some bitterness how one high-ranking news executive had stood in conversation outside Rather's door, not once but twice, and had said in a voice loud enough for Rather to hear, "Rather's bombing out, and it's only a question of time, and it's prolly gonna happen pretty quickly, before they get him out of here." Rather was torn between going outside and "decking the guy" and finding a corner to hide in. He just hadn't expected such breadth and depth of hostility. "I thought that once the decision was made—not everybody thinks I'm terrific, I know—but once in there, I thought, everybody will pull for you because they don't want to pull the house down. I would have thought that everybody would have seen that as being in the best interest of CBS News. But I was wrong."

By summer, just six months after Rather replaced Cronkite, there began to be some talk of replacing Rather. It was furtive hallway chatter at first, but it grew louder and more insistent and eventually made its way into the newspapers. Maybe Mudd could be brought back, or perhaps Charles Kuralt would be teamed with Rather. Maybe Kuralt would simply replace Rather. Kuralt always took pains to dismiss such talk; but it persisted, and it didn't much help Rather's performance.

But at Black Rock the idea of replacing Rather seemed ridiculous. CBS had just made a $22 million "covenant of excellence" with Dan Rather, and if it wasn't working, perhaps it was the fault of the people whose job it was to make it work. That thought had crossed Rather's mind, of course, and it was a view that Richard Leibner, who now had some entrée at Black Rock, was actively expounding. It was just what Leibner had feared; it was why he'd advised Rather to leave CBS for ABC. "The regime didn't understand where television was going, and Leonard thought that you could just put his ass in Cronkite's chair and keep doing Cronkite's show and he'd win," Leibner said. "And nothing could have been wronger, and he went from first to last. It's exactly why I wanted him to leave."

By summer Rather was barely in first place and still downward-bound on a course that eventually put his broadcast in last place. It was an unthinkable circumstance. Something had to change. Something did.

On November 10, 1981, Bill Leonard's daily morning staff meeting was attended by an unscheduled visitor, Gene Jankowski, who, Leonard said, had something he wanted to say to the staff. Leonard's office was crowded with all the senior staff—Fouhy, Lane, Chandler, Colloff, Benjamin, and Margery Baker, a new vice-president of news—people who had been formed by the institution's past and who fully expected to shape its future. Jankowski, normally an amiable man with a salesman's good cheer, appeared nervous, so nervous that he made many in the room feel uncomfortable. This must be bad.

Jankowski got straight to it. There'd been speculation in the organization about Leonard's successor, and in the press, too, and he wanted the staff to know that Black Rock had made a decision. The next president of CBS News was going to be Van Gordon Sauter. There was a breathless moment, and then Jankowski dropped another bomb. "Van's going to be president when Bill leaves next year, and Ed Joyce is going to be coming over here as his executive vice-president."

Jankowski babbled on nervously for a few moments, talking about how both Sauter and Joyce were "part of CBS News," how they were "coming back home" and such, but most of what he said was lost on his audience. When he finished, there was a moment of pained silence, and then John Lane asked the question that was on everybody's tongue: "Are we so bankrupt that you had to bring in *two* people?"

Jankowski didn't answer; he didn't really need to.

Jankowski left, and Leonard's group retreated into a grim silence. They had lost, and their *way* had lost. There wasn't much to say.

"It was like a wake," Ed Fouhy said years later. "And I don't mean an Irish wake."

Chapter

JOHN CALLAWAY WAS SHOCKED. His new national reporter, the star of the WBBM staff, Callaway's *Murrow*, wanted to quit. Van Sauter had gone out on the road almost as soon as he arrived at WBBM, and as far as Callaway was concerned, the guy was perfect, even better than his audition had promised. Sauter had traveled with the antiwar campaign of Eugene McCarthy, he'd reported on black kids from around the country, and his broadcasts had been first-rate. It seemed to Callaway that Sauter was having a grand time, and why not? Sauter had an unlimited expense account, access to airtime, and complete editorial freedom. Callaway had spent a career in broadcasting and had never had such a deal; it was, as Callaway had said before and would say again, the best job in American radio.

But now, just two months after he had started, Sauter wanted to do something else: He wanted, to Callaway's utter amazement, to enter management. "John," Sauter said to Callaway one day early in the summer of 1968, "this fucking place ain't gonna make it through the week after next. You need a managing editor." The WBBM all-news operation, which Callaway had so frantically assembled and put into operation, managed to go on the air and fill the time with news, but it was a very near thing more often than not. Callaway, whose own skill and interest resided in on-air reporting, was terrible at organization, and his newsroom was chaos. The all-news beast he'd created was an insatiable maw. It just devoured material, and there was no system for feeding it; on some days, Sauter said, you could listen to WBBM news and hear the rustling of paper as the anchor actually read one of the local newspapers over the air, desperately trying to fill time. Callaway knew that Sauter was right, the place did need a managing editor, but he was taken aback when Sauter said, "John, let me become the managing editor of this thing; let me get this fucking thing organized."

"Thanks very much," Callaway said, "but you have the greatest job in American broadcasting, and I wouldn't want to do that." Was Sauter crazy?

But Sauter fixed Callaway with a determined look and said, "I want to do this, I'm your boy, I know how newsrooms are run." Put to a vote, that assertion might not have carried any of the newsrooms Sauter had worked in, but it was enough for Callaway. He was convinced, and Sauter was his new managing editor.

The Sauter legend theretofore had borne no hint of management talent or aspiration, no betrayal of any ability to make things work (unless one counted Sauter's remarkable system of converting Vietnamese piasters into dollars on his expense accounts back in his foreign correspondent days, a system, his associates observed, that had the magical effect of making dollars grow). Most of his newspaper associates would have agreed with Sauter's pal Ron Martin that "those of us who knew him were very surprised that he was ever put in charge of anything but himself." But that was only because Sauter had never been in broadcasting.

In the newspaper world Sauter might have been dismissed as a talented but relatively superficial journalist, an admired stylist who'd never win a Pulitzer Prize, but in broadcasting Sauter was the goods, a real journalist. And in the newspaper business a career in management had seemed, except at the highest levels, an exercise in applied penuriousness, not a particularly compelling prospect, but broadcasting, with its fabulous excess, was a fat plum there for the picking. And it was so easy.

As WBBM's managing editor (a newspaper job description casually misapplied, as was the fashion in broadcasting) Sauter made short work of the newsroom confusion, imposing a system that put anchors and reporters on a schedule and put weather, traffic, and sports reports on a regular timetable. He knew nothing about radio ("To the right is louder," he joked), but all that was required was good sense and instinct. He set up his desk in the middle of the newsroom, in the center of the flow, and became a traffic cop, deciding which reporters to dispatch to which stories, coordinating their reports with the volume of wire service copy that was rewritten by the WBBM writing bank and with the taped reports that came in from the station's news services. He beefed up the staff even more, hiring reporters and writers, and almost everything that went on the air went through him.

Most of all, Sauter established a presence. He found that his offbeat personal style—the beard, the glib sayings, the well-measured irreverence—transferred nicely to his role as a boss. It had a certain disarming effect. His self-indulgence, moderated but not vanquished by his new circumstances, translated into a kind of good-time ambience in the newsroom. Sauter planted himself there for twelve-hour workdays; then sometimes he cruised the streets of Chicago with his police reporter in a station car, police radios blaring, until 4:00 A.M. Broadcast management was rich alluvial soil for the Sauter legend; it thrived, and so did WBBM. It was all great fun for Sauter, no mystery to it, really, but to Callaway, what Sauter did in that newsroom seemed a genuine miracle, to be admired even through the distance of twenty years. "He was wonderful," Callaway said. "He got systems set up, and his very presence in the middle of that place brought the turbulent waters down to a simmer."

At the age of thirty-three, Van Gordon Sauter had found his calling, his true métier. In the space of just a few months he had discovered the formula for success in broadcast management: Begin with disaster; apply unlimited resources with a mix of casual charm and intelligence; then wait for results. It was to become a pattern—CBS providing various disasters and the resources, Sauter the charm and intellect—that led Sauter on a fast climb at CBS and one day made him seem the answer for CBS News.

The summer of 1968 was made for an all-news radio station trying to make its mark. It started with the assassination of Robert F. Kennedy and ended with the Democratic National Convention in Chicago, with its police riots, historic political encounters, and the arrest of the Chicago Eight. The year had already seen the assassination of Martin Luther King, Jr., and the "Days of Rage" riots that followed, the Soviet invasion of Czechoslovakia, the Tet offensive in Vietnam. Mr. Paley's all-news format seemed a stroke of genius, or marvelous good luck, and the revenues just poured in at WBBM. Early in the year, when Callaway was called to New York and informed of the change to an all-news format, he was told that if he could keep losses for that first year below a certain amount, he'd be a hero; instead, WBBM turned a profit in that year. Callaway (whose hiring of Sauter as managing editor had happily freed him to go back to some reporting) was moved to New York, in a considerable promotion, to set up a news exchange linkup system between the CBS-owned radio stations that were going the all-news route.

Sauter badly wanted Callaway's job at WBBM—he'd been doing it already—but there was a problem. The station's general manager, William O'Donnell, an arrow-straight family man, apparently didn't trust Sauter, didn't know quite what to make of him. Wasn't Sauter the one with the beard and the long hair, the guy who'd been seen walking up Lake Shore Drive with a six-pack of beer under his arm? Wasn't he, in fact, some sort of left-wing hippie? O'Donnell wasn't at all sure about Sauter, except that he didn't seem to be CBS executive material. What O'Donnell didn't see was the ambitious executive emerging just beneath the newsroom persona. In fact, Sauter was a hard-line political conservative, probably more conservative than O'Donnell himself. It all was great irony, Callaway getting promoted to New York because he seemed the part and Sauter, a true company man in the making, getting stalled because he didn't. That Sauter knack for misdirection—seeming to be one thing, being another—would one day be appreciated by the company as a valuable management asset, but it was all a little subtle for William C. O'Donnell, who needed to be persuaded.

Callaway and Sauter had become good friends. They'd written a book together (Sauter's second; he'd also written a book about the Detroit riots), and Callaway knew Sauter would be perfect for the job. He worked on O'Donnell; the station had to have someone to run the newsroom, after all, and finally, the general manager conceded. Sauter became news director of WBBM, less than a year after coming to the station. He was now squarely in the line of sight of a CBS News executive named

Emerson Stone, who in 1970 happened to be shopping for a bright young radio executive for an important job in New York. Stone, the head of radio operations for CBS News, had just lost the chief of his special-events unit, Ed Joyce, who, after a career in radio, was jumping to the fast track as the news director for the CBS flagship television station, WCBS. Joyce had gone to the special-events job from CBS's all-news radio station in New York, where he'd been news director, and Stone was scouting CBS's all-news stations for his replacement. He didn't know Sauter; but WBBM was soaring, and he offered Sauter the job. After holding out for more money, Sauter accepted and moved his family, temporarily reunited, to New York.

The job wasn't nearly as high-profile as Sauter might have hoped. The radio special-events unit was in charge of all radio news broadcasts except the regular hourly CBS News reports, everything from *Mike Wallace at Large* features to convention coverage. But by the early 1970s radio had long since yielded to television, and it was in television that all the important players at CBS News operated and the CBS News identity resided; radio was a very poor cousin. Although Sauter was as unconventional as ever, creating at radio special events a new edition of the good-time act, with a gang of pals (a hugely important element of the Sauter style) that included the jocular Lane Venardos, imported by Sauter from the WBBM writing bank, none of it was much noticed. It was only radio. To cover the story at the Republican National Convention in Miami in 1972, CBS News dispatched about 400 people, of which Sauter's radio unit constituted fewer than a dozen. (On the other hand, the Miami convention provided a great excuse for a "road trip," which was to become a staple of the Sauter management style; Sauter, Venardos, a desk assistant named George Schweitzer, and radio reporter Christopher Glenn returned to New York by way of the Virgin Islands and Puerto Rico.)

For all that, though, the New York job was an important step for Sauter. He witnessed at close hand the network culture, so different from newspapers, with its limousines, huge staffs, and fat expense accounts, a culture to which Sauter was naturally suited. Beyond that, New York was the place for someone with ambitions. It was where the power was; it was where an ambitious unknown could meet people who counted—people like Robert J. ("Bobby") Wussler.

Wussler was to CBS News in the early 1970s what Van Sauter

had been to the newsrooms of the *Detroit Free Press* and the *Chicago Daily News:* a charmer, a stylist, a semilegend who seemed to inspire doubt and admiration in almost equal measure. He was a creature of television, having started in the CBS mailroom straight out of college and soaring, all smiles and energy, up through the ranks to a considerable position at a very young age. While most important producers at CBS News had a grounding in print journalism, Wussler had a television sensibility, an inclination to make the screen *move* that served him well in his assignments with the CBS News election unit and on the manned space shots, the coverage of which he also organized. When in the mid-sixties CBS News decided to form a special-events unit specifically to cover those big planned news events, Wussler, at the age of twenty-eight, was named its head.

It was a high-cost, big-splash enterprise, and Wussler was perfectly cast. He was tireless in working out the nightmarish logistics of getting hundreds of reporters, technicians, and executives into place, dealing with local unions, putting the big events on the air. It was an enormously important job because the accepted belief in the industry was that whichever network shone brightest at the big events, especially at the conventions, won an edge with viewers until the next big-event showdown. And Wussler came through. The prevailing view at CBS held that it was these special events, particularly the space coverage, that pushed Cronkite to the front to stay.

Wussler was also a world-class spender of network money, cutting no corners on the job and availing himself personally of the considerable perks that network television culture afforded. He was an immensely personable individual who, like Sauter, thoroughly appreciated a good time, all the more if it could be tied in to the work. Dick Salant sometimes grumbled that Wussler and his staff shamelessly padded their budgets, "living high off the hog," but Wussler always delivered the goods; besides, he was so likable. His detractors resented the fact that he'd come so far so fast. Some thought that maybe he was a little *too* smooth (the "Catholic Sammy Glick" Harry Reasoner tagged him); they winced at his unconcealed ambition and the fact that he wasn't really a "journalist"—he'd never written for a paper or a magazine or, for that matter, for television. But being a bright, ambitious television whiz was not alone an indictable offense, even at the staid CBS News of the Cronkite-Salant era.

Wussler was a star, and there were those, including Wussler himself, who thought he'd be president of CBS News someday.

Bobby Wussler was, in short, the Sauter ideal. "Bobby was a big deal," Sauter recalled. "Bobby was bigger than life and operated outside of whatever was perceived to be the normal channels of accountability." So Wussler's promotion to the job of vice-president and general manager of the CBS-owned television station in Chicago, WBBM, was a development that Sauter noted with interest. It was apparent to all that the WBBM-TV job was a step up for Wussler, and a test as well. A local station was traditionally a required stop for a valued young CBS executive, a chance to prove himself at running a business that was expected to be profitable (as opposed, for example, to the news division) before advancing up the corporate ladder. CBS generally chose its station chiefs from the ranks of its sales corps, but by 1972, when Wussler got the WBBM job, it was clear that the most important factor in a local station's success, the center of its profitability, was the local news. That was why Jack Schneider, the president of the CBS Broadcast Group, which controlled both CBS News and the CBS stations, saw in Wussler a timely bet for WBBM-TV. Wussler, for his part, viewed the job as a stepping-stone toward the presidency of CBS News (which, as things turned out, was an underestimate of his destiny).

Wussler got the WBBM-TV job in September 1972; but he still had election night coverage to produce for CBS News before he could go to Chicago full-time, so through the fall he shuttled between the new job and the old. In that time he came to the conclusion that since news was so important to local stations, his own success would depend on the success of his news director, and Wussler made no secret of his utter lack of regard for WBBM-TV's news director, a man named Al Mann. As he shuttled back and forth, he put out the word that he was in the market for a news director for WBBM.

Sauter desperately wanted the Chicago job. His marriage was beginning to break up again, the radio special-events job was limited, and, most of all, he wanted to enter the Wussler orbit. He began angling for it. Sam Zelman, a CBS News executive who'd held a variety of jobs in broadcasting over the years, was a kind of talent scout for the network. Knowing that Sauter had worked in Chicago, Zelman asked him if he knew anyone he could recommend to Wussler. "Sure," Sauter said. "Me."

But as it happened, Wussler had already taken note of Sauter, as few other CBS News executives of importance had. They'd worked together on elections, Sauter and his little unit following Wussler's big-league team around at the conventions and scavenging the sound from the TV reports for the radio side. Wussler had also noticed Sauter's wit, charm, and ambition, the mix of qualities that had served Wussler himself so well. Wussler recognized right away what had eluded Bill O'Donnell back in Chicago: "Sauter's a smart politician. Underneath all that ridiculousness, and the layers of fat and beard and everything else, he's no dumbbell." One day Wussler was exiting through the revolving door at the CBS Broadcast Center, grousing about his unfruitful search to his friend and colleague Margery Baker, just as Sauter was entering. Baker nodded toward Sauter. "You know Van, what about him?"

Much to Sauter's delight, Wussler called; they met for dinner and Wussler asked, Would Sauter like to go back to Chicago? A bit disingenuously Sauter protested that he knew nothing about television; he didn't watch it much, he didn't even own a color set. "That doesn't matter," Wussler said. "It's news we're talking about. You and I will work together." There was just one hurdle: Would CBS News let Sauter go? Wussler said he ran it by Bill Leonard, the vice-president in charge of soft news. "Bobby," Leonard responded, "no one will know if you take him from here."

Leonard and the others at CBS News would know Van Sauter soon enough.

By the end of 1973 Sauter was just where he wanted to be, in television and teamed with Bobby Wussler. The partnership lasted less than two years, but in that time Sauter was formed as a television man, embracing an attitude, style, and set of values—a Sauter "ethic"—that first carried him to the top of CBS News and then made him the focus of bitter division at that institution.

The circumstances awaiting Sauter and Wussler at WBBM-TV were perfect—which is to say, the station was an unqualified disaster. The station's newscasts were impossibly bad, finishing not only behind the local ABC and NBC stations in the ratings but behind one of the independent stations as well. For a network affiliate, especially an affiliate of CBS, beating the independents was routine. CBS had all but given up on the station, and there had even been talk of selling WBBM and buying a strong station in some other market. "I was sort of in a good position in that there was no place to go but up," Wussler recalled. Sauter's recollection is more emphatic: "The station was so badly on its ass that you couldn't fuck it up. It was a junkyard."

Local news hadn't before seen the likes of a Bobby Wussler or a Van Sauter, and together they were a fable in the making. They turned the station, and Chicago television, upside down—challenging form, breaking rules, and spending money with true devotion. They imported old cronies (Wussler's former assistant Clarence Cross and Sauter's traveling buddy Lane Venardos among them), and, of course, a good time was had by all. Wussler ran the station the way he ran special events. "There was no Y class," said Venardos, "not even clipper class. Everything was first class."

The first order of business was to determine what kind of news to do. Sauter and Wussler assessed the marketplace and found that the ABC station employed a happy-talk format—anchors and reporters engaging in insipid chitchat meant to suggest an easy familiarity—and that the NBC station was a fair representation of the standard stolid TV news show. Wussler and Sauter decided to sell the Chicago audience on journalism. Not exactly the staid CBS News approach of Cronkite and Salant, but journalism with a capital *J*, journalism as a kind of theater—the shirtsleeve ambience, the rough-and-tumble pursuit of the big scoop, the *romance* of the newsroom, Chicago style, packaged for television. They commissioned Hugh Raisky, a clever set designer who'd built sets for Wussler for the space shots and conventions, to design a working newsroom for WBBM that could also be used as the studio set. They were looking to capture the "newsroom atmosphere," Sauter said to Raisky in a memo, "with its immediacy, flair and naturalness." They wanted desks, TV monitors, maps, wire machines—all the stuff and noise of a newsroom—right there on camera. "We want to bring the audience into our environment," Sauter continued, "which will be new and different to them, [and] hopefully exciting to them." The set was built, and soon it was emulated across the country.

Next, they went after anchors. The two they wanted—Bill

Kurtis, a CBS News correspondent in the Los Angeles bureau who'd been a local anchor in Chicago with moderate success, and Walter Jacobson, a local anchor and commentator—turned them down flat; WBBM was a problem they wanted no part of. Sauter and Wussler mulled the rejection over drinks and decided not to take no for an answer. They got Jacobson on the phone and worked on him for three or four hours, then went to see him and worked on him some more, until they had him. Then Sauter flew unannounced to Seattle, where Kurtis was working on a story for CBS News, knocked on his hotel door at 3:00 A.M., and refused to leave the room until Kurtis had agreed to come back to Chicago.

Huge contracts were lavished upon Kurtis and Jacobson; but WBBM had its anchors, and it was a marvelous team—Kurtis the smooth, authoritative newsman, Jacobson his scrappy and somewhat controversial counterpart. The station was ready to move, and all stops were pulled. WBBM somehow acquired the only local minicam—a portable camera unit enabling a reporter and crew to feed live coverage from the scene of a story—and it proved to be a huge asset. "I don't know if the gods were just in favor of us or what," Venardos said later, "but elevated trains seemed to collide twenty minutes before we'd go on the air and would hang precipitously off their structure, dozens of feet above the street. And there we'd be with live pictures."

The station exploited its minicam with a huge promotional campaign. Newspaper ads and radio ads and on-air television promotions suggested that any Chicago station that didn't have a minicam (which was to say, every station except WBBM) wasn't giving viewers the best news, the *real* news. "It was as much promotion as it was news," said Clarence Cross, the station's promotion man. "We really showed off." The promotion folks came up with the slogan "It's not pretty, but it's real," which was just perfect, perfect for the realistic newsroom and the live pictures of precipitously hanging trains and perfect for the electric team of Kurtis and Jacobson, whose pictures suddenly seemed to be on everything from billboards to matchbook covers.

The station used Jacobson in a way that CBS News never would have allowed, which is why Sauter and Wussler never asked. They made him a commentator as well as an anchor, and his sometimes outrageous opinions drew even more attention to WBBM. It was strictly against CBS rules for newsmen to insert opinion in their reports, but on that matter Sauter's view was succinct: "Fuck it."

Everything worked. Even when something went wrong, it worked. At one point the minicam was stolen from the station's van. By then, of course, everybody in town knew about WBBM's famous little minicam, and the Chicago papers treated the story like the Lindbergh kidnapping. The minicam caper was a running story for days until the thing was recovered, and if Black Rock wasn't especially amused over the disappearance of an expensive piece of equipment, the whole episode worked nicely into the station's awareness campaign.

It was the perfect environment in which to polish further the Sauter style, and Wussler was a worthy model. He exerted a large presence at WBBM, pulling into the station a little before noon in his company car (a Mercedes-Benz with the license plate "CBS"), all style and grace, and could still be found at the station at ten or eleven at night, after a dinner with some important Chicago politician or journalist. Not that Sauter needed a model. He moved out of the house (for good this time) and bought a BMW, appropriating a station employee as driver on nights of legendary self-indulgence (which included, on one booze-soaked night, the specter of gunplay as the driver escorted Sauter's wobbly companion to her front door and her waiting irate husband). At work Sauter was casual and profane and omnipresent in open-collared shirt and khakis, schmoozing up the crew, working over news copy, or sitting in the center of the newsroom with his feet on the desk and chuckling over one of his favorite newsroom diversions, high-motive crime stories that came across the wire (a guy barbecuing his wife's boyfriend on a charcoal grill and the like). At one point a parrot (a gift from a reporter) was added to the routine. The foul creature, named Sam, perched on a walking stick carried over Sauter's shoulder and screamed "Loretta" and the occasional obscenity as Sauter cruised the newsroom. Sometimes the bird could be heard squawking in the background when the news program was on the air.

It was all very engaging and the most drastic imaginable contrast with the style of the other managements that Black Rock had exported from New York. One of Sauter's old newspaper buddies, Kurt Luedtke, later speculated that some of Sauter's offbeat style was for effect. "An eccentric is a guy who keeps a parrot in his office because he really loves parrots; Bear did it because he knows the value of irreverence." But the Sauter act was a rave in Chicago. It might not have been real, but it sure was pretty.

Sauter had never worked a day in television before WBBM, but his acclimation to the medium, said Wussler, was "instant." How did it show? "Well, by having Sam the parrot wander the newsroom during the show and [by Sauter's] whispering into the director's ear that an interesting cutaway shot would be watching Sam as he's about to attack the anchorperson."

Sauter showed an appreciation of television values (as opposed to CBS News values) in other ways. He had, for example, a trick for boosting ratings during the local sweeps period—a quarterly four-week stretch when local stations' ratings were measured, the results determining how high a station could set its advertising rates until the next sweeps. The "news dummies," as Sauter referred to his reporters and anchors, would come to him with what they thought were compelling ideas for news series but that Sauter invariably found, as he put it, "boring as bat shit." He would turn to his favorite advertising agency, a little boutique operation. "You think up ads that you would love to see for sweeps series," he'd tell them. "If you make up good ads, we'll do the series."

It was an unspeakable breach of standards that would have had Sauter thrown out of the building at CBS News and would have probably even caused an uproar at WBBM had it been widely known. "In the news department, of course, we thought that was the end, that was the worst thing you could possibly do," Kurtis later said. But Sauter had a rationale. "What I tried to do," he said, "was to ensure that we had enough material so that somebody could say in all objectivity that the majority of what they did was of real journalistic value. And the other forty-nine percent was as exploitive as I could make it without embarrassing my mother." It was local news, after all, and he was there to win.

And it all began to work. The station wasn't number one in the ratings—that kind of turnaround took years—but WBBM was on the move. It was easily the most noticed station in the market, and for that, it might as well have been number one. The press was adoring, the TV writers for the local press positively flushed with admiration. For once television had a couple of real guys, people who drank beer and swore out loud—and were always available for interviews. "Van loved to be interviewed," Venardos said. "He and Wussler were as facile with the press as it was possible to be. The station enjoyed a run of good press that I've never seen equaled, anywhere, at a local station or a network."

Wussler's management approach (adopted by Sauter) was to spend first, get approval later; that was how, for example, the WBBM newsroom set was built. It was an enormous project, involving knocking down walls of one of the old radio orchestra studios, and Wussler ordered it done without first getting a capital purchase request approved. He'd leave the details to Chuck Kadlec, the loyal moneyman he'd brought to Chicago as director of finance for the station. "He indeed did go ahead without apparent approval of some [CBS stations] division people and spent money on news equipment or news coverage or all kinds of things, including improving his office, eventually," Kadlec recalled. But it seemed perfectly appropriate to Wussler; after all, wasn't he saving a station? As Wussler recalled it, "By the time I got the job I was in the fortunate position where [Black Rock] said, 'Let this kid do whatever it is he wants to do. If he fucks up, we haven't lost a thing. And if we get lucky, we've just saved a billion-dollar property."

As it happened, that wasn't precisely Black Rock's view. Corporate executives in New York were indeed pleased to have WBBM back in competition, but it was not in their physiology to accept cost overruns casually. They'd have arguments with Kadlec, who explained that it was okay if the station was $300,000 over budget because sales were $1 million over budget, but it was a losing argument. As soon as Sauter and Wussler were gone, Black Rock began to pick off their people one by one, firing, among others, Kadlec. (It was a measure of both his loyalty and of Wussler's and Sauter's charm that years later, after he'd left CBS for a successful consulting career, Kadlec remembered his time at WBBM as "our Camelot.") Eventually Black Rock dispatched to WBBM a general manager who could be counted on to keep things under control, a reliable and responsible news executive from WCBS in New York named Ed Joyce. It was the beginning of what became a kind of unofficial career for Joyce: counterbalancing Van Sauter.

For more than a year Sauter soared at WBBM. Then, in mid-

1974, he nearly crashed. It all began, as many things did, over a somewhat liquid lunch with Bobby Wussler.

The two men were feeling proud of what they'd done at WBBM; they'd turned the station around in a year and had added whole chapters to their respective legends for good measure. The subject turned to the future. What next? Wussler, it was safe to guess, would go back to New York, probably as president of CBS News. But Sauter harbored a rather unexpected ambition. "Why can't I anchor?" Wussler considered. Sauter was smart, he had personality, and he could sure talk— why not? So they invented a new broadcast. It would be something different, something for late afternoon, before the Kurtis-Jacobson newscasts, with Sauter as a kind of anchor-editor-reporter. He would casually stroll through the newsroom (just as he did in real life, sans squawking bird) and debrief reporters about the stories they were working on for that night. It was an extension of the journalism-as-theater concept, and on paper it seemed brilliant.

On the air, however, it was a bomb. Sauter was not quite so charming on television as he was in the newsroom, the pace was awkward, and viewers tuned out in droves. But circumstances made what might have been an easily forgiven misstep into a near disaster for Sauter. Before his first day on the air, Wussler had been summoned by Black Rock to return to New York, not to CBS News, but to become vice-president of the troubled CBS Sports division. It was clear that CBS had bigger things in mind for Wussler than even he had thought, but the move stripped Sauter of his protective shroud. His new boss, Neil Derrough, was no Bobby Wussler. Derrough (like his successor, Joyce) was at WBBM to bring order to the place; the ratings and the attention WBBM were getting were nice, but it was too maverick. The carte blanche was gone. "Neil is about as different from Wussler as night and day," said Venardos, "Y class *is* available. And things sort of changed pretty quickly." Derrough took Sauter off the air and made him a street reporter again, and it was clear to Sauter that his contract wouldn't be renewed. He was miserable covering four-alarm fires in two inches of snow; it was a terrible comedown. As he later told it, "I didn't like being a television reporter, I thought it was a dumb way of making a living. I mean, if you're going to be a reporter, you should write. This is a town where I'd done it the way it should be done."

He cast about for other work and got a bite from the all-news CBS radio station in Philadelphia, which offered him the news director's job—a job he'd left behind in Chicago two positions ago. Out of desperation, he wrote a letter to Bill Small, then the vice-president of news operations at CBS News, asking if he had something for him, anything, he'd go anywhere. Small called soon after. Yes, he had a little something: Would Sauter like to become CBS News' Paris bureau chief? It was a move that startled CBS News, and even Sauter himself was stunned. A local station guy, now a failed anchor, who'd been a minor player for a brief time in a forgotten corner of CBS News, was being handed a plum assignment. But Sauter was known to be close to Wussler, which didn't hurt, and Small, who had himself come up from local stations, had noticed Sauter—again, one of the few who had—when Sauter was head of radio special events. It happened that Small had been partial to radio since his days as Washington bureau chief, when he'd found it a valuable means of getting his correspondents known and an outlet that eased their frustration when their pieces didn't make the Cronkite show, which was often. Despite the prejudice against radio at CBS News, Sauter seemed to have approached his radio job with energy and imagination, and that counted with Small. Even so, years later Small was vague about his selection of Sauter. "Maybe in the best of all worlds you should have looked around and said, 'Maybe somebody else deserves it.' " But if the reasons were mysterious, the result was clear: Small had saved Van Sauter's career.

Sauter, the peerless fabulist, later told interviewers that being Paris bureau chief for CBS News was the "greatest job in the world," that after Paris his CBS career was all downhill. That was just the sort of thing he would be expected to say, and from an orthodox CBS newsman fixed on a career in CBS News, it would have sounded convincing (even though the romantic allure of the Paris job from the days of correspondent-as-statesman, the Murrow days, had long since given way to a routine of administrative and logistic chores). But people who knew Sauter in that time got another impression, one that suggested that he saw Paris as a mere way station. (He may have been the only Paris bureau chief who never learned French.) Sauter's old friend Wussler understood, and he later described Paris as "a shelf" for Sauter, a means of keeping him in play, so to speak, after the disaster in Chicago.

For Wussler himself, the CBS Sports job was only a brief stop.

In 1976, after just twenty months in sports, Wussler was named president of the CBS Television Network, capping his stunning rise through the company. He had stayed in touch with Sauter in Paris, visiting him when he went to Europe on business, reviving the good times in Chicago with a severe strain on the CBS expense account. One day, after he'd been in his new corporate job for just a few weeks, Wussler called Sauter with a question he probably wouldn't have put to any other CBS News journalist: Would Sauter like to leave Paris, and the news business, to become the new CBS censor?

And Sauter gave an answer that probably no other CBS journalist would have given: Yes. Sauter asked Wussler what the job entailed.

"You've got to be responsible for commercial content and you've got to be responsible for program content," Wussler told him. "It has nothing to do with the news division. You'll have no contact with them."

Sauter, Wussler recalled, responded, "That's terrific."

The job of censor—officially vice-president of program practices—was particularly touchy in 1976. The three networks were under intense pressure from Congress and various activist groups to tone down violence and suggestive sexual content in prime-time entertainment programs. The result was the so-called family hour concept, by which the networks promised to schedule family-oriented fare in the early hours of prime time. That, in turn, provoked an outraged reaction from Hollywood's creative community, which was pressing for ever more freedom in television production in the wake of producer Norman Lear's revolutionary sitcom *All in the Family.* A network could afford to alienate neither side in the dispute, which ultimately landed in the lap of the program practices chief. Wussler wanted someone he could trust and work closely with, and Sauter was a proven kindred spirit.

But Sauter's relatively unremarkable stay in Paris hadn't done much to raise his profile at CBS, and Wussler warned him that he'd have to pass muster with Jack Schneider, president of the CBS Broadcast Group and Wussler's boss. "I can do that," Sauter said, and Wussler informed Schneider that he'd found the new CBS censor.

Schneider recalled telling Wussler that he wasn't sure whom he was talking about. The Paris bureau chief for CBS News,

Wussler reminded him. Schneider wasn't convinced. "That's an unusual background for censor," he said.

"Look, he's perfect for the job," Wussler said. "He's written a couple of books; he can bullshit. He will charm the socks off of Norman Lear and those idiots on the West Coast."

Schneider wanted to meet Sauter. A meeting was arranged in New York, and Sauter proceeded to "charm the socks off" Jack Schneider. He got the job. It was a significant moment in the career of Van Sauter, and it offered, to any who cared to look, valuable insight into the man who one day was to be put in charge of that most egocentric institution, CBS News. In the space of five years Sauter had twice left CBS News to move up in the company. That was alien and dangerous behavior in an institution that believed itself to be the ultimate career reward, an institution whose exemplar was Richard Salant, a man who had used a corporate position as a stepladder to get to news; *that* was the proper sense of direction. And Sauter was taking a corporate job—network censor—that was by definition inimical to most journalists, whose interest is to reveal information, not to hold it back. Years later, after both Sauter and Wussler had left CBS, Wussler was asked what made him think Sauter would be interested in the censor's job. "Because I knew that Sauter craved ultimately . . . to write and produce movies. We used to talk about it having pizzas in Geno's in Chicago.

"It was his introduction to Hollywood," Wussler said. "That's how I sold it to him. 'Hey, you're going to become a household name in Hollywood; you may be able to win these people around.' He's a great charmer."

Wussler was right. Sauter became a splendid network censor; he took to it with astonishing ease. He employed the proven Sauter insouciance in a job where buttoned-down worry was the norm. He entertained pals with rollicking tales of the absurdities of his new line of work, such as the time a college professor was hired to replicate baby urine for the purpose of determining the veracity of a diaper manufacturer's claim of superabsorbency. He handled the press smartly, of course, telling interviewers that he saw himself not as a censor but as a publisher or editor and professing a starry-eyed wonderment at how he, Van Sauter, the beer-drinking reporter, ever came to such a position ("I just wish CBS would diversify and buy a family brewery or two; then maybe I could go to work at something more in keeping with my expertise").

But Sauter was best, as Wussler had predicted, at dealing with those on the outside. He was in his element at a Senate committee hearing on the subject of television violence, so disarming, so flawless in his performance that the senators just had to pause and admire. A whole string of network types had come before the committee and, as was their training, their reflex, had rambled and dissembled and had even refused to use the word *violence* when talking about their programs; the shooting and car crashing and other mayhem, they said, were simply a little innocent "hard action." But Sauter's turn came, and you would have thought that he was a TV critic, the way he carried on. Sure, there was violence on TV, Sauter said, too much of it, and *his* network was going to do something about it. That was what the senators wanted to hear—a committee hearing was part show, and a show had to have resolution—and Sauter knew it. Senator Ernest Hollings of South Carolina was so appreciative he was moved to comment on the spot:

> It was almost an unwritten credo, or something that within the discipline and within the broadcast business, you don't even mention [violence] in Washington to a congressional group. You have not only mentioned it, Mr. Sauter, but telling us it's too much and telling us what, for example, your company is doing . . . and that's encouraging to me, because your statement started off like another attack on television and I thought the rest of the statement wouldn't be worth reading. And I found out it was one of the best I have ever read.
>
> Are you typical in CBS? Do you work this hard or are you some fellow they have found that could stand the committee's hearings?

That kind of performance brought Sauter fully to the notice of an appreciative Black Rock, and just in time, because in 1977 there came a corporate upheaval that swept Sauter's friend and guardian angel Bobby Wussler out of power.

The year before, ABC had capped its stunning prime-time surge by winning the season's ratings competition (CBS had finished in first place for a generation), and by the fall of 1977

CBS had slipped to last place in the ratings. Paley and John Backe, the corporate president, removed Jack Schneider as the head of the Broadcast Group and sent Wussler back to sports (both men soon left the network). The new winner was Gene Jankowski, a CBS careerist who'd come up from sales and finance and who, as president of the CBS Broadcast Group, was to shape the course of the network for the next decade.

Jankowski was a competent and abundantly decent man, though not an especially dynamic leader, and what he lacked in intellectual vigor he sought to compensate for by optimism and a consensus approach. He'd developed a vast network of sources inside and outside the company over the years, people who individually embodied the various qualities—such as cunning, guile, and street smarts—that are the components of the ideal network executive but that Jankowski, the pleasant salesman who began each day in church, gloriously lacked.

One of Jankowski's closest assistants was a man named Gene Mater, with whom Sauter developed a close and strong relationship. When they talked about the future (nobody expected Sauter to remain censor for long), what Sauter always told Mater, over and over, was that he wanted to get his hands on a TV station. That, more than anything, would make him happy.

As it happened, CBS had another of those perfect management opportunities—another disaster—in the advanced stages of development. The CBS station in Los Angeles, KNXT (now KCBS), was in horrible shape, and finding a new general manager for it was one of the first matters that Jankowski addressed when he became head of the Broadcast Group. He surveyed his sales corps for a candidate; but there had been a lot of disappointment from those quarters lately, and as was his way, he asked his advisers to advise. Mater put Sauter's name in the ring, and Jankowski was intrigued. Sauter had toned down his act a bit since he'd been in Black Rock (he *had* hired an Irish fiddler to play in his office on St. Patrick's Day, but at least he'd kept the wrestling bears away). Besides, Jankowski thought, style isn't necessarily a bad thing; in fact, he said, "It's a good thing when morale is down." Maybe Sauter could repeat the magic that Wussler had performed at WBBM.

So, in November 1977, just three years after his dismal failure as an anchorman, Sauter went to California, fully resurrected as vice-president and general manager of KNXT. There he was to achieve a spectacular personal triumph, convincing CBS that Van Gordon Sauter was a kind of bearded miracle, a living solution to whose golden touch any problem would yield.

> There is a whole and entire generation right now who never knew anything that didn't come out of this tube! This tube is gospel! This tube is the ultimate revelation! This tube can make or break presidents, popes and prime ministers! This tube is the most awesome goddamned force in the whole godless world! So, listen to me! Television is not the truth! Television is a goddamned amusement park, that's what television is! Television is a circus, a carnival, a traveling troupe of acrobats and storytellers, singers and dancers, jugglers, sideshow freaks, lion-tamers and football players. . . .

When employees entered the office of the new vice-president and general manager of KNXT, that is what they came out with—the famous rant from Howard Beale, the "mad prophet of the airwaves" from Paddy Chayevsky's dark satire on television, *Network*. Sauter had the Beale speech printed and neatly stacked, suitable for framing, and he actually handed out the copies. As a means of letting everyone know that he was something different, it was perhaps a little obvious and a little ridiculous, but in late 1977 subtlety would have been misspent on KNXT. The station was in far worse shape than WBBM had been because not only was it losing in the ratings, but the staff was badly demoralized. In fact, the place would have been mutinous, except that it was so dispirited.

The CBS station in Los Angeles had once known glory, and in the 1960s it had been the prize of the CBS stations, a ratings success that won awards for its journalism, including some of the best documentaries made for television anywhere. Its reporting staff included talent of the first rank, people like Bill Stout, a hard-nosed correspondent as good as any who worked at the network (as, in fact, Stout had done). Jerry Dunphy was the prototype of the avuncular anchorman, snowy-haired and assured, and the behind-the-scenes staff was unmatched in local television. But a series of inept managements, seemingly bent on wrecking the place, had plummeted KNXT into a badly beaten third in the ratings and heaped humiliations upon the staff in the process. When things started going badly, more bad management moves made them worse: One executive ordered that psychological profiles of newsroom personnel be conducted to determine why they weren't "communicating"; Dunphy was declared over the hill and was reassigned (whereupon he jumped to the ABC station and promptly rose to number one); and a new anchor was chosen because he scored so well on galvanic skin tests—a bizarre exercise in which a group of women viewers were wired to devices that measured their physiological responses to the TV image of various male newsmen, the guy causing the sweatiest palms being the winner.

Along the way there were massive newsroom bloodbaths, with twenty or so people being thrown out at a time (on one memorable occasion the targeted employees were called together en masse and informed of their firing as a group). And that wasn't the worst of it. Christopher Desmond, the general manager, came to the surprising conclusion that there was too much news in the marketplace. He knew because he had surveys that showed that the L.A. marketplace was, as he put it, "newsed out." KNXT solved that problem by cutting its news report in half, dropping from two hours of news each night (the output of every other major station in the market) to a single hour. As far as the staff was concerned, that made the ruin complete, and the mood of the place descended from defeat to a kind of despair. Said Stout: "It was a garbage dump."

Yes, it was perfect. And if some were skeptical at first —another ham-fisted rescue squad from New York?—Sauter soon dissolved all doubt. Almost as soon as he arrived, he told the *Los Angeles Times* that what the station needed was more news, lots of it, and he announced that KNXT would go from a one-hour newscast to two and a half hours, from the least news in the market to the most. He would invent a format of "rolling news," waves of news blocks designed to greet L.A. viewers as they rolled off the freeways.

It was just the right touch, and it was just the beginning. The skies seemed to open above KNXT and oddball charm just came down like a redeeming rain.

There would be no confusing Van Sauter with the usual network executive, and if the Howard Beale speech wasn't clue enough, the Sauter life-style was convincing. As station chief Sauter had the right to a company car, but he shunned the

Oldsmobiles and Buicks that bespoke corporate convention and instead bought a big black Jeep, into which he had installed the most ear-rending speakers the vehicle could accommodate. He bought a boat, a forty-five-foot power cruiser named *Casablanca,* and lived on board, so that at night he could come home, unplug the telephone, and put out to sea as the California sun set on the ocean. Sauter didn't just move to Southern California, he *became* Southern California, and he and the culture were perfectly suited. It was a place where executives wore no ties and often no socks, a place where, when Sauter uttered things like "Form without substance, style without meaning," people nodded their heads and *understood.*

At the age of forty-two Sauter had found his native land.

The staffers at KNXT had come to view life at the station as a kind of enemy occupation, and to them, the occasional changing of the commandants usually only meant new forms of anguish. But Sauter worked hard to give the impression that if theirs was a "them versus us" enterprise, he was as much against "them" as anyone. He came to work in boat shoes (when he wore shoes at all), khakis, and a work shirt, and he kept a suit in his office for those occasions when he had to act like a "grown-up," such as when a network executive from New York was in town. (Even then he scored points with the troops by posting FULL MOGUL ALERT signs around the station.) His office, with its rolltop desk and green-shaded editor's lamp, packaged irreverence strewn about (such as the Beale speech, framed and prominently hung), was a testimony to his righteousness. As at WBBM, he was a singular presence at the station, constantly in the newsroom, going over the broadcast lineup, poking his head in during story conferences and editing sessions, talking with writers and reporters and producers, greeting the technicians by name. "He was like a wall-to-wall poultice for the place at a time of great bleeding," said Stout. "His presence in the building was almost magic. He really did work minor wonders in a place that was panting for some kind of help."

Except for those few occasions when he was screening a porn movie in his office (with a few of the guys), his door was always open, and that impressed even Joseph Benti, the anchorman who, like Stout, was a former CBS News correspondent, but one who'd suffered bitter disappointment and had never met a management that he particularly liked. "He opened up the channels of communication, and I felt proud because I could now talk to a general manager who would listen to me," Benti said. "All anchors love to be heard." Sauter was immensely successful with the staff, and he fostered an uncommonly deep loyalty. After he left KNXT, one of his staffers, the station publicist Phyllis Kirk Bush, described her former boss (with no trace of embarrassment) as a "compassionate, humorous, brilliant, eclectic, highly intelligent, intuitive, enthusiastic, first-rate human being."

Benti, and others, later wondered if they'd been taken in a bit by Sauter. Benti said he wished he'd questioned Sauter about that Howard Beale business. "If you really believe this, what the fuck are you doing in this office? Why aren't you out working for the *Village Voice* or writing broadsides?" But at the time the contradiction wasn't so apparent; what was apparent was that KNXT had in Sauter something new and fetching. Maybe the good guys were finally going to win.

That was why most at the station were tolerant of Sauter, even when he allowed his personal life to embroil KNXT in a situation that was, at best, quite awkward. Sauter had met an actress named Barbara Trentham at a party and become completely stricken with her. They began a torrid relationship that would have been no one's business except that somewhere along the way it occurred to Sauter that Barbara Trentham would be an ideal newscaster. He put her on the air, making her a reporter on the weekend newscasts, and asked some of the veterans around the station to help her learn the ropes. Trentham was quite beautiful and apparently quite intelligent, too, but she was not a television news broadcaster. "She was dreadful," said one KNXT staffer. "The whole thing smacked of the old Hollywood studio casting couch," said Stout. "You know, 'This is a dear friend of mine; I'm sure you can find room for her in the chorus line somewhere, can't you?' " Joseph Benti remembered trying to help Trentham on stories. "She was an innocent, but she just wasn't [the right] material. It wasn't there." Before the situation became intolerable, Trentham moved in with Sauter— he sold the boat, and they took a place in the Hollywood Hills— and left the station.

The Trentham episode was a brief lapse in what had been an uncommon run of goodwill at KNXT, an attitude that reflected not only the success of Sauter's personality-driven management style but the success of the station itself. Sauter brought in

Connie Chung, a rising CBS News correspondent, and Brent
Musburger, the CBS Sports reporter, giving KNXT instant star
attractions, and the station was putting on more, and often
better, news reports than any of its competitors. And Sauter did
what he did best, public relations, creating a perception of the
station as a winner, just as he and Wussler had done at WBBM.
Advertising revenues increased dramatically.

In orchestrating the turnaround at KNXT, Sauter employed
the same spend-first-ask-later approach that Wussler had employed at WBBM and, like Wussler, had brought in his own loyal
"smart guy," an M.B.A. named David Percelay, to take care of
details. Sauter was in charge of spending. At one point he concluded that the station needed a helicopter, Los Angeles being
so spread out and all. Maybe he was thinking of the WBBM
minicam. But Sauter had already spent a lot on hiring and expansion, and helicopters weren't cheap; a purchase request
would probably have been stopped at one of the many levels of
approval in the usual channels. So Sauter bypassed the usual
channels and leased a series of helicopter parts from a helicopter dealer, each at a cost just below the price that would have
set off alarms in New York. KNXT got its chopper.

Stories of Sauter's style, the boat and the Jeep and the rest,
filtered back to Black Rock, and there were those who didn't find
it at all appropriate. Jack Schneider, for one, found the Sauter
eccentricities a little tiring. "He worked at his eccentricities; they
were so transparently pasted on him. When Van was living on
a yacht when he was at KNXT, it was an inappropriate bit of
imagery for the head of a CBS-owned-and-operated station. It
was perfectly obvious that he was living the life of a gypsy, and
what you're supposed to do is make the head of a station seem
like a solid citizen, with roots in the community."

Fortunately for Sauter, Schneider didn't count anymore.
Gene Jankowski did, and Jankowski liked what he saw. The
Sauter style was not his style, to be sure. (He had been horrified
on one occasion when, after an important meeting between
Sauter, Jankowski, and Tom Wyman, the new corporate president, at Chasen's in Beverly Hills, Sauter had called for his car
and the attendant pulled up in the black Jeep with Jefferson
Airplane blaring from the monster speakers. "Get in that Willys
and get out of here, before Wyman sees you!" Jankowski had
said.) But Sauter had provided results, he'd turned KNXT

around, and that meant one less problem on Gene Jankowski's plate. So when Sauter decided to celebrate the station's success with a party at a local disco, the USC marching band paraded into the place and the drum major read a congratulatory message to the triumphant staff, a message from Gene Jankowski.

Perhaps the most remarkable measure of Black Rock's faith in Sauter as a manager, the ultimate validation, came a few years after Sauter had left KNXT, when Black Rock commissioned the Sterling Institute, a management consulting firm, to prepare a case study on Sauter's years there. A "turnaround study" it was called in the trade, and it was to be used at the CBS management school to teach CBS executives the Sauter approach. "It may have been his own style or it may have been an act, but he wanted to show he was unique and different," said Sterling Livingston, president of the consulting firm. "It was a style that was appropriate because it was an antiestablishment style, and the establishment had pretty well discredited itself within the news department. It was very effective." Van Gordon Sauter had come the full route; by so effectively seeming not to be, he had become the management ideal.

By 1980 Sauter had been in California for two years, as long as he'd been anyplace for CBS, and he was beginning to become part of the local scenery, more so than Jack Schneider would ever have guessed. To top it off, there was Kathleen Brown Rice. Sauter was watching a TV monitor one evening when a dark-haired woman filled the screen. He was stricken (the Trentham affair had cooled), he had to meet her, and so it was arranged. Rice was as close to royalty as California provided in the post-Navajo age, the daughter of former Governor Pat Brown, the sister of current Governor Jerry Brown, and she was an active politician recently elected to the local school board. They dated, and after a few months they were married, in a ceremony at the posh home (formerly belonging to Howard Hughes) of a Brown friend in the old-money section of Hancock Park. The local gentry was pleased with this perfect match: the TV hero and the California princess.

Sauter was very happy, but he was also very ambitious. When Jankowski would visit, delighted with the progress at KNXT and always eager to keep his promising executives on an upward track, he'd ask Sauter what he had in mind for himself, where he'd like to go in the company, and Sauter would say that he had

no career plan, no particular aspiration, although, he said, he
had noticed that CBS had a serious problem in its sports division. He had no personal interest in sports, he said, no knowledge, either, but if Jankowski was ever to see him as a possible
solution to the sports problem, Van Sauter would be happy to
give it a try. So when Jankowski asked Sauter to come to New
York (which Sauter loathed) as president of CBS Sports in mid-
1980, Sauter accepted, even though he loved California, and
even though Kathleen Brown Rice, his soon-to-be-wife, not only
had deep roots in California but had just been elected to the
school board there.

It was another perfect opportunity, impossible to resist. CBS
Sports was by far the worst sports division of the three networks,
left to seed by the company since a CBS-sponsored winner-take-
all tennis tournament had proved to be slightly phony. In the
late 1970s it had become the province of that bane of the weekend airwaves—"trash" sports. There were strongman contests
and junked-up competitions between "real people" trying to
crash through brick walls and the like, while the other networks
broadcast basketball, football, and baseball. Sauter described
the situation in terms that applied to almost all his CBS assignments: "It was such a shithole that you really couldn't fuck it
up."

Sports was a chance for Sauter to show that he could run an
entire division (that had been Wussler's plan), and he moved
fast to make his mark. He brought college sports back to CBS
for the first time in seventeen years, buying the rights to a
college football package (breaking up ABC's monopoly) and the
college basketball championship tournament (breaking up
NBC's monopoly). He hired away ABC's best sports director,
Terry O'Neill, and he wholly reworked the network's sleepy
weekend sports anthology series, creating a package of sports
journalism and features. He spent money. Suddenly CBS Sports
was back on the map. And inevitably Van Sauter came to the
attention of the national TV press. His first appearance as sports
chief was at the national "press tour," an annual junket spon-
sored by the networks to parade their shows and stars and executives before the TV critics, and Sauter gave a career
performance. He managed to take the stage just as the distinc-
tive green bottle of Heineken's he'd ordered arrived. "Aw, shit,"
he said, and right away he'd won them. He sat there in his safari

jacket and no socks, his full gray beard setting off the display, and one admiring journalist asked another, "Can you imagine him in a boardroom?" Reporters usually arrived at such events with fangs honed and bared, but then, network executives usually arrived at such events wearing socks.

One thing the new president of CBS Sports didn't mention at that press conference in June 1981, something he never mentioned aloud at all, was the keen interest he'd taken in Dan Rather, the struggling anchorman of CBS News. Sauter had known Rather slightly, but when he came to New York, the two men became fairly close friends. The Sauters bought a weekend house in Redding, Connecticut, just twenty minutes from the Rathers' country place, and Sauter and Rather often got together on weekends just to talk. Sauter was a good, sympathetic listener, and he had his own fairly strong opinions about Rather's failure as an anchorman. It wasn't really Rather's failure at all, he thought, but the failure of CBS News, the organization, which was still producing a show that was stuck in the 1960s, a Cronkite show, a show that was out of sync with everything else that was on television. He shared these thoughts with Rather, who, needless to say, was willing to hear them and made the suggestion that he, Sauter, was just the man to make things right. "Van wanted the job, he said so, it was Van at his best," Rather recalled of that time. "He'd say, 'This is a job I want, and I would be good for you and for CBS, too.'"

Sauter was quiet about it, though—nothing could be worse than an open candidacy; the Luddites at CBS News would come out of the woodwork and just kill it—but he said it to Rather, and he said it to Rather's agent, Richard Leibner, who was also a willing listener, and the message made its way to Jankowski. "Dan and I probably put [Sauter] into nomination," Leibner later said, "because there was nobody inside who had a clear-cut image as to how to run the joint." But Jankowski wasn't quite sure what to do about CBS News, and to buy time, he had just extended Bill Leonard's contract for another year, keeping him as news president past the once-mandatory retirement age of sixty-five. Yet Rather really was in a bad way on the *Evening News,* the ratings were dropping steadily, and he'd even publicly said that he would accept a coanchor if that would help. The pressure continued to build.

One day early in the summer of 1981, when Sauter hadn't yet

been in sports for a year, he was out in Los Angeles and got a
call from Gene Mater, Jankowski's trusted aide. Jankowski was
on the Coast and wanted to meet with Sauter the next day at the
Beverly Hills Hotel. It was all very hush-hush, and Sauter soon
found out why: Jankowski had made up his mind. Sauter would
succeed Bill Leonard as president of CBS News, and Ed Joyce
would be his top assistant. But Jankowski insisted that it all be
kept quiet. He hadn't told anyone yet, not even Joyce and certainly not Leonard, who was still operating under the belief that
his yearlong extension actually meant that he had another year
at the helm.

For weeks Sauter didn't say anything, although it wasn't easy,
because he was making deals with the golf organizations and
college basketball, knowing that he was about to leave. He
pressed Jankowski, who, as it happened, needed no pressing; the
Rather ratings spoke for themselves. Jankowski broke the news
to Leonard that Sauter was his successor, and there was something else: Sauter would move into news right away, that fall,
with the newly coined title of deputy president. Leonard realized
that he was being pushed aside, just as Salant had been made
to make way for Leonard, but he didn't fight it; he'd been
around.

So after Jankowski came to that CBS News staff meeting that
November morning in 1981 and broke the news, when the hallways were buzzing with people murmuring, "Why Sauter?" Dan
Rather wasn't among them. It was a red-letter day for Rather,
and he only wished it had come six months earlier. He now had
the man he wanted in the top job; the Dan Rather era could
begin at last.

Chapter

GENE JANKOWSKI BELIEVED THAT the company had certain needs, the needs of the 1980s, but when he looked over at the management team at CBS News, all he saw was the 1960s.

He saw Ed Fouhy, John Lane, Bob Chandler, Sandy Socolow, Bud Benjamin—Leonard's people, Salant's people, Cronkite's people—all good journalists, all wrong for the moment at hand. In 1981, when Gene Jankowski was deciding the future of CBS News, journalism was no longer enough. He wanted a new kind of news management, a management that would be responsive to the company, not always in opposition to it. The world was changing, potent forces were reworking the broadcasting universe, and Black Rock wanted a news division that would help pull the load; the era of news as the spoiled child was over.

The press at the time was frantic with stories forecasting the death of the networks, the "dinosaurs," and indeed, the new technologies of television gleamed with ominous possibility—cable; home videocassette recorders; direct satellite-to-home broadcasting; movie channels; sports channels; news channels; porn channels. There was suddenly new television to watch, lots of it, and the three-cornered monopoly that had defined television for a generation, the status quo that had made the networks so impossibly rich, was suddenly in peril. The Reagan administration would only accelerate the change, deregulating the broadcasting industry and fostering the transformation of television stations from licensed trusts to open-market commodities, to be bought and sold like pork belly futures; huge prices were paid for stations that had been in one family for decades, and even greater prices were paid when the new owners turned around and resold. The number of independent stations in the country was to triple, and a booming program syndication industry was to supply the independents with programs—more alternatives to the networks.

The fabric of network television was starting to give at the seams as the network-affiliated stations began to assert a new independence. The affiliates, long the compliant silent partners in the network business, happily going along and collecting their share of the loot, found new economic power and verve. Their own local newscasts were becoming immensely profitable, and with the rise of ABC, that most sacred bond of the network business, affiliation itself, came under challenge. ABC, consolidating its remarkable gains in the ratings, sought to improve its third-rate lineup of stations by luring away the best stations affiliated with CBS and NBC in the top markets. At one point twenty-two of the most prized CBS-affiliated stations informed the network that they might switch affiliation; canny salesmanship by Jankowski and one of his top lieutenants, James Rosenfield, kept all but one of the stations in the fold (a major selling point in their pitch to the stations being the prestige and allure of CBS News), but the relationship had changed. The affiliates had more leverage now, and the inclination to employ it, as Bill Leonard discovered to his everlasting grief when he tried to sell the affiliates on the idea of an hourlong *CBS Evening News.*

The overall effect was a diminishing of the networks. Suddenly they were less influential, less dominant, less monolithic. Because inflation was still running high and national advertisers had plenty to spend, network revenues continued to grow in double-digit leaps through the late seventies and early eighties; but it was clear to any who cared to look that a curtain was descending on the days of network bounty.

Against this background there was a shifting of the ranks inside CBS that transformed the company. Chairman Paley was getting old, and while he allowed the possibility that he would not live forever (his executives sometimes weren't so sure of it), he wanted his company, CBS, to endure; that meant that someone new, someone other than Paley and his alter ego, Frank Stanton, the two men who had built the company and given it its character and place in the world, would have to be allowed to run things.

Paley forced Stanton to resign when Stanton turned sixty-five in 1973 and thus began an almost comical parade of heirs apparent, each seeming just the right choice at first and each quickly falling short of the expectations of Bill Paley. First in line was Jack Schneider, who'd been a success as the president of the CBS Broadcast Group, which ran all of the company's broadcasting businesses; it was a logical choice, but Paley was convinced that CBS had grown to a size and stature that were beyond the capacity of any mere broadcaster to manage, and there being only one Bill Paley, Schneider wouldn't do. No, Paley determined, the man to run CBS would have to be a captain of industry, one who could manage the CBS that Paley had in mind, a first-rank conglomerate. So, with the help of an executive head-hunting firm, Paley found his new heir, Charles T. Ireland, the number two man at the largest conglomerate in America, International Telephone and Telegraph. Six months after Ireland was made president of CBS, however, he was dead of a heart attack at the age of fifty-one. Another search, another business whiz, this time thirty-seven-year-old Arthur R. Taylor, a former investment banker who'd risen to the post of executive vice-president of International Paper before being embraced by Paley as the inheritor of all that was CBS. The embrace soon became a stranglehold. Even though Taylor was considered a brilliant president, bringing structure and discipline to the company (not to mention record profits), he was at CBS for only four years before Paley demanded his resignation. In his rather gauzy 1979 autobiography, *As It Happened,* Paley explained that Taylor "did not have all the essential qualities to become my successor." Arthur R. Taylor was not, in other words, William S. Paley.

Then Paley turned inside the company for a successor, and he found one, not from within the Broadcast Group, but from CBS Publishing. John D. Backe had in a few short years turned the money-losing publishing operation around, and Paley, who'd had his eye on the rising young executive for some time, was sure he'd finally found his successor. In his memoir he explained that he was still hanging on as CBS chairman (even though he was seventy-eight years old and thirteen years past the mandatory retirement age he'd enforced with Stanton) only "in order to make myself available and as helpful as I can be in achieving a smooth transition of executive management. . . ." He wrote that Backe had been a "wise choice" for president of the company and that he, Paley, could now enjoy "a feeling of pleasure and comfort because my successor is in place." Mr. Paley had said that before, and as John Backe would soon find out, he would say it again.

In June 1980 Backe was out, and in his place came the man who finally succeeded in easing Bill Paley out of the picture. Thomas H. Wyman was something altogether new to the CBS culture. Not only wasn't he a broadcaster (he'd come from the food industry, most recently Pillsbury), but he was emphatically not one. He didn't seem to like television, and he was of a class that didn't much care for television. He was Brahmin to the teeth—Andover, Phi Beta Kappa at Amherst (with a master's in English), the IMED Management Development Institute in Lausanne (cosponsored by the Harvard Business School), the Augusta National Golf Club—a genuine, lockjawed, slightly superior, slightly bored East Coast WASP. High compliment from Tom Wyman was to be deemed "attractive," that was his term for approval, and he apparently did not find a lot of attractive people in television; they were just not his set. With Wyman as president and (beginning in late 1982, when Paley finally agreed to step down) as chairman, CBS took on a distinctly corporate character. People with Roman numerals after their names began to take their place in the company built by the son of an immigrant Russian Jewish cigar maker. Wyman began to assemble a huge corporate staff, with large finance and legal and corporate affairs departments, just like those of the other first-rank conglomerates (a development that had dire consequences for CBS within just a few years).

Wyman's business philosophy followed the accepted model of the best minds of business academia. The company would milk the money cow, the "mature business"—broadcasting, in the case of CBS—in order to feed development in other areas, which would in time, according to the accepted model, augment and replace the revenues of the fading mature business. Wyman would make CBS into a huge multifaceted entertainment and communications empire; he would go into cable and the movie business, CBS would publish magazines and manufacture toys, and gradually the broadcasting money cow would play a relatively smaller and smaller role. With that plan, and given Wyman's own tastes, the network business itself became less important than it had been in the time of William Paley (although Paley himself had pushed for diversification). Wyman spoke often and firmly about the need for cost controls at the network. CBS was spending money as fast as it brought it in, not at all the way the money cow was supposed to behave. Over one period of flash inflation, sales revenues at CBS increased by more than $1 billion; virtually none of it went to the bottom line. Wyman and his staff were acutely aware of their standing in the eyes of Wall Street, and quarterly earnings became the focus of all energies. Wyman would complain about costs, and Gene Jankowski, the Polish Catholic salesman from Buffalo who was not particularly articulate or smooth in Wyman's presence, but who wanted to please him, would pick up on that theme and amplify it to his people. The result was a kind of institutionalized, cyclical panic. "There was never a meeting, not a staff meeting, not a meeting to discuss anything from programming to acquisition or expansion, long-term planning or short-term planning—anything—that didn't start off with 'Okay, now what have we done to cut costs today?' " James ("Jim") Rosenfield remembered. "Gene just was crazed."

And over on West Fifty-seventh Street, eight blocks and a world away, CBS News was chugging along in exactly the wrong direction. News was a place where people went to work in the morning and proceeded to spend the company's money. Gordon Manning, the quintessential CBS News executive, a Salant man, used to tell his people when he was vice-president of hard news that if they went after a story with everything they had and the story just didn't make it to air, that was okay—"But don't ever let me catch you missing a story because you wanted to save money." People like Bill Small, who tried to impose cost-saving disciplines upon the organization, were considered petty and mean.

In the late seventies and early eighties CBS News was spending more than ever. Satellite technology made it possible to cover more stories from more places, and of course, CBS News did, requiring more crews and more correspondents, more equipment and more people to handle the flow. More money. The Iran hostage crisis was a marvelous television story (ABC created a whole new program out of it, *Nightline*) and an incredibly expensive one. John Lane, one of the *Evening News* executives, once authorized an expenditure of $10,000 just to get a taped report—a single report—out of Iran. There was no systematic means of monitoring expenses as they were incurred; news executives would find out weeks after the fact how much they had spent on coverage of a particular event. The CBS News budget swelled from $89 million in 1978 to $108 million in 1979 to $157 million in 1980; by 1982 annual news costs were $212 million.

Lane later recalled that period and supposed that "the Jankowskis of the world must have looked at us and said, 'Holy Christ, look at all the money they're spending; that place is out of fiscal control.'" He was right. That was precisely what Black Rock thought. All that money spent on the *Evening News* and elections and those damned late-night instant news specials that the news division was always demanding time for; CBS News could be a pain in the ass, and Jankowski wasn't sure that Wyman was all that tolerant of news anyway. News made enemies in Washington. Mr. Wyman's top aide and chief Washington operative, William Lilly III, was not regarded as a particular friend of news, and when he was down in Washington lobbying for some pro-network piece of legislation and heard complaints about CBS News from a representative or senator, he was not exactly known to turn away from such talk in anger. CBS News was not fully aware of it at the time, but its place as the favored child was quickly slipping into the folds of the new, emerging CBS.

At one particularly tense budget meeting Tom Wyman spoke the unspeakable, observing that there would be nothing wrong with CBS News' turning a profit for a change, as the other divisions were expected to do; there was no law against it, was there? In fact, *60 Minutes* had proved it could be done. One year Don Hewitt's enormously popular news program had made the difference between profit and loss for the TV network; couldn't CBS News come up with some more shows like *60 Minutes*?

Those were the things on Gene Jankowski's mind when he was deciding the future of CBS News in 1981, and when he looked at the men in position at the news division, he saw people who just didn't seem likely to climb on board. Jankowski's job in the Wyman era was not going to be easy, and the last thing he needed was antagonism from CBS News; what he needed was a little sympathy. Of course, it could have been argued that the very same forces and pressures that prompted Black Rock to demand a new relationship between news and the company, a friendlier, cozier relationship, made it all the more imperative, from the viewpoint of news, that the next president of CBS News be another Dick Salant, fighting Black Rock at every turn, insulating the news division from the bottom-line pressures of the company. It could have been argued, once again, that in network television, news is *not* a business but a public service provided by a company that is licensed to use the public's airwaves to generate numbing quantities of money.

But those arguments weren't made, because in 1981 the great diverting fact of CBS News, the matter that held the attention of the place like a nagging sore, was the daily disaster known as the *CBS Evening News with Dan Rather.* It was a horrible situation, and couldn't be tolerated much longer. The *Evening News* was losing money, but there was more to it than that: The news program, more than any other program, was the daily face of CBS; it was news that gave the network identity, and the failure of the program was not only costly but embarrassing. And there was no doubt at Black Rock, and little argument, that the people in charge of CBS News were not going to make a winner of Dan Rather. They were so straight, so set in their ways, so damned traditional; they weren't trying any of the fancy techniques that were working at the local stations and that Roone Arledge was effectively employing at ABC News. If Rather was going to make it, there would have to be new people running CBS News, people willing to change. Rather believed that, and Richard Leibner certainly believed it; as he said constantly, "Who was gonna save the person [Rather] who had gone from first to third? Another network oldie? Or did you have to go with people with . . . 'now' television fingers?"

Jankowski couldn't have agreed more, and so, when Bill Leonard reeled off his short list of successors, Fouhy and Chandler and Lane, Jankowski listened politely and mentally put Fouhy, Chandler, and Lane on his reject list. Jankowski wanted a turnaround, and he happened to have a turnaround artist, Van Gordon Sauter, standing by. Sauter had acquitted himself nicely as network censor, he'd helped turn WBBM around, and at KNXT, his masterpiece, he'd done so well that the company had modeled a management course after him. There was no doubt in Jankowski's mind that Sauter would foster a more supple relationship between news and the company—Jankowski recognized a company man when he saw one—and moreover, Sauter had a background in news. What's more, Sauter had style. Jankowski wanted change in the most sensitive corner of the company; Van Sauter would make a most accommodating agent of that change. And who knew? With Sauter's legendary style, CBS News might even enjoy it.

Jankowski might have liked Van Sauter, but he didn't necessarily trust him. He had no doubt that Sauter could fix whatever was wrong with Dan Rather—if there was anything Sauter had proved at the CBS stations, it was that he could fix an on-air disaster—but on that other matter, cost management, Jankowski had some serious doubts. Sauter had spent extravagantly in every job where spending was an option, and spending was one of the problems Jankowski was trying to solve at CBS News. At sports Sauter had turned the place around, but he'd spent gobs of money in doing it, the same as he had at KNXT, the same as he and Wussler had at WBBM in Chicago.

That kind of spending didn't go unnoticed by Black Rock. After Sauter was in New York at sports, rewarded for his work at KNXT, the financial director at the Los Angeles station was instructed to inform Black Rock that under Van Sauter, KNXT had gone nearly half a million dollars over budget. There was an accusatory tone of irresponsible management in the communication, and the new station management just wanted Black Rock to know that it was Sauter who'd done it. One day, as Sauter recalled it, an animated Jankowski called and asked Sauter, "Is it true what I'm hearing, that you left that station with a half-million-dollar cost problem?"

Sauter, ever cool, responded, "Gene, might be. Might be six hundred thousand, I don't know what it is. What's the problem?"

"It's a half million dollars!"

"Gene," replied Sauter, "look at the other side of the sheet. It says that we're six million dollars ahead of budget on sales! That means you're five-point-five million dollars to the better." It was exactly what the doomed finance manager of WBBM-TV, Chuck Kadlec, had told Black Rock in trying to explain the Wussler-Sauter cost overruns eight years earlier in Chicago.

Jankowski never mentioned the matter again; but he did re-member it, and he remembered the station executive who'd been thoughtful enough to have the matter brought to Black Rock's attention, Sauter's successor at KNXT in Los Angeles, Edward M. Joyce. Jankowski thought about Sauter's going over to the news division by himself, an outsider in a pack of wolves, and he thought about his record as a spender, and he worried. Ed Joyce, on the other hand, had been a Jankowski man, a company loyalist, and a proven tightfisted manager. For a time Joyce was rumored to be the next president of CBS News, a prospect that made some in the organization shiver; they didn't really know Joyce except by reputation, which was neatly summed up by the unsparing Chicago television critic Gary Deeb, who called him the "Velvet Shiv." All in all, it was a fitting enough description. As general manager of WBBM-TV Joyce quickly closed the lid on the freewheeling, free-spending atti-tude that Wussler and Sauter had brought to the place and that had brought WBBM success. Joyce saw his role as managing that success, which meant cutting spending and imposing strict fi-nancial controls. His time in Chicago did not make him popular in the newsroom, but it made him very popular on the thirty-fourth floor of Black Rock, where Gene Jankowski was not at all offended by the idea of a news manager who, as Deeb put it in a 1980 column, "simply does as his New York bosses tell him."

If only Ed Joyce were a little more like Van Sauter, or Van Sauter a little more like Ed Joyce, Jankowski would have his perfect president of CBS News. Jankowski wasn't God, he couldn't create the perfect news executive, but he was president of the CBS Broadcast Group, so he did what he considered the next best thing. When he had his secret meeting with Sauter at the Beverly Hills Hotel in 1981, he told Sauter that Ed Joyce would be going with him to CBS News. Sauter liked Joyce, what he'd seen of him, and after getting assurances from Jankowski that he, Sauter, would be running the show, he said, "Fine." In fact, Sauter would love to have someone to take care of the detail work. So it was set.

There was one problem, however. Bill Leonard had been scheduled to retire in the spring of 1981, just as Rather was taking over the *CBS Evening News,* but Jankowski had taken the unusual step of asking Leonard to stay as news president for another year, suspending the mandatory retirement policy that had been breached for no one but Bill Paley. As late as the fall of 1981 Jankowski had assured Leonard that even though changes had been planned, Leonard would remain as president through his extension, until the spring of 1982. Friends of Leonard's maintain that Leonard took that assurance to mean that he would remain in charge of CBS News as long as he was president; if so, he was wrong. Bill Leonard had been the man in charge when Dan Rather had dropped into third place, and that wouldn't be forgiven. "Dan was nervous, tight, uptight, and he lost," Leonard later said, "and it was more than [Black Rock] could handle. That hastened my retirement, there's no question about that. They wanted me out of there."

For all the changes in the outside world, and the changes within CBS, for all the subtle forces that were working the equations for CBS News, the overriding concern remained the *Evening News.* And among all the marching orders that Van Sauter carried with him to the news division, his first and most pressing mission was to fix Dan Rather.

Years later, when asked why he had chosen Sauter and Joyce over those who were already at CBS News, Jankowski replied that all the others were fine journalists, all CBS traditionalists— and that they all were losing. Traditional journalism didn't win ratings; effective television won ratings. "It is a question of form," Jankowski said, "not the substance, that was important." He had certainly found his man.

Chapter

SUDDENLY THE NIFTY SAYINGS didn't seem so charming. Van Sauter, the new deputy president of CBS News, was saying things like "Today is the first day of the rest of your career" and "Everything at CBS News is zero-based." He said these things in staff meetings and in private conversations, and in case the point wasn't getting across, he said them in newspaper interviews, too. By the late fall of 1981, although Sauter was technically Bill Leonard's deputy, not due to replace Leonard for six months, no one doubted who was in charge: Sauter was in charge, and it was clear that he wasn't there to validate the glories of CBS News past. He was there to vanquish the past, to repudiate an approach to television that was seen as hidebound and irrelevant and the philosophies of broadcast journalism that fostered that approach. That was his mission, and that is what he did.

The contrast between the old values and the new, between the Leonard era and the Sauter era, was neatly framed by an event that occurred almost as soon as Sauter arrived. The issue was the expansion of the *Evening News* from thirty minutes to an hour, a matter that had become a kind of crucible for Leonard and his people. It had been one of the dreams that Leonard brought to the job, but it was more than just that: It was an expression of the institution's view of itself and of its role in the world. The view held that CBS News was engaged in important work, and the more of it, the better, not just for CBS News but for the country. At the moment it happened that Dan Rather was in deep ratings trouble, and expansion would have presented a convenient opportunity to add a coanchor; but the issue was genuinely larger than Rather, and that fact said a lot about Leonard and his senior staff. For all the pride that the people at CBS News took in their work, for all the talk of the *Evening News* as the "broadcast of record," for all the seriousness and elitist undertones, there was an abiding sense that somehow the work wasn't really quite as important and serious as they sometimes liked to think; they would speak almost apologetically of the limitations of television, its reliance on pictures, for example, and when they spoke of the limitations, the thing they fixed on most doggedly and most often was the limitation of time. Cronkite himself talked about it so much that he became tiresome on the subject, going on about how the *Evening News,* minus commercials, was only twenty-three minutes long and you couldn't possibly impart the day's important events in twenty-three minutes. Cronkite used to say, and he seemed to mean it, that the *Evening News* was really just a headline service. Expanding to an hour could make it more than that.

In November 1981 the moment was at hand. Network executives were meeting in Hawaii with the CBS affiliates board, a group of station managers and owners elected to represent the CBS-affiliated stations across the country, and although a whole range of network-affiliate matters was on the agenda, the *Evening News* issue was clearly the main item. The affiliates had to be sold on the expansion before it could happen because they would have to surrender thirty minutes of local time to accommodate the longer network newscast. Some resistance was expected, of course, but Bill Leonard and his men were ready; they'd worked on a plan for months, fine-tuning it and preparing their pitch, and Jimmy Rosenfield, the network executive who dealt with the affiliates, had made some adjustments to the plan in anticipation of affiliate objections. *CBS Evening News* would be divided into two half-hour parts and designed in such a way that the second half hour could be carried or passed by the individual stations, as each wished. But the newspeople were as confident as it was possible to be, because CBS News had an ace in the hole: The network was behind the expanded format, and the network owned stations in the country's five most powerful markets. If CBS determined to expand the *Evening News* and to carry the expanded broadcast on its big stations, the feeling went, that would pressure stations into providing the same service to viewers in their markets. Viewers would demand it; surely the stations would see that.

The stations, it turned out, didn't see that at all. The world was changing, and they were filling the half hour after (and in some cases before) network news quite nicely with their own programming, mostly syndicated game shows and talk shows, programs that made a lot of money that the stations didn't have to split with the network. What world were these people from CBS News living in? Didn't they read *Variety*? But the affiliates didn't just reject the expanded news plan; they assaulted it. It was a stupid idea, clumsily contrived, they said; how could you end the first half hour without mentioning that another half hour was coming up? And if you did that, what about those viewers whose stations didn't carry the second half hour? It was a disaster for CBS News and especially for Leonard; the affiliates were close to cruel in their attacks on him, and altogether it was the most acrimonious meeting in memory. It was a bitter, heartbreaking disappointment for Leonard, a deep personal humiliation after a long and distinguished career. It was also a major embarrassment for the network, not only because of the defeat itself and what that signified but because CBS had been so certain of success that it had already announced the expansion.

Even as the affiliates were beating up on Bill Leonard and his staff, some of the station managers were perceiving that a new age was dawning at CBS News. One of the leaders of the affiliate rebellion, perhaps its most vocal member, Jim Babb, from the CBS affiliate in Charlotte, North Carolina, got the sense during the Hawaii meetings that the new man at CBS News, Van Sauter, was on their side, or at least he seemed to understand the affiliates' view. In private conversation, in his gestures, Sauter didn't seem quite so intransigent on the expansion as did the others. "I watched him during the presentation," Babb recalled. "I saw a lot of doubt in his mind that I thought I had in my own mind. I think he was grinding through, asking, 'What do they really mean here, what is this?' " It wasn't that Sauter was against the expansion, but he seemed to know instinctively that this wasn't a battle to fight, not with the affiliates, not now. Why risk your chips on trying to make a losing broadcast longer, on a fight that couldn't be won? When the battle was over and Bill Leonard and his dream had lost, it came time to put a public face on it, but neither side would budge. The affiliates and the people from CBS News were just furious at each other, until finally Jim Babb and Van Sauter went off by themselves to work it out. They came up with a statement carefully worded to save face on both sides, to make it seem that the affiliates weren't obstructionists and that CBS News hadn't suffered a defeat, but it was plain to all that what the two men worked out was a total surrender by CBS News. "It was decided that they were all going to have to trust Van and me," Babb said, "and it was no problem once it got down to us." No problem at all.

Ed Fouhy and John Lane and others considered the Hawaii fiasco the sellout of the hour news, which it may have been. But it was certainly more than that: It was the last stand of the Bill Leonard regime and of a value system that had prevailed at CBS News since Richard Salant's time. Something altogether new was about to redefine CBS News, in a way that the John Lanes and Ed Fouhys and Walter Cronkites of the world wouldn't much like. That left Van Sauter with a choice as he took control of CBS News: He could try to win the old line over to his side, to his ways and his vision, or he could ignore the traditionalists and risk dividing the institution. It was a terribly interesting dilemma for a manager whose success had been in winning people over, but it was not, apparently, a terribly difficult one for Sauter. Before he even landed at CBS News, Sauter had made up his mind about many of the people there: Television had passed them by, and so would he.

So Van Sauter and Ed Joyce divided CBS News. They created two classes of people, "yesterday" people and "today" people— two ways of thinking, two visions of broadcasting. Yesterday people were taken out of the mix, transferred to distant or obscure positions, or, if they remained in place, were simply ignored. Their ideas were rejected; their broadcasts were not made. It was an awful and confusing moment, when the insignia of a proud past became a stigma in the new order. There was a lot of pain in store, pain that was to cut deep and wide, for if there was one commodity that CBS News had in full supply, it was yesterday.

Bill Leonard was still the president of CBS News, Van Sauter only his deputy, but Sauter's mandate was clear. When Sauter complained to Jankowski about the awkwardness of the arrangement, Jankowski, Sauter recalled, had assured him, "Your decisions will be the decisions that are executed," and Leonard, himself having experienced a clumsy period when Dick Salant was still technically president, was gracious and accommodating toward Sauter. In fact, in some cases he helped engineer the changes that Sauter wanted, including the change that Sauter wanted most and first—a new executive producer for the *Evening News.*

Sandy Socolow was Walter Cronkite's dear friend, his intimate, his source of gossip, and his caretaker, and at the end of the Cronkite reign Socolow had been Cronkite's executive producer on the *Evening News.* He, like Cronkite, was a former wire service man, and the two of them had been personally and professionally linked for twenty-five years. Socolow had come to CBS News in the 1950s as a writer for Cronkite's daytime newscast, and when Cronkite had become host of the weekly *Eyewitness to History* series, Socolow had been the show's editor and writer. When Cronkite had become anchor of the *Evening News,* Socolow had soon joined the program as a producer. But Socolow was more than just a Cronkite courtier: He was an intelligent and extremely able producer and newsroom manager who became a vice-president of CBS News and the Washington bureau chief before getting the one job he had always wanted, executive producer of Cronkite's *Evening News.* Socolow had lived the television age at CBS News, had, in fact, helped define it. The spare, crisp, straight-ahead style of the *CBS Evening News with Walter Cronkite* was as much a reflection of Sandy Socolow as it was of Cronkite himself, although any distinction would be purely academic, so shared was their vision. Socolow was not overtly ambitious; but he had a strong sense of his abilities and experience, and he secretly wondered why, in the months of speculation over Leonard's successor, his own name was not mentioned. In retrospect, why it wasn't was obvious: Sandy Socolow was the personification of CBS News in the age of Cronkite and Salant. In other words, he had *yesterday* written all over him.

Still, he felt reasonably secure when Sauter was named deputy president. True, things were a little eerie sometimes in the fishbowl, Socolow being a Cronkite man and all, but Socolow was more than solicitous to Rather, always asking the anchorman's opinions, almost always yielding. True, the Rather broadcast had slipped badly, but there were signs that the program was improving, that Rather was becoming more comfortable in the role, and, most important, that the ratings might improve. What's more, Socolow was friendly with Sauter; they'd gotten drunk together when Sauter was Paris bureau chief (lubricating visiting CBS luminaries had been a Sauter specialty in Paris). They even had a former girlfriend in common, a reporter with Knight-Ridder in Washington. When Sauter came to CBS News as boss, one of the first things he did was tell Socolow that the two of them should get together really soon and have a discussion of broadcasting philosophy.

But Socolow was the first to go. One day in the late fall of 1981, just a couple of weeks after Sauter had been named deputy president, Socolow was busy putting together that night's broadcast when he got word that Bill Leonard wanted to see him. It was late in the day, and getting toward the crunch time when hysteria begins to set in, but Socolow stopped what he was doing and went to Leonard's office. Leonard reminded Socolow of a casual conversation they'd had back in September, when they'd discussed various options and possibilities for Socolow in the event of a major change at CBS News. Socolow, a little impatient and rushed, said yes, he remembered, what about it? Leonard reminded him that Socolow had said he loved London and wouldn't mind settling in there for a time if the job and title and pay were right, and Socolow said yes, he remembered. Leonard then said it was happening; Socolow was going to be replaced as executive producer of the *Evening News.*

Socolow, a little annoyed and genuinely worried about the time, said, "Okay, I'll think about it," and turned to leave.

"Hey, you don't understand," Leonard said, nodding toward the anteroom outside his office, where his secretary sat. "The press releases are on the desk out there."

Leonard told Socolow to go see Sauter, who went on in expansive fashion about Socolow's important new duties, his important new title (director of European coverage), and how Socolow would not suffer financially because of his "promotion." Socolow and Sauter never did have that philosophical discussion.

Sauter had known from conversations with Rather that the anchorman was uncomfortable with Socolow, and that was

enough for Sauter; but beyond that Sauter had major, fundamental changes in mind for the *Evening News,* and he didn't think
that Sandy Socolow, who was so closely associated with what the
program had been, would be eager to help transform it. In a
drastic departure from form, Sauter planned to be personally
involved in the broadcast, and he didn't want to get bogged
down, as he put it, "in negotiating change.

"I didn't want to get into a circumstance where after a broadcast I could not go back and stand in the fishbowl and say, 'I
thought this whole thing sucked.' And I didn't want to get involved in 'Oh, God, that's the way this is done, that's the way
that's done.' There wasn't a tolerance for spending a long period of time proving myself. It just needed to be changed."

Replacing Socolow was Howard Stringer, the young, Welsh-
born executive producer of *CBS Reports,* who, as a documentary
maker, had been spared the rigors of daily journalism. But he
had Rather's blessing (Rather had been talking to Stringer about
the job almost since becoming anchor), and that was that. With
the appointment of Stringer, there came a stunning change in
the flow of authority at CBS News, a change that was a direct
repudiation of the structural order Salant had so carefully built.
Sauter eschewed the lordly distance that Salant and even Leonard had kept between the daily broadcasts and themselves and
declared that from then on the *Evening News* would report directly to him. Later, in the light of the traumas yet to come, it
seemed a small thing, but at the time the move came as a shock.

Salant's string of hard-news vice-presidents—Gordon Manning, Bill Small, Bud Benjamin, and their various deputies—had
always had direct authority over both broadcasts and news-
gathering operations, including the bureaus and the foreign and
national desks. The vice-president and director of news was
directly responsible for the content of the *Evening News,* the
Morning News, the weekend editions of news, and the Sunday
show, *Face the Nation.* It was an effective means of distributing
the organization's resources with some equity and of keeping
some check on the naturally acquisitive and expansionist inclinations of the *Evening News.* The news vice-president when Sauter
took charge was Ed Fouhy, Leonard's man, and when Bob Chandler, the vice-president of administration, heard of Sauter's plan
to have the broadcasts report directly to him, he said, "If I'm Ed
Fouhy, I'm mad as hell."

Sauter said, "Listen, if I'm president of CBS News, the most important thing I do is what gets on the air. I wanna take direct charge of that; it's my primary responsibility."

Ed Fouhy later remembered that time sadly, calling it the "destruction of a great system," but of course, it was also the destruction of Fouhy's career at CBS. It became unmistakably and immediately clear to him that he and Sauter were oil and water, they had no common ground, they simply couldn't hold a conversation. Fouhy could pinpoint the moment that he realized he couldn't, or wouldn't, survive in Sauter's CBS News. Sauter was new on the job, and one night he asked Fouhy to dinner. There the two of them sat, the acting president and his most important vice-president (in title, anyway), conversation having been very quickly exhausted, when Sauter got to talking about the future, what each of them might be doing years hence, after CBS News. Fouhy recalled that Sauter said that one day he'd like to become the head of production at a Hollywood film studio. He might as well have told Ed Fouhy that he practiced cannibalism. "If I had any doubts, I certainly didn't after that," Fouhy said. "This was no place for me."

Curiously, Sauter and Joyce never told Fouhy or his deputy, John Lane, or Bob Chandler or the other members of the senior staff just to get out; on the contrary, they asked them to stay. They continued to hold senior staff meetings, and Fouhy and the others gathered in Sauter's office at 6:30 P.M. to watch the three nightly newscasts and break them down and discuss them, just as in the days before Sauter. But the senior staff members soon discovered that it all was something of a charade, that after *their* meetings with Sauter, the acting president then had his real meetings, with Stringer and Rather and the new team he was assembling at the *Evening News,* and the discussions they had were completely different. Fouhy began to lay the groundwork for his departure, and within six months he was gone, to NBC News.

This dual system also effectively shut out John Lane, who, as deputy director of news under first Bud Benjamin and then Fouhy, had been in charge of personnel, the hiring and firing and shifting of correspondents and producers and bureau managers. When Sauter and Joyce came in, they met with Lane and were very friendly. They told him that they liked him, they needed him, they wanted him to stay, and in fact, he was ostensibly to remain in charge of personnel. Shortly thereafter Lane's mother died in Chicago, and while he was there for her funeral, he got a telephone call from Fouhy, who told him that a few changes had just been made by Sauter and Joyce in Lane's absence: Sandy Socolow was the new London bureau chief; Howard Stringer was the new *Evening News* executive producer; to make way for Socolow in London, the current bureau chief there, Peter Kendall, was being moved to Washington (much against his will) to become an *Evening News* producer there; Los Angeles had a new bureau chief, and the *Evening News* had two new producers in New York. "When my mother died," Lane would say, "that's when I knew I was out."

Sauter and Joyce moved very quickly to elbow aside other yesterday people, rarely firing them, usually simply reassigning them to jobs that were either out of the way or imaginary. Within the first month Socolow was out and Lane and Fouhy had been shown the writing on the wall. Then Sauter and Joyce discovered a couple of yesterday people, Ernie Leiser and Russ Bensley, lurking in the special-events unit. Leiser had been at CBS News for twenty-five years, first as a correspondent and then, beginning in the early Salant days, as an executive. He was a man of keen intellect and extreme self-assurance, who'd made an indelible imprint upon the organization. Leiser had graduated from the University of Chicago to the battlefields of World War II, which he covered as a correspondent for the army newspaper *Stars and Stripes,* and after knocking around for a time after the war, he came to CBS as a newswriter. In the late 1950s he became a correspondent in Europe, doing admirable work for CBS News from behind the iron curtain, even landing in jail after the Hungarian uprising. But it was as an executive on Richard Salant's team that Leiser came to flower. It was Leiser who laid the foundation that made CBS News truly a national news-gathering operation, establishing regional bureaus around the country that became showcases for developing talent in the field, such as the young Texan Dan Rather (whom Leiser hired). It was Leiser who drew up a blueprint for a new, expanded half-hour *Evening News* and pressed it upon management so convincingly that it was embraced and sold to the network; Leiser was the father of the half-hour format, which took network news a large step beyond the compressed, tabloid-style broadcast it had been to the form that continues today. In

1964 Ernie Leiser left management to become executive producer of the *Evening News,* and it was under his hand that Cronkite's broadcast developed and grew and finally, in 1967, edged ahead of NBC in the ratings to stay.

In 1981 Ernie Leiser was vice-president of special events at CBS News, the unit that covered elections and big stories as well as special programming, such as the late-night news specials that CBS News regularly spun out of a big breaking story that the *Evening News,* because of limitations of time, could handle only cursorily. Working with Leiser in special events was Russ Bensley, another old hand, who'd joined CBS News as a writer in 1960 and had, like Leiser, once been the executive producer of the *Evening News.* Leiser and Bensley were the very stuff of CBS News, as embedded in the place as the mortar in the brickwork. That, of course, doomed them to the growing stack of professional corpses marked *yesterday.* With the support and advice of Dan Rather, Sauter and Joyce removed both Leiser and Bensley and replaced them with Joan Richman, a former *Evening News* producer and then the executive producer of the weekend news. She assumed both Leiser's and Bensley's titles, becoming vice-president and executive producer of special events, and settled in as a new member of the Sauter circle.

Bensley was made producer of the weekend newscasts; Leiser, who had discovered Dan Rather and still had some capital in that account, was made vice-president and assistant to Sauter. His job, as described at the time in *Variety,* was to "deal with relationships with foreign broadcasts, First Amendment issues, policy questions, etc." Few at CBS News were fooled into thinking it was real work.

Aside from the *Evening News,* the program that best represented the sensibilities of CBS News at the moment before the Sauter/ Joyce revolution was the daily morning news program, *Morning.* The show was a manifestation of two conflicting and irresistible phenomena: the urge at CBS News to be serious and important and the frustrating fact that since the early 1950s CBS had been utterly unable to compete successfully in the morning against NBC's enduring *Today* show. The joke around CBS for years was that its various versions of a morning news program, almost all of them essentially hard-news broadcasts, were designed, produced, and broadcast for a loyal audience of one—William S.

Paley. The rationale for sticking with a straight newscast in the morning—and perhaps the excuse as well—was that Mr. Paley wanted that one time period in the day to be immune from competitive pressures; it also happened that Paley himself watched the broadcast religiously. Dick Salant used to tell how the chairman would call him up afterward with the most niggling suggestions about the show: "You should move the picture to the left or the right" or "You should start the commercials later." Salant wondered why the CBS chairman took such a minute interest in the program until he realized that "he would watch it every morning while his valet served him breakfast in bed."

But by the late 1970s pressures were growing to make CBS more competitive in the mornings, largely because ABC had entered the market from nowhere and found almost instant success with an entertainment program, *Good Morning America.* The show was the antithesis of the CBS view, a lively and glitzy news-and-entertainment mix that was not a news show, in the strict sense, but it accomplished in the space of just a couple of years what CBS had failed to do in a quarter of a century: It found a broad audience in the morning. Morning news, in fact, was booming; NBC's *Today* and ABC's *Good Morning America* were bringing in revenues of $40 to $50 million a year; CBS's morning news revenues were just over one third of that amount. ABC had proved it could be done, so CBS felt obliged to try again. Bill Leonard thought he had the answer, and best, it was practically ready-made.

In 1979 Leonard had made good on one of his dreams by launching a program on Sunday morning designed to be so compelling and thoughtful that it would be watched "by people who don't watch television." The show, *Sunday Morning,* was just what Leonard envisioned: a thoughtful, leisurely, artfully pro-duced and carefully written kind of antitelevision, right there on the same network that gave America *The Incredible Hulk.* Robert Northshield ("Shad" to all who knew him) was the creator and executive producer of the program, and Charles Kuralt, the poet of CBS News and one of the news division's true stars, was the anchor. The show was brilliant from the start, easily the best regularly scheduled news program on television. It was loved by critics, and what's more, it began to build a loyal audience. Leonard was proud of the program, and it occurred to him that if the magic of *Sunday Morning* could be transferred to weekday mornings, he would have solved the CBS morning problem at last; CBS could be classy and successful, too. Neither Northshield nor Kuralt wanted to do it—the *Sunday* workload was enough—but Leonard pressed hard and eventually prevailed upon them. Leonard and Northshield chose as coanchor of the new daily program Diane Sawyer, a relative newcomer whose work in the Washington bureau had been impressive and whose attractiveness and engaging on-camera manner, demonstrated in open-ended exchanges with Kuralt on the *Sunday Morning* program, convinced the executives that a Kuralt-Sawyer teaming would be irresistible. So with high expectations, CBS News launched its new morning hope, called simply *Morning.*

In the view of Van Gordon Sauter, it would have been more appropriately titled *Yesterday Morning.* Sauter hated the program. He thought Kuralt was all wrong for the morning audience (*Good Morning America* had an actor, David Hartman, as its host), and he thought that Shad Northshield was all wrong as a producer. Sauter found *Morning* a ponderous, sleepy, and altogether bad piece of work. What's more, it had failed to improve the CBS ratings position, which remained a distant third (a fact that Kuralt-Northshield defenders blamed at least partly on the fact that *Morning* didn't start until 7:30 A.M., half an hour behind the morning shows on NBC and ABC, to accommodate the moribund *Captain Kangaroo*). But Sauter's mind was made up, and the story got out that *Morning* was in trouble. When Sauter was in Hawaii for the meeting with the affiliates on the hourlong news, less than a week on the job, he was quoted in John Carmody's column in the *Washington Post* as saying that he saw "nothing wrong with interviewing Larry Hagman" on the morning news, a statement that was a fairly undisguised hint to Northshield and Kuralt, who had pointedly refused to include segments with Hollywood celebrities in their broadcast; that was the province of the fluffier *Good Morning America.* Northshield, of course, hadn't been told that he was in trouble. On the contrary, Ed Fouhy and Bill Leonard had only favorable things to say about the broadcast; after all, they had talked Northshield and Kuralt into doing it.

In fact, Sauter and Ed Joyce had already met with Charles Kuralt's replacement, a proven ratings draw who was already a Sauter person in good standing. It was Bill Kurtis, the anchorman at WBBM in Chicago. Sauter and Joyce secreted Kurtis off to an inn in Lake Forest and, in the manner that Kurtis knew so well, convinced the Chicago anchorman to come to New York to coanchor a new-vision morning news program. Sauter made clear to Kurtis that the morning news move was fundamental to the larger plan, which was the remaking of CBS News. "They wanted to break down the arrogance of CBS News," Kurtis said, "and I was on their team."

A Chicago newspaper soon ran a story announcing that Kurtis was going to replace Kuralt, but no one told Kuralt. And even while Northshield was receiving assurances that he was in solid standing, Sauter and Joyce were actively recruiting *his* replacement. They knew whom they wanted, George Merlis, who'd been executive producer of *Good Morning America* for ABC and had played a key role in developing that show's success. But the Merlis talks were taking time, and Northshield kept hearing stories about his own imminent demise. One Sunday Ed Joyce showed up at the *Sunday Morning* set to allay Northshield's anxiety. After a while Sauter joined them, and as Northshield recalled with some bitterness, Joyce said to Sauter, "I just came in to tell Shad that all these stories in the paper are false. I've convinced you, haven't I, Shad?" In fact, Sauter and Joyce had no intention of keeping Northshield as executive producer; they planned changes on the show so drastic they knew Northshield would resist. Indeed, just a couple of days later Northshield was summoned to Leonard's office, where he was informed that he was out as executive producer of *Morning.* Northshield said that Sauter later explained the little charade on the *Sunday Morning* set by saying, "I hope you understand, I had to stretch the truth, but we were able to make this deal with George Merlis. Obviously, he's the right guy."

Finally, it came time to tell Charles Kuralt. A truly beloved figure at CBS News, he enjoyed a huge personal success with his "On the Road" pieces on the *Evening News,* and he was the jewel of *Sunday Morning.* But with his bald pate (there had been talk, briefly, of trying to get him to wear a toupee) and his careful, deliberate manner, he was doomed as a morning anchor in the Sauter era. With Kurtis safely on board, Ed Joyce and Ed Fouhy had an unpleasant meeting with Kuralt. Fouhy remembered that while he and John Lane and the others were cut out of most of the decisions, they were often brought in for the dirty work, "to sort of bless what they were doing." Fouhy hated that meeting with Kuralt. They told the newsman, whose arm had been severely twisted to get him to come to the daily show: "You're off this program, and, by the way, we're reducing your salary." Charles Kuralt had just been zero-based.

"Charlie is the epitome of the decent, honest guy of integrity," Fouhy recalled, "and he looked at Joyce like he couldn't believe what he had just heard. And I just didn't want to be there in the worst way. I just didn't want to have to go through that again. The atmosphere was one of a disconnection between the new and the old, between the news gathering and the programs. It had always been integrated. It became two cultures."

There was some speculation that Diane Sawyer, who in Sauter's view had been as dull and dreary as the rest of the broadcast, would be replaced by Connie Chung, one of Sauter's anchors at KNXT in Los Angeles. Fortunately for Sawyer, Sauter and Joyce decided that she was yesterday only by association. Playing that hunch, Sauter took her to lunch one day, and Sawyer was just delightful, sexy and fetching and coolly intelligent all at once, as only she can be. In the middle of the conversation Sauter asked, "Why don't I see this person on the air? Why aren't you *this* Diane Sawyer on television?" Sawyer said that's just what she'd be, and Sauter had his new morning team: George Merlis, Bill Kurtis, and a "new" Diane Sawyer.

Asked at the time if all the changes meant a new direction for CBS News in the morning, Sauter told the *Wall Street Journal*, "The character of 'Morning' as a serious news broadcast will undergo no fundamental change. We believe hard news in the morning is vital and necessary for the public. While we naturally anticipate some changes in the format, there will be no changes in its objective." Then he proceeded to institute the most drastic fundamental changes conceivable to the character of the show, which was renamed *CBS Morning News.* It was moved to the CBS Sports set, with its flashy rows of television monitors in the background, a snappy, electronic theme song was added, a Hollywood reporter was made a key member of the cast, the anchors and a new weatherman engaged in an incredibly insipid "weather talk" segment, how-to pieces became a staple, and Hollywood celebrities were most definitely no longer taboo. The pace was fast, the style chatty—and the results were mixed, at best. Grumblings were heard on this one, letters sympathetic to Kuralt and the old CBS News way arrived by the hundreds, and in the hallway people observed aloud that the new program had a distinctly *local* look to it, didn't it? At CBS News that was a cold put-down, although it didn't seem to occur to anyone that local news was precisely what Sauter and Joyce intended. They *were* local news. Sauter, apparently annoyed over the sniping, revealed his feelings to a magazine reporter. " 'Looks like local news,' that's what they're saying. Well, hell, that's what it's fucking well supposed to look like! There's a feeling in some quarters that if it doesn't look dull, it's not good journalism. What crap."

As Sauter and Joyce worked their way through CBS News, tearing down the old order and building the new, there was not a lot of effort wasted on diplomacy. The losers in the new CBS News read about how lively and vital this broadcast or that unit was going to be now that the cobwebs had been swept out. It was a true revolution, and it seemed that it was not enough that the people of the old order be vanquished. *What* they had been, their way, had to be exorcised as well. When Leiser and Bensley were replaced at special events, for example, stories about the change noted that Joan Richman was expected to "pump more life into special events broadcasts." Howard Stringer, the new executive producer of the *Evening News,* explained that work was needed with the program's writers to ensure that "Cronkite phrases don't creep in" to the broadcast.

It was a hell of a good story for the television press, this cultural revolution at the House of Murrow, and the new regime was eminently quotable. The broadcast that Rather inherited from Cronkite, Stringer told one reporter, was "stuffy." Sauter told a TV critic from a Chicago paper that what CBS News had to do was develop a broadcast that was "worthy of Dan Rather." Cronkite and his legacy were especially good game because Walter Cronkite was yesterday incarnate. That was why the man who had been the *CBS Evening News,* its force and its face and its voice, was now persona not grata there, effectively banned from the show.

When Cronkite left the broadcast, it was with the explicit understanding that he was going to have fairly open entrée to it (old anchormen "just keep coming back for more," he'd said). He felt he'd earned the right to *Evening News* airtime, and Black Rock as well as news management had encouraged his belief.

The plan was for him to enjoy a kind of working retirement. He welcomed the relief from the daily grind, but he planned to keep a hand in: He was a member of the CBS board of directors, his contract called for a prime-time news series, and he would be a regular contributor to the *Evening News.* Bud Benjamin would be his personal producer, and together they would travel the world, work the big issues, and, with Cronkite's experience and prestige, maybe even score a few scoops.

The very first time out, that is exactly what happened. Cronkite and Benjamin were in Europe when the Solidarity movement became a hot story, so they went to Poland, where they managed to get an interview not only with Solidarity leader Lech Walesa but with the leader of the Soviet-backed military regime, both in the same day. Cronkite and Benjamin were feeling quite proud of themselves, two old dogs on the roam and finding this big bone, and they came back with the story and presented it to the *Evening News* like a gift. A huge gift. The report they gave to the *Evening News* was more than ten minutes long, as long as any piece since the broadcast had done a landmark special report on Watergate. But this wasn't quite Watergate. It was, however, an awkward moment. The *Evening News* had for so long been Cronkite's personal garment that the inclination, the instinct was to suit him. But ten minutes was an awfully long time, no matter how good the story, and Sandy Socolow, who was then still the executive producer, and in a tough position, ordered that the piece be trimmed. He assigned the task to a young producer named Andrew Heyward, who saw his brief career pass before his eyes as he made the cuts; but Benjamin approved the trim, and there was no confrontation over the report. Rather himself had made no open fuss over the piece, but he didn't need to; it was clear that giving Cronkite carte blanche on the broadcast would be a potential source of trouble.

As things developed, though, it was needless worry. Cronkite filed another report or two, but he was thoroughly enjoying his new freedom and was not exactly rushing to the Broadcast Center with daily reports. He did like to pop in now and again, and he and Benjamin continued to plan further adventures and held every expectation of scoring more stories like Poland in the future. Then Van Sauter came to CBS News, and Cronkite's casual entrée suddenly vanished. There were no calls from the *Evening News* for assignments. Big stories came and went. They were stories that Cronkite just itched to get at, but the phone never rang, not his, not Benjamin's. When the United States invaded Grenada, Cronkite, who was famous for his love of sailing and had a particular knowledge of that part of the Caribbean, held his breath in the hope of getting called in; CBS, like the other networks, was having a good deal of logistical difficulty on the story, the press had been shut out, and Cronkite, who had contacts down there, knew he could help. Still nothing.

Cronkite began to sense that something was wrong, and he was bothered by it. "I didn't realize the extent of it for a while, but it was perfectly clear to me that the freeze was on," he recalled. "I thought that it was a more of a sort of personal uptightness on the part of Dan, when I'd come around the shop. . . ." He was right. Cronkite met with Sauter and let him know directly that he was available for an *Evening News* assignment, and Sauter told him that he thought Cronkite was just so busy with his summertime series *Universe* that he didn't have time for *Evening News* work.

The truth was, the new CBS News wanted no part of Walter Cronkite. They didn't want his quaint eight-minute reports on the state of the world, and most important, they didn't want any confusion about whose broadcast, whose CBS News this was. After the Poland report, when Rather's ratings were pointed down and gaining speed, there'd been an item in one of the columns suggesting that maybe Cronkite was coming back to the broadcast in some capacity, and that was just the sort of uncertainty that Sauter wanted to dispel.

Sauter knew that Walter Cronkite made Dan Rather nervous, and Rather was nervous enough already. What's more, Sauter didn't want the audience reminded of Cronkite. He later said, "We could not confuse in the audience's mind whose broadcast that was. We were there promoting Dan Rather, and you could not send through your programming mixed signals to the audience." It was Dan Rather's time, not Cronkite's, and it was Dan Rather's organization, and Sauter wanted no mistaking the point. Whenever he spoke of zero-basing CBS News, he always added that the one exception was Dan Rather. As long as Sauter was there, Dan Rather wasn't going anywhere but up. "I am," said Sauter, making the record as clear as could be, "married to Dan Rather."

Chapter

VAN SAUTER WAS A hands-on manager, just as his press clippings promised, and the first thing he wanted to get his hands on was the *Evening News.* He soon began wandering down to the newsroom after the broadcasts, and one evening he said he wanted to discuss new ways of shooting the show. He asked Sandy Socolow, who was in his final days before exile, to show him some sample formats, each framing the anchorman in a different perspective on the screen. Obliging, Socolow set up on studio monitors three shots that were roughly like those used by the three networks on their nightly newscasts.

The ABC shot mimicked the vogue of local stations: a close-up of the anchor, tightly framed, which gave him an emphatic presence. The NBC approach was a full shot, leaving the anchor visible from head to midsection and making him seem more distant. CBS had been using something in between. Socolow said that Sauter studied the formats and said, "Why don't we do that?" He was pointing to the ABC shot. "After all, what are we selling? We're selling our anchorman, aren't we?"

A more precise declaration of purpose couldn't have been uttered. Van Sauter was making a new universe of CBS News, and squarely at its center he placed a nervous East Texas anchorman whose "covenant of excellence" had begun to seem like a bill of goods. Under Sauter, Dan Rather would no longer struggle to win the hearts and minds of CBS News; his would become the only heart and mind that mattered.

Rather and his *Evening News* became the holy mission of the new CBS News, its animating purpose, as defined by Van Sauter. When Sauter said, "I am married to Dan Rather," he meant it, and whenever he was asked by interviewers or by his staff what his priorities in the job were, he always said "the *Evening News,* the *Evening News,* and the *Evening News.*" That became the official chorus to the metamorphic anthem of Van Gordon Sauter, and the organization was invited to sing along. "There was a single-minded concentration on the *Evening News,*" said Ernie Leiser, Sauter's special assistant and vice-president. "He didn't care about the *Morning News,* didn't care about *Sunday Morning,* didn't care about documentaries or anything else."

The elevation to absolute precedence of Dan Rather and his broadcast ("It was my intention to put him at the center of the universe," Sauter said) was at the heart of Sauter's plan for CBS News. It was a carefully calculated strategy that was designed to bring fast results. And it would. But in the long term it proved to be a disastrous course for CBS News, exacerbating old frictions and creating new ones. It undermined the organizational strength of the institution, once so broad and deep; it devoured one news division president, and ultimately, it provided the rationale for the most devastating cutbacks ever imposed on a broadcast news organization. A business investor named Laurence A. Tisch would one day look at the CBS News budget, swollen to near $300 million, and ask, "All that money for a twenty-three-minute show?" Two hundred and fifteen CBS News employees would answer with their jobs, and in the tumult the unthinkable would be raised: Did CBS really need to have a full-blown, worldwide news-gathering operation of its own? Wouldn't something less do?

The truth is, news and newsmen can be sold to viewers like soap, and Van Sauter knew it. That was why, in the early weeks of 1982, television screens across America were suddenly filled with an artful rendering of Dan Rather's darkly earnest face, etched in black against a gray background, and, below it, the legend: "One news organization sets the standards of excellence in television journalism. One journalist is the nation's leading anchorman. Together, they bring you the best evening news broadcast in America. Experienced. Trusted. Responsive. See the 'CBS Evening News with Dan Rather.' See the difference. The best remains unchanged."

Over and over, day after day and night after night, that message was hammered out over CBS air, in prime time and fringe time, in long versions and short, always with the same payoff theme: "The best remains unchanged." It was a marvelously effective promotion, simple and spare, almost classical in its tones. And of course, it was untrue.

CBS News had, in fact, changed completely, not just in subtle shades and nuances but wholly; it was basic, fundamental, molecular change that Van Sauter brought to CBS News in the late fall of 1981, change in the people who decided and implemented the news, change in the very understanding of what news was. "The best remains unchanged" promotion campaign itself was proof of it. It was something entirely new to CBS News. The advertising and marketing department at CBS News had never come up with such a selling campaign before because there had never before been an advertising and marketing department at CBS News; what promotion there was had always been handled by the network, and it was the sort of thing those people on the network side did. That changed immediately when Sauter and Joyce came to news. They had fought in the wars of local news; their weapons and tactics were local weapons and tactics. The essential local weapon was heavy promotion with a catchy slogan ("It's not pretty, but it's real").

Sauter in particular believed in the magic of imagery and marketing. He had no qualms about a little consumer manipulation in the cause of peddling news to viewers; that's what television was about, wasn't it? Hadn't Cronkite's reign itself been a triumph of perfect casting and marketing—the benign godhead as anchor, selling trust to the American news consumer? True, the Cronkite phenomenon hadn't been planned—it had evolved, the product of journalistic instinct and discipline—but Sauter's CBS News had neither the time nor the inclination for evolution. More expedient means were available.

So it happened that one of the first things Sauter did at CBS News was look for a pitchman to shape a marketing campaign for the new CBS News or, more precisely, for Dan Rather and the *Evening News.* He found his man—Joe Pasarella—in the advertising and marketing department of ABC, a culture as oppo-

site from the pristine sensibilities of the CBS News old guard as
could be conceived. ABC was known for its unsubtle on-air
promotions, which tended to be leering and loud (*The Luuuuuuv
Boat!*). But Pasarella designed a pitch handsomely tailored to
the CBS News image, understated, quiet, and straight, guaranteed to push all the right emotional buttons with viewers.

Sauter had in mind a very specific marketing strategy, designed to exploit perceived weaknesses at NBC and ABC and to
strengthen Rather's uncertain image with viewers. As battered
as Rather and his *CBS Evening News* were in 1981, neither NBC
nor ABC had a strong enough anchor figure to consolidate its
gains and to build a lasting lead. NBC in particular was in a state
of flux at the time, chafing under Bill Small's unpopular leadership and trying to decide who would be the anchor of the *NBC
Nightly News*. John Chancellor had inherited the post from David
Brinkley, but Small had promised an anchor job to Roger Mudd
when he lured the embittered newsman from CBS in 1980.
Moreover, the rising star of NBC News, Tom Brokaw, had
grown impatient with his role as anchor of the *Today* program
and made it clear that he intended that his next job be anchor
of a network evening newscast. The inevitable courtship of Brokaw by Roone Arledge and ABC forced NBC's hand, and as with
Rather, institutional loyalty (and an extravagant contract) won
out. Brokaw stayed at NBC, coanchored with Mudd, while Chancellor was eased into the role of senior commentator. ABC,
having lost out first on Rather and now on Brokaw, was still
without the star centerpiece Arledge wanted for his newly in-
vigorated news division.

With a shifting anchor situation at NBC and an interesting and
competent but not stellar triple anchor team (Frank Reynolds,
Peter Jennings, and Max Robinson) at ABC, it struck Sauter that
the perfect way to sell *his* anchor amid the disarray was to emphasize stability, tradition, experience. Never mind that Dan
Rather at the time no more fully embodied those aspects than
his competitors on the other networks; Sauter had the symbolic
power of CBS News to draw upon, the very characteristics that
he and his team privately found so stuffy and quaint. The old
guard would find a certain irony in the fact that the new order
was selling itself by summoning up echoes of the past, by capital-
izing on the prestige of the old CBS News. The campaign was
classy and smart, suggesting the stark, clean style with which

Frank Stanton had imbued the company (epitomized by the Stanton-designed CBS stationery, gray and buff, with a tiny embossed dot marking the precise spot where the first letter of the first word of each piece of CBS correspondence was to begin). "The best remains unchanged" campaign had CBS written all over it, and it lent Rather a degree of stature and stability.

Selling Dan Rather to the public was the easy part. Selling him inside CBS News might be far more difficult. Sauter knew that Rather was edgy and unhappy, and he'd already heard stories from Rather and Leibner that suggested the anchorman was unable to get the smallest thing accomplished—a shift in editorial emphasis, a personnel request. Sauter was also convinced just from looking at the broadcast that the people who were putting the *Evening News* on the air were not disposed to changing their ways just to make Rather more comfortable. Sauter knew that when Dan Rather was unsure or nervous or angry— and he was all those things in his first year as anchor—it showed on the air. Rather was getting so worked up over his performance that it suffered even more, and as he got worse, the ratings got worse.

Losing did not do much for Rather's standing inside CBS News. Building a consensus would have been challenge enough for him under the best of circumstances, considering the lingering loyalties to Cronkite and Mudd and the considerable baggage Rather himself brought to the task. But the organization had a particularly keen and discriminating nose, and Dan Rather had a scent of doom all over him that discouraged any urge to line up behind him. For all of Walter Cronkite's skills and professional standing, his success was the fabric of the consensus that supported him. By the end of 1981 the internal dynamics at CBS News had considerably lengthened the odds of Rather's lasting another year.

Van Sauter didn't like those odds at all, and he immediately set out to change them, by rather radical means. Sauter had reason to believe that his own test as news president would be the performance of the *Evening News*. That was what the press focused on; that was what Sauter's bosses focused on; that was where journalism's only $2.2 million annual salary was being paid. It was also Sauter's personal inclination to focus on a particular problem, something he could get his hands on; that was the essence of the turnaround psychology. But for the *Eve-*

ning News to succeed, Rather must succeed, and that could not happen as long as people at CBS were wondering aloud who the next anchor of the program was going to be. Sauter genuinely believed in Rather's anchor potential; that was handy because despite the hallway murmurs, replacing Rather was not an option. If Dan Rather had no inside consensus, Sauter would just have to create one for him.

And he did, by giving Rather something that guaranteed the struggling anchorman the institution's full respect, if not its admiration: Sauter gave him power.

It was more than just the power of being managing editor of the *Evening News;* that was television window dressing and in itself meant nothing. Cronkite had had the title, so Richard Leibner had made sure that Rather got it, too. What Sauter gave to Rather was *real* power—a voice in news policy, a direct say in story assignments and staffing, dominion over careers. As managing editor of the *Evening News,* Cronkite had never hesitated to exert his authority over the broadcast, and there were times when "he could be a terror," as Bob Schieffer, one of the Washington bureau stars, put it. Cronkite happily delegated the mundane daily chores to others (Sandy Socolow and his predecessors actually put together the lineup of stories on most days), but he was always the final arbiter of what went out over the air. Marvin Kalb might call him from the State Department fifteen minutes before airtime to complain that the producers hadn't included an important story in the lineup, and if Cronkite agreed, he'd have the broadcast torn apart and restructured. When it came to the *Evening News,* Walter Cronkite was the original 900-pound gorilla.

But Rather's power was something new, something different. Cronkite's authority, and his interest, had resided in and been limited to the *Evening News.* Rather's power in the organization as a whole made Cronkite's influence seem puny by comparison. In the end Cronkite had always been an employee—albeit one well aware of his influence. But Van Sauter brought Rather into management; he ceded a share of his presidency to his anchorman. Rather attended management meetings; he was consulted on all hires; he was clued in to every aspect of the running of the operation. "Nothing happens that he isn't consulted about," said one CBS News executive, "from changing a correspondent in the London bureau who doesn't routinely do *Evening News* work, to everything else, involving, in some cases, other broadcasts which have no bearing on the *Evening News* at all. When he's not consulted, then he's certainly notified in advance. The rule of thumb is, Dan isn't to be surprised by anything. Now, he may not give a shit, or he may be told and not remember that he's been told; but he's to be told, and in advance."

Cronkite had been happy to let the managers manage. He wouldn't especially have cared about a new hire in an outland post; that wasn't his job. People like Bill Small in the Washington bureau, Gordon Manning and Ernie Leiser and Bud Benjamin in New York were paid to make those decisions, with approval from Dick Salant, then president of CBS News. Rather not only cared about who was being hired out there but had approval rights in the matter. It was a drastic departure from form; there was nothing like it anywhere else in broadcast journalism. And among the troops, the joking references to a "900-pound gorilla" gave way to a new, more derisive term: *anchor monster.*

It began to seem that Dan Rather was the reason behind everything CBS News did. The promotion of Rather extended not only to actual on-air commercials but to the news programs themselves. There came to be a rule that anything big, anything special, had to have Dan Rather's face attached to it. Where CBS News once prided itself on its breadth and depth, its touted "bench" of news stars who could step into a documentary or a news special with equal weight, there was now an understanding that Dan Rather alone was to dominate CBS News air. Rather and Rather alone would go on camera when a big news story warranted a late-night thirty-minute special report. What better promotion than showing your anchorman at work on a real news story? It happened that Rather was at his best on a breaking story. However, so were most CBS reporters, and some of them, to their regret, just didn't grasp the new values that were at work. One of them was Morton Dean.

Mort Dean was a member of Rather's generation of CBS News stars, a tough-minded, extremely disciplined reporter whose stubborn adherence to his own particularly demanding standards was sometimes exasperating to those who worked with him. He was not a get-along sort; he'd made his reputation covering state and local politics in New York for local television, and when he came to CBS News in 1967, he chafed at the intensely collaborative process he found. In television news, especially at the network level, much of the real reporting work is done by field producers, who are assigned to stories with correspondents and in some cases report the story, direct the camera crew, and write the script—everything but go on camera. Even with those correspondents who are capable reporters, the producer is a full partner in the shaping of most stories. But Dean preferred to work alone; he trusted his own instincts and didn't particularly welcome the intrusion of a producer. This gave him a reputation for being difficult, but that liability was more than balanced by the quality of his work, which was consistently first-rate.

There had been occasions when Dean's idiosyncrasies had saved the day for CBS News. In 1982, for example, he was dispatched to Buenos Aires to cover the Falklands War, a story that had been as frustrating for the television networks as it was enticing. Britain at war (complete with one of its royal sons, Prince Andrew, seeing combat duty) was great stuff, but because of the complete inaccessibility of the action (camera crews were banned from the scene of the conflict), it was making for some awful television. Dean was the second man into Argentina for CBS News, and by the time he got there, the crew and producers awaiting him were desperate for a score. New York was pressuring them, and there was word that ABC News had somehow gotten its hands on some combat footage. Then CBS seemed to catch a break. One young producer had been feeding a report to New York by satellite from an Argentine television station when a local man simply handed her a videotape containing footage of the Argentine Navy in action. "It's got PT boats and everything," the producer said. The producer and the CBS bureau chief who was running the network's Falklands coverage wanted to put the report on that evening's broadcast. But Dean, typically, resisted. He interrogated the young producer.

"Who was the guy who gave it to you?"

"I don't know, some guy who worked there. It was the most amazing thing, I'm cutting this thing and some young guy comes up to me and we begin talking and he asks whether I want a piece from the Falklands, and subsequently I've got this—"

"How did he get it?"

"I don't know, but—"

"Are you sure it's from the Falklands?"

"Well . . ."

It was a maddening exercise to the harried CBS staffers, who'd been working twelve-hour days to no avail. To have finally struck pay dirt, only to have this hotshot correspondent a day removed from Manhattan questioning their scoop! But Dean insisted on seeing the tape, and then he had the audacity to say that the landscape didn't look at all like the pictures of the Falklands terrain he'd studied on the plane. On the plane! Worse, by this time Van Sauter had been told about the CBS scoop, and New York was panting for the pictures. Dean, however, wanted proof. The haggard bureau chief took the correspondent aside.

"Mort, you know the pressure we've been under here?"

"Yes."

"You know how much shit I've been taking from New York?"

"Yeah, but I am not going to do this."

"Mort, can't we say 'purported'?"

"No, this is wrong. Okay?"

And then Mort Dean walked back to the center of the makeshift CBS News Buenos Aires bureau and made a speech. CBS News stands for something, Dean pontificated, and it doesn't stand for buckling under in the face of competition. And there things stood, growing more tense by the moment, until a naval officer on retainer to CBS News as technical adviser happened to stop by to pick up his paycheck. The journalists hustled the officer over to an editing machine so that he could review the disputed tape, and Dean agreed to accept his verdict. The tape played for just a few seconds, the PT boats whizzed by, and a smile came to the officer's face. Then a chuckle, followed by a roaring laugh. The CBS "scoop" turned out to be an excerpt from an Argentine Navy training film, shot during the war between Argentina and Chile, and was used by a local TV station as its sign-off picture every night. "Whoever spoke to Van Sauter," Dean said as he turned away, "call him up and tell him what an asshole I am."

Morton Dean may have been a singular pain in the ass, but he was as good as he was difficult. He was perfectly suited, in other words, to CBS News. Dean thrived in the Salant era, so much so that he was showcased in one of the prize assignments granted to rising news stars, the anchor chair on the Sunday version of the *Evening News.* He was, in fact, extremely happy, probably as happy as he could expect to be, professionally. That is, until one Sunday in the fall of 1983, when Mort Dean collided head-on with the new order.

Dean was awakened at home at about 4:00 A.M. by a call from the news desk. A suicide bomber had crashed a truck loaded with explosives into the barracks of the U.S. Marine contingent stationed outside the Beirut airport, killing more than two hundred sleeping marines. It was a huge story, of course, and the drill when a big story broke on Sunday was to call Mort Dean. He was the Sunday *Evening News* anchor, as well as the standby substitute for *Sunday Morning* anchor Charles Kuralt, who, as it happened, had already told the desk that he was feeling ill that morning and might not be able to make his broadcast. So Dean, who loved being called into action, hurried down to the Broadcast Center for what promised to be a frantic day. Kuralt recovered enough to do his broadcast; but Dean stood by, and after the show he walked down from the *Sunday* studio to the newsroom to prepare for whatever special coverage CBS would provide that day. When he got downstairs, he knew that CBS News would be interrupting its regular programming for special reports; the troops from the *Evening News* were filing in.

Dean walked into the fishbowl, the windowed office that served as the command post for the *Evening News*. "What's going on?" he asked. "Are we going to do a special?" There was an embarrassed silence. Then someone mumbled, "Uh, no, Dan's coming in. We're just going to see what happens."

A few minutes later John Lane, the emasculated but still titular head of news coverage, called Dean aside. "Look," Lane said, "Dan's coming in, and he's going to do the *Evening News* tonight."

"Why?"

"Well, it's a big story."

"Well, yeah, I know it's a big story. I've covered other big stories."

"Well, he's going to do it," Lane said, adding unnecessarily, "Management wants that."

"Well, that's just fucking obnoxious, that's what that is. Look, it's a story, it's my shift."

Dean went on for a time, letting John Lane know just how he felt about about giving up a big story that had broken on his shift, how'd he'd done just fine for CBS News in Vietnam and in Iran during the hostage crisis, without the help of Dan Rather. "It's belittling, it's stupid," he said, and Lane gave the only answer he had: "Mort, that's what the new management wants, okay? And that's how it's going to be."

And that's how it was. Dan Rather came in that day and went on the air, and Mort Dean didn't. But Dean was so steamed he did something he rarely did: He called his agent at home. "I'm only calling you because I'm going to fucking explode in a minute," Dean said. "This is a goddamn outrage. It shows where this business is going. It's the goddamn star system!" Dean's agent tried to calm him down and pleaded with him not to do anything stupid. It was wise counsel, and anyway, it was really all the response Dean could have expected; his agent is Richard Leibner.

Dean did calm down. He went home for a meal and returned to the studio to do his Sunday afternoon radio newscast ("Is Dan going to do *that* for me, too?" he asked Ernie Leiser), and then he went home for the day. By Monday he was simmering but under control, even when Charles Osgood and Douglas Edwards stopped by his office to commiserate. Osgood's place on the late Sunday night newscast had also been preempted by Rather, and Edwards, the original *Evening News* anchorman, Cronkite's predecessor, had been told that Rather would take over *his* five-minute afternoon newscast on Monday. But Dean kept his feelings in check, he'd had his explosion, and he was rather proud of the restraint he showed when a reporter from *New York* magazine called to ask him about the incident. The reporter was doing a story about the "revolution" at CBS News ostensibly caused by Dan Rather's stepping all over everyone's turf. "I'm not going to say anything" was all Dean said. At first.

But the reporter had heard that Dean was furious, and hadn't he thrown a tantrum? Wasn't there a revolution at CBS News? No, Dean said, adding, "First of all, you can't have a revolution unless you have the arms. . . . You know, I told three or four people I was angry, and the only thing I'll say to you is that like any other reporter, when something happens on my shift I want to do it; when it doesn't happen on my shift, I want to be called in." It was a nice, safe, earnest, reporterlike thing to say, the sort of comment Rather himself might have made under the circumstances, and Dean thought he'd handled it well. But when the story appeared under the headline IMPERIOUS DAN, Mort Dean's quotes looked absolutely seditious, especially inside an institution that was sniffing out sedition. Dean soon heard that what he'd said was considered disloyal, that Rather was quite angry, and that it would be a good idea to seek an audience with the anchorman. Dean did go in to see Rather, but the meeting wasn't very cordial. The anchorman didn't seem to agree at all with the suggestion that he would have responded the same way under the circumstances. Although life went on, Dean felt that Rather never forgave him for his show of temper, and in the short time remaining in his CBS News career, Mort Dean never stopped hearing that he had "a problem" with Rather and the new management. It was very uncomfortable for Dean, which was the predictable effect of having landed on what came to be known as "Dan Rather's shit list."

"You never knew what was going to set Dan off," said one *Evening News* producer. "You could be talking about what we're going to do tomorrow and mention some correspondent that you thought was in favor, and that was the way you found out that he or she wasn't."

Another correspondent who found himself on the shit list was Ed Rabel, a highly regarded New York-based reporter who violated one of the cardinal rules of the new order when he sought and received a transfer to Washington without the blessing of Rather and the *Evening News.* Rabel's fiancée was in Washington, Rabel liked the town, and he implored Ed Joyce for a transfer. "We found out about it when it was a fait accompli," recalled a ranking member of Rather's *Evening News* team. "Nothing will piss off Dan more than not being at least in the consultation stages. He may not give a shit about something, but he sure wants to know it's happening. The best surprise is no surprise." So Ed Rabel turned up in Washington, away from the glow of Rather's favor, and suddenly the quality of his work began to "fall off"—at least, that's the way the *Evening News* judged it. And pretty soon Ed Rabel wasn't making the *Evening News* air, and management offered him a chance to redeem himself: He could transfer to the Dallas bureau. Rabel said no, thank you, and quit CBS, whereupon his services were eagerly snatched up by NBC News.

Both Mort Dean and Ed Rabel had once been on another kind of Dan Rather list, the A List, which meant that their fall from grace was steep, indeed. For to be an A Lister was to sit on the right hand of Dan.

Part of creating an *Evening News* broadcast that was "worthy of Dan Rather," as a member of the Sauter team grandly put it, was weeding from its roster those correspondents whose style was deemed pedestrian or, worse, betrayed a yesterday sensibility. CBS News, like any news organization, had always had a first string among its reporting staff, which had included in the days of Cronkite such names as Rather, Mudd, George Herman, Robert Pierpoint, Fred Graham, and Marvin Kalb, among others. But what occurred under Rather (with Sauter's blessing) was no mere selection of favorites; it was a kind of purifying of the new CBS News breed, and in some cases the consequence of not being chosen for Rather's A List wasn't just not making the *Evening News* as often as desired; it was not making the *Evening News* at all—*ever.*

Just as CBS News producers and executives were classed as yesterday or today people, so there came to be two tiers of on-air correspondents: A List people and everybody else. The people who made Rather's A List did tend to be among the organization's best reporters; but that sort of judgment is highly subjective, and clearly coming into play were other criteria, such elements as youth and looks and, of course, expertise in the new politics. Those not on the A List were best advised to get out of CBS News, to find work at NBC or ABC or (as was eventually the case with one A List reject) to go into real estate. It was not a good time to be merely competent and reliable and loyal to the institution, as Ike Pappas, competent and reliable and loyal to a fault, was to discover. Pappas was one of the workhorses of CBS News, a thickly built Greek who was no movie star but who could always be counted on to answer a call in the middle of the night. He'd been around the lot for CBS News over the years, two tours of Vietnam, tank-town duty in the Midwest. By the time Sauter and Rather came to power, Pappas had worked his way to the prestigious Pentagon beat in the Washington bureau, and his name had become one of the most familiar sign-offs at CBS News. Ike Pappas was good, and that had always been good enough. But the trouble was, Pappas was not a star. With his predictable, workmanlike style, his stocky, blue-collar look, he was simply not considered A List material. So one day Ike Pappas went to work and discovered that he was no longer on the

Pentagon beat; he'd been given the assignment of covering organized labor. It would be fantastic understatement to say that organized labor was not a beat that regularly landed Ike Pappas on the *CBS Evening News with Dan Rather.* He spent the remainder of his CBS News career filing radio reports and peddling stories to the *Morning News.*

Don Webster, another CBS veteran, who, like Pappas, had covered the Vietnam War for the network, was demoted to producer. Other once-familiar CBS names just began to disappear. Marya McLaughlin seldom made the air. Robert Schakne, a brilliant reporter who'd been with CBS news since the 1950s and who had the ability and inclination, rare in the hurried and often cosmetic world of television, to dig deep and do original reporting and to interpret the facts with clarity and perspective— notwithstanding the fact that he wore thick horn-rimmed glasses and looked like a government bureaucrat—vanished from sight. George Herman, a courtly and accomplished broadcaster who'd been with CBS News since the birth of television, did not make the A List. Neither did Robert Pierpoint, another graybeard who'd covered the White House and, twenty years earlier, had been replaced on that beat by a young Dan Rather (at the time Pierpoint displayed the lack of prudence to criticize Rather as a rank opportunist). And it was not just a generational demarcation; younger reporters such as Steve Young, Deborah Potter, and Rita Flynn were "B-Listed," too.

To a degree, the harsh process of selection under Rather and Sauter was a matter of circumstance. Some of those who were rejected by the new CBS News were well past their prime, and others would never have come to a prime. Rather was in an intensely competitive situation, and some of the hard decisions regarding personnel, delayed by the long years of Cronkite's success, could no longer be put off. As one member of the Sauter team put it, "There were people there, whole areas of CBS News, on the weekend and on *Sunday Morning,* on the *Morning News,* where there was waxy yellow buildup in the corners like nobody's business, because nobody wanted to get rid of anybody. There were phalanxes of people who in some cases were just dreadful and shouldn't be in television."

Still, the keeping of lists is not usually the work of people with a benign intent, and it was a terrible time, a kind of living death, professionally, for a lot of people who had put their lives into

CBS News. It was a painful and humiliating exercise, perhaps especially so considering the outsize egos the television news trade breeds, to go to work each day and live as an outcast. If you weren't working for the *Evening News,* it was as if you weren't working at all. The A List was never posted or much discussed aloud, but if you had to ask, you weren't on it. "They just wouldn't put your stories on the air," said Marlene Sanders, who existed outside the periphery of the chosen ones. "They wouldn't talk to you. You know how it showed? You'd call them and they wouldn't return your calls. They just didn't talk to you."

But to be an A List correspondent, to be a Bob Faw or a Bob Simon, a Terry Drinkwater or a Bernard Goldberg, was to be engaged in the most exalted work in television news. *Evening News* correspondents had their own producers and their favorite tape editors (who were kept on overtime, if need be), they earned superstar salaries, and when they went out to do a report, their only concern was the *Evening News*—they didn't have to worry about servicing the lesser outposts of the organization, such as the morning news program.

Dan Rather's personal power, which he hadn't sought but eagerly accepted, was an extension of the absolute primacy of the *Evening News.* The anchorman had fretted over what he saw as a want of resources and attention during his difficult nine months under Bill Leonard, but under Sauter the *Evening News* was like an only child, pampered and the center of attention. Rather not only got all the producers and correspondents he wanted for the *Evening News* but got them exclusively; correspondents on the A List were effectively forbidden to appear on other broadcasts, such as *Sunday Morning* and *Morning News.* Exceptions were made, of course, but only when approved by Rather or by somebody speaking for him.

And so it was that Shad Northshield, the producer of *Sunday Morning,* woke up one day to find not only himself but his broadcast stationed squarely atop Dan Rather's "shit list."

Northshield, who ranked with Don Hewitt and Howard Stringer in the top echelon of CBS's most creative producers, was the executor of Bill Leonard's dream of creating an oasis in the television desert. One Sunday morning in 1978, shortly after Leonard had been named as Dick Salant's successor, he'd called Northshield down to his Washington home and, between bites of his breakfast told Northshield that he wanted a show that "you can curl up with on a Sunday morning," a television equivalent of a Sunday newspaper. Not just any paper, Leonard said, but a great paper, like the *New York Times* or the *Washington Post.* It should have lots of arty features, long and leisurely, lots of lingering retrospectives. It would be commercial, he hoped, but intelligent and classy. Right there, over breakfast and the *Daily Racing Form,* Bill Leonard and Shad Northshield invented a landmark television program. It should be distinguished by its writing, Leonard said, and he insisted that the program have a serious and independent television critic.

In the rarest sort of accomplishment, Northshield managed to create a television show that lived up to this dream. With Charles Kuralt perfectly cast as anchor, *Sunday Morning* quickly established itself as the classiest news program on television, and critics lavished it with unprecedented praise. Even the CBS affiliates, which had made lucrative use of the Sunday morning hours by selling time to religious broadcasters, began to admire the new network offering. It was simply unlike anything else on television; it slowly developed a loyal and growing audience, and inside CBS *Sunday Morning* held a special cachet.

Successful as *Sunday* was becoming, though, Northshield and Kuralt suffered a serious setback when they were pressured into trying to transform *Sunday* into a daily morning news program. That failure, exaggerated by the arrival of the Sauter era and a new set of values, tainted Northshield and Kuralt a bit, and when they returned to full-time *Sunday* duty, their stock was appreciably lower than it had been before their *Morning* foray. Northshield recollected being called into a meeting with Sauter and Joyce in which the two executives asked him to describe his assignment on the weekday *Morning* program. "Well," Northshield said, "the idea was to re-create *Sunday* on a daily basis." "Aha!" the executives said, as if that alone explained the failure of the daily venture. *Sunday Morning,* with its deliberate pace and elitist undertone, was not at all a Sauter-Joyce kind of show, a sentiment that was demonstrated countless times in the coming years. "If you put it on the air today," Sauter said in 1987, "it would probably get booed off television."

By the time Sauter came to CBS News, there was already bad blood between Northshield and Dan Rather. When Rather was struggling on the *Evening News,* he'd spent much of his time

casting about for a new executive producer, and one of the
people he'd considered for the job was Shad Northshield. He
took Northshield to lunch one day and broached the subject:
Would the producer be interested in the job if it were offered?
Northshield, whose ego was as large as his considerable talent,
displayed his customary political ineptitude. "I like what I'm
doing very much," he told Rather. "I could be happy producing
the *Evening News,* I could be happy doing just what I'm doing
now." It was exactly the wrong thing to say to a desperate Dan
Rather, and it set a tone of animosity that would not soon be
dissipated.

What's more, *Sunday Morning* itself had become a source of
friction. It had been Bill Leonard's pet show, and under him it
had usually got the resources it wanted—crews, producers, correspondents—when it wanted them. If *Sunday Morning* needed
a crew in Los Angeles, it got one. It also had correspondents
lining up to get on the show; some of the organization's best
reporters, cramped by the tight restraints of time on the *Evening
News,* delighted in the luxury of telling stories in three, four, and
five minutes. Richard Threlkeld, a distinguished CBS correspondent, essentially made full-time work of *Sunday Morning,*
becoming the regular contributor of the weekly cover story.

The problem was, when correspondents were working on
stories for *Sunday Morning* they were not working for the *Evening
News,* and Rather stewed. The special status of *Sunday Morning*
in the Leonard era backfired on Northshield when the power
balance at CBS News changed.

"When Dan first came on, the *Evening News* would get ready
to do a story and every frontline correspondent we had would
be out working on a piece for *Sunday Morning,*" Bob Schieffer
recalled. "People said, 'We've got to stop this.' Like everything
else, they let it go too far. Instead of cutting back, they said that
no one will do anything for anyone other than *Evening News.*"

Suddenly *Sunday Morning* could get no A List correspondents;
they just became instantly unavailable. Even the second-line
reporters seemed reluctant to work on the show, and with good
reason. After doing a *Sunday* piece one week, one second-line
correspondent in a domestic bureau got a call from Rather, who
reminded him of the need to be ready at all times for the call
from the *Evening News.* The correspondent took it as a repri-
mand and paid heed, despite the fact that he hadn't made the
Evening News in several weeks.

"It was utterly, totally, the end of the world for us," North-shield said. "That's when we became very poor, and we'd use anybody we could get. We had to learn to live without [the A List correspondents]. We couldn't get them. There were many times we couldn't get anybody. Charles Kuralt is perceived by the audience as an expert on contemporary art; that's because he had to narrate so many of those pieces himself, and he did it beautifully; but we just couldn't get people."

No longer struggling for resources, Rather became obsessed with ensuring that the *Evening News* would never again go hungry. A Rather producer recalled the intensity with which the anchorman staked out his turf: "The concept was, 'Even if we don't want you today, we want you ready for tomorrow.' If Dan had his way, every correspondent who works for CBS News would wake up every morning wanting to do something for *Evening News* that night. But that's not practical. I mean, I can remember a big battle over Ike Pappas, who is a C Lister if ever there was one. But Dan was concerned that the *Morning News* had glommed on to Ike Pappas. Who gives a rusty fuck?"

Sunday Morning, Leonard's oasis, became the organization's Siberia, the warehouse for the rejects of the new CBS News. Fortunately for the program, the rejects were solid professionals, people like George Herman and David Culhane and Robert Pierpoint. Still, they were people who couldn't make the *Evening News,* and that sent a clear message about the new standing of *Sunday Morning* in the organization.

Even though the new *CBS Morning News* with Bill Kurtis and the newly buoyant Diane Sawyer was a Sauter brainchild, the morning show also labored under second-class status. A List correspondents quickly got the message that work on the *Morning News* would not only go unrewarded but wasn't to be considered—a restriction that made the morning broadcast's uphill struggle against the more successful *Today* show on NBC and *Good Morning America* on ABC all the more frustrating. While the other networks had mastered the softer, chatty, entertainment-oriented approach in the morning, CBS's morning appeal was ostensibly its edge in hard news; yet a succession of *Morning News* producers discovered to their horror that the best correspondents, producers, camera crews, and editors treated the *Morning News* like a contagion and determinedly avoided it. "The guy who ran the Chicago bureau was a total, unmitigated prick," said George Merlis, Sauter's handpicked *Morning News* executive producer. "If I wanted correspondent A, he'd send correspondent B; anything that was physically possible to thwart us, he did. And Bill Kurtis comes from Chicago, he knew these guys. It was willful."

In the spring of 1982, just as the new *Morning News* was beginning to catch on with viewers, Israel invaded Lebanon, providing the CBS morning program with the perfect opportunity to exploit its supposed news identity with viewers. Yet the show's coverage of the invasion would probably have sent viewers screaming to another channel if they had known how it was pieced together. George Merlis sat in the *Morning News* control booth and watched the news reports on ABC's *Good Morning America*. When ABC correspondent Bill Seaman reported something with an attributed source—"Israeli military radio reported today . . ."—Merlis passed it to Bill Kurtis at the anchor desk, and Kurtis, winging it, reported the story on the air. It was a stunning statement about the new priorities, CBS News having to resort to borrowed information—and from ABC no less. There had been a time when the monitors tuned to ABC broadcasts weren't even turned on in the CBS control rooms.

Why didn't the *Morning News* use reports from its own Tel Aviv correspondent, Bob Faw? "Because Bob Faw and the guy who ran the bureau would say, 'Our priority is the *Evening News,* " Merlis said. "The attitude was, 'You can go fuck yourself."

Then there was the day that a prominent Denver talk show host was murdered as he left the radio station in the early-morning hours (by a group of neo-Nazis, it turned out), and the overnight desk crew on the *Morning News* jumped on the story. It was perfect material for the *Morning News.* It featured a celebrity and violence, and, better because it occurred in the middle of the night, it was *fresh;* viewers hadn't seen the story on the *Evening News* the night before. The *Morning News* staffers raced for the phones to get the Denver correspondent, Robert McNamara, scrambling on the story. But after just a couple of calls they realized they were wasting their time. "We were told that McNamara wasn't to be awakened for a *Morning News* piece," recalled a *Morning News* producer. "We ended up using something from the Denver affiliate." The exclusivity of correspondents to the *Evening News* was taken to absurd extremes, such as the time in 1983 when Dan White, the killer of San

Francisco Mayor George Moscone and Supervisor Harvey Milk, was released from prison. It was a big story, and it was scheduled to happen early in the morning, when the *Morning News* was on the air. The Los Angeles bureau dispatched its top correspondent, Terry Drinkwater, and a crew to the prison, and they were there on the scene as White was led through the prison gates. But the *Morning News* got no live report from Terry Drinkwater, or any report at all. Drinkwater was instructed to do a piece for the *Evening News* alone, a broadcast that would not go on the air for another ten hours. Although a CBS correspondent was on the scene, Bill Kurtis reported the story to CBS viewers from his anchor desk, 3,000 miles away from the event.

"Oh, it was brutal, it was brutal," said Bob Ferrante, who had replaced Merlis as the *Morning News* executive producer, when asked about the caste system. "We'd eventually do things to work around it, so that the public never understood what was going on, but you'd get lesser people doing lesser reports. Second-line correspondents. You couldn't get decent footage."

It was as obvious to the the other networks as it was to many inside CBS News that the policy of single-minded devotion to Rather and the *Evening News* came at the expense of other broadcasts and that it especially hurt the *Morning News*. Timothy J. Russert, a sly and occasionally mischievous NBC News executive, once tallied the number of on-air promotions that each network did for its various newscasts over a period of one week and discovered that NBC broadcast twenty-two promos for its *Nightly News* and twenty for its other newscasts; ABC broadcast thirty-nine promotions for its *World News Tonight* and forty-two promos for its other newscasts. At CBS the breakdown was, predictably, somewhat less egalitarian: twenty-five promotions for the *CBS Evening News with Dan Rather* and for the *Morning News,* a measly four.

"Sauter defined the company as the *Evening News,*" Merlis said, "as opposed to a news-gathering organization the flagship of which is the *Evening News.*"

That philosophy helped ensure that the *Morning News* would remain forever in last place and become a quagmire for CBS News, made worse by what seemed to be terrible management decisions. CBS soon decided to spend a million dollars a year to make Phyllis George a morning news anchor, while at the same time prohibiting its best newspeople from helping the show. The strategy in time led to incalculable embarrassment and humiliation for all of CBS News and ultimately brought about the unthinkable: the news division's loss of the time period altogether.

"The *Evening News* would always squeeze us off, and kick us into second class, and steal the resources," said Kurtis. "But no one was ever thinking that the terrible tragedy would happen, that we would actually lose the time."

Chapter

"YOU SEE BEFORE YOU," Van Sauter used to say, indicating his considerable girth, "a physique that speaks to a lifetime of sloth and self-indulgence." It was his way of explaining, when he was president of CBS Sports, that personally he'd never had the faintest interest in sports. He wasn't a player; he wasn't a fan. As the head of a network sports division Sauter had the best seat in the house at the events CBS covered, but as often as not his place in the VIP boxes sat empty. The president of CBS Sports would be found somewhere in the bowels of the stadium or in the control booth, watching the game on TV. "The game's immaterial," he told his people; "the game doesn't count. This is what counts. This is a television show; it is not a game. And unless you realize this is a television show, you don't realize the importance of our being here."

Although in the world of news Sauter was both a player and a fan, his philosophy as president of CBS News was essentially the same as it had been at sports: CBS was in the television business; its product was television shows. Good journalism that didn't make a point of being good television was, in Sauter's view, doomed to failure.

This was a radical new view at CBS News, and it ran counter to all the high mythology that clung to the walls of the institution, notions of CBS News as the *New York Times* of broadcasting and of the *Evening News* as the "broadcast of record"—the essence of what Bill Leonard called the "grand illusion" of CBS News. It had always been the worst breach of institutional etiquette to refer to a CBS newscast as a "show," Frank Stanton believed (*broadcast* was the term he had deemed fitting for the noble enterprise of Murrow and Collingwood and Sevareid). To Leonard and Salant and their kind this grand illusion was what set CBS News apart, but to Van Sauter, it was more a grand delusion that kept the place dangerously out of touch with the competitive realities of the 1980s.

That was the theme of Sauter's favorite lecture at CBS News, which he delivered whenever he saw evidence of the once-cherished CBS elitism. "This is not the *New York Times,* with a very carefully selected demographic audience," Sauter would say, "it's not the *Los Angeles Times* with its vast news hole, and it's not the *Washington Post,* dealing with a sophisticated, affluent capital city. It's a mass communication medium. And if it's going to fulfill its role in this society, it needs to be able to reach across this country; it needs to tell stories that are pertinent to the audience and are told in a way that the audience can comprehend." That was the essence of the Sauter revolution at CBS News, the heart of the Sauter vision: CBS News was not the *New York Times,* but if it did its job right, it could be *USA Today.*

Such a prospect was abhorrent, of course, to most of the old guard at CBS News; it was a direct assault on the sensibilities represented in Dick Salant's preamble to the CBS News Standards and Practices, which beseeched the institution to pursue "what is important, rather than what is merely interesting."

"The feeling was, we were being paid to make decisions about what was newsworthy, about what was important for the public to know," said Bob Chandler. "It was a little patronizing, a little condescending. But it was our job."

The news that was "important for the public to know," as divined by the high priests of the Salant-Cronkite era, tended to come from Washington, tended to emanate from the routine processes of government, and tended to be dry as sawdust. A typical broadcast in Cronkite's last week as *Evening News* anchor began with a Washington story on federal aid to cities, was followed by two routine Supreme Court stories, a Washington story about a brewing battle over clean-air guidelines, and a report on the Energy Department's plan to recover some money that had been turned over to charity by the Carter administration. An entire section of the broadcast was devoted to foreign news. Of the sixteen stories on that night's broadcast, which was typical, only two were domestic stories deriving from outside Washington.

The *CBS Evening News with Walter Cronkite* had not been, even its most loyal defenders would allow, an overtaxing creative challenge. Cronkite, the former United Press man, would get his first sense of what would be on each night's broadcast by examining the daily UP and Associated Press "budgets"—daily rosters dispatched by the two wire services listing what figured to be the day's top stories. Every hearing, every press conference, every agency announcement that was on the wire service budgets would be fully covered by CBS crews and correspondents, so that at the end of the day Cronkite and his producers could choose from a full, if predictable, menu of stories. For the correspondent and producer, the principal challenge was to capture on film the quote that figured to be in the lead paragraph of the wire service story: "The chairman of the Senate Finance Committee said today . . ." Lane Venardos, who had returned to the Washington bureau as a producer after Sauter's flameout at WBBM in Chicago, described the process of preparing an *Evening News* report: "You'd go to hearings and tick off three or four thousand feet of film, and you'd go through the wires and find the wire service operative lead and assure the people in New York that you could fill the bill on that story. And then you'd make your minute-fifteen piece that was almost exclusively a picture of somebody sitting at a table, a picture of other people sitting at an opposing table, somebody at table one talks, somebody at table two talks, and then one of your correspondents stands in front of an important-looking building telling you what you just heard and what it might mean. The quintessential *Evening News* piece was that."

As prosaic as that approach was, it had been shaped not only by the preferences of Cronkite and his producers but by the events that defined the news during most of the Cronkite era— the Vietnam War and then Watergate. The activist role of the federal government came to its zenith in that time, and those hearings and agency announcements and White House policy statements had a weight that warranted coverage.

But it made Van Gordon Sauter want to scream. The *Evening*

News broadcast that Rather inherited from Cronkite was not only dull, in Sauter's estimation, but irrelevant. Did CBS News really believe that viewers in Toledo gave a rat's ass (as Sauter put it) about a tedious House Ways and Means Committee hearing or about the latest political plans of the moderates in Britain's Labour party?

Sauter knew that he could never get the Ed Fouhys and Bob Chandlers to understand his view of television, and that is why he cast them off into oblivion. But it happened that a whole new generation of newsmen at CBS was hungry for Sauter's vision, and they were soon elbowing their way to the front ranks of the Sauter revolution. They were young producers, most of them, and unlike their predecessors at CBS News, the men (and few women) of the Salant-Cronkite era, they had not grown up in print journalism. Theirs were a discipline and an attitude forged in local television, where the imperative was very much Sauter's imperative: Television news at the very least had to be interesting television. This new CBS News generation of correspondents and producers hated the fact that Roone Arledge at ABC News had the corner on innovation, and their sentiment was shared by Black Rock; that was one of the reasons Sauter was there. "ABC was making a real run," Gene Jankowski said on the subject. "And it was quite clear that we couldn't just continue to present our program in the same form that we had for twenty-some years. We needed to be more contemporary."

Among the young producers who were so eager to sign on with the Sauter campaign were several who were steeped in the sober traditions of CBS News; indeed, they were among the leaders of the new troops that flocked to Sauter's side. One such was a producer named Tom Bettag, who had been a prize student of Fred Friendly, the perpetually aroused conscience-in-exile of CBS News, at Columbia University. Friendly, whose departure from CBS News in 1966 over a matter of principle held a special place in the institution's lore, instilled in Bettag a passion about the news business and the belief that CBS News had a special mission. Yet, as a young producer on the *Evening News,* Bettag was one of the Young Turks in the back of the room, clucking over what he later called the "calcification" that had set in on the Cronkite broadcast. "We were saying, 'Change, change, change,'" Bettag recalled, "and they were saying, 'Look, we've got a winning formula here, nobody wants Walter

Cronkite to change, they're used to him, you shouldn't have radical change in this." So Bettag left the *Evening News* and became a producer on *60 Minutes.*

It only helped Sauter's cause that compared with ABC, CBS News was indefensibly behind the times in terms of the look and pace of its nightly broadcast. Although Roone Arledge had been dismissed as a lightweight glitz peddler when he first came to ABC News from the world of TV sports, he quickly built a hard-driving news organization that usually outhustled and always outmanned the competition at every turn; in short order, his addition of fancy new graphics on *World News Tonight* came to seem less an offense to journalism and more a visual enhancement of a first-rate newscast. CBS, in contrast, seemed like an old gentlemen's club stubbornly refusing to bend its standards while watching its membership steadily drop. Sauter, who possessed no surfeit of tolerance, summed up his feelings about those who stood wringing their hands over the cherished standards in characteristically blunt terms: "Fuck 'em."

"Van realized that CBS News was heading for catastrophe if it didn't hurl itself into the twentieth century," said John Huddy, an outsider who was recruited as a producer for the new Sauter team. "CBS News was coasting and it was living on past glory and its management ranks were getting very old. And there was an arrogance that was going to be the ruination of the whole operation if they didn't retool. It was like Detroit. One day you look around and you've got all these aging, inefficient factories. CBS News was becoming an aging, inefficient place, where the excuse was: 'We don't do that because we're CBS News.' And what I found to be the truth was: 'We don't do that because we don't know how.' "

If the high priests of the institution resisted Sauter, he would simply create a new priesthood. There came to be a new inside clique at CBS News, a Sauter sphere. It included, among others, Sauter's old pal Lane Venardos, who was brought to New York as an *Evening News* senior producer; David Buksbaum, Dan Rather's closest friend and ally inside CBS News, his version of Cronkite's Sandy Socolow, who became vice-president in charge of operations, giving the anchor another pair of eyes and ears inside the power circle; Howard Stringer, the new executive producer of the *Evening News,* who would execute the Sauter vision on the air; Tom Bettag, who was lured back to the *Evening*

News and became an important player on that broadcast; David Percelay, Sauter's "smart guy" at KNXT, who was imported to New York as an adviser on costs; Joan Richman, who replaced the old-liners in special events and built a power base there; and of course, Ed Joyce, who became Sauter's closest friend at CBS.

While for the deposed of CBS News it was a bleak and sorrowful time, for those who were building the new order it was an exciting time of long days and late nights, fueled by the thrill of mission. They could hardly wait to get at it each day. Every morning at eight-fifteen, a CBS car picked up David Buksbaum at his Park Avenue apartment, then traveled down the few blocks to Seventy-fifth Street, where Dan Rather and Lane Venardos, who'd walked the block from the Surrey Hotel, were waiting. The car then swung west and north to Ninety-first Street and Riverside Drive to pick up Howard Stringer, and by eight-fifty on most days the core of the Sauter coterie was at work at the Broadcast Center on West Fifty-seventh Street.

And what they worked on, what they mulled and fretted over and philosophized about for ten and twelve hours every day, was the *CBS Evening News with Dan Rather.* If they were the new priesthood, their temple was the *Evening News.* And it wasn't long before their dogma came into being, a discernible theology of news whose creator was Van Gordon Sauter and which came to be known at CBS News as the doctrine of moments.

If the Sauter legend was to be believed, there existed somewhere in the sand-clay hill country of east-central Mississippi an aged black man who would exert a greater influence upon CBS News than any person since Edward R. Murrow.

As Sauter told the story, he had been down in Mississippi in 1964, writing stories about Freedom Summer for the *Detroit Free Press.* Three young civil rights workers had been missing for several days, and although officials said the disappearance was probably a hoax, there was widespread suspicion of foul play. Sauter was driving through Neshoba County in his rented Oldsmobile when, as he was crossing a bridge, he noticed an old black man in a flat-bottomed rowboat dragging the river for bodies. "The water was brown," Sauter told a writer from *Esquire* years later, "and you just knew from looking at the expression on his face that he knew those kids had been murdered.

"So I started writing right there and I devoted my first six paragraphs to depicting that situation, the color of the water, the total ambience. I was feeling absolutely elated until suddenly I turned around and there, at the other end of the bridge, was a TV crew with a mobile truck getting film of that same guy in the boat and I suddenly realized that no matter how good a writer I was, that TV crew *possessed* that moment in a way I never could." Young Van Sauter knew right then that there was strength and virtue in the lens of a television camera.

Whether the epiphany occurred that neatly or, for that matter, whether it occurred at all was irrelevant; the story perfectly conveyed the doctrine of moments that was to define the new *Evening News* in the Sauter era.

CBS reporters and producers were soon in heated pursuit of moments, looking for that essential, evocative (and, as it turned out, elusive) moment in their farm stories and political stories and foreign stories, the moment that would capture whatever it was that Sauter's old man in the boat had. In a wonderfully ironic and revealing article that appeared at the time, *Esquire* writer Ron Rosenbaum captured the enthusiasm with which the new CBS News had taken up its new doctrine. "Van keeps saying we need stories that reach out and touch people," Rather told him. "Moments. Every broadcast needs moments."

What is a moment?

"When somebody watches something and *feels* it, *smells* it and *knows* it," the anchorman explained. "If a broadcast does not have at least two or three of those moments, it does not have it. I don't know if you noticed it, but the fishbowl people are wearing MOMENTS badges today."

What the moments doctrine amounted to, of course, was a deftly designed cover for the infiltration of entertainment values into the news. It completely changed the way CBS reported the day's news because it completely changed what news was. There were no moments to be found in a minute-fifteen report on unemployment told by a CBS News correspondent standing outside the Department of Labor in Washington, D.C. There was, however, a moment of the highest sort if the CBS News camera studied the strained and expectant face of a young Pittsburgh mother as she stood (babe in arms) beside an employment line as her husband asked for a job. And if the camera was patient enough to remain focused until the husband was told there was no work, it was jackpot city.

Thus did CBS News gently surrender the "grand illusion." A broadcast in pursuit of moments could not also be a broadcast of record. Dan Rather and his colleagues, perhaps without quite knowing it, had given over to the principle that they were, after all, in the television business; the *Evening News* was, they were coming to accept, a television show.

On the day that Rosenbaum visited, he was allowed to see the new philosophy in practice. As managing editor, Rather was pondering the options that he and his producers faced in deciding which story would lead that evening's broadcast and would thereby assume the weight of being the day's most important story. The top three contenders for most important event of the day were the war in the Falklands (CBS News finally had some footage it could use), the war in the Middle East (where the Palestinian refugee camps were being overrun in Beirut), and, from London, the Princess of Wales's new baby. "Had a big fight about it in the lineup meeting," Rather said, "but I decided we had to go with the royal baby. On the back-fence principle."

The back-fence principle?

"The back-fence principle," Rather explained to the visiting journalist, "is, well, you imagine two neighbor ladies leaning over a back fence at the end of the day and one is asking the other what happened today and you figure out which of your stories *they'd* most want to know about. Well, you have to say today it's going to be what happened with the princess—did she have her baby."

It would have been an instructive exercise to stand Rather's back-fence principle next to Richard Salant's dictum set forth in the CBS News Standards: "We in broadcast journalism cannot, should not, and will not base our judgments on what we think the viewers and listeners are 'most interested' in. . . ."

Howard Stringer, the executive producer of the *Evening News,* was a consistent believer in the value of a "soft" story, and over the course of time he revealed a particular inclination for odd-ball animal stories. Once he picked a story from the BBC about a sheep receiving a manicure; on another occasion he ran a piece about a singing sheep who had a hit record in England. "I thought Eric Sevareid would never forgive me for that," Stringer later remarked, recalling his mutton period.

The very selection of Stringer to produce the broadcast was testimony to the new values defining the *Evening News.* Stringer was an accomplished documentary producer at CBS News, a cinematic storyteller whose strength was the visual product; that was what he brought to the *Evening News*. He had no daily news experience at all, but that wasn't the purpose of his new role. He was there to make the *Evening News* look good, to make it visually and sensorially engaging, and that is what he did. He integrated all the new technical gadgets that Sauter had acquired for the organization, machines called Quantel and Chyron that could instantly create graphs and charts of many colors and make a picture on the screen shrink or expand or spin (advances that Roone Arledge, who'd mastered the use of graphics in sports, had already applied to news at ABC).

Stringer, the filmmaker, also changed the way Rather was shot by the cameras. It occurred to him that if he shot the anchor close up, instead of using the standard CBS three-quarter shot, Rather would be more immediate and intimate, freeing him to ease up on his delivery and, it was hoped, to seem less intense. "I don't quite understand the three-quarters shot," Stringer said at the time. "You never see them in the movies."

To help smooth his edge, the anchor began to wear a sweater on the air. It was such an obvious cosmetic ploy that the publicity department dished out the story that Rather was wearing the sweater because he had a cold. So he may have, but the story wore a little thin after a few weeks had passed and the sweaters stayed. The sartorial inclinations of CBS newsmen had never before been of much interest, but then, Walter Cronkite had never had his personality worked on by the wardrobe department; the sweater saga was a running story until finally Rather facetiously addressed the issue. "Manhattan is an island," he told Tony Schwartz of the *New York Times*. "It's cool all year long here, isn't it?"

In the new CBS News, correspondents were told that it was no longer just what they said that mattered, but the way they said it; they were part of the message—performers, in a sense—and they were encouraged to affect a more casual and relaxed style. Those who were most adept at it came to be known as "good broadcasters"; those who were less adept were "good reporters." It was better to be a broadcaster.

Ronald Reagan and Van Sauter both were new presidents, they both were politically conservative, and they both were bent on reducing the power and influence of Washington. In that last regard Sauter would have more immediate success.

Although there was general agreement within CBS News when Cronkite left the broadcast that the *Evening News* should be less dependent upon Washington news, the antennas of the organization before Sauter arrived were still pointed directly at the capital. Ed Fouhy, Sauter's inherited vice-president in charge of hard news, had been Washington bureau chief, and Washington remained his orientation. "El Salvador was the major thing in my tenure in the winter of 1981," Fouhy recalled, "and the Reagan Revolution was really hitting Washington, so Washington was coming back. And things like the tax bill and so on were major issues, and you had to do them. But they thought all that was boring."

Fouhy understated the case. To Sauter and his clique, Washington was the fertile crescent of boring; Washington was full of bureaucrats and bureaucratic news. So CBS News got out of Washington and moved to South Succotash.

"South Succotash" was the name that a misguided Reagan aide gave to the type of story that CBS News began to do in place of the traditional Washington reports. Instead of straight reports on a government policy, CBS News would send a correspondent out into the heartland—South Succotash—to report the consequences of the policy, the way it affected the lives of "real people." There were lots of heartrending scenes of employees standing outside the chained gates of recession-stricken factories, and the Reagan administration, sensing the effectiveness of such reports, complained that CBS was trying to make Reagan look bad. It truth, of course, CBS was only in South Succotash because that's where the moments were, and in that sense the White House criticism was a kind of praise, albeit unintended.

Conservative columnist George Will also got the wrong idea. "[I]f journalism becomes a quest for 'moments,' the point of which is to provoke emotions," he wrote, "then journalism becomes avowedly manipulative. The pursuit of such 'moments' involves editorial judgments that are problematic and, at bottom, political. They are judgments about the emotions that viewers should have, and how to cause viewers to have them." Will, a political animal, endowed Sauter with a grander motive than was there; the new CBS News wasn't interested in bending political opinion, but in wringing emotion, any emotion, from viewers.

In fact, when Sauter did issue a politically motivated instruction, it was pro-Reagan. White House correspondent Leslie Stahl, who was doing some tough reporting on the new administration, heard that Sauter didn't mind that her reporting was severe as long as her tough words were covered by pictures. In a typical piece Stahl would pose both sides of an issue during the videotaped part of her report, and then, looking straight into the camera, she would offer her conclusion, often a stinging assessment that directly contradicted the administration line. But producers in New York began to take the words she'd written for her concluding "stand-up" and move them into the body of the piece, the part that would be covered by pictures. Stahl didn't fully understand this process. After all, New York kept telling her that Sauter didn't mind the toughness; he just wanted it covered by pictures. That is, she didn't understand until the political analyst Martin Schram explained to her that when viewers are presented with conflicting words and pictures—say, pictures of the president cutting a ribbon at a new nursing home accompanied by narration about the negative effects of administration policies on the aged—it was the pictures that registered. Then she understood.

Although there was obvious journalistic value to getting out into the country and showing the effects of government on people's lives, some CBS correspondents worried that substance was being lost in the pursuit of emotion. "What you have to be careful about is, you're doing a story on farms, you tend to go and interview someone who becomes very emotional, but you don't advance the state of knowledge very much," said one veteran Washington correspondent. "Let's face it—abstract things are much tougher to cover than concrete things. And often when you're trying to explain government policy or the rationale behind it, it's easier just to go out and get the emotional response. But maybe that's not always the complete story."

But up in New York the people who were running the broadcast had little pause for such reflections. The small, tight group of producers became like novices in a particularly severe religious order, and their unremittingly stern catechist was Van Gordon Sauter. Every night, after every broadcast, Sauter made his way into the newsroom, took a seat in the fishbowl, rapped his pipe on an ashtray, and consulted his printed story lineup of that night's broadcast, which he had marked with notations. The assembled group—Dan Rather, Ed Joyce, Howard Stringer, and producers Tom Bettag, Mark Harrington, Linda Mason, and Lane Venardos—waited silently. If Sauter wouldn't have felt free, with Socolow as producer, to come down to the newsroom and say, "I thought this whole thing sucked," he certainly had no such inhibitions with this group.

"Why did we choose that story?" Sauter would say, indicating a foreign policy story or some other offense against the ban on boring. "I didn't understand this."

And someone, often Mark Harrington, whose own sensibilities were more akin to those of the old CBS News than to the new, would defend the story: "We chose it because it was news."

"I don't think anybody sitting out there understands the slightest thing about that story. That didn't reach out and touch me."

Down the list they went, picking apart the broadcast. "Some nights he'd be furious with us because he thought we'd betrayed whatever it was we were supposed to be doing," one member of the group said. Sauter left no element unexamined, challenging the story selection, questioning the way graphics were used, and deploring the quality of the writing. These postmortems lasted late into the evening, and often the group was still at it when the shift for the nine o'clock *Newsbreak* broadcast began to wander in.

Inevitably the discussion turned to one of Sauter's favorite peeves, the quality of the reporters themselves. There were too many merely "good reporters," too few "broadcasters." A correspondent would be ridiculed for his or her manner of speech, or facial expression, or vocal tenor—"Why is Ned Potter's voice so deep? He sounds like Ted Baxter," and so on. After a time the others in the fishbowl picked up on the criticisms, and soon the lines that divided the correspondents into A Listers and B Listers, broadcasters and good reporters, deepened even more. Eventually Sauter asked the inevitable: Why have so many reporters on the air in a twenty-two-minute broadcast anyway? In the Sauter ideal only those correspondents who were the best performers, such as Bernard Goldberg, Bob Simon, Bruce Morton, and Bob Schieffer, would be seen on the *Evening News.* And after a time he developed a plan, modeled after the newsmagazines, that would have kept all but the superstars, the cream of the A List, off the air entirely.

The idea was to have a huge team of producer/reporters out gathering material and feeding it to a small, select group of star correspondents (chosen for their ability to write and to perform) in New York, who would spin a story out of the material. The stories that fell in between, such as spot news that had always been reported in pieces from field correspondents, would be told on camera by the ultimate A Lister, Dan Rather. Sauter was never able to effect this plan, but its spirit was felt: Spin masters Goldberg and Simon began to spend a lot less time out covering stories and a lot more time in the studio concocting lump-in-the-throat, reach-out-and-touch-someone pieces, often using material that others had gathered.

The Sauter influence took quite nicely, and his vision became firmly implanted in the instincts of the people who were running the new CBS News. Among the "ins" of the new order, there was often heard (to the point that it became cliché) the chorus "Borrrrr-ring!"—the ultimate put-down of a story or correspondent that didn't meet the new standards.

After a generation in which the top man in the organization had felt obliged to keep his hands off the daily process, CBS News now had a president who was up to his elbows in it. Response to this was sharply divided, depending upon whether one was inside or outside the Sauter circle. Despite the long, exhausting hours, Lane Venardos found the whole thing exhilarating, especially the rigorous postmortems. "I found these sessions to be among the most exciting things I ever participated in. I mean, here we were, with this news vehicle more or less in our command, and the focus of every CBS News employee."

Dick Salant, on the other hand, was horrified by almost everything about the new CBS News. "Those goddamned clinics! They'd critique things immediately after the *Evening News* was finished! A guy works best in our field, which is journalism, who is allowed to do his stuff and not have someone sitting over his shoulder or her shoulder all the time. There are other devices to let people know; there's quiet conversation, little notes, and so on." Salant had a view on moments as well. "The whole purpose of news is not to capture the moment but to explain. And you don't ignore it if you don't have a picture. He [Sauter] said that he went for the emotion, he went for the gut. News, to me, is information that goes to the head and not to the gut."

Although Salant was no longer in the employ of CBS, he felt no reservation about speaking out, a circumstance that hinted at what was to become a most unhappy truth for Van Sauter, one that led to his ultimate undoing. In every other position Sauter had occupied in his broadcasting career, he had been brought in to replace people who were obviously foundering and to invalidate visions that had obviously failed; without exception, the people Sauter had dealt with in his various turnarounds had either leaped aboard or had been obliging enough to disappear into obscurity. But CBS News was different. The people at CBS News were at the top of their profession, and they didn't go quietly. Some, such as Ed Fouhy and John Lane, left CBS, but most stayed; Walter Cronkite was on the CBS board of directors. Network TV news was still a relatively young business, which meant that many of the people who were displaced by the Sauter revolution were the people who'd built the craft from the ground up, and they refused to accept that they were doing it the wrong way. The other side of the supreme CBS News confidence was a fierce, self-important anger, and it began to show.

"[Sauter] came in and one got the feeling that he believed that what had gone before just wasn't good enough," said Mike Wallace. "He knew something new, he knew something better. Well, those of us who were the stewards of what had gone before weren't absolutely certain that he did indeed know something better."

When members of the old guard at CBS News were angry over some new Sauter outrage, and they were angry often, they spoke out—to each other, to the press, in speeches, even to the CBS board. Cronkite, who was among the most restrained of the critics, told Barbara Walters of ABC and other interviewers that he had "some differences in philosophy" with the new CBS News. But privately he spoke for his generation when he railed against what many saw as the sellout of CBS News. His colleagues even persuaded him to speak out at a board meeting, and he did, lighting into the new "show business" values that Sauter and Stringer and Rather had imposed upon the *Evening News.*

From his pulpit at Columbia, Fred Friendly lashed out at the new vision that gripped CBS News. "There was a day when the conscience of CBS insisted that quality and class and seriousness came before ratings," Friendly told the *New York Times*. "That era is ending. The engine that runs it all now is ratings."

Even the mild-mannered Charles Kuralt aired his feelings. "At the networks today," he said in a speech, leaving no doubt about which network he particularly referred to, "there is an unseemly emphasis upon image and flash and the tricks of electronics as substitutes for the hard fact."

Back in California, Sauter's old friends began to hear horror stories about the man who'd been their hero at KNXT and were puzzled. "In many cases they were throwing out people who were nowhere near retirement, who had a lot to offer but didn't fit in with the new," said Bill Stout, the KNXT anchor who was both an admirer of Sauter's and, as a former network man, a friend of many of the dispossessed at CBS News.

"I thought he was absolutely wonderful here, and when he left to go back to the big town, and CBS News, I was astounded when old friends began calling with these horror stories of what was happening, because *none* of that happened here. What had happened here was quite the opposite. He had come in as the great healing force. And it's so strange to have that period followed by stories like Socolow's, stories like John Lane's, Ed Fouhy, dear old friends, I never understood it."

It all gave an air of upheaval and tumult to Sauter's new CBS News, but Sauter himself characteristically dismissed the clamor. "These things are rough, but wounds heal," he was quoted as saying at the time. "Six months from now, nobody will remember any of this."

Six years later the place would still be hemorrhaging.

Chapter

FEW INSTITUTIONS ARE SO accurately described by their environment as CBS News is by the low red-brick building it occupies a block up from the seedy West Side docks at the edge of Hell's Kitchen. The outside of the building, a former dairy, is scrubbed and solid, even a little elegant; the inside is a maze of long, narrow, crisscrossing corridors that lace a series of tiny, mostly windowless offices and editing rooms, all unfailingly drab, spare, and ugly; the stairways leading from the rabbit warrens of the first floor to the studios on the second floor are illogically situated, and a new building, awkwardly adjoining the old, compounds the labyrinthine effect. It is a tricky place and difficult for outsiders to negotiate. So is CBS News.

When Van Sauter took control of CBS News in the fall of 1981, he and Ed Joyce were outsiders. At least they viewed themselves as such, and they believed that was how the organization saw them. They weren't entirely wrong. CBS News was a cloister, bound by faith; Sauter and Joyce were—and the term carried a certain righteous disdain—*local station* people. "We had both been within CBS News, and we left and went out and worked with the heathens," Sauter later said. "And we were always perceived as outsiders. There was a strong sentiment within CBS News that neither Ed nor I should have gotten those jobs." Almost as soon as Sauter was made acting president, he was off to an important meeting with affiliates in Hawaii, leaving Joyce with the chore of finding the two of them office space. The offices that Leonard's people came up with were off in a distant corner of the Broadcast Center, a little display of gamesmanship that Ed Joyce wasn't about to abide; he insisted on offices in the heart of "executive row," and eventually, he got them. The little shoving match didn't amount to much, but it established a tone. "It was like walking into a foreign country," Sauter recalled. "Neither of us knew the players well; we really didn't know the institution well, in terms of how it worked, how it was structured. And obviously we were not there as welcomed guests."

Waiting for Sauter at CBS News was a Mudd camp, a Rather camp, a Cronkite camp, a Fouhy camp, a Lane camp, and a Chandler camp; there was no Van Sauter camp as yet. Ed Joyce was Sauter's constituency, and in a way, Joyce's presence made everything else possible for Sauter. With Joyce in the number two slot, everyone else was essentially demoted, a rung farther from the center of power. With Joyce on the inside with him, effectively administering the organization, Sauter didn't have to negotiate his revolution with the old-line power structure; he and Ed Joyce *were* the power structure. They worked well together, and bonded by their joint mission into hostile territory, each soon became the other's closest and best friend.

It was a friendship to be remembered, a truly odd relationship that bordered on the bizarre. Joyce was Sauter's best friend and, in every discernible way, his opposite. Sauter was a big, blustery politician who stormed the hallways and who, even his detractors allowed, possessed the visionary's flair; Joyce was a slight, taciturn man who kept his door closed and who, even his friends conceded, was essentially a bureaucrat. But that wasn't what made their friendship seem so strange; what made it strange was the near-total subordination of one personality (Joyce's) to the other (Sauter's). On paper, the two men were equally qualified; in fact, their careers so closely tracked each other's that Sauter always suspected that Joyce was disappointed that he, Joyce, hadn't landed the top job. Joyce had been head of radio special events before Sauter got that job; Joyce became news director of a CBS-owned TV station, WCBS in New York, and Sauter became news director of WBBM in Chicago; Joyce became general manager of WBBM, and Sauter became general manager of

KNXT in Los Angeles; when Sauter left KNXT for CBS Sports, he was replaced by Ed Joyce. But if Joyce was disappointed that Sauter got the top CBS News job, it certainly didn't show. On the contrary, Joyce seemed positively enchanted by his new boss and carried his role as subordinate to the extreme. Although they were roughly the same age, Joyce's relationship to Sauter became like that of an adoring kid to his heroic big brother—not subservient, exactly, but utterly emulative. Before the eyes of an astonished CBS News, Ed Joyce became a kind of miniature Van Sauter.

When Joyce had followed Sauter into the job at KNXT, he had spurned the big black Jeep that Sauter had acquired as the station car, characteristically opting for a rented BMW instead. But now Joyce wanted a Jeep, and he and Sauter went shopping together for one. Sauter had a place in Redding, Connecticut, so Joyce bought a place in Redding, Connecticut; but Joyce didn't just buy any house in Redding. He bought Sauter's house when Sauter moved farther out, a source of much amusement to those who knew the two men. Van and Kathleen Sauter's Connecticut house was typical Sauter, a rambling place out in the woods that featured a Jacuzzi off the master bedroom. "We were always afraid that Ed would get sucked down the drain in that thing," one member of the Sauter-Joyce circle cracked. The Joyces even kept the Sauters' old phone number when they moved in.

En route to his new, higher station in life, Sauter had added fly-fishing to his routine, becoming a passionate angler characteristically in advance of the rediscovery of fly-fishing as an "in" sport. So Joyce became a fisherman, too. Sauter took Joyce to his favorite outdoors shop in Westport, where Joyce was completely outfitted. The outdoors look seemed to fit the Hemingwayesque persona that Sauter had fashioned for himself, but the image of the natty Ed Joyce in waders spawned some furtive corridor wisecracking ("Do they come with red suspenders?"). Like Sauter, though, Joyce became quite passionate about the sport. Sauter twice took Joyce to New Mexico on fishing excursions, and he introduced Joyce to his favorite nearby stream, the Housatonic River in western Connecticut.

Sauter, who was perpetually on a diet, was never known to be more than three feet from a cold can of Tab. So Joyce, the wispy little Irishman, drank Tab, too. Tab became the official drink of the new order; there actually came to be a Tab consciousness at CBS News. One morning when the *Morning News* was on the air, there came an urgent call in the control room for Jon Katz, who was the show's executive producer at the time. Ed Joyce was on the phone. Katz thought that Joyce might be calling to complain about that morning's business segment, which had been particularly offbeat. Robert Krulwich, the imaginative business reporter who enlivened his dry and sometimes arcane subject with comic illustrations, had done a segment on the booming soft-drink market, and as he discussed the proliferation of soft drinks in America, he had gradually constructed a pyramid of soda pop cans. But Joyce wasn't calling about that; while building his pyramid, Krulwich had offhandedly read from the product information wordage on a can of Tab: "NutraSweet brand sweetener . . ." Joyce was calling to set things straight; it wasn't NutraSweet that gave Tab its irresistible-to-CBS taste; it was saccharin. Krulwich never made that mistake again.

At one point it seemed that Joyce was carrying his Sauterization to a dangerous extreme. Sauter had gone on a drastic diet, consuming only a protein powder and vitamins and, of course, Tab. Sure enough, Joyce went on the diet, too. He explained to friends that he was on the regimen in sympathy with his wife, Maureen, who was also dieting, but it didn't stop the snickering.

It was quite something to see, this intensely close friendship. "You'd see the two of them walking down the corridor together, the two of them having lunch together, the two of them having breakfast together, the two of them closeted together for meetings," said Gene Mater, the Jankowski aide who came to CBS News at the start of the Sauter tenure. "It was always the two of them, and it was a dual operation in that sense. Oh, they did everything together. The only thing I don't think Van ever convinced Ed to do is smoke cigars." So far as anyone witnessed, anyway. The tandem was considered a bit odd even by admirers, such as Lane Venardos. "That is one of life's sweet mysteries, which perplexed a number of people around here."

Sauter, master of the good-time road trip, and Joyce became inseparable traveling companions. Whenever possible, they traveled together, flying the same-class airfare, staying in the same-class hotel rooms, eating in the same restaurants. They made travel an art form, and sometimes they were so obsessed with it they seemed like fraternity brothers on a marathon road trip. Their ideal journey was one that involved a whole pack of CBS pals traveling together, united by what one conscripted participant termed "a hoo-ha mentality," with lots of side trips "that provided the fun and hilarity that Van particularly enjoyed." Sauter was forever arranging staff retreats near favored fishing spots or vacation resorts and scheduling bureau chief meetings in cities that he wanted to visit. The wives of the top executives—the "mogulettes" they were called—would sometimes go along on the trips, and in the course of time Kathleen Sauter and Maureen Joyce also became good friends.

Occasionally the "hoo-ha" inclination would lead to awkward circumstances, such as the time, after a meeting with affiliates, Sauter got the urge for a side excursion to a strip joint. He put one of his traveling companions, Peter Herford, who was the news vice-president for affiliate relations, in charge of locating a suitable establishment. But Herford, a New Yorker, wasn't precisely a walking guide to the flesh palaces of the greater Phoenix area and could come up with only a topless bar. It was a huge, barnlike place, with a capacity for 500 or so people, with a long central bar and scores of small tables, at which the dozen or so dancers would offer (for a tip) close-up renditions of their erotic art. It happened that on this night one of the members of Sauter and Joyce's group was Ralph Goldberg, the distinguished CBS attorney of long standing who had stood beside Frank Stanton on numerous occasions, defending the independence and integrity of CBS News before hostile members of Congress and other adversaries. "I kept looking at Ralph, and I thought, 'I don't believe that this man is being subjected to this,'" recalled Herford. "I mean, here's a man who has basically been CBS News' lawyer for twenty years; he has been one of the foremost corporate First Amendment lawyers in the country. A straitlaced Jewish husband if there ever was one. He's never been close to a place like this, and what can he do? His boss has dragged him into this place, and we're sitting there, and that's Van's idea of a fun evening." The First Amendment, Goldberg discovered, is for party animals, too.

One of the lessons that any regular member of the Sauter traveling party quickly learned was that Sauter was the field marshal on these excursions, and when his attention span snapped—and it always snapped—it was time to get back on the bus and move on. Herford was along on a Sauter-Joyce trip to

San Antonio when he discovered that essential truth. The CBS News brass had held a bureau chiefs' meeting at a ranch outside town, followed by a night of hobnobbing with CBS affiliates brass, who were attending an industry convention in San Antonio. The next day Herford was put in charge of getting Sauter's and Joyce's baggage together and into the rental car and then transporting the two executives to the airfield for the return to New York. Sauter and Joyce were in a particular hurry because they wanted to be the first to get to the CBS jet—they wanted the pick of seats, so they wouldn't have to sit near a particular network executive on the flight back to New York. While Herford tended to the luggage, Sauter and Joyce were in the hotel lobby, chatting with a couple of colleagues. One of those colleagues described the unfortunate events that followed: "Peter commits the unpardonable sin of locking Ed and Van's luggage in the trunk of this rental car with the keys attached. The hotel refuses to give Herford a tool to break into the car with. Somehow they manage ultimately to get into the car, doing damage to the vehicle. You can see the napalm being sort of spread around the floor and guys with big torches standing around just ready to drop on this napalm. Van, who's watching, Van paces quite well, and Ed is egging him on. Van's ready to explode. There's steam coming out of his ears, like in the cartoon; that would not be an inappropriate image."

Herford finally delivered his high-powered cargo to the CBS jet, but soon after that incident Herford, a twenty-year veteran of CBS News, a former chief of the Saigon bureau, fell out of communication with Sauter and Joyce. Eventually he was demoted to the rank of piece producer on *Sunday Morning*. There was no expressed connection between the San Antonio incident and Herford's exile to Siberia, but future traveling companions took greater care with trunk keys.

As much as Sauter and Joyce loved travel and fishing, they seemed to love shopping even more. Bookstores, shoe stores, gift shops—they hit them all, like two well-heeled matrons. Colleagues remember that in Dallas for the 1984 Republican National Convention, the "boys," as Sauter and Joyce were sometimes called by friendly members of the staff, excused themselves to go shopping for cowboy boots. The Democrats had been obliging enough to hold their convention in San Francisco, a great shopping town. It began to seem that executive trips and bureau chiefs' meetings were really excuses for Sauter-Joyce shopping sprees. For the bureau chiefs' meeting of 1985, which was conducted in Berlin, Sauter and Joyce and their wives planned an adjunct trip to Moscow. Sauter, recalling that correspondent Richard Roth had once been stationed in Moscow, recruited Roth as an advance man for the excursion. "You hate Moscow," Sauter said, knowing that a Muscophobe wouldn't be likely to find charm in the more boring Soviet spots, "you'll be fun." So Roth was appointed to make sure there was plenty of Tab (two cases, imported from the Netherlands) when the boys and the mogulettes arrived, and he conducted personally guided shopping trips. Sauter wanted to find the Soviet version of L. L. Bean; Joyce wanted to know where he could buy new underwear.

But Ed Joyce was much more than Sauter's travel companion: He was in on every Sauter decision, he was part of the nightly *Evening News* postmortem, and he was given direct command of some areas of CBS News that Sauter didn't feel he had time for, such as the *Morning News.* Those who worked with Joyce during this period discovered that despite his kinship with Sauter and his background in local television, he had very strong, traditional journalistic instincts. Where Sauter's after-the-fact analyses of broadcasts tended to focus on aspects of video style and audience appeal, Joyce more often applied the traditional CBS News test to a broadcast: Did we beat the other guys with this story?

But Joyce's editorial strength was somewhat obscured by the role he was assigned in the Sauter administration. Jankowski had wanted Joyce at news to give Sauter an inside sounding board and because he respected Joyce's "administrative skills" ("Van never really had as much cost-control experience as Ed did," Jankowski explained), but what it all boiled down to was that Ed Joyce was there to be Van Sauter's hatchet man. It was Joyce, the "Velvet Shiv," who usually bore bad tidings—there was too much money being spent on this, no budget available for that—and it was Ed Joyce who did the firing and reassigning and demoting of people. "You never saw them apart," Ed Fouhy said of Sauter and Joyce, "except when there was something bad to do, which always fell to Joyce. Joyce got all the shitty jobs."

It was a classic good-cop, bad-cop arrangement, and it served Sauter quite nicely. While few in the organization misunder-

Murrow at the mike, March 1954.

Dan Rather with Murrow's Boys, London, May 1985 (*from left*): Douglas Edwards, Ernie Leiser, Eric Sevareid, Charles Collingwood, Walter Cronkite, Dan Rather, Winston Burdett, Andy Rooney, William Shirer, Richard C. Hottelet.

Walter Cronkite and Dan Rather:
the succession, February 15, 1980.

Portrait of the anchor as a young man:
Dan Rather at KTRH Houston, 1958.

Sauter at WBBM Radio, circa 1968.

Paley at eighty-five: one more time.

CBS◉

Tom Wyman at the top, September 1982,

Van Gordon Sauter as president of CBS Sports.

Richard Salant, while president of CBS News.

Richard Liebner and Carole Cooper:
Ma and Pa or the "General Motors of agents"?

Dan Rather in a relaxed moment.

The Sauter office: a style statement.

The beauty queen miscast: Phyllis George, 1985.

Van Sauter massaging the talent—Bill Kurtis and Diane Sawyer—
on the new set of the *CBS Morning News.*

Ed Joyce, the "Velvet Shiv."

CBS Broadcast president Gene Jankowski,
the man who brought Van Gordon Sauter to News:
"It is a question of form, not…substance."

Rather incognito with wife, Jean, following the "Kenneth" incident.

A triumphant Larry Tisch on the day he ousted Wyman, September 10, 1986.

Howard Stringer: ambition and charm.

Rather walks the picket line with his writers, March 1987.

Beauty and the boss: Diane Sawyer and date, Richard
Holbrooke, with new CBS head, Larry Tisch.

Dan and Van, up country.

stood that the new vision sweeping through the place was entirely Sauter's, on a personal level Joyce deflected much of the antipathy that might have otherwise focused solely on Sauter.

"[Joyce] interpreted, he did what dirty work had to be done," said Mike Wallace. "He gave an opportunity for this guy in the bow tie and beard to have free flights of fancy. This was the technocrat, Joyce." This allowed Sauter a little breathing space and the opportunity to haul out and polish up his old act— Sauter, the fun-loving populist. After just a couple of weeks on the job, he showed up one day at the Broadcast Center wearing a fedora with a huge press card sticking out of the hatband. He roamed the narrow halls campaigning, slapping backs and handing out hearty salutations, "Hi, big fella!" being his standard. He wrote notes, expressing concern or offering congratulations. His door was always open.

Behind that door was a new and improved version of the Sauter office, featuring the rolltop desk and the stand-up telephone from the *Detroit Free Press* days, plus an array of accessories compiled in the serendipitous career of a champion mythmaker. There was an antique cradle, used as a magazine rack; a rubber stamp bearing the words DRUGS, SEX, VIOLENCE, a joking reference to the censor's job; a huge writing table, upon which sat Sauter's well-traveled manual typewriter; an outsize, stained-glass two-dollar bill, with the motto "In Nielsen We Trust"; a framed quotation from the inventor of television, Philo T. Farnsworth, which said, "Television is a gift of God, and God will hold those who utilize his divine instrument accountable to him." Finally, prominently displayed on the wall just above and behind the Sauter desk was the framed excerpt of the Howard Beale speech from *Network:* "Television is a circus, a carnival, a traveling troupe of acrobats," etc.

The old Sauter magic with the press was once again loosed, and although he was dealing with the New York and national press now and the stories were sometimes tempered by a certain skepticism, the act generally played well. Sauter was a great story, an eminently quotable network executive who, with his beard and pipe, bow tie and tweeds, his background in print, and his profane directness, stood out from the long line of corporate gray suits. He had the most marvelous way of darting on and off the record in the course of a conversation with a reporter, casually dropping nuggets in the background pauses, which made it seem as if he were dishing the real dirt. What he was really doing, of course, was framing his own case, but then, dissembling was what most network executives did when they dealt with the press; at least Sauter was engaging.

The press came to serve an almost quasi-official role in the new CBS News, with Sauter, Stringer, and Joyce regularly demonstrating the value of a well-timed leak. There had been a time at CBS News when the top brass made an announcement about personnel or policy, and it came as a surprise to most in the ranks. But in the Sauter-Joyce era, CBS News employees learned to divine what was happening at the news division (and to themselves) by reading the TV columns; that was, after all, the way that Shad Northshield and Charles Kuralt had discovered that they were on their way out, and they were just the first of many. What the press had to say about the new regime was accorded inordinate attention, so much so that a daily press packet was assembled. Every day copies of stories about CBS News from the TV press around the country were gathered and assembled into a neat package (bound in CBS gray) by the CBS News press department and distributed to the top news executives (at a cost later estimated at $40,000 a year.)

There were various valuable uses for the leak, including spreading negative stories about the competition. Geraldine Sharpe-Newton, the head of CBS press information whom Sauter inherited from Bill Leonard, told friends with astonishment that the new head of news had actually asked her if she knew "how to do disinformation."

But it was Sauter who turned the leak into an art form. When he and Joyce were just getting on track in their new jobs in the middle months of 1982, Jankowski came to them with word of an impending economic crisis at the network. The sales department, pressed by Tom Wyman's insistence on ever-increasing stock values, had overestimated ad revenues by a substantial amount (it turned out to be $50 million), and the anticipated shortfall put Jankowski, who was stuck in the middle, in a panic. He asked Sauter and Joyce to help out by cutting costs in the news division, which, because of the Falklands and Lebanon coverage, as well as new *Evening News* costs, was spending well beyond its budget. It also happened that CBS News was an easy target, partly because focusing on news costs deflected attention from where it really belonged (Black Rock) and partly because, while CBS bought its entertainment programs from Hollywood producers, the network owned its news operation and could directly exert cost controls upon it.

This posed a tricky dilemma for the new management team. Part of the Sauter-Joyce mandate had been to impose new cost disciplines upon the organization; its leapfrog budget hikes in the late seventies and early eighties were seen by Black Rock as reckless and intolerable, and Sauter and Joyce had, in fact, brought economies to the place. They brought in a new vice-president of finance, Vince Loncto, who completely restructured the cost system of the organization. In Salant's and Leonard's day the cost-tracking system had been loose and rather lackadaisical—the news division executives wouldn't find out how much they'd spent on coverage of a story until weeks, or sometimes months, after the event—but Sauter and Joyce imposed weekly cost reports, which forced the people on the line, bureau chiefs and show producers and assignment desk people, to weigh costs in their coverage plans. Beyond that they actually put finance types into the field with CBS journalists, both in the bureaus and at the scenes of long-running stories, such as the Falklands Jankowski was delighted, but predictably these measures caused no small amount of discontent in the ranks, not only because they meant new restraints but because they represented a new and what many found to be an uncomfortable alliance of purpose between Black Rock and the news division.

Sauter and Joyce had experienced enough internal public relations problems not to invite more, and according to members of their staff, they were genuinely concerned that the cuts Jankowski asked for (about $10 million in cost reductions) would damage the organization's news coverage. So they resisted, informing Jankowski that any cost-saving measures beyond those they'd already employed would carry too much risk. But Jankowski didn't take no for an answer and forced the issue. That's when Sauter decided to take matters to a new level: He leaked the essence of the dispute to Sally Bedell Smith of the *New York Times*. Fighting Black Rock in the press was a new tactic for a CBS News president, something that even Salant hadn't tried, but it worked. The story was picked up around the country, and suddenly Jankowski, who hated bad press, was on the spot. After a few days he surrendered, drastically amending his request for news cuts and even making an apologetic trek over to the Broadcast Center to announce to the news staff that CBS still held the news division in special regard. It was a major PR triumph for Sauter (although Jankowski, who didn't need help in discerning the source of the leak, took note).

There would come a day when CBS News would regret the intense press attention and in fact pray for respite, but in the early days of the Sauter reign the attention was generally welcomed as a way of promoting the enterprise. It also did wonders for the burgeoning legend of Van Gordon Sauter.

To be sure, Sauter was working the big leagues now, and many inside CBS News, certainly the old hands, viewed his act with jaundiced eyes. Morley Safer, the accomplished and world-weary *60 Minutes* correspondent, saw Sauter as something of a lightweight. "He was trying like hell to create a persona that wasn't there," Safer said. "There's nothing worse than someone trying to affect a persona."

But to others in the organization, maybe even the majority, the Sauter era was beginning to have a certain appeal. Sauter's presence was like a fresh breeze in a place that had invented stuffy, and if one didn't get bogged down in such fine considerations as the fragility of an institutional value system, it was tempting to jump aboard the Sauter bandwagon. A whole generation welcomed the updating of the on-air look, and in fact, some began to notice with satisfaction that CBS's "moments" approach was being emulated by NBC.

Far the happiest consumer of Sauterism was Dan Rather, who was simply reborn during the first year of Sauter's tenure. Gone was the edgy and uncertain combatant, peering around corners for presumed enemies; that Rather was replaced by an authoritative and confident (though still suspicious) anchorman who now seemed perfectly cast in the role. The cosmetic touches, including the sweater, helped, but those who spent time around the anchorman agree that nothing soothed Rather so much as having his very own president of the news division. Sauter was unstinting in his attentions to the anchor, not only soliciting his advice and consulting him on business matters but also cultivating Rather's friendship away from the office; Jean Rather and Kathleen Sauter became quite friendly, and the Sauters and Rathers often weekended together at their respective summer homes, the women playing tennis while the men fished for trout.

Although Sauter denied that he intentionally coddled Rather—
"It's an embracing style, it's a style I've always used. It's not a
style adapted for Dan Rather"—one Black Rock observer of the
relationship reflected the view of many when he said, "Sauter
was an expert at handling Dan; handling Dan was his profession." Rather, of course, loved it and concluded that Sauter's
way was just the right way to run a news organization. The
anchorman publicly declared that Van Sauter was "a surgeon,"
and next to him, Bill Leonard was "a hospital administrator."

What weighed most with Rather and eased whatever doubts
about Sauter and his vision might have been lurking in the
heir-to-Murrow corner of Rather's soul were the ratings.
Through the early months of 1982 Rather's *Evening News* ratings
steadily climbed, and even after a customary CBS summer lull
he remained solidly in front. By the end of the year Rather
had opened a gap over the competition and was en route to a
200-plus-week run at the top. It was an enormously high time
for Rather, a time of immense relief, when all the accumulated
tensions from two long years of sniping and doubt and near
disaster just melted away; he was as close to happy in that time
as any who knew him had ever witnessed, and it showed on the
air, further strengthening the broadcast. Dan Rather was at last
unvexed, if only for a time.

"Sometimes at the end of a day," Rather told an interviewer,
conveying his delight with his new boss, "we'll put our feet up
on his desk and swig on a beer and say, 'Hey, man, this is fine,
ain't it?' "

Chapter

IN RETROSPECT, IT SEEMED that nature must have been seeking a balance and thus ordained that Van Sauter and Bill Moyers would come to CBS News at exactly the same moment in 1981. They arrived together, they were to leave together, and in between, they rained holy torment upon each other. Sauter and Moyers made a kind of perfect symmetry at CBS News, in the way that natural enemies do.

The two men came to CBS News in November 1981—Sauter recruited by Black Rock, Moyers recruited by Bill Leonard—at a time when public affairs programming at CBS News was up for grabs. The great CBS News tradition in public affairs, the tradition of Murrow and the acclaimed *CBS Reports* documentary series, had come to a halting place, and there was intense dispute inside CBS over the issue of what public affairs programming in the 1980s should be.

For Sauter and Moyers, there was no question what it should be. Sauter saw public affairs as entrée to prime time, a fertile ground where his reach-out-and-touch-someone news would prosper and bear the fruit of high ratings. Moyers also saw public affairs as entrée to prime time, where serious issues of social and cultural concern—that is to say, Moyers-style television—would be put before the mass audience. Each man was passionately committed to his vision of broadcasting, and each was determined to win.

Up to this point it had almost been easy for Sauter at CBS News. There had been great trauma and anguish, to be sure, but for others, not for him; in a matter of just several weeks he had imposed his changes upon the hard-news side of CBS and things had fallen quite nicely into place. The *Evening News* was beginning to pick up ratings, Rather was on an even keel, Black Rock was happy—another turnaround was succeeding. But Sauter hadn't yet come up against Bill Moyers.

Moyers was as determined and cunning as Sauter, every bit his match. He was not only a thinker and communicator of enormous power (arousing awe was one of his formidable weapons) but a shrewd political animal who had learned at the knee of Lyndon Johnson. As a young man out of the University of Texas, Moyers left the Peace Corps to join the LBJ White House staff, no inconsiderable assemblage, and quickly rose to a place of influence that belied his age and experience. The guile and instincts that guided the young Moyers through the witchy thickets of 1960s politics were further sharpened as he moved through newspapering (again at an unusually high level, starting as publisher of the Long Island paper *Newsday*) and into broadcasting. Insiders at CBS News, including Moyers's most ardent admirers, were constantly amazed that certain aspects of the man they knew well had never been publicly revealed. Yes, he was "brilliant," his colleagues acknowledged; they also characterized him as "duplicitous," "calculating," and "cunning." Sauter came to have his own assessment: "A truly reprehensible human being."

Sauter, of course, *would* feel strongly. He met his match in Bill Moyers, as did Moyers in him. They were, in a way, opposite sides of the same coin, each the other's bête noire. Between the two men there developed a powerful and ultimately destructive enmity that was bound up with the destiny of public affairs, the most important corner of CBS News. It was a war that nobody was to win. But Bill Moyers fired the last shot.

Never in broadcasting has there been a more suitable pairing of individual and enterprise than the joining of Bill Moyers with the public affairs tradition at CBS News. Moyers, a rare and powerful voice, a kind of secular evangelist, seemed destined for CBS News, where the commitment to the serious social documentary provided a national pulpit of unparalleled reach and influence. The man and the place were drawn to each other, irresistibly, and for a decade Moyers and CBS News struggled desperately to find a fit. Yet the history of Bill Moyers at CBS News is the story of the death of the serious social documentary, and Moyers himself, so suited to the form, came to be an instrument of its demise. It is a history that predates and anticipates Van Sauter, a history of deceit and betrayal, of raw ambitions and poisoned friendships that one day came to an explosive end.

It began in 1974, when the esteemed documentary unit that produced *CBS Reports* was at a crossroads. If CBS News had always enjoyed a certain independence and autonomy from the rest of the company (and, therefore, from such base considerations as profit and romancing the lowest common denominator of the mass audience), the *CBS Reports* unit enjoyed even greater insulation. In fact, the documentary team was housed apart from the hard-news enterprise, and when CBS News moved into its new quarters on the south side of West Fifty-seventh Street, the *CBS Reports* group was stationed across the street, in offices above a Ford showroom.

The physical separation was appropriate, too, because the filmmakers of *CBS Reports* were as distinct in purpose and spirit from the rest of CBS (even CBS News) as a portrait artist is from a house painter. The work of Perry Wolff, among the two dozen or so distinguished documentary makers at the height of *CBS Reports,* was the subject of a retrospective at the Museum of Modern Art, and others of his colleagues were equally regarded. Jay McMullen was considered one of the finest documentary makers working, the creator of such enduring and impactful works as *Biography of a Bookie Joint,* a daring exposé of police corruption in Boston, and a documentary called simply *Tenement,* for which McMullen rented a room in a Chicago tenement for seven months and emerged with one of the most devastating studies of the human condition ever put to film. The documentary makers were loners, for the most part, and often eccentrics, as befitted the nature of their work; they'd spend six months to a year (and sometimes longer) agonizing over a subject and then come forth with a program that lasted for one hour. They were journalists, to be sure, but they and their work were almost completely indifferent to the imperatives of commercial television; deadlines, ratings, profit, and the rest simply had no meaning to them. It was as close as television came to art.

It was no accident that such an enterprise had found a haven at CBS. In the wake of quiz show scandals in the late 1950s

Congress had probed the networks' stewardship of the public airwaves, sending genuine shivers down the spines of William S. Paley and his network president, Dr. Frank Stanton. They feared that CBS might lose its licenses to operate the five TV stations it owned, the cornerstone of the greatest moneymaking machine in the history of communications, the CBS Television Network. Stanton, who sincerely believed that television came closest to fulfilling its weighty obligations with news programs, promised Congress and the Federal Communications Commission that CBS would pay its public debt with a new commitment to public affairs. He turned to Fred Friendly, the dynamic producer who had teamed with Ed Murrow for the epochal public affairs series *See It Now* in the 1950s. It was *See It Now* that had given CBS a reputation for excellence in the emerging television age, the high mark coming in Murrow's 1954 imputation of Senator Joseph McCarthy ("This is no time for men who oppose Senator McCarthy's methods to keep silent. . . . Cassius was right. 'The fault, dear Brutus, is not in our stars, but in ourselves' "), and now Stanton wanted Friendly to build a new franchise, a documentary series that would begin with occasional installments and gradually build first to monthly and then to weekly episodes. Although Murrow would not be the sole correspondent, his association would lend to the series, to be called *CBS Reports,* a weight and identity; as it turned out, the series was the vehicle for the most powerful documentary of Murrow's career, the searing examination of the plight of migrant farm workers, *Harvest of Shame.*

Through the 1960s and into the 1970s the network kept its faith, and *CBS Reports* prospered. Perry Wolff recalled that an early president of CBS News, Sig Mickelson, once spotted a Nielsen pocket ratings book on the desk of Wolff's secretary and said, "If Perry ever sees this again, you're fired. That's not why we do these. I don't want him to know what the ratings are. *I* don't know what the ratings are."

"Nobody knew what the ratings were," Wolff recalled. "That's what documentaries were at CBS once." Wolff's memory may be somewhat colored by romance, but virtually every documentary maker of that time has a similar story. John Sharnik, a producer at CBS News in the 1950s, recalled that as an executive in charge of documentaries he had once approved and scheduled a sure ratings loser about the rise of the Communist party in Western Europe. A few days after the broadcast, he recalled, he was called over to Black Rock by Broadcast Group president Jack Schneider.

Schneider, who was not a sentimental sort ("Murrow's been dead fifteen years," he used to say when exasperated by a particular outburst of CBS News righteousness. "Can't we bury him?"), was reading the Nielsen ratings when Sharnik entered the room and, without looking up, said to the newsman, "Congratulations."

"Uh-oh," replied Sharnik, "what did I do?"

"You have achieved something without precedent in the history of CBS. You've just achieved a single-digit share. Tell me," Schneider continued, "now that you've seen how it came in in the ratings, would you, if you had the decision to make again, commission that documentary again?"

"Oh, sure."

"Why?"

"It fulfills all the criteria," Sharnik explained. "It is a subject of some importance and of some interest. It fulfills an area of need-to-know; not enough people recognized their need to know it, but it falls into that category. The producer who did it has a good track record. If that came to my desk today, I would say, 'Go ahead.' "

"He just shook his head," Sharnik recalled, "and said, 'You know, the wonderful thing about CBS is we can afford it.' "

CBS could afford it, of course, but the documentaries more than paid their freight in prestige and public relations. While CBS reaped tons of money from *The Beverly Hillbillies* and *Gilligan's Island* and other entertainment shows that the network executives themselves wouldn't watch, it was documentaries such as *Harvest of Shame* and *Tenement, The Selling of the Pentagon,* and *Hunger in America* that stirred public debate and had lasting impact. They were what made the place CBS.

By the 1970s, though, pressures were building on the decade-old *CBS Reports* unit. The network's commitment had begun to fade a bit over time, and there was something else: Don Hewitt's magazine show *60 Minutes* was showing signs of attracting a popular audience, a phenomenon that was as unexpected as it was portentous. Black Rock, which had always tolerated the low ratings of the documentaries, but not joyfully, began to wonder aloud if *CBS Reports* couldn't be transformed into something new, something that might tap into the broad audience Hewitt had discovered with *60 Minutes.* Would there be anything so wrong with garnering both prestige *and* ratings?

The people who ran *CBS Reports* were not entirely immune to the idea. By 1974 Bud Benjamin and John Sharnik, the executive and senior producers of *CBS Reports,* had concluded that the documentary series was showing signs of fatigue, that it needed a lift. What it needed, they said, was a maestro, a star correspondent who could give the series an identity that it hadn't really had since Murrow's day. With some difficulty, Bill Leonard, then Salant's vice-president overseeing documentaries, brought Dan Rather from his White House beat to become, as it was described to the dubious Rather, the "son of Ed Murrow." Rather had his suspicions about the move—was he being demoted after his troubles with Nixon?—but after a time (and a sizable salary hike) he adjusted to his new role, and *CBS Reports* did, indeed, begin to take on a new life. But in 1975, just as things were rolling and Rather was coming into form, the enterprise came to a halt.

At the beginning of the year Bud Benjamin was called across the street to become executive producer of Cronkite's *Evening News.* In October Bill Leonard, who had shepherded *CBS Reports* through many of its glory years, was appointed CBS lobbyist in Washington. A month later the unit lost Rather, just a year on the job, who had been invited by Don Hewitt to join Morley Safer and Mike Wallace as the third correspondent on *60 Minutes.* It was a happy break for Rather and for *60 Minutes,* which was about to soar to unimagined ratings success, soon ranking among the top-rated shows on television. But it was a blow for *CBS Reports.*

John Sharnik, now the vice-president in charge of documentaries, knew that if *CBS Reports* was to recover its momentum it would need another strong correspondent to act as its new voice and eyes. It happened that Bill Small, who was then Salant's number two, had heard from a news talent agent that the bright young journalist Bill Moyers had grown disenchanted with the Public Broadcasting Service, where for five years his documentary series *Bill Moyers' Journal* had been the shining centerpiece of public affairs programming. Sharnik and CBS News soon learned that disenchantment was Moyers's particular métier, but at the time Moyers and *CBS Reports* seemed a natural match. In

April 1976 Bill Moyers joined CBS News, as the successor to Rather, the heir to Murrow.

Landing a chief correspondent for the documentary unit was the first step, but Sharnik still held the dream of somehow transforming the traditional hourlong form into something else, something more like a magazine. Moyers, whose canvas had been the traditional hourlong documentary form, resisted the idea, and any chance that Sharnik had of swaying him quickly vanished with Moyers's first documentary.

It was a report called *Born Again*, about the emerging new force of fundamentalist Christians, a subject to which Moyers felt a deep, personal connection. He had been reared in the pews of evangelical churches, and he would say that he still heard the echoes of their hymns and prayers—in fact, that he owed much of his powerful communications skill, the cadence and rhythms of his speech, to that tradition. (Moyers is, among other things, an ordained Baptist minister.) As the lights went up after a special screening for John Sharnik, the executive asked to speak to Moyers and his producers alone. "I won't put that show on the air," Sharnik said. Relying on his instincts as a producer, he told Moyers that the documentary was pulpity and narrow and simply unfit for CBS air. "I want to tell you," Sharnik later recalled, "that was a lousy show."

It was Moyers's first show in his first job in commercial television, and that was just the wrong thing for Sharnik to say. Of that considerable body of journalists and serious thinkers who number themselves among Moyers's fans, it is safe to say that none is more convinced of the worth of Moyers's work than Moyers himself. His zeal was part of what lent his work its fiery conviction; it was also what made him the most difficult journalist at CBS News. John Sharnik had deftly placed himself on Bill Moyers's enemies list, and word was soon out that maybe Sharnik was too much of a producer to be a really good executive. Presented with the chance to produce a pilot for a newsmagazine, Sharnik quickly accepted, and when that failed, he was not reappointed to the vice-president's job. There was little doubt that Sharnik's falling-out with Moyers hurt him in his final years at CBS. "Oh, yeah, it did, very definitely," he later said. "I was determined not to let it, but I knew that it did."

The arrival of Moyers at CBS News might have been a career wrecker for Sharnik, but it was a major factor in the dramatic ascendance of Howard Stringer. Although Stringer had been at

CBS News for more than a decade, he was, in 1976, a very minor player in the organization. *Air Time,* a comprehensive history of CBS News covering the years through 1978, is as good a testament as any to Stringer's relative obscurity. The book, written by a CBS insider, Gary Paul Gates, lists 313 names in the index; Howard Stringer is not mentioned once.

Stringer had been the resident "kid" at *CBS Reports,* the nice, bright Welsh lad who'd come to CBS almost off the boat in 1965. He just showed up at the CBS personnel office one day, eager and earnest and optimistic in the face of the harshest odds—namely, that there were no jobs available, and even if there had been, young Stringer had no experience and no connections. Still, he had come all that way, and the kind ladies in personnel found him a job as a clerk at the CBS-owned radio station, WCBS, where he logged commercials. Then something happened that was an indication of the young Welshman's singular determination: Two months after arriving in America, he was drafted into the United States Army. It seemed a certain end to Stringer's American dream; he was, after all, a foreign resident, the son of a British army careerist who'd attended private prep schools and held a degree (second-class, a good degree) from Oxford University. To avoid the army and the escalating Vietnam War, he had only to return home. Instead, Stringer went into the army and served for two years, including a ten-month tour of Vietnam, where he was a personnel sergeant. Years later, in the course of a lawsuit, he was asked under oath why he allowed himself to be drafted: "Because my desire to . . . stay in this country was stronger than my desire to end what I thought of as a great experience." When he was released from the army in 1967, he returned to CBS and his clerking job.

He got a break in 1968. CBS News was gearing up for the presidential election, and Stringer landed a research job with the expanding election unit. Stringer, who had read modern history at Oxford, performed well in the job, and after the election he was offered a permanent position in the CBS News research department, where he did a lot of work on documentaries for *CBS Reports.* He was happy in his work, but he was also quite ambitious, and when his thirtieth birthday came and went and he was still only a researcher, he began to feel, as he later offhandedly phrased it, "vaguely suicidal." He possessed a kind of self-effacing charm, which was matched by a deeply felt self-confidence, and he knew that he could do more than carry the hod for others who were doing what he wanted to do, which was making documentaries. When he let it be known that he was thinking of leaving CBS for NBC News, where there was an opening, he got a promotion to assistant producer in the *CBS Reports* unit, and he was on his way. He was taken under the wing of Perry Wolff, who proved to be an effective instructor, and Stringer made such progress that Moyers's arrival in 1976 cast mentor and student into an awkward situation. Wolff, the experienced and accomplished producer, was by rights the likely choice as executive producer overseeing Moyers's documentaries. But Stringer was new blood, and he appealed to John Sharnik's sense that *CBS Reports* needed a new direction. Stringer got the job. "I didn't mind Howard going by me," Wolff later said, although as time passed, he had plenty of cause for regret.

The Moyers-Stringer pairing revealed complementary traits in two of CBS's most complicated personalities. Stringer showed his remarkable ability to charm, and Moyers his remarkable willingness to be charmed. "Howard became like the young Bill Moyers," said one *CBS Reports* colleague, "and Bill really adopted this guy." They made a terrific team, and the documentaries that they made together were uniformly first-rate. *The Fire Next Door, Anyplace but Here, The CIA's Secret Army,* and *The Battle for South Africa* were among the products of their collaboration. "Personally I thought the best year of *CBS Reports* ever, maybe including the Murrow period, was that first year that Howard and Moyers had it," John Sharnik said. "They really did venturesome stuff, and they did it with such a sense of immediacy you really felt you were in the midst of life."

But Moyers was becoming disenchanted again. As successful and fruitful as his *CBS Reports* tenure had been, the documentaries were still scheduled irregularly and, when they were scheduled, were invariably placed in the most untenable time periods—opposite coverage of the Oscars or the World Series on another network. Moyers found that intolerable and later explained, "My position has always been consistent: If you're going to have impact in this medium, you must have regularity and frequency." Indeed, that was and would remain Moyers's first rule of broadcasting and the source of his grief at CBS News. Sharnik, who genuinely admired Moyers's abilities despite his own difficulties with him, maintained that Moyers's insistence on a regularly scheduled broadcast could be obliged if Moyers would only agree to do a magazine program. "What I wanted Moyers to do was to turn *CBS Reports* into a genuine *Bill Moyers' Journal,*" Sharnik said, "a journal of current commentary in which he could spend sixty minutes on an idea, or twenty minutes, or twenty seconds. If he had a one-liner, a piece of wisdom that was worth communicating—'You want to know what I think of tax reform, folks?'—or a five-minute interview with a former secretary of treasury." Sharnik even went to Black Rock with his idea and received from Jack Schneider something that *CBS Reports* hadn't had in years: a commitment for a regular monthly slot. But Moyers had a blunt assessment of the magazine idea: "Bullshit." It was a position that Sharnik lamented years later. "If Bill hadn't been so suspicious and resistant to authority and so offended that something of his had been rejected . . ."

Moyers didn't want a magazine, but he apparently wanted a weekly prime-time series. He told Gary Gates at the time, "The problem is not the format, it's the scheduling. If they would give us more air time on a regularly scheduled basis, we'd show them that we could have just as much impact and influence as *60 Minutes* or the *Evening News* or any other news program on television." CBS News executives weren't sure what Moyers wanted. Dick Salant, desperate to keep Moyers, went to Schneider and pulled out all stops; he pleaded, he begged, he cajoled in the effort to get Moyers a series. "So I debased myself," Salant recalled, "I kissed Backe's ass. Finally he said yes, and I was so excited. I was in my office, and I called Bill and said, 'Wait right there, I'm coming over with some wonderful news.' And I told him that he could have what he wanted, and he said, 'Sorry, I have commitments at PBS.' "

Years later, after many at CBS News had wearied of Moyers's vacillations and had made their feelings known, Moyers explained himself. "Everybody calls me Hamlet, but I call it brilliance."

So in 1978 Moyers went back to public television, leaving a void in which *CBS Reports* once again was up for grabs. Stringer, by now a player with real clout, began to exert his vision upon the documentary unit. He believed, as Sharnik had, that the old-style hourlong documentary, the cherished form of his mentors, was tired beyond resuscitation. He wanted to build a new *CBS Reports,* one that would reflect a new generation's television techniques and standards. That generational theme was central to Stringer's view of things and remained so throughout his career at CBS News ("Howard had a problem with generations," Wolff said). Stringer recruited another young producer of like sensibilities, Andrew ("Andy") Lack, a former actor and advertising man who'd spent a brief time at *60 Minutes,* and together they formed the heart of the youth faction at *CBS Reports.* There emerged a new journalistic ideal, the slick reporter-producer, the prototype of whom was a dashing young former magazine editor named George Crile. Stringer and Lack began to think of their unit as the residence of the new video age within CBS. The unit split into old-liners and the new group; the traditionalists, out of favor and often without assignment, began to drop off with increasing frequency.

Stringer, meanwhile, began to experiment in earnest with his idea of a different kind of documentary. Instead of the brooding, year-in-the-making, highly personal oeuvre, he pursued a new concept: the quick-hit, on-top-of-the-news "instant documentary." The new documentary relied on a strong visual style, and it endeavored to spin out of hot news that was still on the public's mind, as Stringer and Moyers had done on the execution of Gary Gilmore. When Ed Bradley replaced Moyers as chief correspondent, the style could be seen in a documentary on the Vietnamese boat people and in a close-up look at the Boston Pops on a tour of China. This form of documentary, while stylish and broadly interesting, was more a news special than an in-depth work with a statement to make.

That was what bothered the old-timers the most: Stringer and Lack were in love with television, not with the documentary. Both had ambitions far beyond the documentary field. They had, in fact, infused a vitality into *CBS Reports* and even fancied themselves in a kind of competition with *60 Minutes.* Some, such as Sharnik, thought that very vitality was the undoing of the serious documentary at CBS News. "It just became a vehicle for ambition, for personal ambition, Howard's and Andy's."

On that subject Lack later said, "There was on the part of people who made documentaries a real tiredness with the form; they didn't want to make any more. There was what Howard and I used to call the 'documentary disease'—after you've made three or four of them, and they're ball-busting programs to produce, they burn you out for a very modest feedback. They're up against stiff competition, and they're irregularly scheduled."

What Lack meant was that he and Stringer had tired of the form. "I hated it, I hated doing it. It was tough work, for which I got no particular satisfaction. It isn't that we turned on them, in the sense that we didn't want to do them because we didn't believe in them; we didn't want to do them because we wanted to do other things. The good people. You could always get bad people to do them." Both Stringer and Lack would be doing other things soon enough.

These were the circumstances that awaited the arrival of Van Sauter in the fall of 1981. If ever there existed yesterday television, it was the traditional, hourlong social documentary, a form that was doomed from the moment Sauter hit the door ("He found them [documentaries] boring," Ernie Leiser understated). Sauter saw in Lack and Stringer the ideal executors of moments television—Stringer at *Evening News* and Lack in public affairs.

The symmetry was perfect, but for one hitch. It happened that the old guard had planted a time bomb for Sauter, albeit unintentionally, in the person of Bill Moyers. In the spring of 1980, at the tail end of Leonard's tenure as president of CBS News, Leonard had heard that Moyers was once again unhappy at PBS, and on Stringer's strong recommendation, he had once again pursued him for CBS. The most urgent need on Leonard's mind was the *Evening News;* he wanted to resurrect the role of commentator that had been vacant since Eric Sevareid's retirement in 1977, and it was believed that Moyers might lend a presence and weight to the broadcast that Rather alone didn't project. Rather himself got involved in the recruitment, telling Moyers that he would have regular airtime on the *Evening News,* a "blank check," as Moyers recollected it, and that "in elections I want you by my side in a partnership." Leonard also mentioned the possibility that Moyers most wanted to hear: a regular series, either in prime time or in the late-night time period.

The negotiations were, typically, long and tortured, conducted by a series of letters, conversations, and exchanges through third parties. Points that Leonard had thought were agreed upon, or at least would work themselves out, were picked apart by Moyers and reconsidered over and over: That late-night half hour, would it be kept on the air long enough to have a real chance? Who would be in charge of it? Would it be like *Bill Moyers' Journal*? On the *Evening News* matter, could Moyers count on appearing at least twice a week? Moyers believed he had been burned in his first tour at CBS News, and he wanted to take no chances.

The heart of Moyers's concern, the clincher, was a regularly scheduled series of his own. Leonard came as close as he could to promising Moyers what he wanted. "We shall make a good-faith effort to make a regularly scheduled program suited to your talents," Leonard told Moyers in a letter. It wouldn't exactly be *Bill Moyers' Journal,* but "differences will be less notice-able than the similarities." That was enough for Moyers; that, and a salary that would reach nearly $1 million a year.

But between the time Moyers began talking to Bill Leonard, in the spring of 1980, and the time, in November 1981, his contract at PBS expired, allowing him to come to CBS News, Bill Leonard became irrelevant. Moyers and Van Sauter came to CBS News together in November 1981, like powder and fuse to a flame.

"It was," said one Sauter associate, "P. T. Barnum meeting Elmer Gantry."

At first there were cautious overtures between the two men. Sauter told Moyers he had a lot of ideas for new shows (one of the first things Sauter did was check the Moyers contract, which revealed that there was no firm commitment to a weekly series, but a gentleman's agreement, enough to warrant an effort), and Moyers happily listened. Sauter, Joyce, and Moyers's old friend and collaborator Howard Stringer asked Moyers to exert his efforts on the *Evening News* first, before diving into any new public affairs series. It seemed fair, and Moyers agreed. He, too, was trying to make nice with the new regime and went so far as to defend the Sauter actions that were causing so much anguish among the old order. The times, Moyers said, were "poignant, perplexing, and painful. It's difficult to redesign a news organization for a new age. But I don't think CBS News is in trouble. Sauter is an intelligent and exciting leader. Dan is a solid news anchor and journalist. I'm still a believer and fan." Although many in the organization were particularly pained and angered by the dumping of Shad Northshield and Charles Kuralt from the *Morning* show, Moyers told an interviewer that such moves were "necessary to strengthen and focus our efforts."

Moyers said that he was happy to do the *Evening News* and the occasional documentary for the time being because "they are good for CBS News and because they have value." However, he told an interviewer, "sooner or later I want the chance to succeed or fail with a prime time news show of my own. And should it fail, I will simply open a bait and tackle shop somewhere in Texas."

Things went smoothly for a time. The Rather broadcast picked up in the ratings, a factor that many (including Moyers) attributed partly to Moyers's contribution. After about six months, in the spring of 1982, Moyers was ready to ask Sauter and Joyce to make good on their part of the bargain, to come across with a series. A meeting was called to discuss Sauter's ideas. The new president of CBS News, it turned out, had something particular in mind: a fourteen-segment, hourlong magazine show, something that although Sauter had the salesmanship not to describe it actually as such, was, in fact, a video version of *People* magazine. It was, in other words, as close to the antithesis of the Moyers style as was conceivable. But Moyers, typically, did not reject the program idea. To the contrary, he seemed amenable to it and said he would consider it. Sauter was delighted. "I thought I had him snookered," he later said. But two days later the other Moyers checked in. He wouldn't do it.

Weeks passed before Moyers went back to Sauter. Why can't we get this thing moving? he asked. In an ideal world what would you like to do? Sauter, ever quick, suggested what seemed the perfect solution. How about a teaming of Moyers and Charles Kuralt in back-to-back half-hour shows? There was something for everybody: Moyers could pursue his vision, Sauter could get some ratings (America *loved* Kuralt), and best, although this part remained unspoken, a regularly scheduled program would allow the virtual elimination of *CBS Reports*. Moyers accepted.

During that brief battle over costs with Jankowski, Sauter and Joyce ordered cutbacks on the *CBS Reports* staff that decimated the unit. Twenty-five people were laid off at CBS News, but far the highest proportion was at *CBS Reports*. When pressed about the death of documentaries by a TV reporter, Sauter and Joyce's response was to point at the planned Moyers and Kuralt shows. That was public affairs, wasn't it? Why, if anything, CBS News was *increasing* its commitment to public affairs.

In the summer of 1983 *Our Times* with Bill Moyers and *On the*

Road with Charles Kuralt went on the air. Gene Jankowski said that the shows would have ten weeks to prove themselves. Moyers protested that ten weeks wasn't nearly enough time, but he needn't have worried. The two shows hit it just right; Kuralt was Kuralt, smart and friendly and evocative all at once, and Moyers did some of the best broadcasting of his career. The half-hour form was perfect for Moyers, better than an hour, which sometimes seemed too much Moyers. *Our Times,* produced by Andy Lack (it was Lack at his best, too), considered serious subjects engagingly, and its ratings were more than respectable. It seemed that Bill Moyers might have found happiness at last.

But at the end of the summer *Our Times* and *On the Road* went off the air, and nothing more was said about it. Moyers finally pressed the issue, and Sauter said that the numbers were not quite convincing; he wanted to try something else. Moyers thought that the numbers were plenty good for a summer news series, but no, Sauter seemed determined. It was a true mystery to many at CBS News, including Andy Lack. "The management answer that I got from Van was that the network doesn't make cakes in that size," Lack recalled. "They said, 'We want an hour show, not a half-hour show. You've given us two half-hour shows.'" It began to seem, especially in light of what came next, that Sauter never really intended *Our Times* to be anything but a temporary diversion.

Ed Joyce asked Moyers if he would consider trying a new broadcast, again cast with Kuralt. Moyers, still eager for a weekly shot (and not quite ready to open that bait-and-tackle shop), agreed. He agreed, that is, until he saw what it was that Sauter had in mind. It was a show called *American Parade,* which was almost exactly the show that Sauter had first tried to sell Moyers more than a year earlier. It would have lots of fast-paced segments, a rock star every week, and a comedy news segment at the end, with Moyers and Art Buchwald. It was to be a slick, breezy grab at the national heartstrings, a play at the new patriotic sentimentality that accompanied the Reagan fever, with lots of flag-waving, patriotic hymns and cornball features. The segments were to be short and fast, a concept that just didn't register with Moyers and his sympathizers, who believed that public affairs TV was something to be laid out carefully and slowly savored, like a fine meal. ("That's like wanting to get laid in a hurry," Perry Wolff said of the fast-paced directive. "Who in hell wants that?") It was as if the new show had been calculated to make Moyers physically ill.

"They killed his baby," said one close associate of Moyers's, "and now they wanted him to do comedy news." This time Moyers didn't just refuse. He offered his resignation.

Moyers was no longer in communication with Sauter, so he wrote a letter to Ed Joyce in which he thoroughly aired his spleen. "Ed," he wrote, "the fact is that *American Parade* is not my kind of journalism. I don't believe in it and I can't do it. It's that simple." But of course, it wasn't that simple. He went on to remind Joyce that "the whole motif of public affairs is to deal with issues of some complexity" and that he and his colleagues had done just that with *Our Times,* a broadcast that "was much talked about and praised.

"Despite all that," Moyers said, "we were now being told it was too good to succeed, that only a magazine appealing to a variety of people with an array of subjects would be given a go-ahead by the network." He added that the program Sauter and Joyce were proposing meant to infuse entertainment with the "ethos of journalism"—which is exactly what it meant to do—and he scornfully recounted some of the proposed segments: a profile of John Cleese, the *Monty Python* star; a profile of rock stars Mick Jagger and Michael Jackson; a segment on the fiftieth anniversary of Muzak; a look at outlaw motorcycle gangs; and an examination of "elegance," whatever that would be. "I find it unthinkable that CBS would be spending more time on celebrities, stars, pop singers, athletes and miscellaneous feature stories" than on the serious consideration of public affairs, Moyers wrote, adding, "Broadcast journalism is increasingly expected to serve the lowest common denominator."

In view of his feelings, Moyers wrote to Joyce, the honorable thing would be for him to leave CBS News; he asked to be released from his contract. Joyce pleaded with Moyers to stay, he said that he and Rather wanted Moyers on the *Evening News* three times a week; Moyers stayed, dejected and angry.

A few months later the worm turned. *American Parade* went on the air without Bill Moyers and was a spectacular flop. It was ridiculed by critics, scorned by the people working on it, and, most important, was rejected by viewers. It looked as if CBS News would lose the hour back to the entertainment side, which had been loath to yield so valuable a time slot to the "amateurs" in news in the first place. Now CBS News needed Moyers, and he played his role to the hilt.

Stringer went to Lack and implored him to take over the show as producer. Lack, who also had had reservations about *American Parade,* had refused to produce it when it was first proposed. Instead, he had asked to be a correspondent; he didn't budge, even when Sauter threatened to fire him. Sauter had relented, and Lack had gone on the air as a CBS News correspondent. Now his friend Stringer was asking him to save the show as a producer. Lack agreed, and the two men went to see Moyers in an effort to pull off the impossible. Stringer and Lack both knew how to pull Moyers's strings: They went to his apartment and humbled themselves, trying to convince Moyers that survival of CBS News and possibly Western civilization depended on his doing the show. (In truth, much did depend on it; it was a very valuable hour of prime time.) They begged, and Moyers said no; but Lack suspected that Moyers was enjoying every minute of it: "He loves it, he just loves it. It's the smoke-filled room and the vote on civil rights legislation is in the morning, and here we are, three power brokers sitting around smoking cigars, drinking brandy. It speaks to the missing ingredient in his relationship with Van. Van never came to him and said, 'I need you,' and you can't work with Bill Moyers and not say, 'I need you.' And here were Bill's two closest professional colleagues, and in some ways pretty close friends as well, who came to him and said, 'I need you.' That means everything. If we said, 'We need you to be Claude Kirchner in a revived version of the three-ring circus [kiddie TV show] and only you can be the master of ceremonies,' I think we could have made the sale."

Throughout the evening Moyers said no, he couldn't do it, he wouldn't do it. Finally Stringer and Lack got up to go. When they got outside, Stringer asked, "What do you think?"

And Lack said, "I think he'll do it."

That night Moyers called Lack and asked how important his decision was to Stringer's future. Lack said it was very important. Moyers said he would do it.

Joyce was delighted, of course, but he needed one more thing from Moyers. He asked the journalist to go to California to sell the damaged goods, now called *Crossroads,* to the CBS affiliates, who were meeting at their annual convention. Moyers, naturally, was loath to go; he didn't believe in the project, they had killed his baby, they had deceived him, and now they were asking him to save this hour for CBS News. But go he did. And with the affiliates' representatives stirring in their seats, awaiting his appearance, Moyers turned to a colleague standing beside him backstage and said, "Watch this."

He went out onstage and became Elmer Gantry, stirring the souls of that polyester crowd, moistening their eyes, making them *believe*. "He walked out and got to that podium, and within thirty seconds he had that audience in the palm of his hand," one witness to the event said. "He became the Baptist preacher. He put on his Baptist preacher's cloak, and he was brilliant. It was a tour de force." The affiliates gave him a standing ovation that lasted five minutes. Moyers himself allowed that he gave the "best speech of my life . . . this on a presentation I didn't want to make about a broadcast I didn't want to do."

With the affiliates in line, Lack and Moyers went to work. After just a couple of weeks' hiatus they went on the air with a reworked *American Parade,* minus the cheap patriotism and the carnival acts but still lacking the spirit and verve of *Our Times.* Moyers wasn't wholly committed to the broadcast, and there was terrible bickering between him and Lack over some of the pieces. Moyers thought that a profile of writer David Mamet, Lack's idea, represented a corruption of values; Lack said the profile "irked" Moyers because he resented being dragged "into a world where he would actually talk to people under forty. . . . He knew that I wanted to involve him in a world of ideas that my generation believed in." The show made a respectable run through the summer, performing as well as anyone might have expected.

But by now Sauter was exasperated with Moyers and had given up on trying to match Moyers with a prime-time show. He wrote a memorandum to his senior staff saying that "we've tried to service a personality-driven broadcast, and it didn't work." As Sauter saw it, CBS had fulfilled its obligation under the "gentleman's agreement," and Moyers had blown his chance. He would get no new chance under Van Sauter.

But Moyers, too, had seen the light. He was convinced that the new CBS News was not only not interested in serious, long-form documentaries but not serious about Bill Moyers. Among the benefits he'd negotiated in his contract with Leonard was a "window," which allowed him to get out in the summer of 1984.

And it happened that an old friend from PBS, Lawrence K. Grossman, was now the president of NBC News. Moyers was sure he could jump from CBS to NBC—that would show them—and he became so convinced of it that he solicited Andy Lack to go along with him; they'd be a team. That would *really* show them. Lack's contract expired later that year, and he said sure, check it out. So Moyers met with Grossman over dinner. But instead of wooing Moyers, Grossman seemed to be stalling. He was new on the job, and NBC had Roger Mudd, and there was a commitment to a weekly series with Mudd, and he didn't know if he could get another piece of prime time. But they'd keep in touch.

Moyers's associates say that he returned to CBS News the next day crestfallen. Within a few weeks *Crossroads* went off the air, and it became apparent that whatever took its place would not be a Bill Moyers vehicle. If it wasn't apparent to Moyers before, it certainly was made crystal clear when Andy Lack came to him with a sobering announcement: Lack wanted to go his own way. CBS had given him a new contract (and a lucrative one, in the $250,000 range) to stay at the network and develop new shows. They would not be shows that included Bill Moyers; one show, to be called *West 57th,* was already being planned. "Bill," Lack said, "I don't think this network as it is currently operating wants the public affairs programming that you do."

Moyers was devastated. The hour he had saved for CBS News was lost to the Sauter vision, and the realization hit him like a punch to the gut. "When it was over," he later said, "the hour I had saved was for *West 57th.*"

Sauter had won. He would have *his* kind of public affairs broadcast, and Andy Lack would produce it. Moyers probably wouldn't have been interested even if he'd been invited to participate. It was conceived as a television *show,* a kind of realistic drama à la NBC's *Hill Street Blues* and *St. Elsewhere,* except it would be real. It would have four news reporters who would star as . . . news reporters. They would be seen discussing their exciting stories; they'd be seen out in the field, undergoing the trials and triumphs of the electronic journalist. It was along these lines that Lack was thinking when, one morning in the shower, he dreamed up the title for his new show: *Hill Street Blues* was named after the place where those fictional cops worked; *St. Elsewhere* was named after the place where those fictional doctors worked; Lack would name his show where his "characters" worked—*West 57th.* It would feature fast cuts, finger-popping theme music, lots of flash and crackle, including inter-jected shots of the behind-the-scenes world of TV journalists, all that electronic wizardry in action. It was the new video, all the way.

But if Sauter had won, it was not without cost. Moyers was seething. Giving up on a regular series of his own, he went back to his commentary role on the *Evening News,* but now he was in no mood to be the good soldier. In January 1985 he wrote a commentary that Lane Venardos, who was by then the executive producer of the *Evening News,* didn't consider airworthy. It was about a pro-Arab political commercial that many radio stations in New York refused to air. But Venardos, reluctant to cross Moyers, never directly told Moyers that the piece wasn't going on the broadcast. Instead, he delayed, telling him that the com-mentary had been pushed off because of breaking events. After several days Moyers discovered that Venardos had never in-tended to run the commentary. That tore it. He refused to go on the air that week, and the next week, and every week there-after through the winter and spring and into the summer. He just disappeared from the *Evening News,* spending his time across the street in the decimated *CBS Reports* unit (which now consisted of a full-time staff of one, executive producer Perry Wolff, and one or two free-lancers hired on for special projects), anguishing over his treatment at the hands of the infidels and trying (some said halfheartedly) to dream up the next Great American Documentary.

Finally, in June, Moyers's producer and friend Marty Koughan went to a a senior producer, Linda Mason, at the *Evening News* and suggested that a way be found to get Moyers on the air. But there was a problem. Dan Rather, who had ambivalent feelings about his towering colleague anyway, was furious that Moyers had put the broadcast (and, therefore, Rather) at risk by aban-doning it. The press had picked up on the feud, there had been Moyers quotes about corrupted news values, and much of the bad publicity naturally devolved upon the *Evening News.* So Koughan and Mason conspired to get the two reluctant Texans into a room together, where they proceeded in characteristic fashion to lather each other with claims of mutual admiration; it was agreed that Moyers would return to the broadcast.

But the *Evening News* episode was minor-league compared

with the grief that Moyers helped cause for Lack and his *West 57th.* There was, understandably, a certain institutional skepticism about a show that relied so much on concept and glitz, and Moyers had hurled oil drums of fuel on that particular fire. Lack was miserable. "My failure is that I didn't go to another network to do a weekly magazine show," he said. "It was the biggest mistake of my career. There's no discussion, there's no question about it, the biggest mistake of my career. I should not have stayed at CBS. I regret it." When Lack heard that Moyers was criticizing his struggling show, he wrote Moyers a letter, suggesting that their close friendship should be worth "a certain silence."

Moyers responded with a letter, handwritten and a half dozen pages in length, that fairly burned with indignation. He laid into Lack, inveighing against the corruption of values, the betrayal of friends and of public affairs, Lack's sellout to Van Sauter (an accusation that particularly offended Lack, coming from a man who was earning roughly four times Lack's salary). "It didn't surprise me, but it hurt me deeply," Lack said. "I was Satan, Adolf Hitler, Goebbels, and Nero. I was everybody rolled into one. It hurt me. I almost cried. It really hurt my feelings. I did cry about it, in fact."

Moyers worked on the *Evening News,* but he made his disaffection evident. "After several long and painful months," Moyers told the *New York Times* after patching things up with Rather, "I have concluded that serious public affairs reporting in depth isn't going to make it in the entertainment milieu of prime time. I have to be a grown up [*sic*] fellow and face the fact that reporting on social issues in depth isn't going to be given a fair shot."

Sauter thought it was all sour grapes. "Moyers," said Sauter, "would have thought me one of the greats of broadcasting if I'd given him a half hour."

Moyers strongly hinted that he would leave CBS News when his contract expired in November 1986, and he spent much of his remaining time at CBS News arranging projects for his next career in public television. But that is not to say that Moyers spent his remaining time at CBS News quietly. Before leaving, he got off one final, devastating blast at Sauter and the new CBS News. It was a parting shot that neither Sauter nor anyone at CBS News would soon forget.

Chapter

11

THE OLD GUARD WAS inflamed and conspiratorial. Moyers was rampaging, Cronkite was indignant, and there was much wailing over the death of documentaries and the sacrifice of values. As anguished as the place was, though, had internal troubles been all there was to contend with, Van Sauter's new order might have stood up. But coinciding with the inside upheavals, and exacerbating them, came a series of assaults from the outside, an onslaught unprecedented in its ferocity and potential for damage, that challenged the integrity of CBS News and then swept the organization into a predatory swirl that eventually consumed the whole company. The fragile coalitions of the new CBS News, which were wide but not deep, flew apart, and the divided House of Murrow descended into a kind of institutional nervous collapse.

The first scent of calamity wafted in on a perfect May morning in 1982, as the CBS affiliates gathered in San Francisco to hear promises of a golden future. The annual convention staged by the network for the owners and managers of its 200 affiliated stations was a glittery three-day party, interrupted by a few business sessions, at which the network and the affiliates would bathe in self-congratulations for the efforts of the past season and hear wildly optimistic projections for the coming fall season. The mood was particularly upbeat at this meeting, not least because CBS had been particularly extravagant in planning the affair, moving it to San Francisco from its usual Los Angeles locale. The network spent hundreds of thousands of dollars on the event, which included a boat trip one evening to the quaint town of Tiburon on the Bay, where affiliates discovered that CBS had bought out the shops and restaurants for the night. At night the network stars, including Walter Cronkite, mingled with the station executives and their wives, and during the day network executives gave details of the CBS triumphs, which, in fact, were compelling. In entertainment CBS had recovered its long-accustomed place as number one in the ratings, and in news Dan Rather was consolidating his lead. Even the *CBS Morning News* had shown signs of ratings life. Overall, the congenital optimism peculiar to these affairs seemed more than usually justified.

It was an important meeting for Van Sauter, his first before the full affiliate body as president of CBS News. His impressive supporting cast included Cronkite, Diane Sawyer, Morley Safer, Charles Kuralt, Ed Bradley, Bill Kurtis, and Dan Rather, who anchored the *Evening News* from San Francisco, and there was every reason to believe that for Sauter, who was magic with a crowd, it would be a showcase occasion.

And then *TV Guide* crashed the party. On the morning of May 24 the CBS affiliate reps, executives, and celebrities who ventured down to the newsstands at the elegant Fairmont Hotel and the Mark Hopkins across the street, some a bit bleary from the night before, were jolted to consciousness by what they saw. That is, they were jolted if they got to the newsstands early enough, for all up and down Nob Hill, the new issue of *TV Guide* was selling out as soon as the bundles it arrived in were unwrapped. On the cover was a headline that would ruin a few expense-account breakfasts that morning: ANATOMY OF A SMEAR: HOW CBS NEWS BROKE THE RULES AND "GOT" GEN. WESTMORELAND. There were three photographs on the cover, including two that everyone among the CBS group recognized instantly: Mike Wallace, the biggest star of the most popular program on television, CBS's *60 Minutes,* and a face from the past, retired General William C. Westmoreland, commander of U.S. forces in Vietnam from 1964 to 1968. The third photo was of a man whom relatively few in the group knew by face, and about whom all would come to know more than they wished. It was George

Crile, the *CBS Reports* producer (and onetime prototype of the new-age producer/reporter) who was responsible for the broadcast that had landed CBS News on the cover of *TV Guide.*

The article was an uncommonly hard-hitting exposé, alleging all manner of journalistic crimes and misdemeanors in the production of a documentary called *The Uncounted Enemy,* which had aired that January. The broadcast, produced by Crile and featuring Mike Wallace as the correspondent, made the case that while in command in Vietnam, General Westmoreland had been so bowed by political pressure to show progress in the war that he had led a conspiracy to misrepresent the size and strength of enemy forces to Congress, President Lyndon B. Johnson, and the American people. A few days after the broadcast General Westmoreland and several supporters had held a press conference at the Army-Navy Club in Washington to defend themselves against the charges, claiming that CBS had taken what had been an entirely appropriate discussion within the American intelligence community over enemy strength and blown it into an "exposé" of military deception. Westmoreland *had* argued for a lower estimate of enemy strength, they said, not in a plot to deceive but rather in an effort to enunciate better a particularly murky aspect of what was a very murky war. Westmoreland, an old warrior aroused from quiet retirement, lit into the broadcast, saying he now had a vivid, if unsought, personal understanding of the film *Absence of Malice,* in which an innocent man's life is ruined "by the unscrupulous use of the media." Westmoreland called the broadcast "a preposterous hoax" and accused the "notorious reporter, Mike Wallace," of staging a "star-chamber procedure with distorted, false, and specious information, plain lies, derived by sinister deception—an attempt to execute me on the guillotine of public opinion."

It was fiery stuff, but the Westmoreland press conference didn't really cause much more than a ripple. It was, after all, more or less the expected thing for exposed wrongdoers to attack the journalism that revealed them. But the *TV Guide* cover story was another matter.

In San Francisco on that warm May morning Van Sauter called a group of his senior staffers into his suite at the Fairmont to discuss the *TV Guide* story. Sauter had known of the broadcast—it had been produced during Bill Leonard's tenure, and it had aired just before Sauter officially became president—and he

had known that *TV Guide* was preparing an article. But he hadn't
expected "Anatomy of a Smear" or anything like it. His in-house
intelligence, gathered from various people at CBS News, some
of whom had talked to the *TV Guide* reporters, had indicated that
the magazine story would be tough but not devastating. As soon
as he read it, however, Sauter knew that damage had been done.
The lengthy article laid out the theme of the broadcast and then
explored in detail the manner in which Crile and his associates
had established their case. The article accused CBS News of
rehearsing one interview subject, of not revealing that the subject was a paid consultant, of allowing another interviewee to see
portions of other interviews, of heavy-handed editing techniques that strengthened the broadcast's case, and of ignoring
evidence that seemed to counter the message of the broadcast.
These were serious charges, implying violations of several CBS
News guidelines, and if they were true, CBS News had a disaster
on its hands. The magazine reporters, Sally Bedell Smith and
Don Kowet, clearly had at least one source inside the news
division who knew a great deal about the documentary's production, and although *TV Guide* was not exactly known for its investigative crusading, the piece had a credibility that demanded
attention. Smith and Kowet were two of the magazine's best
reporters, and although few in the group knew a lot about
Kowet, they knew Smith. She was one of the best reporters on
the TV beat, she had worked at *Time* magazine, she'd written a
book about television, and now she was joining the *New York
Times* as the paper's main television correspondent—a factor
that alone lent her article added weight.

Although the documentary hadn't occurred during Sauter's
"watch," as he put it, the storm it caused certainly did, and it
posed for the new head of CBS News the most exquisite dilemma. If he took the expected course, a quiet review under the
supervision of lawyers, it might seem that CBS was ducking a
charge that Sauter thought was too big to ignore. On the other
hand, the established role of a CBS News president when a
broadcast was under fire was to defend it to the death. Whatever
Sauter did, he had not only the public reaction to gauge but also
that of the news division, with its bowstrung nerves. In the end
Sauter was Sauter: He responded from the gut, and the course
he took also happened to be the one that seemed likeliest to
"play." He ordered that CBS News conduct an in-house inquiry

into the broadcast, a journalistic rather than legal review, at the conclusion of which the news division would take whatever action was appropriate. Some in the hotel room, including CBS lawyer Ralph Goldberg, argued that lawyers should be involved, for all the obvious reasons, not least being the possibility of a lawsuit. But Sauter was convinced that the most compelling response to charges of journalistic wrongdoing was to train a journalistic focus upon itself.

So he picked up the telephone and called Bud Benjamin, who was at home in New York, eating supper. Sauter asked Benjamin if he would conduct the inquiry. Benjamin thought about it, then told Sauter sure, he'd do it. "Somebody had to," Benjamin later explained.

Thus began a long and anguished ordeal that would be called CBS's own Vietnam, and the analogy was entirely apt. Sauter's decision had the desired short-term effect: He was able to review the matter cursorily during his presentation to the affiliates, reminding them that it hadn't happened on his watch and assuring them that it would be taken care of. "The current issue of *TV Guide* has an article, negative, about a recent CBS documentary, initiated more than a year ago and broadcast earlier this year," he said. The charges were serious, he added, and he promised that "upon returning to New York, another CBS News executive and myself, both of us new to that particular broadcast, will thoroughly examine those charges and respond to the management of the CBS Broadcast Group. We will bring to our review of the accusations the same vigor and objectivity we bring to our on-air reporting." A secondary effect of the decision was a buildup of public attention and suspense. A full-scale CBS News investigation into an imputed documentary carried the possibility of a dramatic conclusion, and with the *TV Guide* charges hanging in the air, the press awaited the verdict.

The Benjamin inquiry was unprecedented. Unlike a review by house lawyers, which is usually based on the presumption of a broadcast's essential integrity and is geared to a possible legal defense of the show in case of civil action, Benjamin's mandate was to investigate the broadcast with an independent, objective eye, a mission he took seriously. If there was any concern about a whitewash, the selection of Bud Benjamin was as close to a guarantee against that as could be found. A pleasant and quiet-spoken gentleman, Benjamin was strictly old CBS, with his print

background and a career in documentaries (he had produced
Walter Cronkite's *20th Century* for ten years) and the fetchingly
uncomplicated view of broadcast journalism common to so
many of his generation: News could be interesting, or not, but
it had to be straight.

There were those of Benjamin's generation who partly believed that in the flawed Vietnam broadcast the transgressions
of the new generation at CBS News, the Crile-Stringer-Lack
generation, had come home to roost. Crile had earlier copro-
duced another disputed documentary, *Gay Power, Gay Politics,*
which violated editing rules and for which the National News
Council had chastised CBS (the network ran a correction at the
top of its next documentary broadcast). Crile, for one, was convinced that Benjamin saw his review assignment as a kind of
generational jihad. "I think he felt that there was this whole new
generation of people who either didn't play by the rules or
weren't like he was," Crile later said. "I think he smelled, 'This
is someone who brought the temple into disrepute.' "

There was no demonstrable basis for that assertion. Benjamin
was a maddeningly straight arrow, but in a way that was part of
the problem. Crile was disturbed by what he perceived as a
prosecutorial tone in his sessions with Benjamin. Why hadn't
Crile used more interviews from the other side? Why did it seem
that Westmoreland had been ambushed by Crile and Wallace?
If he interviewed someone a second time because he looked
uncomfortable, how could the interview be "spontaneous and
unrehearsed," as demanded by the CBS News guidelines? In
truth, much of what Benjamin discovered did offend his sensibilities, his old-line notions of fairness and balance, and it
showed.

Crile was, understandably, unnerved by the circumstances in
which he found himself. His journalism was under attack, and he
was alienated from the inquiry process; Benjamin and his re-
searchers, Toby Wertheim and Barbara Pierce, holed up in Benjamin's office for six weeks, granting Crile no special voice. So
he undertook to defend himself. He wrote his own summation
of the controversy, a lengthy defense he called his "White
Paper," and he tried frantically to get an audience with Sauter.
But the last thing Sauter wanted was to engage in a minute
discussion of Vietnam with George Crile, and he repeatedly put
the producer off, telling him to wait for the results of the Benja-

min exercise. Crile was experiencing a terrible isolation inside CBS News, and at one point he wrote a note to Mike Wallace, asking why he, George Crile, seemed to be alone on the docket. What about Howard Stringer? Stringer, as executive producer, had had two and a half months to check out his piece. Shouldn't Stringer, the executive, be held responsible for violations of CBS News standards? Crile demanded a meeting, demanded to be heard; he was told to wait. As the weeks wore on, tensions rose and the whole environment had an air of unspoken conflict that seemed to reflect the larger divisions that were racking the institution.

Finally, in July, Benjamin issued his report, and it was fifty-nine pages of bad news. Benjamin found eleven major flaws in *The Uncounted Enemy,* including Crile's "coddling sympathetic witnesses," his choosing to interview mostly people who supported the program's overall conclusions, and the broadcast's failure to prove that there had been a conspiracy, as alleged. Sam Adams, the former CIA intelligence analyst who had brought the story to Crile and had acted as a sort of associate producer on the project, should have been identified to viewers as a paid consultant, Benjamin wrote. The report noted that eight supporters for the broadcast's premise were shown on air, but only one supporter of Westmoreland, and that single supporter, Lieutenant General Daniel Graham, was given only twenty-one seconds on the air ("Graham was not being candid," Crile had told Benjamin; "he was being demonstrably untruthful." Benjamin had replied, "Then maybe Graham was the wrong man to interview on camera"). The report found that Crile had violated CBS News standards when, worried about how one of his key "witnesses" was coming across on camera, he showed him the filmed interviews of others and then interviewed him a second time to get a better take. (At one point the "witness" himself had expressed surprise that Crile was allowed to rehearse the material, asking, "Is it really kosher to go over this?" and Crile had answered, "Oh, this is what we do.")

The Benjamin report was not to be released to the public, of course; but CBS News was obliged to come forth with some version of the results, so Sauter wrote for public release a carefully worded memorandum, the central statement of which was: "CBS News stands by this broadcast." The Sauter memo added, however, that the broadcast would have been better if Crile had sought out more views disagreeing with the broadcast's premise, if Crile hadn't broken CBS News rules in putting it together, and if the documentary hadn't used the term *conspiracy*.

Although the Sauter memo was nowhere near as damaging as a full release of the Benjamin report would have been, it was pretty strong stuff to declare that a CBS News producer had violated the organization's own standards and that in a documentary alleging a conspiracy at the highest levels of government conspiracy was never proved. It was a blow to the single most valuable asset of the news organization, its credibility; on the other hand, CBS was generally praised by the press for its forthrightness in investigating itself, and if that had been all there was to the Westmoreland matter, CBS News would have gotten off cheaply enough.

Of course, that wasn't all there was to the Westmoreland matter. In September Westmoreland filed a $120 million libel suit against CBS. The general had come by the services of a lawyer named Dan M. Burt, the mention of whose name raised hairs on the necks of CBS News executives long after the case. Burt was a clever, crude, self-proclaimed millionaire lawyer, up from the streets of Philadelphia, who brought to the case a particular edge. Burt claimed that Westmoreland represented to him a personal cause, a symbolic struggle of the little guy versus privilege and power.

The Uncounted Enemy had been a public relations nightmare for CBS News so far, but the really scary part didn't begin until Dan Burt entered the picture. In the long pretrial period, lasting nearly two years, CBS News became the Beirut of journalism, each new day bearing the possibility of a bombshell. Burt deftly worked the press, leaking damaging tidbits here and there, apparently hoping to make a settlement seem more attractive to CBS than the prospect of a public relations war that it couldn't win. When Judge Pierre Leval ruled that CBS would have to turn over the Benjamin report to Westmoreland, Burt had a field day. The flaws of the broadcast got a new round of treatment in the press.

CBS hired as its counsel the Wall Street firm of Cravath, Swaine & Moore, and the lead lawyer on the case was a bright, refined young man named David Boies, Burt's opposite in manner and personality. It had become abundantly clear that Sauter's decision to order an in-house investigation of the documentary had a considerable downside potential: CBS News was now in the position of defending in court a broadcast that its own inquiry had found to be riddled with flaws. Boies decided that CBS would pursue the "truth" defense—that is, the network would claim that Westmoreland wasn't libeled because the documentary was true—and he advised that the forsaken George Crile be allowed to defend himself. So Sauter went into the resurrection business. He allowed the articulate and forceful Crile relatively free rein to answer the Benjamin report, and Crile did, vociferously. Suddenly it was Bud Benjamin who was in quasi-official bad odor at CBS News. CBS News assigned Crile a new documentary on Nicaragua (under the strict supervision of Perry Wolff) as a sort of statement of belief in the beleaguered producer.

But the bombshells continued to explode. While the Nicaragua documentary was in production, some members of the crew raised questions about Crile's conduct, suggesting that he was tilting the broadcast to make his point. It was the last thing CBS News needed from George Crile. But it was not the last thing that CBS News got. It was then revealed (after dogged digging by Dan Burt) that in preparing the Westmoreland documentary, Crile had surreptitiously tape-recorded telephone conversations he had had with several people, including former Secretary of Defense Robert S. McNamara, former Undersecretary of State George Ball, and the former U.S. ambassador to the United Nations, Arthur Goldberg. The Nicaragua documentary was shelved, and George Crile was suspended from all editorial responsibilities.

Dan Burt made hay of that, of course, and it became apparent to Van Sauter that, as Sauter later put it, "Burt was going to eat us alive." So CBS News did something it had never done before: It hired an outside public relations expert to help save the public image of CBS News. Sauter enlisted the services of John Scanlon, who was ideally suited to the task. A glib, smart operator with extremely good media connections, Scanlon worked brilliantly with Crile. On one occasion, when Burt and Westmoreland scheduled a press conference in a Washington hotel, CBS scheduled a counter press conference in the same hotel, with George Crile as featured speaker, to knock down everything that had just been said.

But Scanlon's masterpiece was the killing of a book. Don

Kowet, one of the coauthors of the *TV Guide* article, had early
sensed that the Westmoreland controversy would make a dramatic and juicy book. That precise thought occurred to several
people at CBS, of course, and Kowet's book (few had any doubt
where Kowet would stand on the matter) became the object of
pronounced anxiety at the network. The book was due out just
before the trial was scheduled to begin, and Sauter knew that the
trial would be a media circus. He also believed that a good
portion of the scores of reporters assigned to cover the trial
would not necessarily be expert on the minutiae of intelligence
gathering during the Vietnam War. He feared that Kowet's book
would become a handy primer for the journalists and therefore
set an unfavorable tone in the coverage of the trial.

The Macmillan Publishing Company thought it had a hot
seller on its hands with Kowet's book, *A Matter of Honor,* and
arranged a splashy publicity tour, booking Kowet on radio and
television talk shows around the country. Soon after the tour
started, the program directors of these talk shows began to
receive calls inquiring whether they would be interested in hearing the "other side" of the Westmoreland controversy—the
CBS side—and to present the case, wouldn't they like to book
George Crile, the controversial producer of the disputed broadcast? It was an irresistible offer, the prospect of heated debate
on camera, so George Crile hit the publicity trail, following Don
Kowet on his promotion tour and generally making misery of
Kowet's life. It was an uneven match. Kowet was not, in CBS
parlance, a "broadcaster," and George Crile was. "The decison
was that if this guy [Kowet] went out on the road, we'd go out
on the road," Sauter recalled. "To the best of our ability, we'd
either get these two guys on a broadcast together, or Crile would
follow Kowet. And Kowet's book could not withstand Crile. I
mean, Crile ate Kowet and that book alive."

Crile's shadow tour was not the only stratagem. Scanlon asked
each individual who had a dispute with Kowet's book, a mis-
stated fact here, an incorrectly recounted conversation there, to
write a letter to Macmillan protesting the misrepresentation.
The letter-writing campaign involved not only CBS News people but others outside CBS who had grievances with their por-
trayals. Copies of the letters, naturally, were channeled to
reporters covering the Westmoreland story. It was unpleasant
business, a news organization campaigning to squelch a book,
but it was effective.

After four or five encounters with Crile, Kowet ended his promotion tour. Crile later neatly summed up the effect of the CBS campaign: "We killed the Kowet book."

But Kowet was to get his revenge, with an ill-advised action that indeed hurt George Crile but also brought the scorn of the journalistic community down upon his own head. Understandably angered by the CBS offensive, Kowet struck back by voluntarily complying with a subpoena from Burt for the tape recordings of thirty-seven conversations Kowet had had with CBS News officials. Among the tapes was a conversation with Howard Stringer, whom Kowet had interviewed over the telephone as Stringer was sitting in the *Evening News* fishbowl one afternoon preparing the evening's broadcast. "As you may have gathered," Stringer had told Kowet, "we have our own suspicions about George Crile anyway." Stringer, who had been the executive producer of the disputed broadcast, went on to say that if Kowet was right about Crile, "It does devolve on me because I should have known I wouldn't get fair journalism off him."

It was devastating stuff, which Burt proceeded to leak to the *Los Angeles Times* and ABC News, and it did real damage to all parties. Crile was brought into further disrepute; Stringer, who told the *L.A. Times* that he made the statements about Crile because he was "angry and depressed" and that the statements didn't reflect his true feelings, came off as duplicitous; and Kowet was roundly criticized for turning over his recordings of interviews (some of which were off the record). Scanlon did his best. He called Kowet's action "deceitful" and accused him of having been working with Burt for six months. As good as Scanlon was, though, even he couldn't entirely blunt the impact of the incident.

Meanwhile, the trial loomed. CBS had discussed a settlement with Burt early in 1984, offering a statement saying that it acknowledged Westmoreland's "long and faithful service to his country and never intended to assert, and does not believe," that he "was unpatriotic or disloyal in performing his duties as he saw them." There had been other settlement discussions, too, and at one point CBS even discussed money to help defray Westmoreland's legal costs. But no agreement was reached, and on October 9, 1984, *Westmoreland* v. *CBS et al.* went to trial in a New York federal court. It was, as Sauter had predicted, a media circus of the first order, and it was rough on both sides. It was rougher, however, on Westmoreland, who sat and watched his fellow military officers, the men who had been Crile's witnesses in the documentary, testify against him. After eighteen weeks Westmoreland and CBS reached an agreement: no money and virtually the same statement that Westmoreland could have had a year earlier. CBS celebrated with champagne at the Park Avenue nightclub Régine's; Ed Joyce wrote for distribution a memorandum praising the efforts of Bud Benjamin.

So it was over, but the war with Westmoreland had taken its toll. For nearly three years the institution had sustained a steady barrage of attacks on its credibility and integrity, and although the case was dropped, the findings of the Benjamin report, the charges of *TV Guide*, Westmoreland's accusations of foul play were indelible. The network celebrated the settlement as a victory, but it had its cost in the serious risk of the loss in public confidence.

"We won the case," CBS Chairman Tom Wyman later said, "but we came out of that case with a somewhat damaged image—and all the research we did proved it."

The Westmoreland affair had its personal cost, too. The assault was hard on Crile, of course, but it was particularly difficult for Howard Stringer. Everyone, including Stringer, knew full well that as executive producer of *CBS Reports,* he bore some responsibility for *The Uncounted Enemy.* He also was anxious about the possible effect of the whole matter on his career. He was a success as producer of the *Evening News,* but he had not exactly showcased his leadership qualities in his supervision of the Westmoreland documentary or in the subsequent phone conversation with Kowet in which he admitted having suspicions about George Crile. He worried about that disclosure, fearing he had hurt the company as well as his own career.

The Westmoreland ordeal also took its toll on Mike Wallace. The seemingly indefatigable Wallace was, in fact, consistently in a state of near exhaustion. As the lead correspondent of *60 Minutes,* he was constantly on the road, back and forth from New York to the scene of whatever story he was working on. Usually he had two or three stories going at once, editing one, shooting another, planning yet another. There were also appearances on the increasingly rare but nonetheless demanding special broadcasts, such as *The Uncounted Enemy.* And Wallace was under the strain of a recent separation from his wife. On top of everything, he was a defendant in the Westmoreland suit. The case took a lot out of Wallace, with its long deposition process and the ceaseless attacks by Burt in the press, and as the trial progressed and Wallace's turn to take the witness stand drew nearer, the veteran correspondent became increasingly tense. The famed inquisitor did not look forward to being on the other side of a public grilling.

On a Saturday night in late December Wallace returned to New York weary from a long trip home from assignment in Ethiopia. He went out to dinner with his friend Mary Yates (whom he later married), then returned to his apartment. Sometime later that evening Wallace fell unconscious. Yates found him and quickly summoned Wallace's family doctor of eighteen years, Francis Claps, who put Wallace into an ambulance and had him transported to Lenox Hill Hospital, a few blocks away at Park Avenue and Seventy-seventh Street. The usual Saturday night crisis and chaos prevailed, but Wallace was admitted to the hospital and treated by Dr. Claps. Don Hewitt, Wallace's executive producer at 60 Minutes, learned that his star had collapsed, and there followed a flurry of apprehensive telephone calls among the CBS brass. By this time it was Sunday morning, and Wallace was listed by the hospital as being in stable condition. George Schweitzer, vice-president of communications for CBS, told reporters that Wallace, strained from work and the Westmoreland trial, was suffering from exhaustion.

Twelve days later Wallace was released from Lenox Hill, saying to reporters, "They looked at every part of me and everything is fine." But everything was not fine. A few days later CBS received an anonymous call from someone who said that he knew the real reason why Mike Wallace had collapsed and had been admitted to Lenox Hill: The CBS News star, he said, had taken a drug overdose. What's more, the caller claimed to have proof: a copy of Wallace's medical record. The caller said he wanted to talk about his future in television, or he might have to take his story to the New York Post. Both Wallace and Claps strenuously denied the caller's allegation.

A few days later CBS obtained a copy of the medical report, which contained just what the caller said it did. The small circle of CBS executives who knew about the incident was absolutely fear-struck. They envisioned the headline: 60 MINUTES STAR TAKES OVERDOSE. They imagined what Dan Burt and his team of lawyers would do with Wallace on the witness stand. "They'd

have said, 'Mr. Wallace, isn't it true you tried to kill yourself?' "
said one CBS executive. "That was a frightening prospect."

Not that anyone believed that Wallace *had* tried to kill himself.
He wasn't the type. He was tired, under stress, and sixty-six
years old. Perhaps there had been a mistake, or someone had
stolen Wallace's medical records and altered them. In any event,
a damaging document existed, and something had to be done.
Going to the police was ruled out; too great a chance of a leak.
It was decided that David Fuchs, an aide to Jankowski, would
meet with the caller to get a better sense of the situation.

Handling sticky situations was a David Fuchs specialty, although he was not, on the surface, the fixer type. He was known
around CBS as the "Jesuit," a deep-thinking, somewhat taciturn
CBS lifer who'd come up through the ranks and had served
loyally as a sort of adviser and father confessor first to James
Rosenfield, the head of the CBS network division, and then to
Jankowski. He was, above all, discreet. So it was arranged that
Fuchs would be the contact, and he had several telephone conversations with the caller. There developed a plan to arrange
another meeting and to have Tony Leone, the head of CBS
security, tail the would-be blackmailer and somehow force him
to quit his effort. It was, on one level, the most absurd situation—Van Sauter directing an amateur gumshoe operation;
David Fuchs, a middle-aged TV executive, playing the role of
detective—but it was also a deadly serious business, and the
stakes were high. "It was very dicey," said a CBS executive. "We
really sweated it out." In one of his telephone conversations
the mystery caller told Fuchs that he had some sort of game
show pilot he wanted to discuss. It was terrible, black irony:
CBS, in the middle of a fierce, $120 million war with Westmore-
land, suddenly at the mercy of a frustrated TV producer. Fuchs
assured the man that CBS would not yield to blackmail, and the
proposed setup never came off. Just as mysteriously as he appeared, the caller simply vanished, and neither he nor his copy
of Mike Wallace's medical records was heard from again. It was,
for CBS, a rare and welcome change of luck: for once, a bomb
that didn't go off.

Aside from that break, though, it was beginning to seem like
open season on CBS News. Right in the middle of the Westmoreland ordeal, CBS was drawn into another splashy and difficult lawsuit, a $30 million slander action filed by a California

doctor named Carl A. Galloway who said he'd been wrongly implicated in a 1979 *60 Minutes* exposé of an insurance fraud scheme. The correspondent in that segment, who was also the central figure in the lawsuit, was Dan Rather. The doctor's case carried none of the historical implications of the Westmoreland lawsuit. But it was like Westmoreland in two important aspects; It turned intense public scrutiny on the CBS journalistic process, and it challenged the professional integrity of a major CBS star.

Because the case involved Dan Rather and *60 Minutes,* the proceeding took on the air of a celebrity trial, and the halls of the Los Angeles Superior Court were crowded with reporters and television cameras. The doctor's slander case was not particularly strong; its centerpiece was the contention that he hadn't really signed a phony medical report as Rather had claimed on the broadcast (it was an apparent forgery), but he was shown to have ties with a medical center that was involved in insurance fraud. What made the trial compelling was its minute, very public examination of the *process* of television journalism, which, it turned out, was very much like sausage: Once you've seen how it's made, you'll never think of the finished product in quite the same way again. Galloway's attorney won access from the court to the segment outtakes—that is, all the film footage that was shot but edited out of the piece. What viewers had seen in the finished broadcast was a slick, hard-hitting exposé of fraud, conducted by an authoritative Dan Rather, who had all the loose ends of the case tied up. What the public saw in the outtakes, however, was something rather less pat.

The *60 Minutes* team was seen badgering one interview subject, while being sweetly polite to another. At one point Rather taunted one unwilling interview subject, hollering as the man scurried away, "Adios! See you on television!" The CBS team was shown repeating questions over and over for certain interview subjects, a process commonly used in television to achieve visual variation, but Galloway's attorney represented the process as staging, which put CBS in the position of defending and explaining the nuances of electronic journalism. The courtroom reconstruction of the segment revealed to the public the real nature of the correspondent's role in much of television journalism: While it appeared on television that the star correspondent was wholly in charge of the story, the bulk of the reporting was done by one of Rather's codefendants in the case, the unseen producer, Steve Glauber.

CBS was not very smooth in its public relations effort for the case, Sauter attacking the press coverage (an awkward position at best for a news-gathering organization) and Glauber, the producer, stalking the hallways of the courtroom, collaring reporters and telling them, in subtle fashion, how their coverage of the trial ought to be handled.

But the touchiest portion of the trial, and the most sensational, was Dan Rather on the witness stand. Rather, who anchored the *Evening News* from Los Angeles, had never before been called to testify in his own defense in a lawsuit, and it made for an arresting scene. For three days the anchorman of the most-watched newscast in America, the man who appeared in millions of homes each night seeming to be in complete control, was publicly grilled in a most adversarial circumstance. Of course, television loved the spectacle, and the trial of Dan Rather became a hot TV ticket. All three network newscasts ran pieces, and the cable news channels had a field day. The Cable News Network (CNN), which reached 20 million viewers, had cameras set up in the courtroom for live coverage of Rather's testimony. The Satellite News Channel, with 6 million viewers, carried 175 reports on the trial over a period of six days. ABC's *Nightline* broadcast did two reports on the trial, and the show-business news program *Entertainment Tonight* featured a report every night. Sauter fumed over the coverage, complaining that it was "sporadic" and misrepresented the CBS side of the case. But Ed Turner, a senior vice-president of CNN, responded that his news network's audience was interested in the news-gathering process, and besides, there was "a show-biz angle to the news business, and Mr. Rather's appearance was part of that." (CNN's ratings were up by 20 percent during the trial.)

Rather, now before the camera as a newsmaker rather than an anchor, appeared tight and edgy on the witness stand. Sally Bedell Smith wrote in the *New York Times* that "without flattering lights and stage makeup, he appeared haggard. Away from the anchor desk where he is in constant control, Mr. Rather struggled at times to maintain composure. Much of the time he was confident, articulate and polite. But at other moments Mr. Rather was taut and evasive."

Fortunately for CBS the jury was deciding whether or not there had been a slander rather than judging journalistic technique, and it returned a verdict for CBS. But it was, as the Westmoreland settlement would be, a mixed triumph. Putting the journalism of America's preeminent broadcast news organization before the harshest sort of public scrutiny was becoming part of the national routine. Inside CBS there were fears (and reasonable ones) that the CBS News mystique was falling away, and the organization could only hope that the public's trust was not falling with it.

In December 1984, three men in North Carolina formed a group called Fairness in Media, and in early 1985 they filed papers with the Securities and Exchange Commission (SEC) declaring a drive to purchase enough stock in the company to enable the group to exert an influence upon CBS. Thus began a new round of assaults, an onslaught that was to challenge the independence of the company itself and ultimately to pave the way for change in the control of CBS. It began, fittingly enough, with a controversy over CBS News.

Fairness in Media was organized in part by the archconservative Republican senator from North Carolina Jesse Helms, who sent letters to conservatives around the country urging them to buy stock in CBS. Once the group had gathered enough new shareholders, it would request a meeting with CBS officers to discuss an end to what Fairness in Media believed to be a "liberal bias in news reporting and editorial policies." If CBS dismissed its proposals, Fairness in Media would fight to take control of the company. The group's purpose was most forcefully stated in a simple proposition put forth by Senator Helms in a letter addressing one million American conservatives: Buy CBS stock, he said, and "become Dan Rather's boss."

By February, just as CBS was ending its long, tortured conflict with General Westmoreland, Fairness in Media confirmed that it was considering a proxy fight in order to win seats on the thirteen-member CBS board of directors.

The idea of an ideologically motivated takeover of a major network was not only ominous but absurd. The idea of CBS News as an organ of the left was a caricature of the grossest sort. To be sure, the memory of Rather's sparrings with Richard Nixon lingered indelibly, but that long-running conflict was far less a product of ideology than of personality—both Nixon's and

Rather's. By the 1980s, when conservative chic was in full flower, CBS News was about as left-wing as the Cedar Falls chapter of the American Legion. Rather was, as the conservative *New York Times* columnist William Safire called him, a red-blooded Texas centrist and something of a sentimental patriot. Whether by instruction or by his own instinct, he became even more so during and after the Jesse Helms controversy. In fact, his on-air displays of sentimentality horrified many of his *Evening News* colleagues. After one holiday broadcast he signed off by giving his fellow Americans a hearty salute; while covering the return of the body of an American soldier killed in a terrorist attack, his voice choked and his eyes filled with tears. Anyone who seriously thought that CBS News was excessively liberal in the era of Van Sauter and Dan Rather was not watching television. In fact, the network devised a new flag-waving promotion for the broadcast that vowed to keep "America on top of the world."

But CBS had to take the Helms challenge seriously. Not only was it yet another assault on the integrity of CBS News—why didn't these things happen to ABC and NBC?—but the independence of the company itself was now at stake. Wyman and his management team responded aggressively to the attack, answering Fairness in Media's intentions to wage a proxy fight by filing a lawsuit in federal court to block the group, declaring that the action was essentially political fund-raising and that Fairness in Media had lied to the Securities and Exchange Commission. Two weeks later CBS released to Helms's group a list of CBS stockholders, on the condition that it would not be used for political fund-raising. But Fairness in Media was not able to attract the support it had hoped for, and by the end of March the effort had folded. The group dropped its plans for a proxy fight, saying it hadn't had enough time to organize.

Fairness in Media had dealt CBS a serious blow, however, albeit inadvertently, by putting CBS "into play." On a Wall Street frenzied with mergers and takeovers, CBS seemed to be mentioned in nearly every breath. It was revealed that the arbitrageur Ivan F. Boesky had accumulated 8.7 percent of CBS stock. In April, Wall Street rumors held that the General Electric Company had talked to CBS about a friendly merger; CBS denied the reports (but GE was in the market for a network and eventually bought NBC). In May the Gannett Company, the giant media conglomerate that published *USA Today,* denied rumors that it was involved in an attempted takeover of CBS.

In the swirl of rumors that spring one proved to be abundantly well founded. In March Wall Street investment bankers began to hear that Ted Turner, the Atlanta cable and broadcasting entrepreneur, was organizing his own CBS takeover. It was not the first encounter between CBS and the gentleman from Georgia. In 1981 CBS had been worried enough about the threat from cable TV to dispatch Bill Leonard, who was nearing retirement, and Gene Jankowski down to Atlanta to discuss the possible purchase of CNN by CBS. Turner asked how much of his company CBS wanted to buy, and Jankowski told him that his company wanted controlling interest. Turner refused, and the meeting ended. Bill Leonard later recalled in his memoir that Turner got off a parting shot: "Someday I'm going to own you, you bet I am. Remember I told you so."

In March 1985 Turner came forward with his offer: He would buy CBS with $5.4 billion in stock and debt securities—and no cash. It was a bold and outlandish move, and Tom Wyman promptly declared that Turner's "junk bond" offer had "no financial substance." Still, CBS fought like a fury to defeat Turner, taking steps that some analysts later characterized as foolishly excessive. Turner was "bizarre," Wyman later said. "But you couldn't quite laugh off Robin Hood saying he wanted to buy you."

In July CBS announced a major recapitalization plan, buying back 21 percent of its stock and, in the process, taking on a debt of nearly $1 billion. CBS would foil Turner by burdening itself with such a heavy debt that it would be too expensive for him to take over the company.

The defense ultimately worked, and Ted Turner redirected his attention to the MGM studio, which he eventually purchased. But CBS had defeated Turner at a huge cost; it had gone deeply into debt at a time when its earnings were falling because of a soft advertising marketplace in broadcasting and difficulties in CBS's nonbroadcasting businesses. The circumstance would force CBS to sell one of its five television stations—KMOX in St. Louis, which CBS had owned for thirty years—just when the rest of the industry was buying television stations. And the financial pressures were to have grave implications for hundreds of CBS employees as the company began a major cost-cutting drive.

The spring and summer of 1985 were a dark time for CBS. As the company ricocheted from one crisis to the next, its stock price bouncing and its morale plummeting, there appeared on the scene someone who was in a different league entirely from the Boeskys and Turners and Helmses, someone who was beyond the reach of the defensive strategies of Tom Wyman's management team. To Laurence A. Tisch, billionaire investor, CBS was beginning to seem a most interesting prospect.

In the middle of all this, Van Sauter left CBS News to go to Black Rock. It seemed a good idea at the time.

By the fall of 1983 Sauter had been at CBS News for two years, which was nearing his standard tour of duty in his uniquely varied CBS career. It had always seemed to Sauter's detractors at CBS News that he harbored grandiose ambitions, that he had eyes beyond CBS News; and that spoke for itself. Ambition was sanctioned by the dogma of CBS News, but only normal, healthy ambition—which is to say, ambition to reach the top at CBS News. What else could a broadcast journalist possibly desire? "You either wanted to be the president of CBS News, or you wanted to be the anchorman," said Bob Schieffer. "Those were the things that were the pinnacle of your career; those were the things that everybody wanted to be. I don't know of anybody at CBS News until that time who ever aspired for Black Rock. It's just something that wasn't thought about. It would be like me thinking I'm going to join the circus. It just wasn't something you thought about." What people accused Sauter of was something close to heresy, an ambition for power and position beyond CBS News.

They were right. Sauter did have ambitions beyond CBS News, or more precisely, he had interests in areas of the company beyond news that were fortified by a resolute belief in his own ability to master them. In Sauter's view, he had already mastered CBS News, and he didn't feel particularly bound to the institution, in the way that the priesthood expected; he was, on the whole, rather cynical about CBS News and the people in it. He believed himself to be, and probably was, as capable a journalist as anyone in the place, but he'd done journalism; he was put off by the ceaseless talk of the "sacred trust," which he found irrelevant and, in the face of harsh new competition, dangerously self-deluding. Sauter and Ed Joyce often observed to each other that the people of CBS News were not easy to like, and Sauter took a special delight in those occasions when they'd succeeded in pushing the institution beyond the old bounds, sometimes chortling, "Uh-oh, the flame flickered on that one." The destiny he had in mind was not to be guardian of the flame of Edward R. Murrow.

When Sauter assessed the talents of Gene Jankowski and the heads of the other network divisions, he felt all the more certain of his potential. So, when the network faced a thorny problem, the sales shortfall, for example, Sauter was not hesitant to offer his advice, and he did so voluminously. He dashed out memos by the score, little missives on yellow paper, which came to be known as "Van-grams." "Van wrote memos about everything," said Gene Mater, the former Jankowski aide who became a senior vice-president of news under Sauter. "He was very outspoken. You can wonder whether it was done honestly or otherwise, but I think they were done honestly. Others would look at it and say he was running for something. And maybe he was, I don't know."

What motivated Sauter didn't seem to be strictly ambition, but some trait of personality that was intolerant of constancy. Sauter had a remarkably low boredom threshold, which was sometimes maddening to his friends and colleagues. Outings on group road excursions would last until just the moment Sauter got bored, which was always long before anyone else did. "Believe me," recalled Lane Venardos, "when Van's attention span snapped, the whole group careened back into place." After the European bureau chiefs' meeting in 1985 in Berlin, Sauter's traveling coterie took a tour of East Berlin, and someone suggested that they visit a famed German museum. "And we're in there maybe twenty-five minutes or so and Van gets tired of it," Venardos recollected. "So it's time to leave. It may have been fifteen or twenty minutes. Just as you're sort of thinking, 'Well, maybe we ought to go see all of those things over there,' it's 'Back to the bus!' "

So it was with Sauter's career, too, in newspapering and then in broadcasting; it was always two years on a job and then back to the bus. Once, after he'd risen to a place of high rank at CBS, Sauter was asked by his old friend John Callaway to come back to Chicago to speak to the participants in a fellowship program that Callaway was directing. One of the fellows, noting that

Callaway had turned down an offer from Sauter to join CBS News, asked Sauter why it was that he was always moving on to a new job. "And he said, 'Callaway knows when to quit; I've always been like the kid who followed the string around the corner,' " Callaway recalled. "If he's a power-mad guy, that's his rationalization. But he said it with a certain air of resignation, not proudly, in a moment of reflection, almost despair. It was like 'I can't fucking stop.' "

Whatever it was, pure ambition or a quirk of character, it fit perfectly into Gene Jankowski's plans. As president of the CBS Broadcast Group, Jankowski had a significant empire inside the company, with all the broadcasting divisions—news, entertainment, the radio and television networks, sports, sales, and the CBS-owned radio and television stations—reporting to him. The Broadcast Group was the original business of CBS, broken off into a separate operating group in 1966, after CBS had swelled into a widely diversified company with such concerns as publishing, records, toys, and, for a time, the New York Yankees. Jankowski succeeded Jack Schneider in 1977. But ever since 1982, when Tom Wyman managed to get William Paley finally to move aside, Jankowski had hoped, associates said, to be named president of the parent company, CBS Inc. It seemed to him the obvious course—Wyman as chairman plotting the big picture, complemented by Jankowski, the broadcaster, with a lifetime's experience in the company's core business. Wyman, however, did not think it the obvious course at all. Wyman, the golden boy from Andover and Amherst, the superstar manager who was paid $1 million to come to CBS, was accustomed to winning. "Tom was the one who always got the girl," said one former colleague. On the tennis court Wyman was a ferocious "in-your-face" competitor, who played the net and always took the offensive. At CBS he was the one who finally succeeded in edging the tenacious Paley out of the picture, and he wasn't inclined to share the spoils; he kept the titles of both president and chairman for himself.

Still, Jankowski nourished his dream and, those around him said, he believed that someday Wyman would see that he needed a president to help him run the still-growing company. Apparently to prepare for that day, and perhaps to hasten it, Jankowski began to put into place a line of succession for himself. He devised a plan to restructure the Broadcast Group, expanding the number of executive vice-presidents reporting to him from two to four; the presidents of each of the various broadcast divisions—news, entertainment, stations, and the rest—would report directly to this new management layer, which, in turn, would report to Jankowski. He explained to Wyman that he needed to create these jobs in order to keep the interest of the bright young executives he intended to promote.

A key role in this new structure at the CBS Broadcast Group was designed for the man who was gaining a reputation as the most creative television executive at the network, Jankowski's "turnaround" artist, Van Gordon Sauter. In the summer of 1983 Jankowski proposed to Sauter that he move up to Black Rock to fill one of the new executive vice-president positions Jankowski would create. Sauter would be responsible for the news division (a new president of CBS News would report to him), but he would also have the sales and affiliate relations units reporting to him. Sauter was delighted with the prospect: Sales and affiliate relations were key segments of the television network, they both were new areas to Sauter (and therefore likely to hold his interest for a time), and it was a chance to broaden his experience for whatever came next—possibly even Jankowski's job as head of the Broadcast Group.

But the proposed structure meant a considerable loss of power to James H. Rosenfield, who had been the executive vice-president of the Broadcast Group and who had considered himself the top contender for Jankowski's job. Rosenfield, like Jankowski a former network salesman, had been clearly cast as Jankowski's number two, in charge of entertainment, sports, sales, and affiliate relations. Rosenfield later recalled that he was so outraged by Jankowski's proposal that he walked into the senior executive's office and threatened to sue him for breach of contract. He argued, among other things, that Jankowski's proposed realignment represented the worst sort of threat to the integrity of CBS News. An executive in charge of both sales and news would be as beholden to the network's clients—advertisers—as to that corner of the company most likely to cause those clients grief, the news division. "News is encapsulated as a separate entity not influenced by sales or business or any other extraneous influence," Rosenfield later explained.

"The whole concept of big business having an influence over what gets on news—it's mind-boggling."

Sauter didn't buy Rosenfield's position; but Jankowski was swayed, and he devised another structure. Sales and affiliate relations would remain together, under the authority of Thomas F. Leahy, an executive vice-president who was also given responsibility for the CBS Entertainment division, the part of the network that developed and scheduled programs (another province formerly Rosenfield's). Rosenfield was appointed senior executive vice-president in charge of finance, operations, and development, a lofty title that did not obscure his comedown (but he had won his point about news and sales). Neal Pilson, who'd been president of CBS Sports since Sauter left that job for news, was given responsibility for the sports and radio divisions. Sauter would supervise the news division and the CBS-owned television stations.

Sauter was not at all pleased with the new configuration. He was currently president of CBS News, and he had already run or helped to run two network-owned stations, WBBM and KNXT. He saw nothing new in the Jankowski plan for him, and he told his boss that he'd rather just remain president of CBS News. But Jankowski persisted, Sauter relented, and on September 16, 1983, the CBS Broadcast Group announced its realignment. To the surprise of no one, Sauter's friend and closest colleague Ed Joyce was appointed the new president of CBS News.

It was apparently lost on Jankowski that in adding another management layer between CBS News and the top of the company, he risked the ire of the most temperamental and outspoken division of the company. CBS News had never been just another operating division of the company, but the favored child, with special access to the top. The news division presidents, and many of the key players in news as well, were accustomed to reporting directly to Frank Stanton and William Paley and, later, to Jack Schneider and Gene Jankowski. That access was a dear issue at CBS News, and not just for reasons of ego: It underscored the news division's essential exemption from the cold profit-and-loss imperatives of the commercial environment. The CBS Broadcast Group had been created, and Jack Schneider named its president, in January 1966. By February that new layer had cost CBS News one president: Fred Friendly, who quit in a fit of pique when Schneider refused to interrupt the regular daytime schedule to allow CBS News to provide live coverage of the Senate Vietnam hearings. But what really galled Friendly, what set the stage for his inflamed exit, was the fact that he had to take orders from Schneider at all. Now Jankowski was creating a structure that would put a layer of management between news and the Broadcast Group, which was itself a layer beneath the president-chairman of the company. On the flow charts CBS News would now be on a par with any other operating division of CBS Inc.

The dangers of that arrangement were not lost on Ed Joyce and Van Sauter. They shared their doubts about it, but in the end they were convinced they could make a go of it. After all, they were not just any two network executives. They were soul mates, best friends, believers in a shared vision. They thought they could make it work. Just how wrong they were soon became strikingly plain.

Chapter

IN THE SPRING OF 1987, long after the cataclysms had ended, Tom Wyman sat in an office on Fifth Avenue, removed from CBS but not yet quite separated, picking through the ashes of his ruined incumbency. He considered CBS News. "The critical mistake," he said, "was the day that Sauter got in the car and drove over to Black Rock." In retrospect it seemed clear: The Sauter revolution at CBS News had been doomed from the moment Ed Joyce took rein.

Perhaps it should have been foreseen. But it wasn't, and in the fall of 1983 Ed Joyce became president of CBS News. No job could have pleased him more, and no circumstance could have been more charged with catastrophic possibility. Joyce became president of CBS News just in time for the worst of the outside assaults: the Westmoreland trial, the Jesse Helms attack, the takeover attempts, and drastic company-wide retrenchments prompted by the fight against Ted Turner. He was also met by a new round of internal upheavals, unprecedented in their ferocity even for CBS News, an institution prone to revolts and rebellions. The combination of these forces, inside and out, were to devour Ed Joyce within two years.

The odds were all against him from the beginning. He was president of CBS News, but his boss and best friend, Sauter, was cast in the role of "superpresident," with power over the news division and nothing much else to do but to exercise it—or seem to. In the first several weeks of Joyce's presidency, in fact, Sauter still maintained an office at the Broadcast Center, and that more or less set the tone. Who was really president of CBS News? "I don't know where Sauter ends and Joyce begins," correspondent Morley Safer said at the time, and he spoke for most at CBS News.

There was for the first time in the organization a real ambiguity in the lines of authority. At the Republican National Convention in 1984, for example, there was some dispute about whether CBS News would stay on the air past 11:00 P.M. in the East to cover the renomination of George Bush as the Republican vice-presidential candidate. For the CBS-affiliated stations in the East, the network coverage would cut into local news broadcasts and would mean losing local advertising revenues. But Dan Rather and his news organization were in Dallas to cover the convention; if they weren't going to stay on the air for Bush's renomination, what were they there for? Rather argued the case to Joyce, who agreed. But no one really knew what Joyce's decision was worth. Would Joyce, speaking for news, have the final say? Or would it be Sauter, who was responsible not only for news but for the CBS owned stations, some of which stood to lose money if CBS News stayed on the air? "If Ed had had the same brief as Dick Salant," Rather recalled, "he'd have said this or that and everyone would have known what the decision was. But in this configuration it was unclear." In the end CBS News stayed on the air. "But it wasn't clear to me, I don't think it was clear to others, it might not have been clear to Ed himself, whether that was his decision or whether that had to go to higher authority," Rather said. "I didn't know then; I don't know now."

It was not the soundest grounding for someone trying to take charge of a volatile organization, and Joyce's precarious situation was only worsened by his own personality and management style. Joyce was a bright, articulate man, and although he didn't have a college degree, he was extremely well read and more than held his intellectual ground with most in the organization. But he was also exceedingly aloof, Sauter's opposite in personal approach. Where Sauter roamed the halls, pressing the flesh and dispensing breezy salutations ("Hi, big fella!"), Joyce kept to his office much of the time, often with the door shut. "He couldn't get along with people; he didn't know how to get along with people," said Bob Chandler, vice-president of administration for Sauter and Joyce. "He was shy, afraid, or, in compensation, he'd go the other way and suddenly get very tough, needlessly so, abrasively so."

Many managers succeed without winning personalities, and CBS News had certainly had its share of examples over the years; but Joyce's "people problem," as his staff called it, was a particularly unfortunate shortcoming, considering the baggage he brought to the job. Not only had he coauthored the new age at CBS News, but he had served as Sauter's hatchet man, the designated bearer of bad news, and the resentments still simmered. To the degree that Sauter had succeeded at CBS News, it was in no small part due to his ability to avoid open insurrection, by force of personality and by his well-advertised alliance with Dan Rather. Joyce had neither asset. That was part of the reason why Sauter decided fairly early in Joyce's tenure that Joyce needed help, and Howard Stringer, the executive producer of Rather's *Evening News,* was chosen to be Joyce's executive vice-president.

Stringer resisted the promotion at first and later told colleagues that he took the job partly because he feared that if he didn't, Rather's closest confrere, David Buksbaum, would get the job—the anchorman had enough power as it was. Stringer, who'd spent his life at CBS News and was naturally given to the role of mediator, was to become a sort of liaison between Joyce and the people of CBS News. In fact, Stringer did do a good deal of mediating in his time as Joyce's assistant, which was part of the reason why his elevation to management at just that time proved to be such a huge mistake. Not only did it remove Stringer from the *Evening News* before either he or the broadcast was ready, but it made him a partner in a bitterly despised management and cost him a good deal of capital among the ranks.

More immediately, the move triggered the first real internal controversy of Joyce's tenure, a helter-skelter realignment of the power structure at CBS News that again brought Walter Cronkite's old friend and producer Sandy Socolow into the spotlight.

Stringer's ascension to management left the *Evening News* without an executive producer, although it seemed likely to most in the organization that the job would go to the senior producer, Mark Harrington. Harrington had been the nuts-and-bolts man on Stringer's *Evening News,* the producer who made the hard decisions under deadline pressure. Stringer crafted the new *Evening News,* giving it his visual and philosophical touch, but he wasn't a daily news producer; it was Harrington who got the broadcast on the air each night. The Harvard-educated Harrington also brought a strong journalistic instinct to the table and was perhaps the most cerebral journalist within the *Evening News* circle.

But Sauter and Joyce had reservations about Harrington. He was talented, true, but he was perceived, as one in the Sauter circle put it, as being "intellectually aloof," presumably meaning he wasn't as enthusiastic a disciple of moments television as he might have been. He had a supreme confidence in his own editorial instincts, which tended to be old-line; in those intense postmortems, for example, when Sauter would ask, "Why did we do *that* piece?" it was often Harrington who replied, "Because it's a news story." What clinched it was that Rather wasn't especially comfortable with Harrington. It was therefore decided that Sauter's old traveling buddy Lane Venardos would become the next executive producer of the *Evening News*—a move that surprised everyone, not least Venardos himself. Venardos was a capable producer, but not quite as strong or experienced as Harrington.

Meanwhile, there remained the matter of Rather's friend and unflinching supporter David Buksbaum. "Buks," as he was called, was a gruff, somewhat coarse individual, a solid journalist who, in the days when CBS News was divided into Rather and Mudd camps, aligned himself squarely behind the ultimate winner. He was extremely loyal to Rather, and Rather, who was excessively concerned with loyalty, was extremely grateful for Buksbaum's fealty. Although Rather did not demand further promotion for Buksbaum (Sauter had put him in charge of news operations in 1981), it was understood that Dan would be happy if Buks were taken care of. And if he was not to be made Joyce's number two or the *Evening News* executive producer (a passing suggestion that caused Sauter to shudder), then what? It was decided that Buksbaum should get the job Gordon Manning, Bill Small, and Ed Fouhy had held, vice-president in charge of news gathering. The job had been somewhat watered down in the Sauter era; it also happened to be occupied at the moment by John Lane. So one day Sauter called Lane over to his office at Black Rock for a friendly talk, during the course of which the subject of London came up. Lane, who had once been the CBS bureau chief in London, mentioned how he loved that city, and the next thing he knew, he'd been dispatched to London to look for a place to live.

There was one hitch: Sandy Socolow was London bureau chief and director of European coverage for CBS News, and he was, all things considered, happy in the job. But Socolow was also a card-carrying member of the old order, perceived by Sauter and Joyce as a seditious government-in-exile, and he was, therefore, eminently expendable. "Sandy was very close to Cronkite," Don Hewitt said, "and they were trying to do away with the Cronkite influence." One night Socolow got a phone call from Ed Joyce, and he was stunned to hear that CBS News had a reassignment in mind for him—Tel Aviv. Tel Aviv was a "hot" bureau, a travel bureau, a place for someone with young legs; it was not an assignment for a former vice-president of news, one of the architects of the Cronkite era. Socolow was so distressed by the news that he emptied the better part of a bottle of scotch and made a few calls to friends, including Cronkite. Socolow was a respected and beloved figure at CBS News, a true symbol of what had distinguished the organization, and word of his reassignment quickly spread and became something of a cause. Socolow refused the assignment and hired a lawyer. He suggested that CBS settle his no-cut contract; in exchange, he would vow silence. Ed Joyce, Socolow later recalled, "went through the goddamned roof." What was Socolow trying to do, skewer Joyce? Didn't he know how Tom Wyman felt about severance pay? Incensed, the president of CBS News stopped speaking to his London bureau chief.

Meanwhile, John Lane visited London (Socolow assuring him there were no hard feelings) and found a place to live on Sloane Street, near the CBS News bureau. But on the plane back to New York, Lane, uncomfortable with the way events were unfolding, decided that he didn't want to accept the assignment. As it happened, when he returned to his office, he found three telephone messages awaiting him from Larry Grossman, the new president of NBC News. "It was a gift from God," Lane recalled. He soon left CBS to become vice-president of NBC News.

That development might have resolved the Socolow situation, but it didn't; Sauter and Joyce now considered the London bureau chief's job vacant, providing a convenient answer to the Mark Harrington question. Harrington accepted the assignment. Socolow, meanwhile, remained out of communication with his bosses; after nine weeks he got a call from Stringer asking him to come to New York. It happened that Don Hewitt, the *60 Minutes* producer, had run into his former CBS colleague Bill Small at a social function, and Small, having heard about the Socolow situation (it was the outrage of the day), suggested that Hewitt had the solution at his fingertips: He could hire Socolow as a *60 Minutes* producer. Hewitt, who enjoyed playing power baron at CBS News, loved the idea, and sold it to Ed Joyce. Socolow flew to New York, met with Joyce and Stringer, and it was done.

Socolow was saved, but the affair left a bitter taste. The attempt to force reassignment upon Socolow was widely seen as an effort to squeeze out of CBS News a respected veteran whose principal sin was a close friendship with Walter Cronkite.

Ed Joyce wasn't exactly building a broad constituency inside the organization, and Stringer, his alter ego, was only moderately successful in oiling the churning waters; after all, Stringer, too, had accumulated his share of detractors, and no amount of Stringer charm was going to sway Walter Cronkite, for instance, from the conviction that CBS News was bound swiftly for hell. Sauter, at least, had had his personal style and the commotion of change to deflect resentment, but Joyce had been cast in a most unlovable role, that of the postrevolutionary bureaucrat. He had to answer not only for his own actions but for those of Sauter as well, and it didn't help that Joyce was increasingly finding himself in disagreement with his closest friend, the "other" president, on matters regarding the news division.

As it happened, their differences came to a head over what turned out to be a hugely significant matter—the *CBS Morning News,* which was becoming a battleground where the new corporate culture and the fading "grand illusion" were colliding head-on.

Whatever combination of genius and luck was required for the creation of a successful morning television program, it had escaped the grasp of CBS executives for thirty years. CBS simply couldn't do morning television. It had tried with Walter Cronkite, teaming him with a puppet lion named Charlemane in 1954; it had tried with Jack Paar, Dick Van Dyke, Will Rogers, Jr., and Mike Wallace; it had tried, over the years, with twenty-five different anchors and nearly as many formats, to compete with NBC's successful mix of entertainment and news, the *Today* show, which went on the air in January 1952 and tormented CBS programmers from that moment on. After a time CBS developed a rationale of sorts about the morning time period and more or less contented itself with a respectable, if low-rated, news and information broadcast that followed *Captain Kangaroo.* Paley, its legendary "audience of one," was satisfied, and because there was only NBC's *Today* show to compete with, the CBS morning news programs in their various incarnations more or less paid their freight.

In the mid-1970s all that changed. ABC invented *Good Morning America,* whose ratings promptly breezed by not only CBS's morning program but *Today,* thus proving that there was an audience (and, therefore, profit) in the morning for the right program. That discovery led to Bill Leonard's attempt to develop a weekday version of *Sunday Morning,* with Diane Sawyer and Charles Kuralt, a program Sauter hated and quickly set about replacing with a new version of the *CBS Morning News* in March 1982.

But the institution was terribly resistant to Sauter's plans for the morning broadcast, so much so that Joyce, then Sauter's deputy, told the program's new producer, George Merlis, that he couldn't have the title of executive producer; he would be called "senior producer," a rank below executive producer. Merlis, who had helped make a hit of *Good Morning America* at ABC, recalled that he was insulted by the suggestion—Shad Northshield, his predecessor on *Morning,* had been a full executive producer—and Merlis demanded to know why he was being asked to settle for less. By CBS logic, the reason was obvious: Merlis had come from ABC, that lesser journalistic light; worse, *Good Morning America* was produced by ABC's *entertainment* division, the quintessence (in the minds of many at CBS News) of all that was craven and base in television. "The problem," Merlis quoted Joyce as saying, "is your journalistic credentials." Merlis was asked to make an appearance before the senior staff of CBS News, in which, as he put it, "I had to show my journalistic spurs." He explained to his "review board" that although he had been in public relations at ABC News for a time, he had a journalism degree from Columbia, he'd been an assistant city editor at the *New York World Journal and Tribune,* he'd written two books and had published articles in the *New Republic, Nation,* and *National Review.* He got his executive producer credit.

Merlis knew that people at CBS News considered themselves journalists who just happened to work in television, but he was surprised to discover firsthand just how indifferent the place was to the cosmetic aspects of the medium. The *Morning News* set was improperly lit, the equipment and facilities were out-dated, and even his star, Diane Sawyer, needed work. She would one day be a cover girl, but on the *Morning News* Diane Sawyer came across as a bit of a frump. Merlis didn't like her makeup, he hated her hair, and she dressed like a member of the Welles-ley debate squad. Merlis hired a makeup artist to redesign the Sawyer look, enlivened the look and pace of the broadcast, and in general brought a distinctly commercial sensibility to his cor-ner of CBS News.

Although Merlis was in charge of more CBS News airtime than any other producer in the organization, he was, as the bearer of change, an outsider at the network, a vantage point that gave him a particularly vivid view of the institution's person-ality. "It's a tough place. . . . Everything's a struggle. Nothing comes easy. . . . It's the most inhumane place to work on the face of the earth. My office was a little cinder-block cell, no windows, fluorescent lights. Everything about the place—narrow corri-dors with junk bins in them all the time, harsh fluorescent light-ing, the whole place—it's calculated to be hard. It's not a nice environment. I don't know if people reflect that or if that reflects the people, or what, but it's a hard place."

Merlis had come from *Good Morning America,* an information show produced by ABC's entertainment division that sometimes had to fight for help on news stories from the news division. But CBS was a shock. "To battle your own tape editors to get them to cut a piece, it's ridiculous," he recalled. "I mean, everyone in the place thinks they're Edward R. Murrow. Edward R. Mur-row's dead! Everyone's Edward R. Murrow."

He was criticized at the time, but the irony was that Merlis's version of the *CBS Morning News* was later recognized as the closest CBS had ever come to real success in the morning. The show managed to find an accommodation between the institu-tion's self-image and the competitive realities of the morning time period—namely, that viewers wanted their news served up with some fluff in the morning. Bill Kurtis was derided as a slick local news reader (he'd been a star anchor at WBBM in Chi-cago), but he proved an effective and credible newsman, in some ways stronger than his competitors on the other networks. And, more significant for CBS News, Merlis's show made Diane Sawyer a star; within just a few years she would seem to CBS a compelling alternative to Rather himself for the *Evening News.*

Sawyer had overcome the odds at CBS News. On the one hand, she was bright, blond, and beautiful, attributes that at CBS News didn't necessarily count for much; on the other hand, her professional experience consisted of a couple of years as a local TV weather forecaster in Louisville and eight years as an aide to Richard Nixon, and those things did count—negatively. The Nixon White House had openly warred with CBS News and there was strong sentiment against Sawyer on that ground alone. She had been not only a Nixon aide but a Nixon loyalist of the highest order; when Nixon finally resigned in disgrace, she was one of the faithful on the plane that took Nixon on his long journey to exile at San Clemente. She and her boyfriend, Nixon aide Frank Gannon, spent the next four years at San Clemente, researching Nixon's autobiography, *RN.* In 1978 she was hired at CBS News by Bill Small, who remembered her early days doing the weather in Louisville (at the same CBS affiliate where Small had worked) and gave her a general assignment job in the Washington bureau.

Sawyer got all the expected low-level rookie assignments, but she quickly showed herself to be something more than a run-of-the-mill blond striver, which both Washington and television had in abundance. That she had good connections was no surprise—she'd been a Washington insider—but as a journalist she was a hard worker and, it turned out, a very good reporter. What's more, she stood out from the crowd; she had an inner surety that bespoke her upbringing in a professional-class home in the near South, where beauty contests and Chopin preludes were two sides of the same coin. Sawyer was as ambitious as the next young network correspondent, but she packaged it so much better. She was flirtatious but not coquettish; powerful men, including her own bosses, were turned by her good looks. It would become part of the Sawyer legend that in a meeting with several male executives she was told that Mr. Paley was on the line for her. "Tell him I'll call him back," she responded as every jaw in the room hit the floor. Other women network reporters dated and married other journalists, or agents, or, more rarely, businessmen; Diane Sawyer dated a secretary of state (Henry Kissinger).

Sawyer worked her way to the State Department beat, an assignment that showcased her star potential. On the *Sunday Morning* segment when Charles Kuralt would debrief various beat correspondents, Sawyer's breezy, spontaneous exchanges with Kuralt convinced Bill Leonard and *Sunday* producer Shad Northshield that all Diane Sawyer needed was a vehicle and she would soar. On the *Morning News,* however, she became suddenly more reserved and withdrawn. Part of it was the format, which was precisely plotted and didn't allow for a lot of spontaneity, but part of it, many who worked on the broadcast believed, was the large shadow cast by Kuralt.

Sawyer believed that she would be dropped along with Northshield and Kuralt when Sauter arrived—"Absolutely, I think there was no doubt they were going to," she later said—and in fact, there had been discussion of bringing in a new female coanchor for the *CBS Morning News,* Connie Chung being among those mentioned. But Sauter was taken with Sawyer's potential ("The woman is a real treasure," he told Merlis), and given a new life, Sawyer took off. She became the star that Leonard and Northshield predicted she would be, and if she became a little too much the star for Bill Kurtis's liking, it didn't hurt the show. The new *CBS Morning News* steadily rose in the ratings, attracting a larger audience than it ever had, and within a year, by the spring of 1983, it seemed that CBS had finally beaten its morning curse.

But the magic didn't last. Merlis was the perfect producer for the *Morning News,* the one producer the broadcast ever had who actually caused concern to the producer of the *Today* show, Steve Friedman. Merlis knew morning television, knew television period; but he was a difficult personality, at times abrasive and arrogant, and as the months passed, he became less communicative with his staff just when Diane Sawyer was beginning to feel particularly communicative. As her stature grew, so did her belief in her own ideas about the broadcast and her inclination to express them. When she lost arguments, she complained. For Van Sauter, a choice between keeping his morning star and his morning producer happy was no choice at all; the woman was, after all, a treasure. Kurtis was unhappy, too, and although he made more money than Sawyer and was billed first in the show, it was evident to him that Sawyer was cast in the starring role. Although Merlis didn't know it, he was on very shaky ground just as his broadcast was taking CBS to unimagined success in the morning.

The tensions came to a head one week in February 1983 when the CBS television network was building up publicity for special final episodes of its long-running hit show *M*A*S*H.* Sawyer saw the event as an epochal pop culture event; Merlis saw it as the overdue end of a TV rip-off that had grown pedantic and tired. Sawyer wanted to make a splash over the event, to book several *M*A*S*H* segments on the show; Merlis wanted to blow it off with one or two references, preferably not involving the show's star, Alan Alda, whom Merlis considered a sanctimonious wimp. Sawyer pushed; Merlis pushed back. Merlis later told friends that he believed that Sawyer took her side of the argument to Sauter; Sawyer declined to discuss George Merlis. Whatever happened, Merlis recalled that Sauter called him into his office one day and said, "Brother Merlis, we just don't think you have the management skills to run the organization you've put together. So I'm taking you off the *Morning News.*" Merlis was shocked. The *Morning News* ratings that week were the highest they had ever been; two days earlier Ed Joyce had run into Merlis's agent at lunch and told him that he and Sauter couldn't have been more pleased with the show. And now Merlis was being relieved of his post because he lacked "management skills." It was an obvious political move; but it was done, and Sauter told Merlis that he had other plans for the producer.

What Sauter had in mind was for Merlis to develop a prime-time magazine show with the potential for broad popular appeal. As hosts, Merlis recalled Sauter saying, it would feature "someone like Phyllis George and Ken Howard." George was the former Miss America from Texas who was a hostess of CBS's *NFL Today* pregame show; Howard was the amiable star of the former CBS show *White Shadow.* Sauter said the program would be done under the umbrella of the news division, except that it would be staffed by free-lance people from outside CBS News. "So you'll get a feel for what it is," Merlis quoted Sauter as saying, "it would have an *Entertainment Tonight* pace." *Entertainment Tonight* was the entertainment news show syndicated by Paramount Television, a nightly half hour that managed to treat every twitch of the show business world as if it mattered and was probably far closer to Sauter's ideal than *Our Times* with Bill Moyers ever was. Merlis didn't accept Sauter's invitation to produce a new show; instead, he moved to Hollywood, where he became executive producer, at significantly higher pay, of the original *Entertainment Tonight,* and with him disappeared CBS's last best chance in the morning.

Although the *Morning News* remained fairly strong in the ratings for a time after Merlis's departure, behind the scenes it began to descend into a tangle of political maneuvering and backbiting, which coincided with the rising influence of a new CBS executive named Jon Katz. He was one of two newspapermen brought to the *Morning News* by Van Sauter in 1982, with the unspecific title of manager of news planning. Both Katz and the other planning manager, Steve Isaacs, had had varied and highly controversial careers in newspapers, Isaacs being the last editor of the *Minneapolis Star* before it folded and Katz acting as a managing editor of the *Dallas Times Herald* (his brief tenure was a subject of nightmarish lore) before being relieved from that post and joining CBS. The two men were strange additions to the CBS culture; both were extremely intelligent, extremely overweight, and extremely confident of their intellectual superiority. "Four hundred fifty pounds of Jewish bullshit" was how Katz jokingly referred to himself and Isaacs, and the term occasionally was applied to Katz alone. Both men were assigned to the *Morning News,* where they were supposed to generate ideas, and in fact, each was a fount of ideas. Isaacs, especially, had strong notions about broadcast journalism and just how CBS News might be improved, and one day at lunch with Dan Rather he made the mistake of telling the anchorman just what he thought. He was soon thereafter dispatched to the organization's netherworld, *Sunday Morning,* where he became a useful producer and actually learned a great deal about television.

That was more than could be said for Jon Katz, who made a running gag of his ignorance of the mechanics and sensibilities of television, perhaps partly to emphasize that he was there to provide ideas and an editorial edge, not video expertise. Katz came to CBS with a reputation as a newsroom operator, and in that regard he made a swift adjustment to television. He had regular access to Sauter and was unsparing in his observations of the shortcomings of George Merlis and his successor as executive producer, Bob Ferrante. "Katz was a real politician," Merlis recalled. "You know, he's the kind of guy who confidentially tells you something that helps you put your own head in the noose." Although under Ferrante the *Morning News* continued to prosper, reaching record ratings and even beating the *Today* show by the end of 1983, Ferrante's head soon found its way into a noose, and he was removed from the show in March 1984. His replacement as executive producer, to no one's surprise, was Jon Katz.

In the space of two years CBS had mismanaged its way from having a rising morning program with an experienced and successful producer to having a morning program rife with behind-the-scenes intrigue, produced by a television novice. By early 1984 the decline of the *CBS Morning News* had begun, and it would be one of the most spectacular, publicly embarrassing, and ultimately portentous program failures in broadcasting history.

Katz bore a large portion of the responsibility, but the collapse of the *Morning News* was by no means his doing alone. Although he was singularly ill equipped to be a television producer, he was a creative thinker and had a strong journalistic instinct; he brought an intellectual curiosity to his broadcast, and occasionally insipience, too. "The low point of my existence on the *Morning News,*" recalled Diane Sawyer, "was when I interviewed the yo-yo queen of America for about five minutes. I did that. That was a Jon Katz special, which I never let him forget."

By the middle of 1984 Sawyer was seriously thinking of leaving the *Morning News.* It had become clear to her that the broadcast did not have the attention and commitment from Sauter that it needed to succeed in the long run. As she later put it, "I don't think Van was particularly interested in the morning. I don't think he cared very much. . . . It was clear to me they were going to rotate in and out a lot of producers." Sawyer was in the rare position of having a choice: Don Hewitt had let it be known that he wanted her to be the fifth correspondent on *60 Minutes.* Neither Joyce nor Sauter—nor Jankowski or Wyman, for that matter—was inclined to say no to Hewitt, and in the large picture Sawyer's move made sense. She was a bright young star, and *60 Minutes* was a hugely valuable CBS News franchise that looked as if it might need the help. After years as one of the most popular shows on television, it seemed vulnerable in 1984. Its stars were aging, Mike Wallace was showing the strain of the Westmoreland matter, and the program suffered a worrisome dip in the ratings.

Joyce insisted that Sawyer not be moved off the *Morning News* until the end of the year, after the political conventions and the presidential elections. By then, Joyce told a management staff meeting Black Rock, CBS News would have had time to select her replacement, and Stringer and Katz would have had time to develop a new format. It was agreed: Sawyer would stay at the *Morning News* through 1984, and her move to *60 Minutes* would be kept secret until then.

The next week the story that Diane Sawyer was leaving the *Morning News* for *60 Minutes* was leaked to the *New York Daily News.* Joyce was furious. He called Sawyer into his office and told her that he resented being pressured by her and Hewitt into making the change precipitously, that he didn't like being steamrollered. "The upshot was he decided very impetuously just to announce that I was going on *60 Minutes,*" Sawyer recalled. "And when I said, 'I'd like to come back and say just a farewell on the *Morning News* he said no."

So Diane Sawyer just disappeared one day from the *CBS Morning News.* It was a clumsy bit of management and an affront to the audience, but it meant much more than that: Sawyer's departure posed again the question of what the *Morning News* would be, and this time the answer shook CBS News to its foundation.

Most inside CBS News assumed that Sawyer's replacement would come from within the organization, and in the summer of 1984 there was a kind of open audition on the *Morning News.* The two likeliest candidates, it seemed to most, were Meredith Vieira, an attractive and promising correspondent in the Chicago bureau, and Jane Wallace, a brassy, ambitious star in the making, who was assigned to the Miami bureau and had been reporting on El Salvador for CBS News. Wallace bought five dresses and moved to New York for the summer, staying at the Parker Meridien Hotel, three blocks from the Broadcast Center on West Fifty-seventh Street.

Katz, meanwhile, drew up plans for a new format, which would be unveiled at the beginning of the year when the new coanchor joined Kurtis on the show. It was going to be a daily newsmagazine, with an emphasis on hard-news coverage. There'd be a news anchor—Kurtis—and a half dozen or so beat reporters who would become regulars on the program. The coanchor would help Kurtis tie it all together. Stringer, who had been put in charge of the *Morning News,* approved the plan, and so did Joyce. As the interim period progressed, it became increasingly evident that the format was best suited to Jane Wallace, who was working well with Kurtis and had shown real personality during her tryout appearances. Although Wallace was a hard-nosed reporter, she was not at all averse to this development in her career (after all, look what the *Morning News* had done for Diane Sawyer), and she took advice about her performance and even agreed to go to CBS's regular performance coach, Lilyan Wilder. In a particularly unfortunate episode Wilder suggested that Wallace's hair was all wrong and, Wallace said, sent her to a salon for a new cut. The stylist apparently was having a bad day, and Wallace arrived at the *Morning News* the next day in a do that sent the place into paroxysms. The subject of her haircut would be raised in the angry postmortems that were to come.

Katz, Stringer, and the news division believed that Wallace was the obvious choice to succeed Sawyer. But Jankowski didn't think she was the obvious choice at all. Jankowski thought the show needed a star, and it happened that someone who had Jankowski's ear had a particular star in mind. Jankowski had a close relationship with a California agent named E. Gregory Hookstratten, who told Jankowski that one of his clients could become the next Barbara Walters. What's more, she already worked for CBS: Phyllis George, the former Miss America turned sports feature reporter. So one day, when Sauter and Jankowski were discussing Sawyer's replacement, Jankowski asked, "What about Phyllis George?" Soon Sauter was in California breakfasting with Hookstratten, and when the agent proposed George for the *Morning News,* Sauter said, "Why not?"

"We had no woman within the organization who would bring anything to the table," Sauter recalled. "They brought journalistic expertise and skill, but nothing else. And we were never going to get a woman journalist as good as Diane Sawyer, and we know where the top [in the ratings] was on that. So it didn't make any sense to go with a Jane Wallace or a Meredith Vieira. It wasn't going to do anything except make us feel better." It was decided to give George a week's tryout. To keep the press from recognizing it as an audition (and possibly starting a drumbeat from within the news division against her), the CBS News press department put out the word that George's contract required that she fill in on the *Morning News* for two weeks. Those were just the circumstances that Hookstratten wanted, very low pressure, and George did quite well; of course, the new hard-news-oriented format hadn't yet been installed, but her tryout impressed Black Rock.

Still, Katz and Stringer and Joyce believed in Jane Wallace, who remained their first choice. "She was far and away the most qualified; she was far and away the best," Katz said. In fact, they led her to believe that the job would be hers. Then, one day in the late fall of 1984, Sauter called a meeting of his news executives to discuss the new *Morning News*. It was the day before Stringer, Katz, and Joyce were to meet at Black Rock with Jankowski, unveil the new format, and decide on Sawyer's replacement. As Katz remembered it, Sauter told his subordinates, "Do not present Jane Wallace to Gene Jankowski; just don't." Joyce argued strongly in favor of Wallace, but Sauter said, "I'm telling you, if you go in there with Jane Wallace, it's not gonna fly."

"The rest of us," Katz later said, "just caved." The next day the news executives went to Black Rock to make their presentation. Jane Wallace's name was not brought up. Phyllis George would be the new coanchor of the *CBS Morning News*.

Wallace knew that the decision was to be made that day, and she planned a celebration in her hotel room. Her sister and a friend were there, and a bottle of champagne was on ice. Then Stringer and Katz arrived with the bad news, and Wallace, who could do a fair impression of a longshoreman, let the executives have it with both barrels. She was so distraught that on the broadcast the next day she made the worst on-air gaffe of her career. She and Bill Plante, who was sitting in for Kurtis, were chatting after doing a segment on toys and games, and when it came time for a commercial, Wallace teasingly aimed a toy gun at Plante and fired, saying, "I'll be back alone for the last half hour. Stay with us, will you?" Plante laughed, Jane laughed, and then she looked at Plante, and indicating the toy, she asked, "What the hell is this supposed to be? Would you give that to somebody? You can shoot me back, we still have to stretch. I couldn't bullshit about anything." The laughter turned to panic when Plante and Wallace realized that their mikes were still live and that her "bullshit" had gone tumbling into homes of millions of breakfast-hour CBS viewers.

The hallway lore held that Wallace had blown her chance for the *Morning News* job with her "bullshit" gaffe and barber-college hairdo, but in truth, Wallace was simply caught in the larger shifts that were changing the whole company. As Jon Katz later put it, "A program that for thirty years existed as an information service, protected by the individual who had started the company, suddenly became, as did everything else in the company, something that made no economic sense. And overnight it became something that had to make money."

Sauter, armed with audience research and a showman's instinct, was convinced that the very reputation and tradition that CBS News cherished were hurting the network's chances in the morning, that as long as viewers associated the *Morning News* with the sober, serious journalism they usually got from CBS, the program was doomed. That's why he agreed with Jankowski that the *Morning News* needed a star, someone who could "light up the screen," as Sauter put it at the time.

"And so," Sauter later explained, "we hired Phyllis George, and the institution killed her."

She had been through a tough Hollywood divorce, she had been the first lady of a state, but at heart she was still Phyllis Ann George of Denton, Texas, the beauty queen who believed that with a cheery smile, wholesome good looks, and a little talent, a girl could do anything. She was proof of it. Although she'd never been a journalist, the former Miss America was now being paid $1 million a year by the preeminent news organization in broadcasting to be the anchor of a daily two-hour news program.

She arrived at CBS News in a limousine, trailed by an entourage, all smiles and sincerity, and as she met her colleagues in news, she looked them in the eyes and said, "This is going to be wonderful, I just know it! This is going to be fun, y'all, you'll see!" And CBS News went into a state of shock.

The contradiction that Phyllis George represented at CBS News was beyond articulation. There was, for example, Mr. Vincent—a nice, quiet little man who scurried about after her with makeup and a comb, keeping the Phyllis George "look" in constant repair. There was the limousine. Other news anchors were driven to work in a taxi, contracted to CBS News, but Phyllis George was escorted to and from her Trump Plaza penthouse in a big black limousine, a contractual perk. There was the money: George was being paid $1 million a year to do something she'd never done before; in contrast, Jane Wallace, the news correspondent who lost out on the job, was earning $77,000 a year. Through no fault of her own, Phyllis George became the embodiment of Black Rock's rejection of the old values, and she was made to pay for it.

Very early Bill Kurtis had let it be known that he disapproved of the choice of Phyllis George as his *Morning News* coanchor. It hadn't helped anchor relations that Kurtis found out about her hiring by reading about it in the newspapers; now he was telling reporters that CBS had abandoned its commitment to news in the morning, as, in fact, it had. CBS News was a very insular culture, with a common language and attitude, and the accepted attitude toward Phyllis George was utter rejection. The president of CBS News, Joyce, the executive vice-president, Stringer, and the *Morning News* executive producer, Katz, all opposed their new million-dollar coanchor, and their attitude filtered down through the ranks, to the producers and bookers and newswriters whose job it was to make Phyllis George look good. The production staffers worked hard, in fact, but even as they worked, they openly ridiculed the new star, dismissing her as an inconsequential fluff artist too dumb to succeed.

It became a self-fulfilling prophecy, of course, a disaster of unprecedented scale. Although CBS was abandoning serious news in the morning, it did not, for some reason, abandon its new hard-news format, the precise circumstance in which Phyllis George was least likely to succeed. Hookstratten, her agent, didn't help matters, insisting that she get her fair share of the hard-news interviews and "serious" segments. When Hookstratten was in town, he'd go over to the Broadcast Center, sometimes even entering the control room, where he lectured Katz and the producers and the director on how a morning show should be done. When he wasn't in town, he'd call his client every day after the broadcast, consulting, advising, telling her not to relent on her demand that she get her share of the serious stuff.

None of that helped George's standing inside the organization, and her cause was further hurt when her apparent inadequacy as a newscaster became a running story in the newspapers. Television writers discovered that they could always get good dirt on George from practically anybody inside CBS News, including Katz. Although he publicly defended her, privately Katz absolutely lambasted Phyllis George, not only to the staff but to newspaper columnists looking for a good off-the-record quote from an unnamed *Morning News* insider.

She hurt her own cause with her performance, of course, committing a series of on-air goofs that culminated in one of the most storied incidents in CBS News history. One of the hot, if somewhat dubious, news stories of the early summer of 1984 was the case of Cathy Webb, an Illinois woman who found God and recanted her testimony that had sent Gary Dotson to prison for rape. Illinois Governor James Thompson commuted the sentence of the convicted rapist, and Dotson and Webb became the objects of a frenzied competition among the three morning news programs. It was a low display by all three networks, with NBC chartering a plane to bring the odd couple to New York, putting them up in a hotel, and then squiring them to the studio in a limousine. On one frantic morning Webb and Dotson appeared on *Today, Good Morning America,* and the *CBS Morning News.* George did the CBS interview, and at its end, sensing that reconciliation was what this story was all about, she smiled and ingenuously asked the pair, "How 'bout a hug?"

A loud, collective groan rumbled through the CBS Broadcast Center. Then many fingers were suddenly busy, dialing the phone numbers of TV reporters who might have missed the latest Phyllis George gaffe. That night George talked to Tom Shales of the *Washington Post,* and then stayed up all night drinking wine, uncharacteristically, and, more characteristically, crying. Her eyes were red and her face was puffy the next morning as she went on the air, and the TV columns, including Shales in the *Post,* were devoted to her slip. "If Barbara Walters would have asked that question," said Hookstratten, "the CBS News people would have said, 'Jesus Christ, does that woman have balls!' But because it was Phyllis who did it, they twisted it on her." In truth, it was a horrible mistake, and in truth, another anchor might have gotten away with it. But Phyllis was Phyllis, and it was becoming increasingly clear, in the parlance of CBS News at the time, that she would soon be "toast."

The institution just seethed over Phyllis George. As Bill Moyers later put it, "Real damage came with the Phyllis George hiring. Because [Sauter] was so wholly a corporate man, instead of saying no and going to the mat, he accepted Gene's bad impulse. It was a blow to the young women here. They're asking,

'Are they saying we've got to be Miss America?' " The situation became a horrible embarrassment, and worse, the ratings began to slide. The show became an ongoing daily disaster, which a strong executive producer might have averted; but Katz was completely ineffective. He didn't believe in the broadcast he was producing, the organization didn't believe in him, and to make things worse, he had alienated Van Sauter.

Sauter had taken Katz to lunch, and in the course of their conversation Sauter told Katz he was disappointed in the performance of Howard Stringer as executive vice-president. Stringer didn't seem to be quelling the various controversies, and he didn't seem to be helping much with the *Morning News.* Sauter spoke to Katz in confidence, or so he thought; but Katz returned to the Broadcast Center and proceeded to repeat the conversation to Howard Stringer. Sauter was furious. "Katz," he told him, "you have gone through one miserable event after another in your career because you are an inept politician with a loud mouth, and now you've done it to me. Our relationship is over." So, through almost the entire Phyllis George episode, the man who had hired her was not speaking to the man who was supposed to be producing her show. The *Morning News* staff, which had had to struggle for resources and help anyway, now found its task impossible. "The *Evening News* by this point would no longer allow us to have a piece of stationery," Katz recalled. "We couldn't get crews; correspondents would refuse to go on the program, they thought it was so awful."

To make things worse, in the middle of all this, Ed Joyce went to war with his other *Morning News* anchor, Bill Kurtis. Kurtis had realized at about the time that Sawyer did that the morning time period was being terribly mismanaged by CBS, and he was quoted in a newspaper story as saying that Sauter and Joyce, after a promising start, had "taken their hands off" the broadcast. When George was hired, Kurtis was quoted as saying the show was becoming a clone of the entertainment-oriented *Good Morning America.* That, predictably, infuriated Joyce, who quit speaking to Kurtis—directly, anyway. Shortly after Phyllis George joined the broadcast, CBS News management let its feelings be known in a story leaked to the *New York Daily News,* in which an unnamed news executive was quoted as saying that CBS News felt "disillusionment" over Kurtis's performance and was upset by his "lack of team spirit."

Kurtis, certain that the anonymous *Daily News* source was Ed Joyce, tried to confront the president of CBS News about the matter. But Joyce refused to see him. So Kurtis asked his lawyer to begin to negotiate an out; within a few months Kurtis had returned to WBBM in Chicago, from which he had been wooed by Sauter and Joyce three and a half years earlier with promises of glory in the new CBS News.

"In one respect," Kurtis later said, "I was lucky. I simply had to choose between journalism and television at an early stage, and I was lucky to get out."

Kurtis was temporarily replaced by Bob Schieffer in the summer, and things calmed down for a time, but it was clear that Phyllis George would never succeed in CBS News. As Schieffer later put it, "I could never bring myself to dislike [George], but it was like sending me out to build a nuclear plant. I wouldn't know where to start. Poor Phyllis."

Finally, Ed Joyce took action. He told Black Rock that the situation was beyond repair and that he intended to fire George. He got no resistance from Sauter or Jankowski. On the Labor Day weekend, when Phyllis George was at home in Kentucky on vacation with her family, Joyce telephoned Ed Hookstratten in California and told him he was making a change. Hookstratten didn't argue; he just reminded Joyce that he expected her three-year guaranteed contract to be honored by CBS. Joyce agreed. A statement for the press was worked out, in which George said, "I have come to the conclusion to rearrange my priorities." Ed Joyce said, "We will miss her."

So, after eight months, Phyllis George's career as a CBS News anchor ended (although her salary would continue for another two years). For Joyce, it had been a bitter lesson, and both he and the institution paid for it dearly. Aside from the public embarrassment and the further deepening of the internal rifts, CBS had lost a potentially valuable franchise in the *Morning News,* which never recovered from the Phyllis George fiasco.

But as terrible as the episode was, it was, for Ed Joyce, not nearly so damaging as the troubles he was having with the one man whose enmity no one at CBS News could survive—his anchorman, Dan Rather.

Chapter

CBS REGULARLY DENIED THAT it commissioned, possessed, or reacted to research on its news programs or news personalities, but in fact, such data did exist, and what they said about Dan Rather explained a lot. They said that Americans were passionate about Rather but were divided into polar extremes of admiration and disdain. Dan Rather was either a beloved and trusted American or he was a clear and present danger to the Republic. There was scant middle ground. That explained why Rather was a ratings winner; it also explained why he had to travel with bodyguards and wear disguises to take a walk.

There was to Dan Rather a kind of innate vehemence, a quality that tempted crackpots to stalk him, prompted strangers to accost him, and urged cabbies to drive wildly through city streets with him screaming for help in the back seat. Things happened to Dan Rather, odd things, mysterious things, sometimes frightening things. And through the years Rather's actions caused embarrassments and controversies that baffled those around him and gave him a reputation (perhaps not fully earned) for being something of a loose cannon. He himself seemed to be baffled by the reactions he triggered and by the frays he incited. "Only in recent times," he said, after a particularly stormy period, "have I come to understand, 'Dan, try as you may, you're never going to be just Old Dan. Your public doesn't perceive you that way, your colleagues don't perceive you that way. Some like you, some don't, but you're never going to be just Old Dan.' "

No, he wouldn't, and that fact was much more than just an interesting quirk. It was hugely portentous, especially when the elders of CBS News in 1980 picked Dan Rather over Roger Mudd to succeed Walter Cronkite. They weren't just choosing who would sit (or not sit, as it happened) in Cronkite's chair to read the news for twenty-three minutes each night; in a way they were deciding what CBS News itself would be. CBS News, much more than the other network news organizations, was defined by its most visible newsman; the institution was peculiarly given to a "cult of personality," as Cronkite himself derisively called it, a one-man mantle of influence that began with Murrow and continued through Cronkite to Rather. By the end of Cronkite's time the mantle had acquired even more power and influence, thanks to the increased importance of the *Evening News.* So in taking over for Cronkite, Rather became the personification of CBS News. His personality, to a degree, became its personality; his values, its values; his fortunes, the fortunes of CBS News.

In retrospect, it would seem remarkable how accurately each man reflected the character and temperature of the organization during his time. Although Cronkite presided in the turbulent 1960s and 1970s, through Vietnam and Watergate, he himself was the steady Dutchman, sure and constant and serene, and CBS News during his time was a relatively ordered and prosperous place. Rather, in contrast, exuded inner turmoil, and his era at CBS News would come to seem like one long, ceaseless storm.

Storms just seemed to gather up around him, and after a time the fact that Dan Rather was a remarkably good reporter, one of the best ever in television, became almost obscured. He wasn't the smartest, or the deepest, or the most polished, but from the beginning his instinct and drive set him apart—his drive especially. It was the up-from-poverty ardor of one who believed himself always a step from going bust, long past the time that his going bust was even a remote possibility. It was the hardscrabble ambition of a ditchdigger's son, bound to make it past the oil fields of East Texas; a boy who tried to get to college on football, only to be pummeled and defeated, and who hung on anyway, piecing together his passage through Sam Houston

State Teachers College with an assortment of odd jobs that included part-time announcing work at the 250-watt Huntsville radio station.

Rather's CBS News career, fittingly enough, was born in a storm, Hurricane Carla, which swept onto the shores of the Texas Gulf Coast in September 1961. Rather was the twenty-nine-year-old anchor and news director of KHOU in Houston, not the best station in the market but newly successful in the ratings, thanks partly to Rather and partly to the employment of what he described as the "fuzz and wuz" approach: the liberal use of film showing police action (fuzz) and dead bodies (wuz). It was Rather's way even then, with a full-time news staff of fewer than a dozen people, to swarm all over a big story, and as Carla slid across the Gulf of Mexico, Rather convinced his station manager that KHOU should set up a camera and crew and correspondent (Rather) down in Galveston, fifty miles away, where the storm was likely to hit. For three days Rather and the crew stayed their ground in the face of what became a terrible storm, Rather broadcasting his reports even as the winds and tides lashed at their building. Legends sprang up about Rather's work (including the yarn that he had saved a drowning horse), but in fact, his work needed no embellishment; he'd come through in the clutch. CBS News had monitored KHOU's coverage, noticed Rather ("He was ass-deep in water moccasins," Cronkite said), and soon offered him a job as a network reporter. Rather, early showing an ability to get what he wanted from CBS, held out for the loftier position of correspondent, which carried higher status and more money and was rarely bestowed upon newcomers. CBS, showing an early inclination to give in to Rather, yielded, making the young anchorman from local TV a full-fledged correspondent. The "child of the storm," as Rather called himself in his autobiography, had arrived.

For two years Rather worked the civil rights story in the Deep South, showing himself to be a first-rate field reporter and a ceaseless worker and establishing for CBS a commanding presence on a story that was a test of network television news itself. It was the first running story of national importance that television fully covered, and the story and the developing medium interacted to lasting effect. Television brought home to the nation the civil rights struggle in vivid images that were difficult to ignore, and for television, it was a story that finally proved the value of news *gathering* as opposed to mere news dissemination. It was the perfect TV story, with the clash of abstract notions— freedom, equality, regionalism, heritage—manifesting itself in the most visually compelling ways. The young newspaperman Van Gordon Sauter, who watched from a bridge in Neshoba County, Mississippi, as an old black man dragged the river for three slain youths and ceded the moment to a TV crew, would testify to that.

A natural disaster had given Rather his first break with CBS, and another calamity, in November 1963, again boosted his career. He was in Dallas when President John F. Kennedy was assassinated, and it was Rather who gave CBS a seventeen-minute beat on the president's death. There was an edgy moment to the event; Rather had (inadvertently, he later said) reported Kennedy's death before getting official confirmation, and he and CBS sweated out the next several minutes until the story was confirmed. But it was a memorable "beat," and in the next frantic days Rather continued to shine; he was rewarded with the top CBS spot on the White House beat.

The promotion caused resentment among some Washington veterans—Rather was, after all, only two years removed from covering double murders in Houston—and in fact, the promotion proved to be too much too soon for the young correspondent. He was transferred first to London and then to Vietnam, but he had entered the fast track at CBS News, and when the White House opened up again in 1966, Dan Rather was ready. On a beat where the scores are publicly tallied every day, Rather was a ferocious player who hated to be bested; he worked the beat like the best of the print reporters, not contenting himself with White House handouts and presidential aides as sources of information. For example, Rather developed a source in the Mississippi congressional delegation who, after attending private White House briefings, sometimes leaked information to Rather, giving CBS important edges on major stories. (There were also occasions when Rather's zeal exceeded the facts; he twice permaturely reported the retirement of FBI Director J. Edgar Hoover and three times the resignation of Ellsworth Bunker, the American ambassador to South Vietnam.)

After just five years Rather had pretty well covered the stations of the cross at CBS: He'd been a war correspondent, he'd held the sacred London post (of Murrow, Collingwood, et al.), he'd excelled as a field correspondent, and he was on his second tour at the White House. By his mid-thirties he was an established CBS star of the first rank, and it was clear that whatever the future of CBS News would be, Dan Rather would be one of its key authors.

Yet in some fundamental respects Dan Rather and CBS News were an awkward fit. Although Rather deeply coveted success at CBS and deeply revered the near-mystical emblems and myths of the place (he had his suits made by Murrow's Savile Row tailor), somehow he did not seem fully at ease with his place in the institution. CBS News was an elitist subculture, the exclusive club of broadcast journalism; Rather was, at root, a poor boy out of Sam Houston State. The Murrow club, Sevareid and Smith and Collingwood and the others, had been fiercely intellectual and grounded in the written word; Rather was the star example of the new breed, a product of local TV. He was sensitive about these things, and perhaps that is why he developed such a deep and abiding suspiciousness; it sometimes seemed that fear and suspicion had become his prime motivating forces. When asked to recount his ascent at CBS News, Rather framed each major advance with an anecdote that featured an innocent and naïve Dan Rather suddenly awakening to the realization that he was about to done in by unfriendly forces inside CBS.

For example, regarding his first CBS anchor job, the late-night Sunday newscast that Rather eventually won away from John Hart in 1969, Rather said he'd been perfectly content as the White House correspondent until somebody told him that he'd lost out on something big, that Hart had been promoted ahead of him, and if Rather said he didn't care, he was either a fool or a liar. "And then I began asking around, and I was somewhat shocked to find the unanimity of thought saying, 'Yeah, that's right. You're at an age and stage where they're considering who's going to move forward, who's standing still, and who's going to slide back. Clearly this is a signal that you're going to stay still.' Now I didn't like to hear that. That got me hot." That was when Rather confronted Bill Small. "You've got trouble with me, beginning now," he said, and within a few weeks Hart was out and Rather was in.

A decade later, according to Rather, he was happy at *60 Minutes* when he began to hear similar stories about how he'd lost out in the race to replace Walter Cronkite. "Once again I didn't like it a bit when it reached the point when somebody would say, 'Well, you're way above your station already, I'm not surprised you've lost this race.' It was a version of 'We got you, you son of a bitch.' I'd say to myself, 'Hey, what the hell is this? I don't like this.' And I began to feel sort of the sting of that." That, he said, was what prompted him to go to Leibner and touch off the most frantic and expensive talent derby in the history of the news business. "It may or may not reflect well on me," Rather later said of his motivation to become Cronkite's successor, "but this is the truth of the situation. It was less wanting to do this job, far less that, than that I didn't want to be told, 'You're second to anybody.' That's what it was. Now I could take being second; I could take being fifteenth, if I'm given a fair shot and I've given my best. Where I have my dark moments is when I didn't have a shot."

It seemed to Rather that some people within the organization were working against him—at CBS News that was by no means an entirely unreasonable assumption—but Rather greeted nearly every development in his career at CBS with suspicion. When he first left the White House in 1964, after just ten months on the job, he worried that CBS was transferring him either because LBJ had pressured the network into it or because his bosses no longer thought well of him. When he left the White House beat the second time, to become chief correspondent for *CBS Reports* in 1974, he was again suspicious. Was he being punished for having stood up to Nixon? Was he being sacrificed for the affiliates? He was so upset about the transfer that he almost quit CBS News; he abruptly left for a vacation and gave Leibner permission to put out feelers to the competition (NBC showed strong interest). Finally CBS persuaded him that he was being promoted, not punished, and as a measure of its sincerity, the network threw in a salary raise that brought his annual pay above the $100,000 point. Rather went to *CBS Reports,* but not entirely happily, and he harbored suspicions about the move for years.

Just a year later Rather's bosses asked him to join *60 Minutes.* John Sharnik, the senior producer in charge of *CBS Reports,* didn't want to lose Rather just as the broadcast was gaining momentum, but he told Bill Leonard that he couldn't stand in the way of what was an obvious promotion for Rather. "And Rather came to me," recalled Sharnik, "he went to everybody, and with great suspiciousness and paranoia, he said, 'I guess I flunked, huh? You didn't like my work.' I said, 'Jeez, Dan, I'd love to keep you. . . . But *60 Minutes* is the best game in town.''

Most people reached a point in their careers at which they knew they'd made it, that they could relax a little without risking catastrophe. But the people who have worked with Rather over the years maintain that Rather has never come close to such contentment, even as anchor of the *Evening News*. "He never, in all the time I've known him, has ever been comfortable, at ease," said producer Tom Bettag, one of Rather's friends and allies in the organization. "Anytime that he's feeling good about something, he starts to worry about it. He's just always pitching from this side to that side, and he sees his role in life [as being] to question. And he just keeps pitching, back and forth, doing that all the time." Friends recall that the closest they ever saw Rather come to real contentment was in 1982, that first year under Sauter, when the *Evening News* bounced back from the long post-Cronkite ratings slide and Rather felt the euphoria of resurrection. "But I guarantee you, during that year, he was not laid-back," said Bettag. "That was just not his style."

Possibly because of his suspicions, Rather particularly valued loyalty, perhaps overvalued it; his close friendship with David Buksbaum, for example, led to promotions for Buksbaum that CBS News management later regretted—largely because Buksbaum continued to function as Rather's personal rabbi after he'd joined the senior management staff. Of course, there was another side to dogged loyalty, too, which showed itself in Rather's inclination to hold fast to a negative opinion. Once he became anchor, that was a quality to be feared for the career damage it could do. The only way out of disfavor was to face Rather with it. Usually it worked; sometimes it didn't.

But if Rather harbored suspicions about the organization, many inside the organization were doubtful, and even contemptuous, of him. They found something slightly false in his exaggerated Texas courtesies ("Yes, ma'am," "No, sir"), and his extraordinarily solicitous behavior was seen by some as cheap office politicking. When he was in Washington, for example, Rather regularly brought doughnuts and coffee to the technicians and secretaries before recording his radio commentaries, a ritual that seemed oddly off-base to his colleagues. Whenever some CBS staffer whom Rather knew even slightly fell ill, or had a baby, or got married, Rather always sent flowers, and his was always the largest bouquet. Some Rather defenders believed that his solicitations were sincere and were simply misconstrued by his colleagues in a profession in which courtesy is not exactly a prerequisite; Ernie Leiser, the executive who hired Rather, was one of those. "When my wife was in the hospital having her hips replaced, there was absolutely no reason for Rather to call her," Leiser recalled. "He called her several times to make sure she was okay. Absolutely no reason. I was no longer at CBS News. He cared. He's a caring person, overly sentimental perhaps." Others, though, refused to buy it. Dick Salant, for example, believed that Rather never forgave him for saying in a closed meeting in the early 1970s that if Walter Cronkite were to get hit by a truck, he would probably be replaced by Roger Mudd. Asked if Rather had ever discussed the incident with him, Salant said, "No, Dan never does that. Face to face, Dan is your best friend. After I left, I had a major operation. Dan heard about it and called up my wife and said, 'I'd go through fire for that man.' Bullshit."

Sandy Socolow stewed for years over Rather's apparent duplicity regarding Socolow's status as executive producer of the *Evening News.* When Rather was named Cronkite's successor, he personally asked Socolow to remain as producer of the broadcast, and in the course of their nine months together on the broadcast, Rather never wavered in his expressed support of his executive producer; but, as Socolow later discovered, the anchorman had been auditioning candidates for Socolow's job almost from the moment he took over the broadcast. "He's tricky," Salant said of Rather; "he plays client's golf."

An oft-cited example was Rather's refusal in the Nixon years to sign a letter protesting Paley's banning of "instant analysis" after presidential speeches and then rushing to join the protest after learning of Salant's tacit approval of the letter. Rather was a mystery to many of his colleagues; he could be as tough as anyone on the air—tougher usually—and yet in the most baffling ways he would back down. Although Rather's greatest strength was his performance on big breaking stories—he had few equals there—one of the low points of his career came on a story that should have been his showcase, the resignation of Richard Nixon. Cronkite anchored the network's coverage, and Sevareid, Mudd, and Rather offered commentary. After Nixon's speech, which offered no apology for Watergate and associated misdeeds, and no explanation, Rather, who had faced down Nixon and had thereby added to his reputation in doing it, became suddenly magnanimous. "Walter," Rather said, "I think it may very well go down, when history takes a look at it, as one of Richard Nixon's if not his finest hour." Rather went on to say that the disgraced but unrepentant president "gave this moment a touch of class—more than that, a touch of majesty—touching that nerve in most people that says to their brain: Revere the presidency, and respect the president. The Republic and the country comes [*sic*] first."

Roger Mudd, cool and incisive, put the speech in more realistic perspective. "Just from a pure congressional point of view, I really wouldn't think that was a very satisfactory speech. It did not deal with the realities of why he was leaving. There was no accounting in the speech of how he got there and why he was leaving that Oval Room. That whole question of Watergate is all that anybody in the Congress has had on their minds for the better part of a year. Half the Congress has defended him; half the Congress has gone out on a limb for him. In the absence of any explanation or any acknowledgment of the president's responsibility in the Watergate cover-up, the viewer is left to conclude that it was simply some craven politicians in the Congress who collapsed in their defense of the president, and solely because of that, he was having to leave the presidency."

It is possible, even likely, that Rather's uncharacteristically milquetoast performance came from a sense of fair play, a reluctance to be seeming to gloat. However, there was no stopping the less generous interpretation, which was widespread, that Rather was covering his flank, mollifying the many CBS affiliates that believed he had become too politicized in his coverage of Nixon and wanted him off the White House beat.

Rather was not a natural performer, or at least he was not a naturally good performer. He had to work at smiling, for example; it was not his natural expression. He knew that he came across as a bit harsh, a little "intense," as people were always telling him, and over the years he worked on developing an on-air persona that had a touch of warmth and humor. Rather was not a graceful writer, like Sevareid or Collingwood or Safer, but he came to be known for his colorful Texasisms. He'd spice up a report on a congressional race, say, by observing that Candidate A's chances of winning were about as likely "as a stick with one end," or of a notion with little chance of success, he'd say, "That dog won't hunt." Such embellishments were meant to seem to viewers like a natural flair for colorful talk, but even they were taken by some as a sign of Rather's phoniness. Many of Rather's "spontaneous" sayings were, in fact, written out beforehand, and some of them weren't even written by Rather, but by his writers. There was certainly nothing immoral or unethical about it, but to a lot of people it was one of those things about Dan Rather that just stuck in the craw.

After he became anchor, Rather longed to be taken seriously as the managing editor, and sometimes, when there was a visitor from the outside, a reporter or an official, he would launch into a routine of important-seeming activity and hands-on involvement that was, to say the least, a marked departure from routine. One day early in Rather's tenure as anchor/managing editor, Fred Rothenberg, the young television columnist from the Associated Press, came to do a profile on Rather. Rothenberg, who was new to the beat, got quite a treat: Rather on the phone, caucusing with producers, going over the script, giving orders— being the managing editor. Howard Stringer, then the executive producer, and Lane Venardos, a senior producer, were in stitches. "Just think," Venardos said to Stringer, "people are paying fifty dollars a seat for theater tickets just ten blocks away, and we're getting it for free." Although Rather did, in fact, exert his influence on the broadcast, he wasn't the one-man whirligig he seemed to Rothenberg that afternoon. From that day on, whenever Rather went into his managing editor routine, Stringer and Venardos would exchange knowing glances and say, "The full Rothenberg." The term stuck.

Such behavior was seen as part of Rather's mythmaking, like the story he told about Eric Sevareid and Sevareid's list of books. Rather often referred to Sevareid as one of his mentors (his "guru in television" Rather once called him), and he liked to tell how Sevareid had once taken the callow, unpolished Rather under his wing in Saigon. As Rather related the story, he was concerned about his prospects of becoming anything more than merely a good or adequate correspondent. He wanted to be a great correspondent, and he asked Sevareid just what it would take. The two of them were eating dinner at the restaurant on the roof of the Caravelle Hotel (where CBS News had its office and where one could be reasonably sure, Rather said, "that the meat you were being served wasn't dog meat"). In the background (Rather has it) flares were going off, artillery was sounding, and in the very far distance an air strike was being waged. Sevareid said that Rather ought to think about taking a year off, enrolling in courses at Harvard, and mostly just spending some time with books. Sevareid said that Rather should read all the books that he hadn't read in high school or at Sam Houston State—the classics, the philosophers, the ancient thinkers. He listed them: Machiavelli, Montaigne, Henry James, Thomas Jefferson, Aristotle, Plato, and Herodotus. Herodotus stuck out in Rather's mind especially, because Sevareid (as Rather told the story) had often discussed Herodotus in the context of the Vietnam War and was rather surprised that Rather's knowledge of the Greek father of history was so scant.

Rather recalled that he thanked Sevareid for his advice, and when he got back to the United States, he discussed it with his wife, Jean, and decided that because of his family obligations (son, Dan, and daughter, Robin), he couldn't take a leave from CBS to go back to college. But he could read Sevareid's list of books. He bought the Chicago Great Books series, the legend goes, and read every one of the books on Sevareid's list.

Richard Leibner later said that when, as a young agent in the N. S. Bienstock firm, he heard that story about Rather, he was lastingly impressed. It showed Leibner something of Rather's drive, his urge to better himself, his desire to expand his possibilities. It was, in fact, a marvelous anecdote, compelling in every regard but one: When asked about it years later, Eric Sevareid said, "I'm not sure that's true."

But didn't he remember the supper at the Caravelle Hotel? The advice about the ancient philosophers? Montaigne? Herodotus?

"No," said Sevareid, "I don't."

What's more, Sevareid said, there had been an article recently in the *New York Times Magazine* quoting Rather as saying that on the advice of Sevareid, he had for years carried around in his pocket a copy of *The Elements of Style,* William Strunk, Jr., and E. B. White's primer on economical writing. There was a problem with that story, Sevareid said. "I've never read the book in my life."

But why would Rather be so specific about the Caravelle Hotel account or the Strunk and White book? "I think Dan has little flights of fancy once in a while," Sevareid said.

Of course, it may have been Sevareid, not Rather, who misremembered the incidents, but the salient point is that Sevareid, the man whom Rather calls his "guru," would fall so easily to the conclusion that Rather was just engaging in a little myth making. That was the institutional impression of Dan Rather. In telling the story of his career at CBS News, Rather would give a detailed account of the first time he was offered an anchor position. It was early 1963. Rather was a new correspondent with the network, he'd just opened the New Orleans bureau, and Blair Clark and another executive (Rather remembered its being his friend and mentor Ernie Leiser) approached him about coming to New York to anchor a new version of the morning newscast. Rather paints the picture in some detail: They met in his motel room, and he remembers being a little embarrassed at the modesty of the place ("your early Holiday Inn"). Clark pointed out that while Rather was doing very well in the field, the move to New York could be a big career break, could put him on a track to become *Evening News* anchor someday. Rather thought about it and thanked the men but said no, what he wanted to be just then was what he was—a field correspondent, honing his craft. Years later, when Ernie Leiser was asked about that incident, he said that he had no recollection of such a meeting or of Rather's being asked to come to New York at that stage of his career. Clark remembered the story, but only as an anecdote in Rather's autobiography. "You have," said Clark, someone who "invents legends about himself and embroiders them delightfully."

Myth making, of course, is not an uncommon exercise among men who pull themselves up from humble means to positions of power and influence, and Rather was particularly sensitive about his background, his modest education and intellectual foundation. He knew that scholarliness was a revered trait among the CBS icons (with the possible exception of Cronkite), and he knew that inside CBS News, deep thinking would not be included in even the most generous assessments of Dan Rather. (Oxford-educated Howard Stringer, Rather's executive producer and later his boss, used to joke about Rather's lack of depth. He told an especially wicked story about a time he and Rather were at the London airport awaiting their flight to New York. To kill time, they stopped at the bookstall at Heathrow, where Rather spotted a copy of *The Decline and Fall of the Roman Empire,* the famed work by the English historian Edward Gibbon. Indicating the book, Rather turned to Stringer and said, "You read that in the original Latin, I suppose.") And as he moved through his career, constantly redefining himself, Rather acquired aspects of a persona that didn't quite fit but that he awkwardly wore anyway, like a vain matron in ill-fitting shoes. When Rather first became anchor, the most noticeable of the new furnishings in his redone office was a tall, formal lectern, with a large leather-bound Bible perched open on it. None of Rather's colleagues had known him to be particularly religious or a student of the Scriptures, so they came to the inevitable conclusion that the Bible was there for effect, a holy prop in the ever-unfolding saga of Dan Rather.

And then there was his Sir Edward Creasy period. For a time visitors to Rather's office (which was spare—a fishtank, a desk, and little else) found, conspicuously handy on Rather's desk, an antique copy of Creasy's dense history *Fifteen Decisive Battles of the World.* Sometimes, without prompting, Rather picked up the book and began a discourse on the lessons to be learned from Sir Edward's work, or he used it as source material for his occasional staff pep rallies in the newsroom. On one particularly gloomy day, when the *Evening News* ratings had slipped, Rather called the staff together and gave a rousing locker-room speech. "All right," he said, "this is when we're best, it's a fight now! We're not going to feel sorry for ourselves, and we're not going to let this get us down. I only have one thing to say to all of you people." A long dramatic pause. "Syracuse four-thirteen. Read it." Rather turned on his heels, and returned to his office as his staffers scratched their heads and looked at one another in puzzlement. Syracuse 413? No one was about to ask Rather what he meant, so a couple of the curious pressed *Evening News* researcher Toby Wertheim (the "minister of truth," as she was known) for a clue. It turned out that Rather's obscure reference was taken from Chapter Two of Creasy's tome, recounting the "Defeat of the Athenians at Syracuse, 413 B.C." It tells of the near destruction of the Syracusans at the hands of the Athenians and how, battered and divided by factions within, the Syracusans nearly surrendered before turning the tide and prevailing against the odds. The staff dined out on that Rather story for days.

Unshaved, wearing a hat and dark sunglasses and his collar turned up, Rather could walk right by one of his colleagues on the street without being recognized. In fact, he got to be pretty good at disguising himself. It wasn't precisely the image that the CBS promotion department would have chosen, but for Rather, it was entirely fitting. Asked about Rather's disguises, Van Sauter shrugged it off. "A guy likes to have his privacy and get around, so he develops a cover. It's perfectly natural."

Rather needed a disguise for the same reason that in a restaurant he preferred to sit with his back to the room, for the same reason that he needed Toby Chandler, an amiable gentleman occasionally described as Rather's "traveling companion," who was, in fact, one of Rather's bodyguards (a former head of security for the National Football League also did bodyguard work for Rather occasionally). Simply put, in the term used by several of his colleagues, Dan Rather was something of a "lightning rod." Things happened to him that didn't happen to other journalists, even famous TV journalists. Walter Cronkite didn't have two bodyguards. Tom Brokaw didn't wear disguises. But throughout his career, and then with increasing frequency after he became anchor of the *Evening News,* Rather was prone to bizarre incidents. After a time they became a kind of Rather signature.

Sometimes the incidents arose from his extremely aggressive reportorial style and could obscure his first-rate work as a reporter. For example, Rather did genuinely good work for CBS News during the long-running Watergate story, but it was his confrontation with Richard Nixon ("Are you running for something?" "No, sir, Mr. President, are you?") that was remembered. In 1972, a few months before the Watergate break-in, Rather's Georgetown home was broken into, and after Watergate had begun to unfold, with its tales of White House "plumbers units" and dirty tricks, Rather asked the police to reinvestigate his break-in, on the theory that he'd been a target of the White House (a suspicion that was never proved). In 1968 many reporters worked the Democratic National Convention in Chicago under tough circumstances, but it was Rather who took a punch in the belly from one of Mayor Richard Daley's security people in full view of a national television audience (prompting a rare outburst of anger from Walter Cronkite, who said, "It looks like we've got a bunch of thugs in here"). Joe Benti, who was a floor correspondent with Rather that night, later assessed one curious result of such incidents. "He got roughed up,"

Benti said, "and it had the perverse effect of making Dan Rather better known to television viewers."

When Rather was at *60 Minutes,* just before going to the *Evening News* as anchor, he was sent to Afghanistan to do a report on the struggling rebel movement there. With Andy Lack as his producer, he walked dozens of miles across the Afghan border and into no-man's-land to get his story. It was a brutal assignment and quite dangerous, but when it aired, Rather wasn't hailed as an adventurer-journalist. Instead, he was ridiculed by TV critics across the country as "Gunga Dan," a derisive reference to the disguise he wore on his journey, which was meant to make the middle-aged American TV star look like an Afghan peasant. To the television press Rather's great adventure came off as a clumsy piece of show-biz hokum, and he was hurt by it. Tom Shales of the *Washington Post,* who could hurl a barb with devastating precision, observed that Rather looked in his getup like an extra from *Doctor Zhivago.*

In fact, that interlude between Rather's being named successor to Cronkite and his actually moving into the job proved particularly hazard-strewn. The organization was rife with second-guessing, Rather was beginning to feel unsure, and his unfortunate knack for landing in bizarre circumstances continued unabated. In November 1980, for example, Rather went to Chicago for what should have been a routine assignment, an interview with author Studs Terkel for *60 Minutes.* Rather caught a cab from O'Hare International Airport. After a time it became apparent that the driver was unable to find Terkel's house from the directions that Rather gave him. Rather asked the cabbie to stop and let him out, but the driver, fearing that he was about to get stiffed, took off, tearing wildly through the streets of Chicago at high speed as Rather leaned out the window, screaming for help. Rather pressed disorderly conduct charges against the driver, who, for his part, said that he had only been looking for a policeman and accused Rather of ruining his "professional reputation." Rather ultimately let the matter drop, citing the press of a "mounting schedule of reporting assignments"—but not before the incident had been thoroughly considered in the national press.

Sometimes Rather had no one but himself to blame for the frays he got tangled in. At the time of the infamous Chicago cab ride the furor caused by another incident involving him was just dying down. There had been, predictably, a rush of newspaper and magazine articles about the man who was replacing Cronkite, and in one of those interviews, with the *Ladies' Home Journal,* Rather imprudently allowed that he had once taken drugs in the 1950s. It was under police supervision, and he'd done it for the purpose of a story; but what rang across the countryside like a bulletin was that Walter Cronkite's successor had admitted doing drugs. And it wasn't just any drug that Rather had taken; it was *heroin.* Rather had just been trying to be frank with the interviewer, but it was a measure of his poor judgment that in the town of Portage, Indiana, the City Council unanimously passed a resolution declaring that he should not become the anchor of the *Evening News.* Bill Leonard tried to shrug off the incident, saying he "couldn't get excited about a reportorial experiment by Dan Rather or any other young newsman that took place a quarter of a century ago," but in fact, the episode was a huge embarrassment for CBS and for Rather.

Bad judgment also got Rather in trouble after the Galloway trial. Being grilled on the witness stand on national television had been a strain on the anchorman, and several weeks later, when one of the reporters who'd covered the trial showed up in New York for an interview, Rather lost his composure in most memorable fashion. The reporter, Steve Wilson, who worked for a syndicated show called *Breakaway,* had repeatedly tried to contact Rather for an interview. When Rather didn't respond, Wilson put his request in a registered letter, and when that brought no result, Wilson decided to stake out the Broadcast Center until he spotted Rather and to interview him on the run—an "ambush interview," in the style, ironically enough, of *60 Minutes.* After a while Rather walked up to the Broadcast Center with Howard Stringer, and Wilson and his camera crew hustled over. Rather objected. "I've sent you a registered letter," Wilson told Rather, "I don't know how else to do it." Rather, appearing calm, put his hand on Wilson's shoulder, looked at Wilson's sound man, and said with a smile, "Get the microphone right up, will you?" Then, cameras and sound rolling, Rather put his face close to Wilson's, looked him in the eye, and said, "Fuck you. You got it?"

Stringer smiled weakly, perhaps anticipating the inevitable headlines, which, in fact, rained down in abundance. Wilson ran a clip of the confrontation (with Rather's message bleeped out) on his show, and a nationwide audience witnessed the scene. There was the expected outrage, of course, enough to warrant a response from Rather. The anchorman wrote Wilson an apology that stirred nearly as much comment as the incident itself. "I mistook who you were and what you were doing," Rather said. "That was inexcusable, rude and un-Christian behavior, for which I am remorseful." To say the least, many who saw the clip (and *everyone* saw it; it became a segment in an in-house production of on-air bloopers) had some reservations about the sincerity of Rather's expression of remorse over his "un-Christian" behavior. Christian or un-Christian, behaving that way *in front of a television camera*—now *that* was cause for remorse.

There were also incidents over which Rather had no control, flashes of violence that he seemed to touch off just by being Dan Rather. At an affiliates' convention in San Francisco Rather was walking across Nob Hill with Sauter, a few paces behind some other CBS News people, when a man suddenly accosted Rather and began verbally abusing him, screaming violent threats and accusing Rather of various imagined misdeeds. Sauter and the others hustled Rather off to the meeting room and summoned the police.

It was a frightening incident, but it didn't end there. In 1986 the same individual made his way to New York, where he checked into the New York Hilton Hotel and delivered to Black Rock the message that he intended to kill Dan Rather. Again the man was arrested, but he'd caused a genuine chill. It was an extreme case but by no means isolated. At Kennedy Airport in New York once Rather was walking through a crowded area with Stringer and Lane Venardos. There was some jostling, and a man suddenly approached him and just knocked him down, flat. "He's the kind of person things seem to happen to," said Venardos. "You think anybody recognizes Tom Brokaw when he walks down the street?"

When CBS chose Dan Rather as its heir to Murrow and Cronkite, it took a risk that perhaps Bill Leonard and the others hadn't even considered. It wasn't a journalistic risk—Rather was a strong reporter, as strong in his way as either Murrow or Cronkite—but Rather was a tightly wound, complex, and sometimes unpredictable individual, about whom the institution clearly had deeply mixed feelings. It was a setup for conflict, exacerbated by the profound changes taking place in the company, especially in the news division. When, through the conscious decision of management, Rather was given the strongest voice inside CBS News, the potential for disaster was created.

The risk came home in dramatic fashion on the evening of September 11, 1987, when Rather's hubris caused a historic embarrassment for CBS. The *Evening News* was on location in Miami to give a big-event "feel" to its coverage of the visit of the pope. Just fifteen minutes before the broadcast was to go on the air, word came from New York that CBS's coverage of a semifinal match in the U.S. Open tennis tournament might run long, cutting into some of the allotted *Evening News* time. Rather was furious and informed New York that if his broadcast didn't air as scheduled, he wouldn't be at the anchor desk when it did go on. Sure enough, tennis ran long, and Rather stood up, unhooked his mike, and walked off the set. When, just a moment later tennis went off the air, and the network went to Miami for the *Evening News,* Rather wasn't there. For more than six minutes, an eternity in broadcasting, CBS went "black"—no picture being transmitted by the network. Such an occurrence had never happened before at CBS, or anywhere else, so far as anyone knew. The incident was a terrible embarrassment for CBS News, as well for the network, which had to answer not only to confused viewers but to outraged affiliates. Going black is the elemental sin in broadcasting, an eventuality to be guarded against at all costs.

The most telling aspect of the Miami incident was that at the key instant, when Rather said he would leave his anchor chair if the tennis match ran long, no one in authority—not the executive producer, not the president of CBS News, not Gene Jankowski, the president of the CBS Broadcast Group—felt he had the weight to order the $2.2 million anchorman to get back in his chair and read the news. What's more, no one dared exercise the option of putting someone else in the anchor chair in Rather's stead, although two veteran newsmen, Bernie Goldberg and Richard Roth, were at the studio. Explained one producer on the scene: "The managing editor [Rather] had told the president of CBS News that we were were not going on at all if we couldn't go on at six-thirty. Under those circumstances, you just can't take the air."

The incident crystallized six years of unease over Dan Rather and perfectly framed a central conflict of the Sauter-Rather era: the tradition of a broad-based, team-oriented organization on the one side and the accretion of power and authority in the anchorman on the other. "It was everyone's worse fear come true," said one *Evening News* producer; "it was like the great East Coast blackout. It all came down to one two-dollar transistor, except it was a two-million-dollar anchorman. He was the petulant anchorman and the boss at the same time."

Walter Cronkite said bluntly that Rather should have been fired. The *Times* of London asked in an article if Rather was "losing his marbles." The *New York Post* ran a front-page photo of Rather on the *Evening News* set with his face missing and above it the banner headline TV TANTRUM!

Some close to Rather said that he was surprised and hurt by reactions to the incident, that he had expected it to be taken as a Murrow-like stand on behalf of news. In truth, Rather did care fiercely about his newscast and was ceaselessly vigilant in protecting it. But many in the organization agreed with the assessment of Bill Leonard, the man who had given Rather his managing editor's title during the frantic anchor derby of 1980. "It's not healthy for him to be the final decision maker," Leonard told Harry Waters of *Newsweek*. "I simply gave in to him, and I've regretted it ever since."

And up in Redding, Connecticut, Ed Joyce, long removed from CBS, read the accounts of the latest embarrassment with a kind of grim recognition and perhaps some degree of vindication. As president of CBS News, Ed Joyce had come to the rather stunning conclusion that his anchorman was not completely stable. It thus occurred to Joyce, as Leonard would later say, that having Rather as final decision maker at CBS News was not a healthy thing. Ed Joyce had tried to do something about that, and in the end, he would always believe, it cost him his career.

Chapter

ED JOYCE CAME AS a complete surprise to Dan Rather, and Rather didn't like surprises.

Rather was in Boston in September 1983 when he began to hear from his *Evening News* grapevine that something big was happening and that it involved Sauter, Joyce, and the news division. That made it Rather's business, and he was more than a little bit surprised that any development of consequence would be undertaken without his being clued in, especially when he was on the road. (He later suspected that CBS did what it did when it did precisely *because* he was on the road.) Curious, he called Sauter, but Sauter was unusually evasive. There was nothing he could tell Rather right then, Sauter said, the whole thing might not come off, and Sauter would let the anchorman know just as soon as he could. That made Rather all the more nervous, and by the time he got back to the New York office, on Friday afternoon, September 16, he was on edge. His people were asking him what was going on, and he had nothing to tell them. Then Gene Jankowski called, and what Jankowski had to say, Rather recalled, "came like a bolt out of the proverbial blue for me—that Van was going to Black Rock, that Ed was going to become news division president."

Jankowski told Rather that he planned to make the announcement that afternoon and would explain it all to Rather over dinner. Rather was not pleased. He called Sauter. "I told him, one, I was surprised. I didn't appreciate being surprised. I remember saying to him, 'I've got very few rules of thumb around here, and one is, if I'm expected to be in on the landings, then you'd better have me around for takeoffs. It's okay with me if I'm not gonna be around for the landing, fine. But if you expect me to be in on the landing and all through the flight, then I want to be around for the takeoff. I'm not complaining about this. I'm telling you exactly how I feel. I'm surprised. Somewhat disappointed. I'm pleased for you.' "

Rather recalled that Sauter said he wasn't really leaving news, that his duties were just being expanded, but that worried Rather, too. He talked to Ed Joyce about the blurred lines of authority, and, as Rather recalled it, Joyce said there could be some value in ambiguity. "I didn't agree," Rather later said. "I'm elemental man in that sense. When I get off the truck in the morning, I like to say, 'This guy's boss, this guy's a tool pusher, and this guy's who you report to.' I don't value ambiguity in such things much. But it was no argument. We got off to a good start."

And so they did, and at first it seemed possible that Rather and Joyce would come to an amiable and workable relationship, if not the marriage that Rather had enjoyed with Sauter. In fact, Joyce's real problem, it seemed, was not with Rather or any individual but with containment of the general agitation that was tearing at the place. It was hard to overstate the institutional anxiety that gripped CBS News in 1984 and 1985. From the outside came the pressures of Westmoreland, Helms, and Turner. Internally the glitzy new *West 57th* further polarized the organization into its increasingly familiar camps of yesterday and today; there was morbid unease in the decimated documentary unit and the messy departure of Diane Sawyer from the *Morning News;* Bill Kurtis was angry and alienated; Jane Wallace was fuming; Howard Stringer was isolated; the Cronkite-Socolow wing was deeply embittered; and Phyllis George was giving rise to endless hand wringing and hair tugging. Each new day brought the possibility of new disasters.

Ed Joyce's answer was to get tough. He was by nature a structure-conscious person, and if Sauter liked to talk about running CBS News like the People's Army, with no insignia showing, Joyce was more inclined to run it like the U.S. Army, with insignia prominently displayed. He—not Bill Moyers, not Don Hewitt, not Diane Sawyer, and certainly not Dan Rather—was president of CBS News. "I think he consistently made a point of the animals not being in charge of the asylum," said Lane Venardos. *"He* was in charge of the asylum. He was the president of CBS News."

It was an approach that reflected Joyce's rather rigid nature and that, very quickly, had an unfortunate effect. Joyce held fewer meetings with his staff, the *Evening News* postmortems dropped off, and access to Joyce narrowed, and as he became less visible, he became more the focus of the accumulated uneasiness. He had already aroused the wrath of many with the Socolow affair, and as he sought to impose new efficiencies and economies upon the organization, the general uneasiness erupted into fairly open disdain. There was, for example, the case of Perry Wolff, the documentary producer and executive who, as executive producer of *CBS Reports,* was master of a phantom empire. Wolff's long and impressive list of documentary credits is blank for the year 1983, and in 1984 his name was on only one documentary. Wolff had absolutely nothing to do at CBS News in that period, so when a friend asked his advice on a public television project called "Civilization and the Jews," Wolff happily obliged. Joyce, having heard about it, apparently believed that Wolff was getting paid for his consultations; he was said to be furious. "And Joyce, who was looking for a way to cut salaries and people, demoted me from executive producer to producer," Wolff recalled, "and I just wouldn't take that crap." Wolff, who was not known as a brawler, walked across the street and confronted Joyce, who relented. "It was the only time I ever saw him," Wolff said. "I never got a lunch with him. He wouldn't go to lunch with me. That's the way he ran it; he ran it out of the back office."

Joyce was so aloof, so invisible that he became the subject of a kind of black humor. Peter Herford, his vice-president in charge of affiliate relations, had thought he was getting along with Joyce as well or as poorly as anyone else—which was to say he couldn't get his phone calls answered. Stringer, who was Joyce's top assistant, would tell him, "That's okay, I can't get my calls answered either," so Herford didn't worry until he went one particularly long stretch, more than a month, without talking to his boss. Herford concluded that the only way to get a meeting with Ed Joyce was to hang around the men's toilet outside executive row, "Because of all the damned Tab he drank," Herford said, "he went to the men's room literally every twenty to thirty minutes."

Herford decided that ambushing Joyce in the men's room was going too far, but he continued to be plagued by his circumstance. Then one day Dan Rather called. He and Herford had worked together years before, and the anchorman asked, "Hey, are you okay?" Herford explained that he didn't know, that he hadn't been able to talk to Joyce to find out what, if anything, was wrong. Rather told him to wait right there; he'd go to Joyce himself. Within just a few minutes Herford was in Joyce's office, with Stringer present. Joyce told Herford that he needed someone with "different skills" in the affiliates' job. Herford recalled saying to his boss, " 'Ed, all I can ask you is one thing: If you didn't want me in this job, why didn't you tell me? I don't want to work for you if you didn't want me. Why didn't you tell me? I've been in management long enough. I know the rules of this game, and there's no point in hanging around if your boss doesn't want you hanging around.' To which I got no response whatsoever, and all I got was a laugh out of Howard."

Joyce told Herford, who'd been with CBS News for twenty-five years, who'd been the Saigon bureau chief at the height of the Vietnam War, that he didn't have to leave CBS News; he could be a producer on *Sunday Morning.* "Ed's line was a classic," Herford recalled. "He said, 'We think you'll love it on *Sunday Morning,* doing pieces on deer running through the woods.' That's it. That's the quote, I'll never forget that one. 'You'll love doing pieces on deer running through the woods.' "

Herford was not the only CBS News staffer who had problems with access to Joyce. Rather was almost always able to get through—Joyce wasn't suicidal—but other anchors were not. Bill Kurtis went through the most difficult year in his career in 1985, the year that Phyllis George joined him on the *Morning News,* and during that time he was constantly amazed at his inability to gain access to the president of CBS News. "Joyce becomes president, and we don't see him for six months," Kurtis recalled. "We don't see him for *six months.* Six months. Doesn't pick up the phone. Doesn't walk down the hall. I thought he was mentally ill."

At the time of Charles Collingwood's death, when grief mingled with the institutional anger in a particularly bitter moment, Andy Rooney wrote Joyce a note accusing him of having mistreated the late reporter, of having isolated him in a remote office and allowed him to wither in his final years. Joyce, who habitually wrote memos to the file (giving him fodder for the book he would one day write), wrote Rooney back, including a copy of a note that he had sent along with flowers to Collingwood in the hospital. "Jeez," Rooney later observed, "that's caring for the image of the future."

Ed Joyce was isolated and unpopular almost from the start, but his long and agonized downfall as president of CBS News had a far more definite trajectory than that. Over the course of his two-year tenure, he made a series of terrible political blunders that put him squarely at odds with Dan Rather and thus assured his unhappy end.

The first of the missteps, and perhaps the worst, came when Joyce tried to tighten the burgeoning CBS News talent payroll. The high price of CBS journalists—the average annual salary was well above $100,000, with many earning $500,000 and more—was the largest single expense in the CBS News budget, which, in turn, was the largest source of concern to Black Rock. Both Sauter and Joyce were incessantly badgered about the cost of news by Jankowski, who, in turn, felt the heat from Wyman. In contrast to Dick Salant, however, Sauter and Joyce were much inclined to try to accommodate the corporate demands for cost control. In fairness, Salant had never had to cope with runaway payroll costs brought on by talent raids, which was a constant concern to his successors, to the point of near obsession with Joyce. And if there was one person most associated with the skyrocketing salaries, it was Richard Leibner, the canny accountant who maneuvered CBS into a $22 million deal with Dan Rather and in effect created a free agency system for network news reporters. Leibner represented so many CBS News correspondents so well that Van Sauter once said he "almost constitutes a bargaining unit in the context of a labor union."

When Ed Joyce became president of CBS News in the fall of 1983, he was determined that Leibner would not whipsaw him as successfully as he had Bill Leonard; soon enough he was presented with the opportunity to assert himself. Two of Leibner's clients—Los Angeles correspondent Gary Shepard and Paris correspondent Don Kladstrup—came to the ends of their contracts, and Leibner shopped them all to the other net-works. Joyce wasn't willing to go the route with either Shepard or Kladstrup (for whom Leibner was asking raises in the $20,000-plus range), and both went to ABC. Although Joyce and Sauter were willing to let Kladstrup go, they hated to lose Shepard, and the departures were particularly ominous because another group of Leibner stars—Andy Rooney, Bob Simon, and Barry Petersen—was also coming up for contract negotiation. Foreseeing a new round of talent raids coming and torn between the prospect of losing some of his best people and the chilling notion of explaining salary leaps to Black Rock, Joyce embarked on an ill-considered course: He publicly declared war on Richard Leibner.

The news business had never seen anything like it. The banner headline of the November 30, 1983, issue of *Variety,* the show-business trade paper, loudly proclaimed: CBS NEWS DECLARES WAR ON AGENT. Every Wednesday morning Leibner and his wife, Carole, picked up the weekly trade paper at the newsstand on Columbus Circle; Leibner later said that when he saw that headline, "I almost had a heart attack." In the article Joyce attacked Leibner for not bargaining in good faith, and provided *Variety* writer Jack Loftus with the information that each year Leibner negotiated from CBS News $15 million in salaries, which, with commissions from Leibner's other clients elsewhere, brought his gross annual income to $2.25 million. "We're not talking here about some Ma and Pa operation," Joyce said. "We're talking about the General Motors of agents." Joyce said he feared a new round of talent raids, pointing to the Kladstrup and Shepard defections, at the same time hinting that CBS hadn't planned to renew Kladstrup anyway. (In truth, CBS News had intended to keep Kladstrup but had planned to reassign him to the Chicago bureau; Kladstrup, who was reluctant to relocate his children, declined the reassignment, and joined ABC News.)

Joyce's tactic was apparently meant to reveal Leibner as a corrupting force in television news (and possibly to intimidate CBS News people into dropping Leibner as their agent), but whatever his aim, it backfired terribly. Kladstrup, who happened to be on hazard duty in Beirut when the story broke, fired off a cable to Joyce in New York. "I can hardly believe what I just read in Variety," Kladstrup wrote. "Nor can I hardly believe that the president of CBS News, or any organization, would resort to such petty nastiness. If your intention was to hurt and embarrass me, you have succeeded. Not only were the things you said about me false and misleading, they were vicious. Congratulations on a terrific hatchet job.

"And to think," Kladstrup concluded, "I was worried that Beirut was the only place I had to watch my back." The cable immediately made its way to *Variety,* and Joyce's attack became a full-blown public controversy.

What most stunned people inside CBS, and across the television business, was not the headline of the article or the attacks on Kladstrup and Leibner, but Ed Joyce's statement in the second paragraph of the story. "I am determined," Joyce told Loftus, "not to let the flesh peddlers affect the caliber of our broadcasts."

The phrase, Rather later said, "hit me like a thud in the pit of the stomach." It was a shocking choice of words, which the Leibners (and many others) interpreted as blatant anti-Semitism and which raised the intensity of anti-Joyce sentiment at least one notch. In a rare display of public intramural sniping, ABC correspondents Betsy Aaron and Richard Threlkeld (both CBS defectors) wrote an angry article-length letter to *Variety,* lambasting the president of CBS News. "Rather than cursing the flesh in his own employ and defaming two decent people," the journalists wrote, "Mr. Joyce and his superiors would be better advised to discover why some of his most talented employees are quitting CBS News and moving to ABC News. If he thinks it is all about money, Mr. Joyce is surely going to lose his war against Leibner."

Leibner, devastated by the attack, later claimed that he had been genuinely worried about damage to his business. But he was smart enough not to strike back in the newspapers. As he later put it (in his inimitable fashion), "It's my greatest philosophy that I try to teach all my new young clients: Squat on the campfire and piss, and it smokes and it smells. Walk away, think about it, don't shoot off your mouth, and there's nothing that can stop you from coming back a day, two days later and *then* pissing on the fire. But piss on it while you're hot, and try to relight it, and all you're going to get is smoke and smell. That's my basic philosophy I teach." There was, of course, smoke and smell enough without Leibner's contribution. Joyce took a lot of heat in the hallways, some of it coming from his most famous journalists (and Leibner clients), such as Mike Wallace, Diane Sawyer, and Andy Rooney. Rooney asked him how he had ever let himself be put in such a position of such ambiguous authority (and Leibner exploited the situation to win for Rooney a new contract that brought his annual salary to more than $400,000, while allowing him to continue to write his lucrative newspaper column).

Joyce had made a serious mistake, one that not only was embarrassing to CBS and to himself but threatened to impair his ability to function as president. To declare war on Leibner was to declare war on Leibner's clients, and in Joyce's case, that meant practically his entire first string and most of his bench. It was also clear that Leibner was not about to blithely forgive and forget. *Flesh peddler* were words that were seared into Leibner's brain, and he must have an apology before business could return to normal. Leibner fretted and stewed, he appealed to Sauter (who tried to distance himself from the affair), and finally he formed what he called his "war council"—a group of his clients and friends who acted as his advisers during the "flesh peddler" period. It was no insignificant collection, including Rather, Wallace, Morley Safer, the historian and journalist Theodore White, and Robert Sack, a noted First Amendment attorney.

After several weeks of frustration White advised Leibner to demand a meeting with Sauter and Joyce to clear the air. Leibner prepared for the arranged meeting as intensely as he prepared for the biggest negotiation, plotting tactics down to the details of who would sit where. The one thing he wanted to hit Joyce with, what stayed with him and gnawed at him, was the matter of anti-Semitism. But that wasn't a charge to be thrown around lightly, and so Leibner huddled for hours with Sack, the free speech specialist, over just the right way to broach the subject. Finally they struck upon the right way to fire what Leibner called his "secret weapon," and he was ready.

The night of the meeting arrived, and when the Leibners made a dramatic entrance at the Broadcast Center—everyone in the building knew why they were there—some of Leibner's most important clients made a show of support. Howard Stringer (for whom Leibner had negotiated a $250,000 contract as executive producer) and Dan Rather both were on hand, with Rather leaning over his anchor desk to give Carole a kiss. The tension was thick.

The meeting began, and, as Leibner recalled it, Joyce apologized for his incautious remark (he later steadfastly denied that he'd meant any anti-Semitism), but he defended his anger over what he saw as Leibner's unfair negotiating ploys, such as misrepresenting CBS's side to his clients and his clients' feelings to CBS. Leibner listened for a time, and then unloaded with his "secret weapon." He recalled: "I look across the room and I raise my voice. I said, 'Ed, let's get off it for a minute because this discussion goes no place else until you two say you believe me, that I've never lied to you. As long as you believe I was doing this, then we can't solve anything tonight. But there's something you have to know, Ed Joyce!' And I raise my voice even louder, and I point across the room. 'We received dozens, even hundreds, of *phone calls,* Ed, in the three days after that incident. And I want you to know that many of those people asked . . . 'Why didn't he call you *Shylock?*' "

"I now know why they put a mask on somebody in the electric chair," Leibner later said. "The blood rushed to his face. His hair stood up on the back of his neck. His hands shot up like Elsa Lanchester's hands in *The Bride of Frankenstein.* His ass left the couch. He was a man who had just received two hundred volts of raw electricity through his body."

Sauter tried to move the meeting along. As he later put it, "I didn't want to spend the evening witnessing anguish." After a time Joyce agreed to tell the staff that the war was over and, Leibner said, to offer a public apology. Leibner accepted the resolution, and the "flesh peddler" incident was over.

But it was not forgotten. Leibner, a highly emotional man given to histrionics, was understandably inclined to assign to the incident a large place in the brief and troubled history of Ed Joyce at CBS News. "He was dead the day he used an expression like that," Leibner later said. "He was never the same. That was the beginning of the end. That was the end of the end. It only took time." Leibner did not exaggerate by much. The incident marked a turning point in Joyce's relationship with Dan Rather, a poisoning from which it would never recover.

As Rather later put it, "The flesh peddler thing was one of those wounds, one of those deep cuts, that no matter how much scar tissue heals over it, is always tender. We had that. It never really left me."

The ultimate futility of Joyce's strategy was seen eight months later, when it came time to negotiate again with Dan Rather. Unlike the public spectacle that attended Rather's first negotiation, his renegotiation in the summer and fall of 1984 was conducted in near-total secrecy—so much so that not even Tom Wyman knew the details of the deal until it was completed.

Technically it wasn't exactly a renegotiation. One of the incentives that Bill Leonard had granted to Rather in 1980 was a "window" at the five-year point of his ten-year $22 million contract. At that point either party could seek a new deal; the window didn't actually open until December 1984, but both sides were eager to come to an agreement, so the discussions began months in advance of the deadline, with Joyce and Gene Jankowski guiding the negotiations for CBS.

Leibner realized that it was the perfect moment for Rather. Not only was he on top in the ratings, but with so much tumult at CBS, the last thing the network needed was a defection by its winning anchorman. So Leibner suggested a starting number: $5 million a year. Jankowski and Joyce were stunned. Nobody in journalism—and few in *show business*—earned $5 million a year. It was suggested to Leibner that his request, if granted, could very well backfire if word got out that the heir to Ed Murrow was earning more money to be a journalist than Hollywood stars were getting. Leibner backed away from his first figure, and after some quiet back and forth, a deal was made. Dan Rather got a new contract, calling for more than $3 million a year, a healthy $800,000-a-year raise (which was roughly the amount of the annual salary earned by his counterpart at ABC, Peter Jennings).

Jankowski and Joyce felt good about bargaining Leibner and Rather "down" to $3 million a year. Asked two years later whether he would have gone to the higher figure to keep Rather, Jankowski said, "No way. We'd put somebody else in the anchor slot and fall into third place before we would pay the amount of money that was being asked."

But there would be some question of who actually won the negotiation. Three million dollars a year was a record sum. Leibner, while not directly confirming the numbers (others did confirm them), slyly noted that if the $3 million figure was correct, "There's never been a bigger personal services contract in the history of the Western world."

In 1987 Leibner told an interviewer:

"You know what you think the number is. Is that a blown negotiation?"

What's more, there was at the time CBS gave Rather his new contract no external force driving the anchorman's price up—NBC had Tom Brokaw, ABC had settled on Peter Jennings, and Rather had instructed Leibner not even to talk to the other networks. Recalled Rather: "I told Richard, somewhat to Richard's chagrin, 'I don't want to fight over this contract. In 1980 my ship came in. I'm happy, I like this job, I want to stay.' Richard always hates that because it takes the cards out of his hand." CBS didn't know that, of course, but under the circumstances, giving Rather an $800,000 annual raise would not seem to be the height of restraint. Beyond that, CBS gave Rather a long-term renewal that would keep him at the CBS anchor desk until 1990—a commitment that later CBS News executives, desperate for leverage in dealing with Rather, came to lament.

Ed Joyce had helped give Dan Rather the richest contract in the history of the business, but he was determined not to give his anchorman any more power or even as much power as he'd enjoyed under Sauter. Lane Venardos, who replaced Stringer as the *Evening News* executive producer when Stringer became Joyce's executive vice-president, later explained Joyce's attitude. "It was okay if Dan Rather knew about things when they happened, but we're running CBS News—he and Howard—and there's no reason to be consulting with Dan. These things [such as hiring and firing and other personnel decisions] are not Dan's purview. We're in charge of these things."

Joyce thought that there was a danger in letting any anchorman have too much power and a particular danger with Dan Rather. Joyce was especially sensitive to the bizarre incidents Rather was prone to and to the anchorman's volatility in general. Van Sauter, later asked about the relationship between Joyce and Rather, underscored Joyce's uneasy feeling about Rather. "There's no doubt in my mind," Sauter said, "that Ed thought Dan was unstable. That explains part of the estrangement."

Joyce himself confirmed that assessment and joked, "The little red light on that camera—in it is some sort of gamma ray, and prolonged exposure causes genetic damage."

One of the things that gave Joyce particular concern was

Rather's susceptibility to illness just before big events, such as elections. Rather would develop a cold or a sore throat or partially lose his voice, and panic would set in. As CBS was preparing for its coverage of the 1984 elections—a big event in Rather's life, his first election as anchor—he suddenly developed a sore throat, and there was real concern that he might not be able to go on. CBS lost tens of thousands of dollars in missed rehearsal time that had to be rescheduled because of Rather's affliction. Van Sauter, who was generally relaxed about quirks of personality, never was particularly worried. "I knew that when the red light went on, he'd be in the chair, and his voice would be fine," he later said. "And there may be minions putting up tea with sugar and honey in it, or whatever, but he'd be there, with the energy and stamina and voice and the clarity necessary to get through the broadcast. I never gave a shit about that." But Joyce and others were considerably worried that Rather, under the pressure, would bend.

Rather, for his part, was aware of that fear, and he deeply resented it. "I had real throat problems," Rather said. "It wasn't anything psychosomatic; it wasn't anything to do with pressure; it was I had real problems. Now, Ed came to believe, this much I did know, that there's something kind of strange about it."

The suggestion that pressure got to him infuriated Rather, who prided himself on his long hours and his record of always answering the bell. "It pisses me off a little, yeah. On the sore throat thing, I got sore at him. God damn it, I work, I don't malinger, I may work too much. I work hurt; I work ill. If I can work, I work. I've never been any tender little flower. You tell me how you're going to survive Afghanistan, Vietnam, dueling with presidents if you're some fragile hothouse flower. My view was, 'Fuck you, Jack, I've been in all kind of places. When I say I've got a sore throat, I've got a sore throat.' Ed had this sort of thing that maybe it's the pressure, even when there wasn't any pressure. Pressure? I mean, hell, with your job on the line with Richard Nixon and a bunch of thieves and knaves, that's pressure."

At one point it was decided that Rather should see a team of specialists, and a weekend session was set up for him (at a hefty cost, estimated by one CBS executive at $20,000) in the comfortable surroundings of the Hamptons on Long Island. Ed Joyce, who was due for dinner at the White House, was designated to accompany Rather, and he sat in as Rather was put through a series of voice exercises and a battery of tests. Joyce made it to Washington; but Rather later got word that Joyce had resented the intrusion on his weekend, and that, too, became a source of friction.

"I knew he resented that," Rather said. "The fact of the matter is, it was his idea to go. I didn't want to go. I'm the guy who didn't want to go. Ed encouraged me to go. He insisted that he go along. I was a little embarrassed by the whole thing, to tell you the truth." Rather later went to a doctor in New York who told him that the problem was in the chilled, dirty air of the old Cronkite newsroom, which was still being used by the *Evening News*.

"All of this [sore throat problem], for the first time in my life, I now know why," Rather later explained. "We were in a fucking filthy hole over here, with no air moving around. It cost me a lot of my own money, not to mention some of CBS's money, to finally find it. I never had throat trouble to amount to anything in my life before I got in this job."

Reconstructing the deterioration of his relationship with Joyce in retrospect, Rather said that he became aware of Joyce's doubts about his stability after the incident at Kennedy Airport when Rather, accompanied by Stringer and Lane Venardos, was knocked to the ground by a total stranger. "Maybe in Lane's retelling the story, for some reason, Ed kind of latched on to that, I remember that. 'This is not good.' You have the Chicago taxicab thing, you have this madman out in San Francisco, the guy came out of nowhere. I'm not complaining; this is the unpleasant part of being somebody who's in the public eye. Now Ed Joyce, I guess, said, 'This guy has real problems.' "

For his part Rather had his doubts about Ed Joyce. "I wanted to like him, I wanted him to succeed, but I keep thinking, 'He's pretty strange.' [Considering] my feeling that way about him, I guess I shouldn't be surprised to find that his receiver was picking up from me some vibrations that I found him strange."

It was not, to say the least, the healthiest circumstance, the president of CBS News thinking his anchorman unstable, the anchorman thinking his boss strange, and it created an atmosphere in which Joyce's mistakes were magnified into major issues.

After the "flesh peddler" incident, Joyce's next controversial assertion of rank came when Rather wanted to hire a new producer for the *Evening News.* It was a seemingly minor matter—there were more than a dozen producers assigned exclusively to the *Evening News,* and one of the slots had been empty for a time—but Rather was fiercely protective of the program, and for weeks he badgered Venardos and Joyce about hiring someone, and for weeks, they smiled and said yes, they were looking. Rather fretted and stewed and thought that Joyce was stalling to save money. Finally someone came up with a candidate, a woman who had once worked for CBS and had left to have a family and was now available again. She interviewed with Linda Mason, an *Evening News* senior producer, and with Venardos, and both producers liked her. A meeting with Rather was arranged. He talked with her, they got along fine, and the deal was set—Rather had his producer.

But in the end she wasn't hired. Joyce claimed to know that her work wasn't satisfactory, and he vetoed her. Rather, of course, was furious. He wasn't asking for new perks, or more time off, or more money; he was asking for resources that he believed would help the *Evening News* competitively. The producer position was eventually filled, but the tension level between Rather and Joyce had been lifted another notch.

The next eruption in the Joyce-Rather relationship was born of a genuine tragedy, the death of two CBS journalists in southern Lebanon. Tafik Chazawi, a cameraman, and Bahij Metni, a sound man, were covering an Israeli sweep of Muslim villages believed to be bases for hit-and-run terrorists when they were killed by a shell fired from an Israeli tank. There had been some criticism of Israel over the question of press access to its military operations, so the incident occurred in an atmosphere of tension, which was exacerbated when early reports from the Associated Press suggested that the attack on the journalists might have been deliberate.

Joyce, Sauter, and the CBS News senior staff were in Europe for the bureau chiefs' meeting in Berlin when the incident occurred, and their common reaction was outrage. Joyce ordered that a protest be registered with the Israeli government, so Bob Chandler and Ernie Leiser drafted a strongly worded cable and sent it to Prime Minister Shimon Peres. The protest, which was sent in Joyce's name, was scathing, accusing the Israeli tank crew of "wanton" killing in an "unprovoked and deliberate" attack on the CBS journalists. The cable called the matter a "tragic and shameful affair," and Joyce decided to cancel a trip by the *CBS Morning News* to Israel that had been planned for the Easter and Passover season.

Many were stunned by the vehemence of Joyce's response, especially considering that it was based on unsubstantiated wire service reports, and concerns were heightened after Peres had released the results of an Israeli investigation that concluded that the Israeli tank crew was not at fault in the incident. The Israelis said that their tank crew had fired at some men who were running from a building and was too far away from the scene to have known that its targets were actually journalists. That night President Reagan told a press conference that he was "quite sure" that "this was not a deliberate killing." Ed Joyce suddenly began to seem a bit incautious; he was roundly criticized by the Anti-Defamation League of B'nai B'rith, which expressed regret that "an organization upon which the American public depends for its news should first make an accusation, then take punitive action [the cancellation of the *Morning News* trip], and later examine the facts." Coming after the "flesh peddler" incident, there was a good deal of sensitivity inside CBS News to even the remotest suggestion of anti-Semitism, and the B'nai B'rith charges added pressure to the situation.

It became clear that CBS News would have to investigate the deaths of its crewmen before taking further steps, and Rather wanted his friend Ernie Leiser to conduct the inquiry. Joyce had doubts about sending Leiser; but Rather pushed, and Leiser, who had some old connections in the Middle East from his days as a correspondent, was dispatched to Israel. He made his connections and researched the incident, even flying over the scene, and came to the conclusion that what Peres had said was right: The Israeli tank crew had not been at fault. As he was leaving Jerusalem for London, where he planned to file his report, Leiser told reporters, "I now believe, even without complete information, that it was certainly not a deliberate attempt to fire guns against our camera people."

Joyce was furious. It now appeared to the world that Ed Joyce was an intemperate hothead, inclined to jump to the wrong conclusion about Israel (no one outside CBS News knew that Ernie Leiser and Bob Chandler had written the original CBS protest, although Joyce had agreed with its message). He cabled

London, ordering Leiser to keep quiet about his conclusions, and according to Rather, he lambasted his anchorman for having forced Leiser upon him in the first place. "He did castigate me and criticized me for suggesting Ernie," Rather later said. "He said, 'This was a mistake, Ernie was a disaster, Ernie was exactly the wrong guy to send there, he's blown us out of the water, he kissed their ass, I can't imagine anybody doing this to CBS News.'"

Joyce accepted Leiser's report and issued a new statement, backing away from the earlier, harsher protest, allowing that "it is entirely possible that the tank crew was unable to make out the camera and the press signs on the [journalists'] car." The matter eventually faded, but the alienation between Joyce and Rather was deepened.

Then came the final clash, the conflict from which the Rather-Joyce relationship would not recover. It began, fittingly, as a turf fight.

Rather's incessant theme, his constant obsession, was the matter of resources for the *Evening News.* It seemed to Joyce, and to many others inside CBS News, a ludicrous concern, in view of the centrality that Rather's broadcast had been accorded by Van Sauter, but to Rather it was entirely appropriate. The *CBS Evening News* was an extension of him. It was his identity, and its health and well-being were his own. His intense competitiveness infused the broadcast; inside the news reader was a reporter struggling to get out.

In June 1985 Rather's constant refrain was a lament over the hiring of Meredith Vieira and Jane Wallace, two bright coming stars at CBS News, for Andy Lack's new magazine show *West 57th.* If Vieira and Wallace were going to be in prime time, that meant they were not going to be on Rather's *Evening News.* What's more, the two correspondents had been given the assignment without his being consulted. He was predictably angry and seldom missed the chance in the *Evening News* postmortem sessions to remind all that his broadcast had been hurt by the loss of the two correspondents. "Every thirty seconds," said one *Evening News* producer, "we were reminded that we were missing those two people." Rather constantly worried that the broadcast had too few A List correspondents on the air on any given night, that it had to rely too often on the work of mere

"reporters" rather than the skilled craftwork of the "broadcasters."

One Wednesday in June, after an uneventful evening broadcast, Rather's complaint had more of an edge than usual. He was
particularly upset with that evening's newscast, he said. Of the
nine correspondents who had been on the air that night, only
four were genuine A Listers. Of the rest, one, Bruce Hall, was
a CBS veteran whose work was respected but considered pedestrian; another, Bill Whittaker, was a young reporter from local
television who'd been with the network for less than a year; and
the others, Ned Potter, Steve Young, and Mike O'Connor, were
B Listeners, and not among Rather's favorites.

Rather went on about how the broadcast just couldn't make
it through many more such nights, how it would "disappear
without a trace." Howard Stringer strongly disagreed. Stringer,
who was sensitive about *West 57th,* having acted as its midwife,
reminded Rather that the *Evening News* already had most of the
resources of CBS News. Ed Joyce agreed. The meeting ended,
as most did, without resolution of Rather's pet issue, and most
of the participants went home. There was some electricity in the
air, but no one expected what came next.

Ed Joyce didn't go directly home that night. Instead, he returned to his office and wrote a memorandum that would be
seen by Rather and his staff as an act roughly equivalent in its
hostile implications to the bombing of Pearl Harbor.

Early the next morning, June 12, Joyce's secretary, Josephine
Frank, hand delivered the memorandum. Recipients were
Rather, Venardos, and senior producers Tom Bettag, Andrew
Heyward, Steve Jacobs, and Linda Mason. Copies were sent to
David Buksbaum and to Stringer. Attached to the memorandum
was a list of correspondents, seventy-six in all, in twenty-two
locations around the world. The infamous memo read:

> Take a close-hand look at the extensive list of correspon-
> dents available, almost exclusively, to the CBS EVENING
> NEWS. ABC or NBC can't come close to this group. I have
> not included in the list other CBS correspondents attached
> to 60 MINUTES, WEST 57th, SUNDAY MORNING,
> NIGHTWATCH or Radio. The people on this list work at
> virtually nothing other than your twenty-two minutes a
> night. Three years ago, not only did fewer people do this,

but they were heavily involved in the MORNING NEWS. If you end up on as many nights as you claim without the presence of correspondents whose work you most admire, it's time for a serious review of how you are managing for us what may have become a disproportionate share of the total resources of CBS News.

Joyce later reflected on the thunderous impact of his memo and said, with a trace of bitterness, "Mild, isn't it? I was busy trying to readjust a balance at that time. As it turns out, not very successfully, but that's what I was trying to do."

In fact, the memorandum wasn't, on its face, as inflammatory as it came to be taken—there was no tirade, no name-calling— but its subtext was a direct challenge to Dan Rather and the absolute preeminence of the anchor and his newscast within the organization. The fire storm that Joyce's memo caused was, in an ironic way, proof of his point, a measure of the animus toward him and of the disproportionate sense of power that resided in Rather's corner of CBS News.

Howard Stringer knew what a minefield Joyce was stepping into. He recalled that when he saw the memo the morning it was distributed, he said to Joyce, "Yes, very good . . . you're not going to send it, are you?" Joyce said that he already had.

Rather came in, saw the memo on his desk, and read it. His reaction, he later said, was "sulfuric." He summoned Venardos to his office and said, "This is a load of shit, we don't need this. This is not leadership."

The anchorman called Stringer, who said that Rather misunderstood Joyce's intent. Then Rather had a meeting with Joyce that, as Rather later told it, did not go well. "This is a load of shit," Rather said to the president of CBS News, "and this won't do. I really don't like this. We don't need this. And, particularly, set aside how I may feel about it, I'm just not going to have you coming down on people who work as hard as they do back there and give you and me and give the outfit what they do." Rather said that he told Joyce he wouldn't have minded a private rebuke but that he saw Joyce's memo as a putdown of the entire *Evening News* staff.

Joyce stood by his words, and Rather stormed out to meet with his troops, who were by this time up in arms over the memo. Rather expected some apology from Joyce, some back-

ing away from the memo, "at the very least a conciliatory visit."
When it became apparent that Joyce had no such intention,
Rather asked Stringer to intervene, to persuade Joyce to make
an appearance. "You'd damned well better do something,"
Rather told Stringer, "and let us see something before the sun
goes down, or it isn't just me on the warpath."

Joyce did not make an appearance or an apology of any sort,
and Rather and his *Evening News* staff did go on the warpath. The
Evening News meetings now were no longer about the broadcast
but about Joyce; the intense reaction on the part of Rather and
his staff could hardly be overstated. "I hated the memo," said
Rather. "I thought it was terrible for Ed to put out this public
thing to crap all over our people."

Tom Bettag agreed. "What lost Joyce was it shocked us when
he came back and fired the memo at us, because it was a 'You
people stepped out of your place' kind of memo, rather than
as a colleague to colleague, 'Let me tell you what the tough
realities are from the position that I'm sitting in' kind of thing.
It was: 'You mind your place.'"

Bettag and Andrew Heyward felt so strongly that they agreed
they couldn't work for someone who could write such a memo,
and on at least two occasions the inner core of the staff—Venardos and the senior producers, those people who'd been sent
copies of the memo—came close to staging a walkout.

In the days and weeks that followed, the tensions escalated.
Joyce wasn't apologizing, Rather and his staff were simmering,
and matters got worse when someone leaked word of the memo
to reporter Kevin Goldman of *Variety*. The feud was now public.
Richard Leibner was so worried about what might happen that
he arranged a lunch with Sauter and asked him to intervene. It
was the first time that the Rather camp had broached the subject
of Ed Joyce's removal as president. "I sit down at lunch with
Sauter, and I say, 'You don't understand it,'" Leibner recalled.
"I feel like Dean with Nixon. I say, 'You've got a cancer in your
administration.' I say, 'You've got an albatross around your
neck.' I said, 'Your days are numbered if you don't cut this
cancer out and cut it out quick.'"

Stringer, whose unarticulated role was mediation of the many
internal disputes, tried to bring Rather and Joyce together but
failed, partly because he was deeply involved in preparation for
the Westmoreland case. After several weeks the conflict re-

mained unresolved, and attention was eventually diverted to the various other crises that were rocking CBS News that summer. But the die had been cast. As one member of Rather's circle put it, "There was a clear sense for any of us who'd been around Dan for a long time that Ed had signed his death warrant. That we all knew that CBS had millions and millions of dollars invested in Dan Rather, and it sure as hell wasn't going to be him out the door first."

By the end of the summer of 1985 CBS News was a place thoroughly in torment and desperately in need of some kind of uplift. Instead, it got more torment.

In September it became clear that Tom Wyman's defeat of Ted Turner had had its Pyrrhic aspects, and one of them was an order from Black Rock for severe cost cuts as part of the drive to offset the billion-dollar debt the company swallowed to chase away Turner. CBS News was ordered to eliminate one out of ten jobs, a terrible blow to an already sullen and anxious organization, made worse by the grossly insensitive way the action was handled by news management.

In the days before the cuts, supervisors, such as the executive producers of each broadcast, were asked to draw up lists of their staffers in inverse order to their value to the operation. Those listed by their supervisors as being of least importance were put on the master hit list, which was kept by Howard Stringer. This system was, of course, an invitation to mischief, allowing the placement on the lists of some people who'd simply failed to master office politics.

After the hit list was drawn, the supervisors, about thirty-five in all, were called together on a Wednesday night, to meet with Joyce and Stringer. Vince Loncto, the vice-president of finance, kept going in and out of the room with papers, and the moment was very tense. Stringer and Joyce kept saying how fair the process had been, painful but fair, and then each of the supervisors was handed an envelope containing the names of the doomed employees in his area. "It was like a reverse Oscar," said one executive producer. "You opened the envelope to find out who the losers were." In the envelope were also written instructions on how the individuals were to be told of their firings, a kind of script, meant to minimize public statements of outrage.

The instructions on procedure became a case study in insensitive management. Each dismissed employee was to be first advised of his or her termination and then asked to be out by the close of business the next day. If a key had not been turned in, the lock was to be changed. Seventy-four CBS News employees (another fifty were urged into early retirement), some of whom had been with the company for all their working lives, were told on Thursday that they were to be off the premises by Friday, never to return. That was the way it was handled.

The next two days at CBS News were truly terrible to witness. There was wailing in the corridors, with people embracing one another in tears as they said good-bye. The worst of it, to some, was that for the first time there was no apparent recourse, no angel in the company to turn to. Who could it be? Van Sauter? Jankowski? Jankowski was conveniently out of town; others were unavailable.

"To let people go who'd been there for years and years, and they had nobody to appeal to," recalled Bob Schieffer. "It was awful. People running up and down halls, crying . . . it was just awful."

For television and media columns there was no other story in the early weeks of the autumn of 1985, and each fresh story heightened the anxiety and deepened the despair. Rumors fed upon rumors, Joyce was locked away in his office, and the closed, narrow corridors of CBS News became a kind of bedlam. "Things could scarcely appear to be worse," wrote Tom Shales in the *Washington Post.* "CBS is suffering from more than a head cold, more than deep depression and more than bottom-line fever. And with much of its internal combat going public, it has lost something that was near and dear to the company during its golden years: a sense of decorum, an aura of dignity, a semblance of stability."

That is why the death of Charles Collingwood three weeks later was so overwhelmingly poignant and why the memorial service at St. Bartholomew's and the gathering afterward at the Century Club were so charged with morbid associations. To Moyers and Hewitt, Safer and Cronkite, Kuralt and Rooney and the rest, it really did seem, as Hewitt had said, that "we were all at our own funeral," that something worthy and rare was gone forever.

Chapter

RATHER WAS ALWAYS A little sensitive about the legend that he had single-handedly dethroned Ed Joyce. "If I was his only problem," Rather said, "he'd have been here a lot longer and might still be here." He had a point: Joyce had other enemies inside CBS News, including one who was nearly as powerful as Rather, Don Hewitt.

On the day of the Collingwood memorial, at the melancholy gathering at the Century Club, Hewitt was at the center of the insurrectionary talk, and that evening he went back to the Broadcast Center to pick up the theme with Rather. The anchor-man, who was truly shaken by the emotions of the day, de-murred, but early the next morning Hewitt was back. He and Rather met in Rather's office, on the edge of the newsroom where Cronkite had presided over the glory years of CBS News. They talked about what a marvelous occasion the Collingwood memorial had been, about how special his legacy was; they also talked about how the friends he left behind should feel ashamed for having let things come to their present state.

"We never should have let the likes of him in the building," Hewitt said of Ed Joyce. "That's not what we're about. We've let this go too far. We have to do something, even if it's at great cost to ourselves." CBS had prostituted itself, and Joyce, the two agreed, was the symbol of its degradation. Joyce would have to go, and soon.

Rather later said of that conversation, "It's what makes this place different from other places; those kinds of conversations don't happen elsewhere." He was right.

Certainly no other organization in broadcast news had so many competing baronies, lorded over by so many powerful barons, as CBS News. Of these, Don Hewitt was among the most powerful and, in a way, the least likely.

Of the parallel instincts driving CBS News, television and journalism, Hewitt was a creature almost wholly belonging to television. He loved the medium. He joyed in its dazzling possibilities with a childlike enthusiasm that was as fully charged in 1987 as it had been in 1957, when as the first permanent director of CBS's evening television newscast, *Douglas Edwards with the News* (forerunner to the *Evening News*) he wired Ping-Pong balls to a globe to illustrate the Soviets' orbiting sputnik. When he combined the responsibilities for both the look and the editorial content of the program into one job, he called himself "producer," and the term became part of the broadcasting dictionary.

Hewitt was a CBS pioneer who was decidedly not of the Murrow-Collingwood-Sevareid breed of scholar-journalist, that elegant elite grounded in radio and words. From the beginning Hewitt was given to the show-business aspects of television—he identified with Hollywood more than with the *New York Times*— and he would probably have achieved as great a success, or greater, if he had gone into the entertainment field rather than journalism. As it was, he carved for himself a unique position within CBS News and forged with the organization a truly symbiotic relationship: He brought a television sensibility to CBS News, and the institution, in turn, put a necessary check on his more outlandish instincts.

Even so, there was a time in the 1960s when it seemed that the flamboyant and impetuous Hewitt would not survive in the solemn culture of CBS. Many in the organization considered him too shallow and too susceptible to the crass temptations of the medium; the nightly newscast, now called the *CBS Evening News with Walter Cronkite,* was developing into a serious "broadcast of record," and Hewitt, the producer, was seen as just a little too flaky for such a high calling, even if he had basically invented the newscast. In late 1964 he was fired from the show by Fred

Friendly, and for several years he languished at CBS and even considered leaving the company.

Then something happened that changed Hewitt's life, and television news, forever. It was called *60 Minutes,* a long shot idea that brought the magazine format to public affairs television. *60 Minutes* was the perfect synthesis of Hewitt and CBS: fluff and serious journalism, in compelling union.

When *60 Minutes* went on the air in 1968, Dick Salant was in charge of news and Bill Paley was still chairman of the company—which is to say, there was a firmer commitment to public affairs programs than there came to be—and *60 Minutes* was allowed to live despite early low ratings. It bounced around on the schedule for a few years, and then, in 1975, CBS moved the program to Sunday at 7:00 P.M., a time period that provided a kind of hothouse for Hewitt's creation. The seven o'clock Sunday time slot was reserved by the networks for public affairs and family programming—in other words, relatively weak competition. In it all the latent commerciality of *60 Minutes* came blooming forth.

Oddly, when Van Sauter and his commercial instincts first arrived at the more austere culture of CBS News, Don Hewitt became an opponent, part of the chorus of old guard detractors who gathered around the Murrow flame. Although Sauter's attitude toward Hewitt and *60 Minutes* was one of utter laissez-faire, there was antagonism between the two men that eventually became bitter. Sauter thought Hewitt a crude vulgarian who, but for his extraordinary television talent, would be working in the garment district; Hewitt found Sauter a grasping manipulator, and he was offended by Sauter's refusal to see CBS News as the ultimate mountaintop. "I always felt that for the first time we had people running CBS News, Sauter and Joyce, who saw it as a stepping-stone to something higher in the company," Hewitt said. "They made decisions not based on what is best for CBS News; they made decisions based on 'What is best for my career?' "

The antagonism between Hewitt and Sauter belied their essential agreement in philosophy—namely, that CBS News could be a kind of production house of popular programming. The irony of Hewitt's latter-day position as news traditionalist was widely appreciated by his colleagues. "I know we're in trouble,"

Andy Rooney once joked, "when Don Hewitt becomes the best practitioner of serious journalism around here."

From the first, *60 Minutes* was a news-entertainment hybrid, news as a *show.* "It's the oldest form of entertainment in the world," Hewitt would say of his program; "they're little morality plays, only they're real. Nobody wrote a script. So you do a doctor. Did he rape those women? Or didn't he rape those women? It's a morality play." Hewitt thought of himself as a cross between Hildy Johnson and the Broadway producer Julian Marsh, and of his correspondents as "a repertory group of reporters."

60 Minutes concerned itself not only with serious subjects but with fluff, too. The very first broadcast included a discussion with foreign journalists about the American election process, but it also turned that process into high drama by putting cameras inside the hotel suites of Richard Nixon and Hubert Humphrey as they awaited their parties' presidential nominations. There was also an interview with political humorist Art Buchwald, the first of what was to become a *60 Minutes* staple—the celebrity interview.

Even serious investigative reports were entertaining, presented in the famed *60 Minutes* exposé style: the nervous culprit, cornered by the tightly framed *60 Minutes* camera, suggesting his guilt with the twitch of a sweaty brow, or Mike Wallace, the avenging angel in a trench coat, pursuing baddies out of their homes and down the street, cameras rolling all the while—the patented *60 Minutes* "ambush interview."

At the end of the 1976 season *60 Minutes* became a hit show, and everything changed. It suddenly became apparent that a hit prime-time news program was a property of unimagined worth, infinitely more valuable than a hit entertainment show. Where the network essentially "leased" the sitcoms and dramas that it broadcast, paying a licensing fee to the studios that produced them, CBS owned *60 Minutes.* Where an entertainment hour in 1976 might cost the network $750,000 for the rights to two airings, *60 Minutes* at the time cost about half that much—and CBS could rerun it forever, for free. What's more, the CBS sales department discovered that advertisers, who'd shunned low-rated documentaries and news specials, were begging for commercial time on *60 Minutes,* with its educated, money-spending, upscale audience.

News became a gold mine, which was a source of great anxiety to Richard Salant and others, who worried that the commercial success of one news program would erode network tolerance for news broadcasts that weren't ratings winners, such as documentaries—a fear that proved well grounded.

After a time it gnawed at Hewitt that other creators of television shows, those on the entertainment side, such as his friend Norman Lear, made such an enormous amount of money. Hewitt's *60 Minutes* was on the air before and after all of Lear's hits, but Lear owned his shows and sold them into syndication for hundreds of millions of dollars. Hewitt's show was far more valuable to CBS than any single hit produced by Hollywood; although complicated bookkeeping methods made it difficult to say for certain, it was estimated that CBS made upwards of $70 million a year from *60 Minutes,* and in at least one year Hewitt's program meant the difference between profit and loss for the network. In time it dawned on Hewitt that maybe *he* should own a percentage of *his* show, and that became a constant theme in his dealings with the network.

But CBS shuddered at the thought of giving away pieces of its news programs to employees—and an employee, after all, was ultimately what Hewitt was—so instead, to keep Hewitt happy, they made him incredibly rich. Not Norman Lear rich, but the network gave Hewitt a contract that dwarfed any that had ever before been given to a news producer. It included terms that made it potentially worth more than $2.5 million a year, over a ten-year period.

It was an unprecedented deal and a matter of enormous sensitivity at CBS—so much so that, as with the Rather contract, Gene Jankowski didn't tell Wyman about it until it was completed. Wyman loathed Hewitt—he didn't like the way Hewitt cozied up to Paley; he didn't like the way Hewitt whispered insurrection—and he was outraged when Jankowski told him about the contract. It was the cause of one of the few truly heated disagreements between the two men, made worse when Wyman realized that Jankowski himself hadn't even been directly involved but that the deal had been negotiated by Jankowski's longtime aide David Fuchs. Wyman had particularly wanted a say in the Hewitt deal because he knew that Jankowski shrank from confrontation. "I think Gene was really frightened of that, threatened by him, and just hoped that it kept making its forty million dollars or whatever, and he was not in any supervisory role," Wyman said.

Jankowski, for his part, later defended the contract. "You have to understand that *60 Minutes* is the most successful program in history," he said. "Norman Lear sold his company [Tandem/T.A.T.] for four hundred thirty-five million dollars. People obtain their value. If you can't get it one way, get it another way."

But Wyman worried about the corollary effect the deal would have on Hewitt. He believed that Hewitt knew that Wyman himself would never have given him such a deal and worried that having got it anyway would give the producer, as Wyman put it, a pronounced "sense of independence." It did. Instead of buying Don Hewitt's cooperation and sympathy, the deals he got in the era of Wyman and Sauter and Joyce became a kind of license for outspokenness or what management viewed as mischief. ("He became bored with the other stuff," Wyman later said of Hewitt, "and he became a little bit the revolutionary folk hero. He was basically safe.") Said Hewitt himself in 1987: "I have a contract now that's ten years. I have the most unique contract in the history of the world. My contract's up when I'm seventy-four years old. It's unbreakable. They signed me for ten years. Like the president. I'll prolly be as nutty as he is by the time it's over. But seventy-four years old. Who gets a ten-year contract until they're seventy-four?"

The producer of the most lucrative show in television did, and he was the first to declare its liberating effect: "I'm in that wonderful position of [having] a ten-year firm contract and [producing] a show they can't do without. I can say, 'You're doing wrong.' I've done a lot of that." Yes, he had, to the unending annoyance of Sauter, Wyman, Jankowski, and Joyce.

In 1985, the most difficult year for CBS News, Hewitt was particularly aggrieved, working the hallways and news columns with complaints, and the people ostensibly in charge of CBS couldn't understand his discomfort. What could he want? To reopen his contract? More money?

Apparently, what was bothering Hewitt was simple, unadorned insecurity. In 1984, *60 Minutes* had dropped off noticeably in quality. Wallace was deeply involved in and disturbed by preparation for the Westmoreland case, and overall the broadcast was showing signs of tiring. Its correspondents were getting older, as was its audience, and it occurred to some in CBS News, including Sauter, Stringer, and Joyce, that the broadcast might be coming to the end of its string.

Hewitt had incredibly sensitive antennae when it came to a

piece of institutional gossip, a new wrinkle ("I Knew It" Hewitt was one of his nicknames), and his perception was doubly acute when it came to *60 Minutes.* By 1985 he had known that he was no longer the fair-haired boy of the Sauter-Joyce era, no longer the only wunderkind producer in the company. And in case he'd had any doubts, Stringer and Lack and their circle made it abundantly evident. They spoke openly and often of *West 57th* as the program of the future; there was quiet (and not so quiet, in some cases) scoffing at the quaint old *60 Minutes* way of doing things, with its stark sets, its use of film, even its old-fashioned hand-operated crank device for rolling credits.

West 57th, on the other hand, was praised as hip and new, and its staff comprised not only the up-from-the-ranks CBS veterans (as was the case with *60 Minutes*) but also staffers from MTV and *Entertainment Tonight.* (There had even been much discussion over whether to downplay the association between Lack's new show and CBS News, to the horror of Bill Moyers and others. Van Sauter later said of *West 57th,* "We made a conscious effort in the advertising campaign we developed for it to position it as other than a news documentary broadcast. And we worked extensively with the agency to develop prints and an on-air campaign that would not lead the viewers to suspect that they were getting a conventional news documentary broadcast.")

The television columns of newspapers began to run stories suggesting that *West 57th* would be coming into its prime just as *60 Minutes* was fading, and those stories, Hewitt knew, didn't just materialize from thin air. He was furious. "See, Howard was guilty of it," he later said of the hyping of *West 57th* at the expense of *60 Minutes.* "During *West 57th,* they started that yesterday people, today people thing." Hewitt said he went to Jankowski at one point and asked him, "Why didn't you, when you were reading this, just say, 'Will you cut out this shit? Those people [*60 Minutes*] support this company. What are you doing?' "

West 57th became a generational flash point at CBS News in 1985, the focus of anger for Moyers, Hewitt, and other influential players who, by generation or disposition, fell into the ranks of the old guard. Andy Rooney was so annoyed he made a *West 57th* parody segment for *60 Minutes,* in which he dressed up in suspenders (mocking the rather obvious yuppie-pandering garb of *West 57th*'s John Ferrugia), mimicked the finger-snapping, fast-cut *West 57th* opening, and did a fully produced eight-minute piece. Ed Joyce found little amusement in the Rooney segment and ordered it killed.

For his part Hewitt struck back in the press, saying that *West 57th* was "light summer fare." Both shows were located in the Ford auto dealership across the street from the CBS Broadcast Center, Lack's broadcast on the eighth floor, Hewitt's on the ninth. At one point Hewitt posted signs in the elevator, mocking the generation gap. One said, EIGHTH FLOOR. VIDEO FLUENT PEOPLE GET OFF HERE. The other read, NINTH FLOOR. YESTERDAY'S PEOPLE GET OFF HERE.

So it was a very disgruntled Don Hewitt who met with his old friends that October afternoon at the Century Club, a Don Hewitt inclined to dramatic gesture. That he would do something big was inevitable; the only question was what.

On the morning of October 11, 1985, James H. Rosenfield stood at the mirror in the bathroom of his pricey Fifth Avenue apartment, carefully shaving his face. It was 7:45, and in the adjacent room, a comfortable, book-crammed study, the *CBS Morning News* was on. The big story of the morning was that some American fighter jets had downed an Air Egypt plane bearing the Lebanese terrorists who engineered the hijacking of an Italian cruise ship. But on this particular morning Rosenfield, the senior executive vice-president of the CBS Broadcast Group, was not thinking about the news. His mind was on the things that he liked in his life, the comforts, such as his chauffeur, his executive dining room privileges, his personal chef. These things were good, and they were part of why he liked the particular game he was in, network television, and why he had to think long and hard about leaving it. Leaving had become a real possibility for Rosenfield because of the company's lucrative, one-time-only early retirement plan, a head count reduction effort prompted by the Turner takeover fight.

Those were the thoughts on Rosenfield's mind when the phone outside the bathroom door sounded its pleasant chime. He reached around the corner into the cozy study and picked up the receiver.

"Hello, Rosenfield," he said.

"Jimmy, where are you?"

It was the excited voice of Don Hewitt. "Don," Rosenfield said, "it's quarter to eight in the morning, I'm in the bathroom, shaving."

"I'm outside your office," Hewitt told the executive. "I gotta talk to you immediately."

"It'll take me half an hour."

"Can't wait half an hour."

"All right, I'll be there in fifteen or twenty minutes."

Rosenfield smiled to himself and dressed. He knew what Hewitt wanted, and as he left for Black Rock, he said to his wife, "Mark this day—Hewitt has hijacked the hijackers."

Rosenfield, who had been around CBS for a long time and who had been witness to countless Hewitt adventures, assumed that the maestro had somehow managed to get an interview with the terrorists for that Sunday's broadcast. But Hewitt wasn't thinking about getting any scoops for *60 Minutes* that day. He had bigger fish to fry.

Rosenfield rode the few blocks down to Black Rock at Fifty-second Street and Sixth Avenue and got off the elevator on the thirty-fourth floor, where he was greeted by Hewitt. Inside Rosenfield's office, Hewitt wasted no time. He told the executive what was on his mind. It was a bombshell.

"Don Hewitt, Bill Moyers, Dan Rather, Mike Wallace, Morley Safer, and Diane Sawyer," Hewitt said, "want to buy CBS News."

Leaving Rather the morning after the Collingwood memorial, Hewitt had returned across the street to his office, a large corner space in the Ford building, with a view of Manhattan's West Side and, across the Hudson River, the sprawl of New Jersey. He'd put his feet up on his desk, and as he gazed out the window toward the car dealerships and body shops of Eleventh Avenue, his thoughts had drifted to the troubles of recent months and the melancholy mood of the Collingwood gathering the day before.

And, looking down, his gaze fixed on the roof of the Potamkin Cadillac dealership across the street. The wheels in Hewitt's head began to turn, and suddenly it struck him: Put a satellite dish on the roof of Potamkin Cadillac, and you've got a broadcast center. Potamkin Village, Hewitt thought. Potamkin Village Productions. One receiver, one transmitter, and—he'd need names. That's what Cable News Network lacked, he thought, big-name journalists. But big names were something Hewitt had access to. Rather, Moyers, the stars of *60 Minutes,* maybe even ABC's Ted Koppel and Sam Donaldson, NBC's Tom Brokaw, too. But would they go along? Of course, Hewitt thought. As co-owners of Potamkin Village Productions they'd sell their services back to CBS or to the highest bidder.

Hewitt went home bubbling over his brainstorm, and early the next morning he was on the phone with Rather and his *60 Minutes* stars. Could he use their names in pitching his idea? Their responses varied, depending upon their individual experiences with Hewitt's occasional schemes: Wallace thought it was harebrained; Rather thought it had possibilities. No one said no.

Hewitt then dashed over to Black Rock, hoping to find Jankowski, who, Hewitt knew, always arrived before the others after attending early-morning mass. But Jankowski was not in; he was out of town, attending a function at his alma mater, Michigan State. Rosenfield was next in command, and Hewitt called him.

Sitting in his office, listening to the ebullient Hewitt outline his plan, Rosenfield wasn't sure he was hearing right. "I said, we want to buy CBS News," Hewitt repeated.

"What makes you think we would sell CBS News?"

"I never thought you would sell an affiliate," Hewitt said, referring to the recent sale of the CBS station in St. Louis, KMOX. "Obviously you're trying to get money, and I can get the capital to buy CBS News." In fact, Hewitt later said, he had already talked to some venture capitalists, who were encouraging.

"Have you run this by your guys yet?" Rosenfield asked.

"Yeah, I called them at six o'clock this morning to see if I could use their names. I woke them up."

"Don, this is very serious," Rosenfield said. "If you're serious, let me think about it, and I'll be in touch with you in an hour."

Rosenfield immediately tracked down Jankowski in East Lansing, Michigan, and, after assuring him that he was cold sober, told him of Hewitt's proposal. In the next couple of hours a good many anxious phone calls were exchanged between highly nervous CBS executives (Rosenfield delivered the news to Sauter, whose response, Rosenfield recalled, was succinct: "Oh, shit!"). Rosenfield told Hewitt that Jankowski wanted to meet with him when he returned to New York.

Hewitt and Jankowski met early the following week. Hewitt had wanted Rather to accompany him to the Jankowski lunch, but Rather (to Hewitt's annoyance) begged off, explaining that he had a long-standing lunch date with Leslie Stahl and promising that he'd try to join Hewitt and Jankowski for coffee.

Rather and Stahl lunched at Maurice, the restaurant at the Parker Meridien Hotel on West Fifty-seventh Street, and they got to talking and ordered late. The food had just arrived when, to their surprise, Hewitt joined them. To their amazement Hewitt launched right into a recap of his conversation with Jankowski. Stahl, who'd covered palace revolutions in her years as a correspondent in Washington, was astonished to find herself in the middle of a coup at her own company. She didn't know what to say. Should she leave the table?

Hewitt said no, and he proceeded to detail the grievances that he'd presented to Jankowski, the central theme being the urgent need to remove Sauter and Joyce. Rather and Stahl nodded in agreement (although Rather, the loyalist, was silent as Hewitt lambasted Sauter).

In his meeting with Hewitt, Jankowski had assured the producer that CBS News was not for sale. In the public statements about that meeting, Jankowski was assigned the old cliché about the place of CBS News in the scheme of things. "CBS News," he was supposed to have assured Hewitt, "is the jewel in the crown of CBS."

Hewitt probably was not entirely serious about his scheme, and he later said that he had made the proposal simply because he and his colleagues were genuinely concerned that CBS might sell off the news division—an eventuality that Hewitt well knew was highly unlikely. There was a symbolic importance to Hewitt's buyout scheme that was lost on no one. As Rosenfield later put it, "The sense I got was that this was open revolt. This was the senior talent and management [Hewitt] of CBS News saying, 'You'd better do something about what's going on here at the news division or there's no telling what's going to happen. We are at our wits' end, nobody's listening.' And that's focused on Ed Joyce."

Within a week Kevin Goldman, the ubiquitous *Variety* reporter, had picked up on the buyout story and published it in *Daily Variety*. Predictably the report triggered a storm inside CBS and, of course, a host of follow-up stories, and it was soon clear that something would have to be done.

At Black Rock Sauter and Jankowski decided there should be

one last effort to save Ed Joyce. The reluctant front man would be Dan Rather.

It fell to Stringer, the smooth operator, to enlist Rather in the cause. He dropped by the anchorman's office and gave a little speech, saying how Joyce really wasn't such a bad fellow, he'd given his whole career to CBS, and he'd really worked hard, no matter what Rather thought of him. Rather wondered what in the world Stringer was talking about. "It was so tactfully and subtly put that I didn't get it," Rather recalled. "In many ways I'm too dumb to deal with Howard; he's too sophisticated a person."

Then Sauter, who was better at coming directly to the point when he needed to, called Rather and laid it out: Ed Joyce was in deep trouble. He was besieged and beleaguered, and he needed someone (such as Rather) to say something good about him publicly. Rather said he'd think about it. He hated the idea ("I'm just country enough to feel uncomfortable about praising the boss," he said) and brooded about it all day. He knew that his own credibility was at stake, not only on the outside but, much more important, inside the organization, where the temperature was running high against Joyce, and everyone knew precisely where Dan Rather stood on the subject. Sauter called back and pressed again. Rather said okay.

So Kevin Goldman was called over to the Broadcast Center and ushered into Howard Stringer's private anteroom for a truly bizarre session. Stringer, Eric Ober, the vice-president in charge of public affairs, John Richman, the vice-president in charge of special events, and Goldman sat in the office and waited for the main event, which was Dan Rather. After a while Rather came in and began his command performance. CBS News was an "unruly family," Rather said, and criticism of Joyce must "be placed in the context of all he has done for the news division." Rather dragged out his usual bone to Joyce—that he'd stood up against the affiliates at the Republican National Convention in 1984 on the matter of running late—and added, "Joyce has also been among the most vocal supporters on First Amendment issues." It was lukewarm praise at best, but Rather had been right to be suspicious. After Goldman had printed his story, Rather's new nickname around the Broadcast Center (whispered, of course) was "180-Degree" Dan.

Rather resented having been manipulated into defending Joyce, and it later occurred to him that even though Stringer and

Sauter had asked him to, both had something to gain in Joyce's demise. "Both Howard and Van, I thought, were playing a double game, at least to a degree." If Joyce lost his job, who stood to get it? Sauter or Stringer.

In any event, the "dog-and-pony show," as Leibner described the session with Goldman, fooled no one. Animosity toward Joyce ran deep and wide and was no longer possible to overcome.

It was obvious that Ed Joyce had become a lost cause, and soon Sauter's efforts on his friend's behalf became less than wholehearted. His position was complicated by his own extreme discomfort in his job at Black Rock, a job that had proved so untenable for him that cynics later speculated, somewhat generously, that Jankowski had deliberately put Sauter in the job to neutralize him.

That was unlikely, but Sauter had in any case lost all effectiveness as a manager. He was the supervisor of the presidents of the news and stations divisions, which meant that he bore responsibility for those two enterprises but had no hand in their daily operations. None of the executive vice-presidents, that extra management layer Jankowski had created, were at all comfortable in their jobs, and the division presidents below them were just as uncomfortable.

Sauter, the gregarious rouster, particularly chafed in the sterile and formal atmosphere of Black Rock, especially after it had become apparent that Wyman had no intention of moving Jankowski into the corporate president's job. With Jankowski staying put, there was nothing to wish for, and Sauter and another of the executives in the dead layer sometimes pined aloud for their former jobs. "I'd have gone back to news, anywhere," Sauter later said.

Through much of the difficult year, 1985, Sauter had defended Joyce, but by the time of Rather's disaffection Sauter had begun to back away from the beleaguered news division president. It was evident to him that Joyce was losing the news division, and what was worse, he was bringing down Sauter with him.

As Sauter spent more and more time with Rather, weekends in the country, fishing excursions, long walks in the city, Joyce became more and more suspicious of his friend's intentions. Sauter wrote Joyce a new long-term contract ("for his protection"), but it must have been clear to Joyce that Sauter was thinking about returning to CBS News as president. By autumn the two men were no longer speaking. As Sauter saw it, Joyce's tenure was in an irreversible death spiral, and he finally declared his opinion that Joyce would have to go.

Joyce would see Sauter's pronouncement as an act of treachery and betrayal, and in fact, the story of the two men's friendship had had its melodramatic aspects. Sauter and Joyce had been close, almost comically so—Sauter had taught Joyce to fish; Joyce was living in Sauter's house, even still using Sauter's old phone number—but by the end of 1985 Van Sauter would be trying to convince Jankowski to force Joyce to sign a "muzzle" agreement, preventing him from talking or writing about CBS after he left.

Sauter told Jankowski that there was no way that Ed Joyce could survive, that CBS News was being damaged each day, but Jankowski was loath to be seen as having been stampeded into a decision.

In October Sauter wrote a memorandum to Jankowski and David Fuchs, saying that the situation at CBS News was unprecedented and that action must be taken to protect the organization as well as Ed Joyce. "I know the group is resistant to any action that indicates the employees have forced the hand of management," Sauter wrote. "But the reality of our situation is that a variety of converging influences have resulted in a massive display of discontent which has led to a psychological trauma in the news division. Either through covert activism or passivity, the employees have sent a message."

That message, Sauter said, was clear:

> Ed Joyce is not perceived as a leader; Ed Joyce and I are perceived as willing lackeys of the corporation and unwilling/unable to withstand Black Rock pressure; the news presidency is now a stepping stone to higher position and those who occupy it tilt toward paths that best achieve advancement rather than best represent the division; the news division should report to the group president (at least); the division is exhausted by economic anguish, layoffs and concern about its future and that of the company; the quality of the news division product has been eroded (this position is unique to the so-called "old guard," though most employees have grave concerns about the Morning News).

It was a remarkably frank and accurate assessment of the situation at CBS News. Sauter went on to suggest to Jankowski two possible actions. The first, Sauter wrote, would be to "halt the turmoil and keep Ed Joyce in place." It was apparent, however, that Sauter didn't think this the best course. He said that Jankowski had great credibility in the news division and that he, if anyone, could sway the newspeople to Joyce's side, but, he went on to say, Eric Ober, Joan Richman, David Buksbaum, Lane Venardos, and Howard Stringer all "fear that Ed is permanently crippled." The only way to find out would be for Jankowski to put himself on the line and see. Of course, Sauter pointed out (just in case Jankowski missed the point), "if the effort is made, and six months from now there is still an acute malaise, then you and the division have lost important credibility."

The second option Sauter suggested was the one he obviously favored. "Halt the turmoil, replace Ed Joyce, but protect him." Here Sauter offered several scenarios, all involving his own return to news. "I could take his place and through a combination of love, reason and brute force restore the ambience the division needs to function," he wrote. "This would not be a primary career choice for me, but if it served the group and the division, I would do it."

Still another possibility Sauter posed would be for "me to become an executive vice president of the group and president of the news division. In this role, I would move to the Broadcast Center, restore the balance there and expedite the development of Stringer so he could . . . as soon as possible . . . assume the presidency."

Naturally, Sauter added, there was the possibility of making Stringer president right away, but he made evident his belief that Stringer was not yet ready. "We could also take a flyer on Stringer assuming the job. With close supervision, he could muddle through. But if there is a new president, that person should report to you, and you don't have the time to guide the process."

As for Joyce, Sauter suggested offering long-term financial protection (the new contract), a new job, possibly an executive vice-president's job within the Broadcast Group, to let him save face and stay on the payroll until he reached the age of fifty-five, at which point he could take early retirement or a consultancy.

Sauter ended his memo by recounting his own "anguish" over recent events. "Balancing the Ed-Dan relationship has been complex," he wrote, "and Ed is now growing suspicious that Dan and I are forging a deal to unseat him. At this point, Ed is encouraging Howard to ask some CND [CBS News Division] people to call you with their support for Ed. Howard is hesitant. . . ."

Sauter said that his own preference was to stay at Black Rock "to see what new challenges and opportunities developed over the years." However, he added, unnecessarily, he would be willing to return to news. In any event, he concluded, "I strongly recommend we make a decision in the very near future. The focus in all this could soon shift to Dan and we can't afford to have him damaged."

Jankowski knew that Sauter was right about the need to act, but still, he hesitated. Ed Joyce, totally besieged now, had launched one last desperate effort to save himself, and it was having some effect on Jankowski. Joyce had convinced Bill Moyers and Don Hewitt, two of his chief antagonists that year, that if he left, Van Sauter would return as president. That was enough to make instant Ed Joyce fans of both Moyers and Hewitt. "I sided with Joyce at the end," Hewitt recalled. I'd rather have Joyce than Sauter because I found Joyce to be less ambitious than Sauter. . . . I thought he was the lesser of two evils."

The effect on Jankowski, the consensus artist, was paralysis. Asked later why he didn't act sooner on the Joyce matter, he explained, "What you have to understand is that when you're over on this side of town, you get a lot of crosscurrents. And there were a lot of critics of Van; I was picking up a lot of that. And there were supporters of Ed's, and I was picking up a lot of that information. I would hear one story about Ed Joyce and Dan Rather, and then I would hear a completely different story coming from different sources. And the one thing you learn if you're a manager for a while is you don't jump to hasty conclusions."

Sauter, meanwhile, grew increasingly anxious. At an affiliates' meeting in California in late November he told Jankowski that if he didn't remove Ed Joyce, he, Sauter, might have to quit. A few weeks later he did.

In yet another memo to Jankowski, Sauter said, "I hate to burden you at this time with yet another problem, but I increasingly feel it appropriate to end my relationship with CBS." In the current situation, he said, his management skills were not being realized, a problem complicated by his soured relationship with Joyce. He said that he and his wife, Kathleen, were going off for the weekend with the Rathers, during which time they would decide what steps to take. If he left CBS, he promised, he would speak only praise for "you and the company."

That may have been the move that finally sealed Ed Joyce's fate. Within days Jankowski had agreed that Joyce would be replaced. The question was, Who would fire him? Jankowski thought Sauter, Sauter thought Jankowski. After some back and forth, Sauter just decided to do it. But even the firing of Ed Joyce was complicated and filled with tragicomedy.

Sauter called Joyce (one of the few conversations they'd had in weeks) and asked him to come to Black Rock at 2:30 P.M. to discuss "something important." At 2:00 Sauter went to Jankowski and told him that Joyce was coming to Black Rock. Jankowski, as was his way, said that he wanted to run it by Mr. Paley first; Tom Wyman had already agreed to it. So Sauter was waiting in David Fuchs's office, and 2:15 came and went, and then 2:30, and still no word from Jankowski. Sauter called down to his office and told his secretary to have Joyce "read a magazine or something," Sauter was tied up. And 2:45 came and went, and then 3:00, and still, no Jankowski.

Finally Jankowski appeared, and he was shaken. Paley, he said, had vetoed the Joyce firing; he didn't want Van Sauter named the new president of CBS News. He wanted a search committee formed, comprised of such CBS elder statesmen as Walter Cronkite and Frank Stanton, to find a suitable new president of CBS News. That was that.

So, Joyce was sent back to the Broadcast Center, never knowing, apparently, why he'd been summoned.

But the momentum was too much to stop, and just a few days later, at the annual CBS gathering at the Pierre Hotel honoring longtime employees of the company, word that Ed Joyce was going to be fired was leaked. That sealed it, and the next day Jankowski told Joyce he was finished as president of CBS News. He was given Option C in Sauter's October memo, a face-saving job at Black Rock.

And Van Gordon Sauter, to the dismay of many and the delight of few, was back at CBS News.

Chapter

GENE JANKOWSKI HAD BEEN faced with an opportunity to restore calm to his harrowed news division, but in sending Van Sauter back to news, he virtually assured new tumult. With Sauter's reappointment in December 1985, there was within CBS News a sense of triumph thwarted, of resolution denied. Dan Rather aside, much of the animosity toward Ed Joyce had been deflected from Sauter, and now Black Rock was solving the problem by bringing back Sauter himself. "That is typical," said one member of the *60 Minutes* team upon hearing the news. "They've just thrown out the symptoms and installed the disease."

Sauter had his own reservations about going back. While rescue work had been his forte at CBS, it hadn't been this kind of rescue work, going into a bad situation that he'd had a hand in creating. Besides, Sauter had already spent his real enthusiasm for CBS News, and going back to it, as he'd said in his memorandum to Jankowski, was not his career move of choice. Also, Sauter was not unaware of his standing in the sentiments of the organization; he, not Ed Joyce, had been the agent of change, and he was the living symbol of its agony. Of his first tour at CBS News, Sauter himself later said, "I accumulated a fair amount of baggage in terms of haters."

It almost seemed that the Sauter move was designed to agitate. If a principal complaint during the Sauter-Joyce era had been that the two executives represented the interests of Black Rock rather than news, Sauter's new incarnation made it official: He held dual titles, president of CBS News *and* executive vice-president of the CBS Broadcast Group. Representing the interests of the corporation was now the job of the president of CBS News.

Given the circumstances, the cataclysms that followed were probably inevitable and certainly predictable. What could not have been anticipated, however, was the intensity of this new upheaval at CBS News and its reach. This time the shocks and rebellions of CBS News would be felt across town at Black Rock and would play into a boardroom revolt that would change the company forever.

Sauter may have had reservations about returning to CBS News, but his survival at CBS in any capacity had been a near thing. Sauter had not succeeded at Black Rock—both the divisions he oversaw, news and the CBS stations, were trouble zones for CBS—and Jankowski had been disappointed by Sauter's inability, or disinclination, to adapt to the corporate culture. Jankowski also apparently believed that Sauter remained too much involved with news, and that added to his, and the news division's, problems. "They've done studies on why managers fail," Jankowski later said. "People have grown up in one function or skill, then they become a general manager, and the tendency has been for those who have failed to run back to the area they know best and, as a result, ignore some of those other areas they should be involved with. A general manager can't have too much of that specialist mentality; he has to develop a broader scope. The question [for Sauter at Black Rock was], Can I do this? Can I determine to do it? Or am I so unhappy that if somebody doesn't find something for me, I leave?"

Jankowski also had reservations about sending Sauter back to news, and he worried—correctly, it turned out—that the resentments Sauter had stirred by dividing the institution in his first tour at news would mean trouble the second time around. So Jankowski sent along his own trusted aide, the confessor-adviser David Fuchs, as a senior vice-president under Sauter, to provide a conduit for Jankowski inside the news division and to pour oil on the waters when necessary.

Jankowski also instructed Sauter to try to make amends with key members of the old guard, with Salant and Leonard, Hewitt and Cronkite and the others, in the hope of forestalling revolt. Sauter found the prospect demeaning and refused. He did, however, make some halfhearted statements in the press that were meant to be seen as gestures to the traditionalists. He said, for example, that he'd made a mistake about documentaries the first time around, and now that he was back, CBS News was going to go back into the business of serious documentaries and public affairs; it didn't fly.

Sauter spoke of the need to restore morale at CBS News, and in staff meetings he told a story about how, when he was a child, his hero had been the circus master Clyde Beatty. Beatty's first rule was that when you were in a cage with a bunch of hungry big cats, the trick was to keep them on their stools; once they were off, no cap gun and whip could save you from being devoured. That, Sauter said, was what he had to do at CBS News: keep the cats on their stools.

But in 1986, after everything that had happened, the old Sauter charm was of limited use. The accumulated resentments had hardened into a resolute disdain, and not only on the part of the old guard. "I think he embarrassed us," said Leslie Stahl. "I think the content on the air, Phyllis George, the content on the *Evening News, West 57th*—he embarrassed us. I think we had all come to CBS News because we all thought we were going to work for the best, the *New York Times* of television, and he destroyed it."

Sauter's deputy, Howard Stringer, later succinctly framed Sauter's difficulty in trying to win back the institution: "They'd already seen the act."

To some of those around him, it seemed that Sauter had little of the enthusiasm for the job the second time around that he had shown in 1981, and none of the hands-on fervor. He still roamed the halls, but less frequently, and he was quite literally removed from the mix. One of the things he had done as news president the first time, and then at Black Rock, was to plan a new, $12 million newsroom in the building adjacent to the Broadcast Center, a huge, cavernous set shaped like a horseshoe, with glassed-in executive offices on the balcony above, overlooking the newsroom. It was quite an extravagance (which included an open elevator spanning the twelve feet or so between the first and second floors and, presumably, cleaner air for the anchorman's sensitive throat), and because it was completed at a time of painful retrenchment, it was the source of some embarrassment.

But it was no embarrassment for Sauter, who moved right into the new facility, and through the early months of 1986 he was essentially alone there.

Van Sauter did have a plan for his second tour at CBS News. If he was going to survive, if he was going to effect another turnaround, it would come through the programs; if the programs were winning, morale might take care of itself. He had paid lip service to documentaries, but the two areas that most concerned and interested him were the *Evening News* and the *Morning News*. Sauter thought that in his absence the *Evening News* had begun to drift, and there was disturbing new research suggesting that Rather's five-year lead in the ratings might be in danger. But more pressing was the beleaguered *CBS Morning News*, which had come to a state of emergency.

Phyllis George had left the broadcast in September 1985, and soon thereafter Jon Katz was replaced as executive producer by a bright young news executive named Johnathan Rodgers, who had been executive producer of the *CBS Weekend News*. Rodgers inherited an anchor team of Forrest Sawyer, the Atlanta newscaster who had been the anchor of the *CBS Early Morning News*, and Maria Shriver, who had been a West Coast correspondent for the *Morning News*, specializing in Hollywood news. Shriver was a member of the Kennedy clan, and consequently possessed some celebrity, but as television personalities both she and Sawyer were relatively unknown. They worked well together, Sawyer in the role of straight newsman and Shriver an engaging and bubbly presence, and in the aftermath of the Phyllis George experience, they brought the broadcast a needed stability.

But their ratings remained dismally low, and key affiliated stations clamoring for success in the morning were convinced that an anchor team of Forrest Sawyer and Maria Shriver would never bring it. What's more, turbulence in another corner of CBS prompted the unexpected departure of Johnathan Rodgers from the broadcast.

When Bill Kurtis left the *Morning News*, he and his agent arranged a lucrative deal that would return him to Chicago, where he would anchor the local news, produce documentaries,

and anchor the network's prime-time news breaks. To make
room for Kurtis in Chicago, a veteran black anchorman, Harry
Porterfield, was demoted. Angered, Porterfield left WBBM for
an anchor job at a rival station. The matter did not end there.
WBBM and CBS had become the target of an effort by Jesse
Jackson's Operation PUSH (People United to Save Humanity)
to bring equal opportunity to blacks and other minorities in the
media. Porterfield's treatment at WBBM became a handy cause,
and PUSH launched a viewer boycott against the station. WBBM
was suffering a decline in ratings as it was, and a boycott was the
last thing it needed. As it happened, Johnathan Rodgers, who
is black, had experience on the local-station level, and he was
dispatched to Chicago to become the first black vice-president
and general manager of a CBS-owned station.

But Rodgers's departure forced another major change on the
Morning News. In view of the affiliates' sentiments about Sawyer
and Shriver, it seemed to Sauter an opportunity to try one last
time for a major revamping of the morning broadcast.

Sauter had just the solution in mind. Six months earlier, in the
depths of the Katz-Kurtis-George debacle, Sauter had wanted to
bring to CBS an accomplished television producer named Susan
Winston. The move would have carried certain risks, not the
least being that Winston's professional identity was largely outside news. She had been the producer of ABC's *Good Morning
America* at the height of its popularity. She had gone on from
ABC to Hollywood, where she was head of her own television
production company. When Sauter first suggested Winston for
the *Morning News,* the idea met with a good deal of resistance,
including from Ed Joyce, who thought that her appointment
would fuel the already raging fires.

But by the spring of 1986 Joyce was gone, Sauter was back,
and the opportunity was at hand. So Susan Winston was brought
in to produce the *CBS Morning News,* becoming the show's fourth
executive producer in two years. She was given a two-year contract, worth $250,000 for the first six months, at which point
there was a window through which either she or the network
could escape. As things turned out, Winston's time at CBS News
was brief, but during her tenure she was to get a memorable
firsthand perspective on the innate conflicts that were tearing
the institution apart.

Winston's presence both excited and intimidated the staff,

many of whom felt that for the first time since George Merlis had gone the broadcast was in the hands of a true television professional. Winston said publicly that she found the morning broadcasts on all three networks to be clones of one another and altogether "boring." She would do another type of show, she said, but she knew from the beginning that it wouldn't be easy, that the traditions and standards of the place would make for hazardous going. "It works for you and against you," she said at the time, when asked about the rigid traditions of CBS News. "For you, in that in this marvelous institution is a history that others don't have. Against you in that anytime you deviate from the norm the perception is you're deviating from the institution. They don't like change very much."

The company—Sauter and Jankowski and Wyman, that is— had hired her to do whatever she wanted in the morning, something radical, something that could win. "I'm not here to make people glad," she said. "I'm here to get ratings."

In fact, there was a rather stunning premise underlying the Winston hiring, unknown to the organization at large: Sauter and Jankowski had come to the conclusion that the CBS News legacy, that hallowed tradition of Murrow and Cronkite, was a kind of hex in the morning. They were banking on Winston, who'd produced game shows as well as a news and information program, to break that spell. "From day one," Winston later said, "CBS brass told me that the words 'CBS News' were a turnoff to people, that audiences didn't want to watch something from CBS News."

Winston developed all kinds of new-format ideas, including a "rolling format" that would have had anchors around the country introducing live segments. But when she started suggesting people such as Geraldo Rivera, the flamboyant "me" journalist from ABC News, or Frank Gifford, the ABC sportscaster, CBS executives blanched. "What happened," said David Fuchs, by then Sauter's vice-president at news, "was every time you began to say that you're going to make Geraldo Rivera a CBS News correspondent, you had to take a deep breath. And you realize that you can't quite face up to hiring the kinds of names that are consistent with this concept." Winston and CBS began considering compromises. They talked to Linda Ellerbee, who was leaving NBC News, and Charles Osgood, of CBS, and Winston continued to develop format ideas. This process went on through the spring of 1986; meanwhile, each new step or new candidate for the show was leaked to the press, inspiring a swirl of controversy and confusion inside CBS News. Winston's six-month window began to seem inviting.

Sauter's other project upon returning to news was the Rather broadcast, which, while still in first place, was beginning to show signs of serious vulnerability. It turned out that moments television didn't age very well, and in the Joyce era, with the *Evening News* staff preoccupied by infighting, the broadcast had drifted so badly that it had become a bad parody of itself.

Lane Venardos, though a capable producer, had never secured as strong a position in the executive producer's slot as Stringer had, either with Rather or with the broadcast's writers.

Journalist Michael Massing studied more than a month's worth of *Evening News* broadcasts for an article in the *Columbia Journalism Review* and found not only that the broadcast was less serious than it had been under Cronkite—that was old news by then—but that it wasn't even doing moments journalism very well. The production was undisciplined, relying upon whiz-bang editing that obscured meaning, and the writing was sophomoric or often unintelligible. The Sauter dictum about reaching out and touching someone, about engaging the audience, had atrophied into a kind of license for self-indulgence. In an apparent effort to make Rather seem friendly and chatty, the anchor was given such lines as this: "Don't stop me if you've heard this one, because you have. It's time-warp time again in the nation's capital. From out of nowhere fast, guess what's back on the fast track tonight from the White House to Congress? Phil Jones reports the House, after a personal house call and arm-twisting session for Republicans from President Reagan yesterday, yup, the House is again getting ready to vote again tonight on a bracket-to-bracket, top-to-bottom, coast-to-coast federal tax overhaul bill."

What was worse, Sauter's research showed that changes in the sample audience used by the A. C. Nielsen Company, which tallied the ratings for the networks, indicated that NBC's *Nightly News* with Tom Brokaw was on the rise and would gain audience at Rather's expense.

So, just weeks after he had returned to news, Sauter convened a meeting of the senior *Evening News* staffers, including Rather, at the Captiva Island resort off Florida. He brought along a marketing and research expert named Doug Clemenson, whom

Sauter had hired for CBS News. Clemenson convinced the gathering that change was needed, but there was serious division over what those changes should be. Rather had been resistant to the newcomer's presence at CBS News. He thought of Clemenson as a news consultant ("You want somebody who works hand in glove with consultants, then you've got the wrong anchorman," he said to Sauter); instead, he was listening more and more to Tom Bettag, the senior producer who ranked just below Venardos on the broadcast. Bettag had been one of the Young Turks in the back of the room crying for change at the tail end of Cronkite's time, but he had come to believe that the *Evening News* under Sauter and after had strayed too far from its mission of delivering the day's serious news.

Sauter's hope had been to convince the staff that the targets of the *Evening News* needed to be broad and, truth be told, relatively low; they should think of it as a well-produced electronic tabloid, not the *New York Times.* But the Bettag-Rather faction was becoming increasingly strident in its contention that the *Evening News* needed to become a harder, more serious broadcast. What was most significant about the disagreements was that Sauter held such little sway with his staff.

Several weeks later Venardos was moved into the special-events unit, and the selection of his successor presented another test of Sauter's influence. The two obvious choices were Bettag and Andrew Heyward, an extremely capable producer who'd come up from local news and had a reputation for being flexible when it came to news philosophy. Heyward was Sauter's choice for the job; Sauter thought that Bettag, a prize student of Fred Friendly's at Columbia, leaned a bit too much toward the old style. But Rather wanted Bettag, and Stringer told Sauter that Bettag would leave the broadcast if he didn't get the job. So Bettag was it, and the anchor and his new producer formed a bond that led the broadcast in the very direction Sauter believed would doom the *Evening News* to third place.

Sauter's influence on the *Evening News* was far less significant in his second tour than it had been during his first, and by the late spring of 1986 events had distracted his attention away from the *Evening News* altogether.

In 1985 NBC surged past ABC in the prime-time ratings and finished just behind CBS, and in the 1985–86 television season NBC established itself as the viewers' favorite entertainment network. NBC had scored huge hits with such programs as *The Cosby Show* and *Family Ties,* and its programming lineup was proving the most popular with advertisers as well. CBS's top shows, on the other hand, were old mainstays such as *60 Minutes,* shows that didn't bring new viewers to the living room. With slick, offbeat programs like *Miami Vice,* NBC was clearly building toward a period of dominance in prime time, which would have a beneficial effect for NBC News.

Just as CBS was losing its prime-time lead to NBC, all network television was hit hard by a sudden and dramatic slump in the advertising marketplace. In the 1970s and early 1980s, years of runaway inflation, the networks had always operated on an inflation-plus basis—that is, each year they added to the cost of their commercials by the amount of inflation, plus another 3 or 4 percent increase. By 1986, though, the gravy train had hit a dead end. Because rapid inflation in the national economy had long since ended, major network advertisers, such as producers of packaged goods, were not taking in inflation-plus revenues to offset increases in the cost of commercial time on the networks. What's more, the overall network audience was declining, thus relatively diminishing the value of network commercials. So advertisers resisted higher prices, and in 1986 there was a huge shortfall for CBS and ABC. It became clear that two of the networks would lose money—a previously unimaginable circumstance.

For CBS the predicament was particularly pointed, in light of its costly fight with Ted Turner and disappointing returns in some of its other businesses. In May 1986 Gene Jankowski and his top executives in the Broadcast Group, including Van Sauter, met and decided on a new round of cutbacks: Seven hundred jobs in the CBS Broadcast Group would be eliminated. Jankowski wrote a memo to all employees, talking about "disinflation in the national economy" and the need for "downsizing."

Sauter knew that "downsizing" was risky business in an organization that had undergone such devastating cutbacks just nine months earlier. If fat had been trimmed away in that first cutback, how much more could CBS News pare down before it began to lose muscle and bone?

The news division was instructed to eliminate another 90 jobs (out of about 1,350). In staff meetings at Black Rock, Sauter spoke of the anguish that came when a company broke its "social contract" with its employees; but he was, after all, an officer in the corporation, and he readily acquiesced. "In my opinion," Sauter later explained, "CBS News was perfectly capable of losing more jobs."

It sometimes seemed that Sauter found in nearly any matter an excuse for a "working retreat," and the cutbacks before him in 1986 were no different. In the late spring, just as the fishing was getting good in the Catskills, he convened a retreat of his senior staff at the Beaverkill resort. There was conceived what came to be known inside CBS News as the "Doomsday Book." It was a list, from top to bottom, of all CBS News employees, along with their job descriptions, their salaries, and the value of their tasks. As with the original *Doomsday Book,* the report provided a handy ordering of the parcels of the realm; from that list were chosen the names of those who soon were to lose their jobs.

Sauter was aware of the outrage the earlier cutbacks had caused within the news division. This time he was determined to do it more sensitively, construing it as a reorganization, not leaking the names of those who would be fired, and even arranging for job placement counseling.

On July 17 "doomsday" arrived, and despite all the plans, the layoffs hit like a bombshell. Among those dismissed, as in the earlier round, were several CBS News employees of long and worthy service, such as George Herman. Herman was a network fixture. He'd been hired in 1944 by Paul White, one of the founding fathers of CBS News, and had worked as a writer for Murrow and Collingwood and LeSueur; he'd covered conventions since 1948, the Korean War, the White House under Eisenhower and Kennedy. In 1986, at the age of sixty-six, he was still a productive employee, reporting the cover story on *Sunday Morning* each week as well as the daily afternoon news breaks.

CBS News said that it had reached "an arrangement" with Herman. Herman didn't care for the sugarcoating, asked about the "arrangement" he and the network had come to, he said, "If you mean being fired is coming to an arrangement, that's what it is. I have a contract that runs to January twenty-seventh. They have told me that as of January twenty-seventh, I'm fired. Laid off. Not renewed. Whatever you want to call it. . . . I'm a little paralyzed right now."

Several reporters, including Sandy Gilmour (who went on to

a successful career at NBC News), Carlos Aguilar, Nadine
Berger, and Gary Schuster, along with several veteran producers, were also dismissed.

Sauter wrote a memo—a "sensitive" memo, one of his aides
pointed out—saying that "the date that distresses all of us is
here." He wrote of the "wrenching changes in the economy"
that prompted the cuts and reminded the news staffers that "the
work you do, individually and collectively, is of importance to
our society." Those who were leaving, he said, "have not been
irrelevant to our purpose."

That warm summer evening Sauter met in his elegant new
office with a circle of his senior staff. They drank Samuel Smith
ale (Sauter's brand) and told stories, some involving people who
had been fired that day by CBS. Sauter told the anecdote that
got the biggest response. It was about Don Webster, a former
CBS News correspondent in Vietnam (he spent seven years
there and was once captured by the Vietcong) who had become
a news producer covering the Arab side of the Middle East for
CBS.

It seemed that Sauter as Paris bureau chief found himself in
Marrakesh with a cameraman when he got a telex from the
foreign desk in New York asking him and the crew to go to
Angola, where some American mercenaries were being tried.
Sauter's cameraman, who was also a close pal, took him aside
and told him, "This will be very, very bad." The chances of
getting out of Angola without any problems, said the cameraman, who had experience in such things, were no better than
one in five.

Sauter recounted that it had quickly occurred to him that he
had matters to attend to in Paris, urgent matters, and he responded to New York with the message that Don Webster, who
was in Morocco with him, would be going to Angola with a crew
that worked for CBS down in Salisbury, Rhodesia. New York
approved, and Sauter explained to Webster that this could be
a breakthrough in his career, his big chance. Off Webster went
to Angola, where he was taken into custody by military police
and put in prison, which in Angola is apparently an even less
pleasant experience than incarceration elsewhere. Then came
the punch line. Sauter had arranged to have supplies sent in to
Webster in Angola, and finding himself in need, Webster had
sent an oblique message: "Now is the time to ship the precious

quantities"—meaning drinking water. "But the goddamned military thought, 'Uh-oh, he's calling in the special forces!' " Webster ended up in jail for nearly three weeks.

Reached in London in 1986, Don Webster, fifty-two years old and suddenly out of work, was diplomatic about his circumstance. "The crisis is real in television news," he said. "They have to change the nature of the whole operation, and the Middle East is not one of their high priorities," he said. As for himself, he said, "I'll come back and look for work. I'll work for anybody. Do you know of a job?"

In the new age of austerity in network television, there came to be a kind of cost-cutting chic—ABC went through severe cutbacks when it was acquired by Capital Cities Communications, Inc., and now CBS was experiencing the belt tightening— that played to the analysts on Wall Street who always believed that leaner was better. Asked about the 1986 cutbacks at CBS News, Sauter later stoutly defended them: "I must say, I think it was one of the better things that the Broadcast Group did in years, in terms of addressing a core problem and addressing it in a very thoughtful, productive manner. I think we did it better than Cap Cities, much better."

However, the institution was not inclined to such abstract analyses. The layoffs, as Sauter had suggested, did represent a breach of the social contract, and in a creative business such things count heavily. People had made deliberate choices along the way in their careers to come to or stay at CBS; talk of "disinflation" didn't blunt the loss of a drinking buddy or the sacking of someone you'd been under fire with out in the field. It did not help, either, that Phyllis George was still being paid $1 million a year by CBS News to stay at home or that the man who had ordered the layoffs, Gene Jankowski (who, after all, was at least partly responsible for the company's circumstance competitively), was being paid a base annual salary of $475,000 with bonuses adding at minimum another $350,000 in 1986. Both Sauter and Ed Joyce, many in the institution noted, had been given new long-term contracts in the past year.

The organization was still reeling from the cutbacks when, just eight days later on July 25, the second bombshell went off. Sauter announced that the *CBS Morning News* would be canceled, the bulk of the morning time period taken away from the news division, and the slot filled by an entertainment program.

The view that CBS News had cast a "curse" on the morning appeared to have triumphed.

It was a bizarre and stunning turn, arrived at after a series of bizarre turns. In early July Sauter, Jankowski, Fuchs, and Stringer had met for a long debate about the *Morning News* at the Ritz Carlton Hotel on Central Park South. The executives concluded that even the Phyllis George experience hadn't convinced the institution that the morning time period was not suitable ground for traditional news, and the evidence was the uproar that attended each of the various plans for Susan Winston's show. Sauter and Jankowski, with Stringer acquiescing, agreed that the thing to do was to remove the time period from news altogether. Winston's new show would be produced by the Broadcast Group, with Sauter supervising. Under those circumstances, it was thought, Winston would be freed from the narrow restrictions imposed by CBS News. She could break the curse; she could produce a "show" instead of a broadcast.

Sauter flew to London, where the *Morning News* was on location for the wedding of Prince Andrew and Sarah Ferguson, and revealed his plan to Winston. To Sauter's amazement, Winston said no. She had already seen the fury of the news division at work, and that was just over plans; she told Sauter that to take the morning time period away from news would be a mistake. If done right, she said, a morning broadcast that would get ratings and satisfy the news division could be produced. Sauter disagreed and returned to New York.

Three days later, while vacationing in Britain, Winston was surprised when her staff read to her stories in the *New York Times* and *Newsday* that she planned to leave the show. Obviously the morning time period was leaving the news division, with or without Winston.

Sauter needed some victories, and the possibility of another long and tormented tryout of yet another version of the *CBS Morning News* left him numb. Black Rock was pressing for some success in the morning, and as significant, CBS affiliates were clamoring, too (some had threatened to drop the program if Shriver and Sawyer continued as coanchors). So, on July 25, just a week and a day after the layoffs, he issued another memo to the staff. He said what everyone at CBS News already knew, that the *Morning News* was not managing to compete with NBC and ABC and added, "[I]t is imperative to the news division, the company and the affiliates that we do so." To succeed in the morning, he continued, "we must have as much flexibility as possible," and to achieve that, "we have decided to eliminate the traditional boundaries that experience after experience have convinced us are too restrictive."

Sauter's deft phrasing aside, the message was clear: CBS News had just relinquished its biggest single block of news time, ten hours a week, to entertainment. The move, coming just behind the cutbacks, had a devastating effect on morale. But the mood that swept the news division was not melancholy; it was fierce anger.

Andy Rooney, the popular *60 Minutes* commentator, gave voice to the feelings of many inside CBS News in a newspaper column he wrote the next week. "CBS, which used to stand for the Columbia Broadcasting System," Rooney wrote, "no longer stands for anything. They're just corporate initials now."

Rooney told his readers about the cutbacks and about the *Morning News,* and then he wrote:

> At CBS, a committee of executives made the firing decisions. It would be interesting in any company that has to cut down to save money to take a vote of all the employees and find out who they think should be fired. At CBS, the list would have included several members of the firing committee. CBS News has, for example, at least 12 vice presidents, none of whom were dumped overboard.
>
> If it was the money the company wanted to save, firing a couple of $150,000 a year VP's would have saved more than firing a lot of $50,000 a year people. . . . The real tragedy is that CBS News will never again be as good as it once was.

Sauter and Stringer tried to deflect the criticism by pointing out that Rooney hadn't offered to give back any of his considerable salary at layoff time, but their efforts didn't take. Rooney's comments had struck a chord in the organization, and a measure of the depth of people's feelings emerged one afternoon when Rooney walked into the company cafeteria in the basement of the Broadcast Center to be greeted with a standing ovation. "It was the damnedest thing that ever happened to me in my life," he said. "I guess I struck a nerve."

The intense ill will toward Sauter, Stringer, and management

as a whole was almost beyond measure, but a good indication
of Sauter's standing was a *TV Guide* editorial that virtually demanded his resignation. In his supervision of CBS News, the
magazine pointed out, Sauter had:

> —Presided over the largest personnel cuts ever to hit a
> network news division.
> —Seen the historic ratings leadership of the CBS Evening
> News dwindle to almost nothing.
> —Eviscerated CBS's hard-hitting and controversial docu-
> mentary and public-affairs units.
> —Hired a former Miss America with no journalistic creden-
> tials as Diane Sawyer's successor.

"Sauter's antics," the editorial continued, "have outraged
many who take their television journalism seriously. . . ."

There was a rising chorus of anti-Sauter talk in the hallways
and calls for his resignation, a swelling mood of sedition. And
what gave it strength and momentum was the feeling that a real
alternative was at hand; in the background of all the chaos stood
a figure who, many in the news division were beginning to believe, could free them not only from Van Sauter, the executor
of such unpopular policies, but from Tom Wyman and the
whole CBS management structure. That man was Laurence A.
Tisch.

On July 3, 1985, when CBS was at the height of its fight with Ted
Turner, the Loews Corporation, which was controlled by the
successful financier and philanthropist Laurence A. Tisch,
began to buy CBS stock. In three weeks it had acquired 2.9
million shares, giving Tisch more CBS stock than William Paley
owned.

By October, Loews owned nearly 12 percent of the stock, and
suddenly Larry Tisch was the largest CBS stockholder; that
month he was invited to join the CBS board. At the time Wyman
publicly welcomed Tisch, noting his "well-deserved reputation
as a successful, long-term investor in publicly held companies,"
and Wyman's aide and spokesman, William Lilly III, said, "It
was obviously a very friendly arrangement; we have been inviting him for a long time to be an investor." The statements were
meant to distinguish Tisch from the many unfriendly investors

that CBS had been battling through the year, and in fact, Tisch had come to CBS under friendly circumstances. He'd first considered CBS at the time of Jesse Helms's move against the company, nearly a year earlier, when he discussed the matter with a friend and member of the CBS board, James Wolfensohn. In a move interpreted by some as courtship, Wyman had come to Tisch six months later, asking advice about the buyback plan as a strategy for holding back Turner.

Still, Wyman and some members of the board were wary. Wyman had not invited Tisch to become an investor and didn't know that Loews was buying stock until it already owned 5 percent, when Tisch telephoned him to assure him of his peaceful intent.

Tisch's history warranted some caution. Although he declared that his purpose was to help keep a great and important American company independent, he was not a broadcaster, any more than Loews' ownership of hotels meant that he was an innkeeper or his ownership of Bulova made him a watchmaker. Tisch was a financier, his profession was making money, and such men do not usually attach much sentiment to their investments. (When the deal was right, Tisch had sold the Americana Hotel in Bal Harbour, Florida, the place where his children had grown up.) At the time of Tisch's election to the CBS board, *Broadcasting* magazine reminded readers that in early 1974 Loews had announced that it had acquired just more than 5 percent of CNA, the Chicago-based insurance company, and that the *New York Times* at the time had said, "[Tisch] is known to have personally reassured a former board chairman of CNA, Howard C. Reeder, that he had no intention of making a bid for the company." Loews had then proceeded to wage a successful hostile takeover of CNA.

Tom Wyman personally extended to Tisch the invitation to join the board and, in doing so, hinted that he and the CBS board would feel a lot less antsy about things if Tisch would make his peaceful intentions official by signing a "standstill" agreement—a written promise not to purchase more than 25 percent of the CBS stock. Tisch refused.

Tisch's presence had an immediate and profound impact on the dynamics of the CBS power structure, the two most important elements of which were Paley, the founder, and Wyman, the chairman. There had been some tension between the two men almost from the day Tom Wyman, with the help of the board, urged the somewhat reluctant Paley finally to surrender the chairmanship in late 1982.

Having consolidated his power and secured for himself the titles of chairman, president, and chief executive officer, Wyman seemed to shut Paley out. He was polite and deferential to the founder in his presence, but he was not, associates say, solicitous of Paley when it came to running the company. Gene Jankowski became Paley's principal conduit to the daily operations of the broadcasting portion of the CBS empire, bringing the founder videocassettes of new CBS programs and asking Paley's advice on programming matters. Wyman, on the other hand, believed Paley to be well past his full capacity (he later told people stories about Paley's infirmities, cocking his head to the side and crossing his eyes to suggest the image of an addled old man) and resented Paley's disinclination (or inability) to let go of the company he had founded.

Paley, for his part, came to harbor the same doubts about Wyman that he'd felt about most of the other potential successors he'd chosen over the years. Paley was said to be understandably disappointed with Wyman's running of the company's nonbroadcasting ventures, many of which had soured by 1986; CBS had overpaid by a considerable sum for twelve Ziff-Davis Publishing Company magazines and had then turned around and filed suit against the seller; the CBS theatrical films division was losing money, and the toy division was a notorious money loser ($67 million in the wrong direction in 1984). But with Wyman, unlike his predecessors, there seemed to be little that Paley could do about his disappointment.

Larry Tisch, meanwhile, declared that he had no interest in controlling CBS, but almost immediately after joining the board, he began to show a proprietary interest in the company. At his first board meeting, in November 1985, he jumped right in and offered his opinion that there seemed to be too thick a layer of management at CBS; fittingly, his remarks pertained to CBS News, which was going through public torment in the final weeks of Ed Joyce's tenure.

Still, through the first half of 1986 Wyman felt secure enough, under the circumstances, and in April the board underscored that sense of security by voting him a raise. His annual salary of $675,000 was boosted to $750,000, which would have been a sizable leap even in a year when the company was not going through economic agony. In granting Wyman the raise, the board members spoke of his stout stewardship in a brutal time, the successful fight against Turner, and the reestablishment of CBS's credit line in the face of huge debt. Wyman had reason to believe that his position with the board was strong.

But soon things began to heat up. Wyman had not succeeded in getting a standstill agreement from Tisch, and when, in late spring, Loews increased its holdings to just under 25 percent, there was a new wave of concern on the part of Wyman and his supporters.

The concern was not likely to have been allayed by Ken Auletta's compelling and studiously detailed account of Larry Tisch's CBS involvement for the *New York Times*. The article made it clear that Tisch was thoroughly enjoying his CBS involvement and that his intentions were more than those of a casual friendly investor. Auletta referred to Tisch as the possible "heir to William S. Paley as the guiding force behind one of the nation's premier communications companies." Days later, on June 12, Tisch wrote to Wyman, meaning to assure him once again of his essential friendliness:

> Dear Tom,
> I've been concerned in this period of various articles in the press regarding Loews interest in CBS. I want to reiterate to you that I continue to have full confidence in you and your management.
> Last October, when I accepted your invitation to join the CBS board, I advised you that Loews intended to purchase up to 25% of outstanding shares of CBS. There has been no change at all in our intentions.
> Sincerely,
> LT (Larry)

Wyman was not reassured, and in July a group of board members again tried to secure a standstill agreement. They were beginning to feel that Larry Tisch was shrewdly taking over CBS at bargain prices, paying the current stock market price rather than the premium of $40 to $50 a share he would pay in a declared takeover. Once again Tisch declined to sign a standstill agreement.

But as influential as Tisch was becoming, as impressive as his CBS holdings were, he did not control CBS. He was only a single member of a thirteen-member board (fourteen counting Wyman). To control CBS, he didn't need to buy more stock. He needed a revolt on the CBS board. And that would come, triggered, in part, by CBS News.

Sauter, for his part, remained amazingly calm through the turbulent summer of 1986. He knew that if Wyman and the current management survived, he would survive, and if Tisch prevailed, what would it matter? CBS would be a different company.

He was also aware that Larry Tisch had insinuated himself into the sentiments of the news division, acquiring nearly the status of a folk hero among the troops and of a friend among the CBS News barons. Mike Wallace and Don Hewitt numbered themselves among Tisch's social acquaintances, and Tisch's son, Tommy, began to develop a social relationship with some younger members of the news division. Tisch, a man with a pronounced social conscience, genuinely liked the people at CBS News, and he said that he thought news should be treated as something special, not as just another part of the company. All around, the name Tisch came to resonate with the promise of an alternative and a safe haven.

The end of the famous *TV Guide* editorial blasting Sauter fairly well expressed the common sentiment at CBS News: "Still, things may soon change for the better: businessman Laurence A. Tisch, a strong leader, has increased his investments in CBS stock. We hope that if Tisch takes control, which is altogether possible, he will restore to CBS News some of the honor and glory it knew in Edward R. Murrow's time."

Meanwhile, Sauter just seemed to shrug it all off with his characteristic insouciance. In August he greeted a visitor to his plush office, with his big oak desk, his oriental carpets, two N. C. Wyeths hanging on the wall, and, looking out his balcony window at the humming news operation below, said he knew that people wondered how he could take the current circumstances so calmly. He said that he told them he had grown up in a household in which illness, hard times, and death were part of the expected course of events.

"Bad things happen in this life," he said. "And so I have come to a place in life that is quite exalted by the standards of Middletown, Ohio, but I still have that in me. I am completely unaffected. I learned long ago to compartmentalize my life, and what is going on around here has no impact whatsoever on the rest of my life."

In fact, Sauter seemed to be feeling almost buoyant. He spoke hopefully of a *Wall Street Journal* article that was in the works and that, he had heard, would portray him as a good manager. "I *am* a great goddamn manager," Sauter said, looking out over the newsroom below. "This place is like a movie studio in the 1930s. Money isn't everything, but it's an indication. We have more than a hundred twenty employees to whom we pay more than a hundred thousand dollars a year. We have several employees to whom we pay more than one million dollars a year. This is like a thirties movie studio, with producers and stars and huge egos clashing and greed. And what we do every day is tell the world 'This is what is important to you, this is a public responsibility, and what we do here has nothing to do with greed and ego.' "

Of course, it did have to do with ego and greed, and for all his studied indifference to the turmoil surrounding him, Sauter was keenly aware of that fact. By this time he knew that his detractors were not just the big-time players Moyers and Hewitt and Cronkite, but the rank and file and such key producers as the born-again radicals Tom Bettag and Richard Cohen on the *Evening News.* Two days after that August visit he spent a day off up in his Connecticut home, writing a speech for the coming bureau chiefs' meeting in Park City, Utah, in which he planned to address the opposition head-on.

It was a memorable speech. For the first time Sauter openly faced his detractors and stared them down. The economic realities of the company, he said, were painful and unprecedented, and "it is unrealistic for people within the News Division to assume that they can in some fashion be hermetically sealed off from this reality. They can't." He defended the cancellation of the *Morning News,* while acknowledging the "powerful storm cloud" it had caused. "And the disillusionment, lack of confidence, and anger resulting from this has focused on me, which is fine."

Then he let his audience of employees know that they would not run him out. "I'm more than constitutionally capable of dealing with negative attitudes about me, with unflattering publicity, with dissatisfaction about how I run the News Division and my continued employment at CBS."

Sauter spoke as the corporate man. "[T]here are some who feel I should have thrown my body in front of budget cuts or layoffs or The Morning News decision. There is a feeling I did not adequately represent the News Division at Black Rock. I increasingly feel I did not adequately represent the forces of the outside world to the News Division."

In a final blast Sauter said that the hallway gossip and speculation had reached a point where it threatened to compromise the work of CBS News. "As we all know, the anger, the anxiety, and the apprehension have also hatched an unbecoming strain of petulance and self-righteousness in our organization. This could prove far more damaging to our purpose than the emotions which have provoked these feelings. I thus urge you to urge those who work for you to tighten the focus of their work."

Lest anyone miss the message, Sauter had a copy of the speech distributed to every employee in CBS News.

After the speech there was open confrontation. Bettag, Cohen, and Andrew Heyward got involved in heated discussions with Sauter and among themselves and their co-workers over the propriety and tone of Sauter's speech and the direction in which he was steering CBS News.

Later the newspeople got a rare visit to the Park City gathering from Tom Wyman. The chairman made it clear that he recognized the key role of the news division in all the turmoil, that it was the news division, not entertainment or records or any other part of the company, which kept the waters churning and thus made his own position tenuous.

But Wyman was facing a hostile crowd in Park City, and his visit only made things worse. As he worked his way through the milling newspeople, falling into conversations here and there, one of the things he mentioned was Larry Tisch's stout support of Israel. He may not have meant to imply that Tisch's feelings about Israel could compromise the integrity of CBS News; but that was the inference that was taken, and word of it spread like wildfire. The story eventually reached Tisch and was said to have hardened his growing contempt for Wyman.

Increasingly, all events seemed to point to the September 10 meeting of the CBS board. In August, Tisch had cast off his posture as a Wyman supporter and directly asked the chairman to move aside for the good of the company; Wyman refused.

Wyman still felt the company was being hustled by this erstwhile "white knight," so he went to see his friend Francis Vincent, president of Coca-Cola's entertainment division. Wyman and Vincent were of the same class, the same world (Vincent was, in Wyman's book, "one of the most attractive people in the city"). Over lunch Wyman discussed the options, and Vincent posed an interesting one. If Larry Tisch was indeed taking control of the company at a bargain, as Wyman suspected, would the CBS board be interested in getting paid a fair price for something that was happening anyway? A "fair price" being $170 a share?

Yes, of course, it would, Wyman thought. Remaining independent had been the whole objective of the long, hard fight against Turner and the others, but perhaps acquisition was inevitable. It was the way of the times. ABC had merged with Capital Cities, NBC had been acquired by the General Electric Company, and CBS seemed to be in the process of being taken over by Loews. If CBS were going to be acquired, shouldn't it go to the highest bidder? Tisch had acquired nearly 25 percent of the company's stock, paying an average price of only $127 a share. That spring the CBS board had turned down an offer from Marvin Davis at $160 per share. Now Coca-Cola was talking about $170 per share. Why shouldn't the board have the option of choosing Coca-Cola, a classy corporation which, with its own Hollywood studio (Columbia Pictures) and other ventures, had experience in the entertainment world?

Wyman decided to present to the board Vincent's request for a ten-day look at the CBS books, during which time neither CBS nor Coca-Cola would be under any obligation; after that period, if the CBS board was amenable, Coca-Cola would present its offer. As Wyman saw it, there was no risk, and in the days before the board meeting he briefed eight members of the board about the Coca-Cola matter. He didn't want to stir opposition, so he did not inform either Tisch or Paley, nor did he speak to Paley's closest supporters, Walter Cronkite and Marietta Tree, the philanthropist who was one of Paley's closest friends on the board. Wyman felt that he had the others in his camp, and as September 10 approached, he was confident. It was, after all, his board.

But something happened, something from CBS News—Bill

Moyers decided to bow out with a splash, and Dan Rather, the public symbol of CBS News, began to behave particularly strangely on the air.

On Monday night, Labor Day, Rather caught the *Evening News* staff quite unawares when he ended his broadcast by signing off with the word "courage." He'd told no one he was going to say it, and explained it to no one afterward. The place was abuzz, but many people assumed that maybe it was just a one-time holiday greeting, and let it go. But on Tuesday, Rather said it again. "Courage." This time Bettag talked to him about it, telling him if he'd wanted to come up with a signoff, like Cronkite's "That's the way it is," that that was fine, but they should discuss it first. Bettag assured the curious that Rather wouldn't say it again.

And then on Wednesday, Rather once more signed off with "courage," and by this time, people were beginning to notice. Was it some sort of insider's code meant to bolster the troops in the face of all the company's turmoil? If so, was it appropriate to use the *Evening News* airwaves for that purpose? The senior staff of the broadcast sat down with Rather and tried to talk him out of his new signature; the CBS publicity department, which was beginning to get calls from TV columnists about it, explained that Rather had long signed letters and autographs with "Courage," and that it was just something he was trying out. Off the record, CBS News officials allowed that Rather seemed to be getting, as one put it, "a little fuzzy around the edges."

On Thursday night of "courage" week, he didn't say "courage." Instead, he said, "coraje." The CBS News phone system lit up with calls. "What the hell did he say?" asked one bureau chief, speaking to a New York producer. "I don't know," replied the producer. "He either said the Spanish word for 'courage,' or an Asian form of the martial arts." (The last report on the broadcast had been a piece by Bill Moyers about the Mexican-American border and, apparently, it put Rather in a Latin mood.) Friday, Rather switched back to English, signing off with "courage" one more time, and on Monday, Rather ended his broadcast without saying it at all. Some of the people in the Broadcast Center broke into applause.

It was a strange episode, but it seemed particularly symbolic coming just when it did, when the board, Black Rock, the press, and much of the outside world was beginning to think that CBS

News was on the verge of flying apart at the seams. If the Rather "courage" episode hadn't been convincing, there was Bill Moyers to seal it.

The turmoil at CBS News had been a big story, and Moyers had led reporters covering the beat to believe that he might go out with a bang, with some "resignation in protest" type of action, before going back to public television. The *New York Times* and Jonathan Alter, the media reporter for *Newsweek,* were particularly interested in getting Moyers's feelings about CBS News, knowing that they would make for good copy; Moyers, typically, was on the fence about whether to cooperate. Finally he decided that he would not say anything to the *Times* because, he said, he knew that it would feel obliged to include a response from management. "This is too sensitive a matter, too large an issue, too great an organization for someone to be quoted out of context," he said; in other words, Moyers wanted to write the article himself.

However, Moyers did tell Alter that he might oblige him. It happened that *Newsweek* was preparing a big story on the difficulties at CBS in anticipation of the September 10 board meeting, as was almost every major news organization. The possibility of a showdown loomed, and *Newsweek* wanted a scene setter, just in case. But going into the week of publication, the magazine wasn't sure how big to play the story, and through the week Alter kept going back and forth with Moyers. On Friday night, when the magazine closed its issue for the next week, Moyers told Alter that he still wasn't sure, that he'd let Alter know in the morning. As the reporter was leaving the *Newsweek* building after working on his CBS piece until 3:00 A.M., an editor told him the staff still hadn't decided how to play the story. There were two other stories competing for the cover that week, including a major story on Middle East terror.

Saturday morning Alter was awakened by a call from Moyers. He'd been up half the night, Moyers said, and he'd decided to do it. Alter, half asleep and sitting in his underwear, frantically took down what Moyers dictated, which amounted to an essay on CBS. Moyers said that over the years the managers of CBS News had always protected the news division not only from outside intruders but from the encroachment of entertainment values from within. But in recent years, he said, that had changed. "Not only were those values invited in, they were exalted," Moyers said. "The line between entertainment and news was steadily blurred. Our center of gravity shifted from the standards and practices of the news business to show business.

"Pretty soon," Moyers added, "tax policy had to compete with stories about three-legged sheep, and the three-legged sheep won."

Moyers went on to decry the subversion of news to a level of "small talk" and expressed his fear that obsession with pleasing the viewers had created a "video version of the drug culture. . . ." He ended by recounting a dinner he'd had with Gene Jankowski, in which Jankowski had asked what it would take to keep Moyers at CBS, and Moyers had told him he would stay for a weekly series and a one-year commitment to keep it on the air. Moyers said that he had promised that at the end of the year, if CBS decided the project had failed, it would owe Moyers just a dollar, and he would quietly go away. He concluded with a final dig. "He looked at me," Moyers said of Jankowski, "and said, 'Bill, I'm going to stick with *West 57th.*'" (Learning the content of Alter's story from another reporter in advance of publication, Sauter had a barb or two of his own to hurl in Moyers's direction: "He wanted his own vehicle, done his way. When that was not forthcoming, he became very bitter and angry, though not bitter and angry enough to resign and relinquish $20,000 a week.")

Alter immediately called *Newsweek,* interrupting a meeting in which his editors were deciding which story to put on the cover, to tell them he had Moyers. They went with CBS for the cover, and what a stark, dramatic cover it was—the black CBS trademark eye against a white background, with a jagged crack streaking across it. CIVIL WAR AT CBS the headline read in bold black letters, and beneath was the subhead: "The Struggle for the Soul of a Legendary Network."

It was devastating stuff. Alter reported the story about Wyman and his imprudent conversations with newspeople on the subject of Israel, and the body of the article reported that if Tisch opposed Wyman, he would have Bill Paley as an ally. If so, Wyman wouldn't stand a chance with the board. Hewitt got an advance copy of the story, and its various sidebars, which he showed to Wyman in Wyman's private box at the U.S. Open. At his Fifth Avenue apartment Paley got his own advance copy of the *Newsweek* article. There on the cover was the shattered image of his beloved company; it seemed to symbolize all the turbulence and trouble of the last five years.

On Tuesday, the night before the board meeting, there was a rump meeting of the board, all members except Tisch and Wyman. Mr. Paley revealed that it was true, he favored a change in management. The months of turmoil—particularly the troubles at CBS News—could not be allowed to continue. The board members seemed to agree, and Wyman's Coca-Cola strategy was dead before it was delivered. (One board member later said that the Coca-Cola offer looked good but noted that if CBS had seriously considered it, the company would be "opened up for auction.")

The next day Wyman's big moment arrived. After the presentation of reports by the division heads, they left, and Wyman noticed something queer; there had not been the usual round of questions from the board. But he pressed on and put his case for Coca-Cola. It was a good company, he said, a classy bunch of people, and it wanted to consider an acquisition. It'd pay $170 a share (as opposed, he didn't need to add, to the average $127 per share that Tisch had paid). He wasn't asking the board to vote on that for now, just on the matter of yielding to Coca-Cola certain information about CBS for a ten-day examination period, which, if all went well, would be followed by an offer.

Paley said no, Tisch said no, and Wyman was asked to leave the room. By the end of the day he was out. William Paley was chairman again, and Laurence Tisch was named acting chief executive officer.

Wednesday was a routine day for Sauter—yet not routine at all. He'd had breakfast at the Dorset Hotel with Dan Rather and Jim Babb, the manager of the CBS affiliate in Charlotte, with whom Sauter had pounded out that agreement about the hourlong news so long ago. People wandered by and wished Sauter luck, and there was some commiseration, but Sauter was characteristically sanguine and resigned to his fate. Three weeks earlier, as he prepared to make his Park City speech, he had speculated with a visitor about his chances under Tisch. "Well," he said, "Fred Friendly's wife is a close friend of the Tisches. He listens to Bill Moyers. He and Hewitt are close. And I am very, very much associated with Gene Jankowski and Tom Wyman. In that speech this weekend I will associate *myself* even more with them. Tisch thinks that Jankowski is a smiling salesman and that Wyman is a total incompetent." Then he had laughed, as if to ask, "Where does that leave me?"

He had lunch that day at a favorite restaurant across from Central Park, with his old pal Bobby Wussler, now a top executive at Ted Turner's Cable News Network, and they had discussed the prospect of CBS's buying a minority interest in CNN. Through the day and into the early evening Sauter had monitored the progress of the board meeting. When he heard that the meeting was still going on after his lunch with Wussler ended, at two-thirty, he knew that something big was happening. En route to the Broadcast Center, Sauter called Stringer on his car phone and told him, "Something's happening, I'll call you." Stringer was at home with a bad back, and Sauter was afraid that his call from the car phone could be picked up by outsiders. But another caller told Stringer that Wyman was out, to which Stringer replied, "Oh, shit, it's happening. Well, it's better. The place was paralyzed."

Sauter returned to the Broadcast Center and spent much of the rest of the day on the phone. That evening he got the call he was waiting for. He hung up quickly and rang up Tom Bettag in the CBS newsroom below. The *Evening News* was on the air. Sauter relayed his news to Bettag, and during a commercial break Bettag relayed it to Rather. Back on the air Rather looked into the camera, and ad-libbed, "The CBS corporate board met today. After that meeting the chairman of the board and the chief executive officer, Thomas Wyman, is reported to be out." Even as Sauter spoke to Bettag, he knew that his career at CBS, a time of soaring highs and crashing lows, had ended.

After the broadcast a few Sauter pals gathered around. Rather stopped by, but he had to run; he was attending a party that night at the Park Avenue apartment of social maven Mollie Parnis, honoring Mike Wallace and his new bride, Mary Yates. So Sauter went out that night with one of his diehard loyalists, Ann Morfogen, who'd been with him as a publicity director since the days at KNXT in Los Angeles. They went to one of Sauter's favorite dives and got drunk on wine.

The next morning Sauter went to Black Rock for Gene Jankowski's usual Thursday morning staff meeting. It was an awkward moment at best. Jankowski wasn't there, though; he was upstairs in a meeting with Tisch, so Leahy and Pilson and Sauter hung around George Schweitzer's office, exchanging pieces of gallows humor. Sauter joked that he was going to love returning to California. His birthday was the following Sunday, and to cheer him up, Schweitzer gave him a funny hat—one of those baseball caps with a contraption on top to hold a cold one. Finally Jankowski sent a message to the executives that they were to return to their jobs, there would be no staff meeting that day, and Sauter went to the Broadcast Center, where he shuffled papers and killed time until he went out to lunch.

He told a reporter waiting outside the door that no, he wasn't going to Black Rock to be fired, just to the Jackson Hole (another favorite Sauter hangout, on Sixty-fourth Street) to eat lunch. But on the way to lunch Sauter got a call from Jankowski. It was important.

"I'll be right there," Sauter said, and he made his way to Black Rock.

There Jankowski asked for his resignation. Sauter, who believed that Tisch owed a debt to the news division and would pay it with Sauter's head, knew at whose direction it had come. He said sure, he'd resign, but he assumed that the five-year contract he'd just signed would be honored. Yes, Jankowski assured him, it would be.

Sauter went home, got together his fishing gear, and dictated a memo to Ann Morfogen: "My eighteen years at CBS were joyful and rewarding, and while the difficulties of the past ten months constituted an irreversible end game, I leave with pride in my work and respect and fondness for my former colleagues. CBS is a glorious place for creative people to work, and I feel honored to have been a part of that organization."

Then he left for Montana.

So Van Gordon Sauter and CBS News were finished with each other, and both were pleased. Sauter said of the place, "I didn't like some of the people. I thought there was a basic hypocrisy inherent to it, and there were a lot of what I called self-appointed priests of self-serving piousness, who were everywhere. And who would posture themselves to be representing the best values of the news division when they were really representing themselves. And I thought some of these people were terribly distasteful."

Bill Moyers, who'd had the last word, said of Sauter that final day: "Unfortunately, he was shaped as a corporate man. We journalists are outsiders; Van wasn't . . . [They should have] put him in charge of entertainment; he's not of the bone and marrow of news. Somebody miscast these people. Van's conditioned to listening to the people above him, not around him. That's part of his nature. He was simply the wrong choice. . . . They thought a little journalism made him a journalist. That's Greek tragedy."

But Sauter had sounded a warning about Larry Tisch, about life after the revolution, if there was to be a revolution. In his Park City speech to CBS News staffers, he said that the unpopular steps he'd taken were necessary for the good of the news division, adding, "And no matter who was sitting in my chair, the same steps would have been necessary. You can change the players, but let me assure you, you don't change the rules."

On that September night, though, CBS News wasn't inclined to hear warnings. It was too busy rejoicing. Some sang the song from the *Wizard of Oz,* "Ding-dong, the witch is dead. Which old witch? The wicked witch!"

Their hero, Larry Tisch, was in power now. Hadn't he told the waiting reporters at the conclusion of that decisive board meeting, "Everybody in the news division is a friend of mine"? Hadn't he assured the old guard, Cronkite and Hewitt and Wallace and the others, that he believed in the total independence of CBS News from the company? On the night of his boardroom triumph, had he gone straight home to celebrate? No, he had gone to the party for Mike Wallace at Molly Parnis's apartment, to mingle with Cronkite and Hewitt and Wallace and Andy Rooney.

CBS News, it seemed, was saved at last.

Chapter

ON LARRY TISCH'S FIRST day as the acting chief executive officer of CBS, in his first official communication with the company he now ran, he issued a memorandum saying that he had met with the heads of three CBS operating groups and had personally assured them of his "complete confidence in them and in the organizations they head." The first person mentioned in this inaugural memo, which was dated September 11, 1986, was Peter A. Derow, president of the CBS Publishing Group. Three and a half weeks later Tisch dismissed Derow along with fourteen members of his staff. Their positions, deemed an unnecessary layer, were eliminated.

Shortly after ousting Wyman at CBS, Tisch was asked in an interview if he would sell CBS's publishing arm to help reduce the company's debt. Tisch said no. A few weeks later, on October 24, the *New York Times* reported that CBS had a deal with Harcourt Brace Jovanovich to sell it most of its book publishing operations. The rest of the CBS publishing operations were also eventually sold.

In an interview with *Broadcasting* magazine the same week, Tisch was asked about rumors that CBS might pull out of Trintex, its joint venture with IBM and Sears to develop a nationwide videotex system. "No," Tisch said, "CBS will remain in Trintex. It's just a question of on what basis it will remain in Trintex." Three weeks later CBS pulled out of Trintex.

The broadcasting world didn't know quite what to make of this man of finance, and at CBS people crossed their fingers and hoped that Tisch meant what he'd said when he spoke so reverently of Mr. Paley's "great company" and the CBS family of which he was now so honored to be a part. Had they been searching for clues, they might have read a brief profile of Tisch's operating style published in *Fortune* magazine just after Tisch's CBS boardroom triumph. "It is worth noting," Stratford P. Sherman wrote, "that Tisch's unchallenged reputation as a man of his word depends partly on the lawyerly care with which he sometimes chooses his words. His commitments are often sharply limited. When he says he *isn't considering* something, he is expressing only a transient state of mind subject to infinite later change."

As for CBS News, which had been his personal cheerleading section during his rise to power at CBS, what Larry Tisch had to say was clear, and emphatic: "We're not touching news."

Howard Stringer, like Van Sauter, had ambitions that his considerable charm deftly obscured. When he heard about the boardroom coup of Larry Tisch and William Paley, he was at home with a bad back and heavily medicated, but that didn't deter him from handicapping the race for Sauter's soon-to-be-vacant job. With Paley back, Stringer figured, the old guard would be in ascent: "Everyone under sixty will be in trouble."

That meant Stringer, for one. At forty-four he had spent half his life at CBS, much of that time in close association with pioneers of television journalism, and he had a rather complex relationship with his many professional fathers. They'd been the mentors of his youth, they had taught him his trade, and Stringer regarded them with affection. On the other hand, he came to believe that both time and Howard Stringer had passed the older generation by at CBS News, and he developed an acute generational awareness that sometimes seemed to border on obsession. During the Sauter-Joyce era, when intergenerational tensions were acute, Stringer was often torn between those who'd reared him professionally—among them Perry Wolff, Bill Moyers, and Bill Leonard—and his own instincts, which were, in fact, quite attuned to Sauter's. In a way Howard Stringer personified the conflict racking CBS News: He wanted desperately to push the organization into the new video age, but he remained hypersensitive to the reversionary chorus of the old believers. He would champion *West 57th,* while at the same time begging Bill Moyers to stay at the network. (At one point he even mulled over the possibility of having Moyers on *West 57th.*)

Stringer's premonition about the ascension of the old guard was quickly borne out. After Sauter was fired, Stringer was put in charge of the news division, but only on a provisional basis. A search committee composed of Walter Cronkite, Frank Stanton, and Richard Salant—a triumvirate of elders—was formed to find a permanent successor to Sauter, and no one fell easily to the assumption that it would be Howard Stringer. Quickly the names of candidates began to flood in. David Burke, Roone Arledge's respected assistant at ABC, was put into contention (at least in the rumor mills), and there was strong sentiment for bringing Bud Benjamin back from his fellowship at Columbia University to serve as interim president; even Don Hewitt was mentioned as a possibility. Bill Paley talked to Moyers about the notion of a kind of dual presidency, a "publisher"/"managing editor" scenario with Moyers in one of the roles, which Moyers found interesting but declined.

For his part, Stringer was in a tricky political position. He had been the immediate subordinate of the two least popular presidents of CBS News, and his fingerprints were all over the various policies and decisions that had brought the place twice to revolt. It was Stringer who had re-created the *Evening News* in Van Sauter's image, alienating the Cronkite crowd; it was Stringer, yielding to the imperatives of management, who had defended Joyce, alienating some of the *Evening News* crowd. Stringer had been part of the decision to kill the *Morning News,* and it had been Stringer who had kept the lists during the rounds of cutbacks. Although he considered himself the natural candidate for the future of CBS News, representing the young correspondents and broadcast producers, the distrust and anger felt toward Stringer in the fall of 1986 were broad and knew no generational bounds.

But if the formation of a committee to find a permanent president was a snub to Stringer, he was unbowed, and almost immediately he began to campaign openly for the permanent appointment. Like any good politician, he brought many promises to the campaign.

He made grand postrevolutionary gestures, telling people on

the inside, and reporters on the outside, that he would bring back some of the people who'd been fired. He said that he would divide up Sauter's lavish quarters in the new studio and parcel them out to producers for office space. He said that he would eliminate at least two vice-presidents' positions. And he promised to bombard the network with program ideas, which he would take directly to Tisch himself—no Black Rock layering for him. He even spoke of taking over an entire night of prime time (Tuesdays, a terrible performer for CBS Entertainment) for news programs, perhaps using some of the ideas (such as a nostalgia show that would follow up on news stories of the past) he'd kept to himself during the dark times in case he jumped to another network.

"I'm just so fucking liberated!" he said at the time. "My God, there's no one here to say no, at least, not at the moment."

Some found the blatancy of Stringer's campaign distasteful, but Stringer shrugged it off ("What have I got to lose?") and dashed blithely ahead. He was happy to do what Sauter had found too demeaning nine months earlier, actively wooing the old guard. Within seventy-two hours of Sauter's ouster, Stringer had set up lunch or dinner appointments with Cronkite, Bud Benjamin, and Bill Leonard for the following week, and he had talked by phone with Fred Friendly and Dick Salant. His tactic was to massage the older generation, while reminding the younger generation of the vision he'd demonstrated on the *Evening News,* on *West 57th* and in a slick, instant documentary about drugs he'd produced that summer called *48 Hours on Crack Street,* which was vintage Stringer.

Stringer had been right to worry about his standing with the old guard. Early in the campaign Cronkite, Stanton, and Salant met for lunch to discuss the prospects. When they got to Stringer there was unanimity: Howard Stringer would be a disaster for the news division. That message had to be gotten to Tisch somehow, and it fell to Cronkite, a member of the board, to inform the new chief executive that Stringer would be exactly the wrong guy to head CBS News after all that had happened. There was just too much bad blood.

Bill Leonard, one of the flag bearers of the old guard, was asked at the time about Stringer as a potential president, and his diplomatic answer pretty well expressed the feelings of a generation. "Howard's young," Leonard said. "He's a very good producer. I'm not sure he's not better off as a producer. I've never said this to him, we talk all the time and I'm really terribly fond of him, but I get the sense that he hasn't, that it's not his style to . . ."—Leonard struggled for a delicate way to put it—"I don't know how to say this, but he's been sort of laid-back as the number two guy there, as a manager, so that his impression, his impact on the organization is not as much as it maybe should have been."

What Leonard was trying politely to articulate was the belief of many at CBS News that Howard Stringer had had a chance to stand up for the values of the system that had nurtured him, and he'd passed it up. Dick Salant was less reserved on the subject.

"He's a dishonest son of a bitch," Salant once said of Stringer. "He's so ambitious that he's manipulative."

Stringer had, in fact, shown remarkable skill at dissociating himself from the more unpopular features of the Sauter-Joyce regimes, even while he served as their principal architect; it was something that everyone in the organization realized, but it was somehow forgiven in Stringer, with his easy laugh and engaging personal manner. Of the old guard, perhaps Salant was the least seduced by Stringer.

"I'll tell you about Stringer," Salant said in the fall of 1986. "I never knew him well, but I had one adventure and one experience with him that I found unforgivable." Salant recalled that Stringer had asked him to lunch during a particularly anguished moment at CBS News under Sauter and Joyce. Salant had no reserve of admiration for Sauter and Joyce, but what he heard from Stringer that day disturbed him. "He spent the entire lunch distancing himself from all the turmoil," Salant said, "tearing down Van, tearing down Ed, saying all the things that were happening weren't his fault. That was typical of him." It was a trait that Salant couldn't abide, a refusal to own up to one's actions, and it was one of Stringer's key weapons of survival.

But it wasn't up to Dick Salant to choose the next president of CBS News, or Frank Stanton, or Walter Cronkite. It was up to Larry Tisch. And Larry Tisch liked what he saw in Howard Stringer.

Stringer, whose instincts were good in such matters, sensed the value of spending time alone with Tisch, and just a week after the takeover Stringer proposed to Tisch that the two of them take a little trip together. The *Evening News* had been out on the West Coast for most of the week, and it was going to Washington for the Friday broadcast. Stringer suggested that it might be a nice chance for Tisch to meet some of the troops. Of course, it would also be a nice chance for Tisch to get to know Howard Stringer. Tisch liked the idea, and he suggested that the two of them take the train down to Washington. It would give them time to talk.

It had been an exhausting week for both men, but Stringer was nonetheless surprised when as soon as they settled into their seats, Tisch suggested that they take naps and proceeded to fall sound asleep. This was very disarming for Stringer, who didn't quite know what to do in such a circumstance, so he dozed off himself. He awoke a few minutes later in a panic, sure for a moment that three hours had passed and that he had slept through his big chance with Tisch. But there was still plenty of time, and Tisch awoke from his catnap refreshed and ready to start firing questions.

Stringer had come prepared. He'd studied flow charts, derived from Sauter's "Doomsday Book," and was ready to explain to Tisch all the jobs at CBS News as well as cost figures and the budget for the coming year. Apparently it was just the sort of conversation Tisch had in mind for his first serious encounter with the prospective president of CBS News, and Stringer had been clever enough to perceive it. Tisch made Stringer wait another month (and put him through great anxiety), but Tisch had his news president. Stringer was appointed to the job on October 29.

Stringer had the job, but not necessarily the hearts and minds of the organization, and he knew that the place was deeply divided in its feelings about him. So he continued his campaign through the fall. He began to draw up preliminary plans for an hourlong *Evening News* broadcast, which, unlikely as it was to come to fruition, gained him valuable points for right thinking. And as ambivalent as he was about Bill Moyers, Stringer made a frenzied late-hour effort to keep Moyers at CBS.

Stringer shared Sauter's and Lack's frustrations regarding Moyers, and he sensed that the institution had generally wearied of Moyers's Hamlet routine. So there were times when Stringer expressed relief that after five years of incessant agitation, Moyers planned once again to return to public television. But there was also reason to keep Moyers. He was a potent institutional symbol, and if his departure from CBS News was in some part a personal protest over lost values, then his remaining could be taken as a kind of validation of the Stringer regime. Also, to his credit, Stringer had genuine feeling for Moyers; he knew that for all Moyers's crankiness, there really was no more powerful thinker on television, or so devotedly serious a journalist. If Stringer could interest Moyers in one of his new programming ideas, the combination of Moyers's weight and Stringer's production touch had fetching possibilities.

Perhaps the most compelling reason to try to keep Moyers, however, was the fact that Larry Tisch and Bill Paley wanted him. Both men appreciated the prestige that Moyers lent the institution, and each met privately with him in the late fall of 1986 in individual efforts to persuade him to stay. Moyers, who did not mind the wooing at all, protested to Stringer that his commitments at PBS obliged him to leave, and indeed, they did: One part of his deal at PBS, a $1 million grant from a public television fund, was contingent upon his making a clean break from CBS. But that didn't stop him from listening as Stringer presented various program packages as enticement. Stringer offered Moyers a weekly hour, and he later said that Andy Lack had even offered to produce a show with Moyers and the *West 57th* correspondents. Moyers listened, and at several points Paley and Tisch were convinced that he would stay. But Stringer, who'd seen the act, knew that Moyers would leave, and in November he did.

(Moyers was to have a glorious first year in public television, putting ten times more programming on the air than he had in his final year at CBS News. Yet by the fall of 1987 there were signs of new disenchantment. Moyers was frustrated by the fact that many of the PBS stations refused to air some of his programs in prime time, finding them too narrow in their appeal, and soon enough there began to circulate a rumor that Moyers would be returning, once again, to CBS. Moyers denied it; Stringer said that he'd asked Moyers and continued to hope for his return.)

Stringer had lost Moyers, but there were other victories, including one that in other times would have seemed a matter of routine. With the November off-year elections coming up, Stringer petitioned Black Rock for a full night of airtime to cover the returns, and Tisch and Jankowski consented. It was an easy enough decision, Tuesday night being one of CBS's worst nights competitively in prime time; but Stringer took his victories where he found them, and he milked for all it was worth the fact that CBS alone was opting for "wall-to-wall" election coverage. In fact, it was an uplift for the organization, just the right signal from Tisch and Stringer, and spirits ran high at the Broadcast Center that night.

Stringer was in his element, performing the traditional presidential chore of hosting the top brass from Black Rock, Tisch and Jankowski, in the second-floor VIP room at the Broadcast Center. Almost unnoticed by most staffers amid the excitement and festivity was the presence in the Stringer party of someone who had nothing to do with that night's election coverage, or with journalism at all, but who was about to exert a significant influence upon CBS. He was a mild, balding, middle-aged man named Thomas C. Flanagan, a management consultant from the accounting firm of Coopers & Lybrand. Less formally he was known at Black Rock as "Larry's big stick."

On October 1, 1986, three weeks after CBS became his, Laurence Tisch had distributed to the entire company a two-paragraph memorandum that a good many CBS employees likely glanced at and deposited into the nearest trash can. It was a densely worded communication announcing that CBS had engaged the management consulting group of Coopers & Lybrand "to assist in a review of financial and operating systems and procedures within CBS." The memo said that the group would "address such aspects as paperwork flows, financial systems, data processing functions, reports, forms and organizational structures in order to obtain an understanding of overall operations." The inelegant phrasing of the memo obscured its portent: CBS was about to be "Tisched."

CBS had been a certain kind of company, with its polished granite Eero Saarinen headquarters, the priceless artworks lining the walls of its corporate suites, the personal chefs for senior executives, and not one but two corporate jets. It was a place of style and class, not only for the executive corps but for most employees. Pay and benefits were more than generous, medical facilities were provided at both Black Rock and the Broadcast Center, and there was even a company store where employees could buy CBS products at a discount. It was a place to spend a career, a lifetime even.

But to Larry Tisch, CBS was first and foremost a business—and heretofore a rather poorly managed one. Tisch, who was not only a shrewd investor but a hard-nosed businessman who prized efficiency, was astonished at the fat, layers and layers of it, that he found at CBS. With its huge corporate staff, its public relations and personnel departments, its legal and investor relations staffs, CBS seemed to think that it was IBM or General Motors. As a member of the board of directors Tisch had thought that the cutbacks instigated by Thomas Wyman were "piddling," as he put it, and he was determined to put the company in order.

Through the month of October 1986 Thomas Flanagan and his band of management consultants worked their way through Mr. Paley's empire, scrutinizing flow charts, counting heads, and, when supervisors showed up with preliminary lists of cuts, calmly instructing them to go back and try again—for bigger lists. Flanagan himself was stationed in an office on the twentieth floor, with no nameplate on the door and no one to answer his phone, a symbol of austerity in an environment where abundance had been the norm. When Flanagan moved in, his floor-mates had included the CBS personnel department. By the time he left, there was plenty of room; personnel was cut by seventy people during his stay. The CBS medical department, comprising two doctors and four nurses who attended on-the-job injuries and illnesses, was shut down. The CBS store was closed.

Twenty-six CBS pages, mostly young people just out of school and looking for entrée into the business, were fired, saving CBS their hourly wages of $6 (and no benefits). Hit, too, were the company's in-house social services operations, including the minority development program, causing concern that it would become that much harder for blacks and women to make careers at CBS. (It was that concern, perhaps, that prompted a memorandum from Tisch to the whole organization some months later reaffirming the company's commitment to the "principles of equal employment opportunity"; few noticed that the four-paragraph memo was, word for word, a repeat of a 1983 memorandum issued by Thomas Wyman). Orders went out to all department heads that newspaper and magazine subscriptions were to be curtailed, private copiers eliminated, limousines and first-class air travel banned, new furniture and rented typewriters prohibited.

Even the United Way was "Tisched." Wyman had been a member of the national board of the charity, and CBS had been a major contributor. In early October a United Way officer wrote a memorandum expressing concern about that year's CBS contribution. "The CBS corporate and employee campaign appears to be an unqualified disaster," he wrote, adding that "it was Tisch's policy that giving is a private matter and not the responsibility of private companies." The year before, the combined CBS corporate and employee contribution from CBS to the United Way had totaled nearly $850,000; the charity official estimated that in 1986 it would probably plummet to $200,000.

Suddenly CBS was a different company, and inside CBS the dreamy aura that had surrounded the return of Paley and the rise of Tisch quickly began to fade. People began to mull aloud some hard facts about Tisch's ascent, the most eye-opening being that he had taken over the company. True, it wasn't technically a takeover in the eyes of the regulatory agencies because Tisch hadn't gone beyond the 25 percent level in his acquisition of CBS stock. (For that matter, Tisch owned only 24.9 percent of Loews, the Tisch family holding company.) No one doubted any longer that CBS was Tisch's, and all at once there was a firsthand, if somewhat embittered, admiration for the storied shrewdness of Larry Tisch. He had indeed, as Wyman had warned, taken over the company at bargain-basement prices— twenty-three dollars a share less than Ted Turner had offered, thirty-three dollars a share less than Marvin Davis had offered, and forty-three dollars a share less than the Coke proposal. "In the world of takeovers," said *Manhattan Inc.* magazine, a year after the Tisch coup, "his bagging of CBS is the steal of the century. An all-timer."

It also began to dawn on people that Larry Tisch was doing precisely those things that had caused so much panic over the Turner takeover attempt—namely, dismantling the company. Although he said he wouldn't sell publishing, or Trintex, he did; and in the fall of 1987, in a move that clearly articulated the changed nature of CBS, the company sold its prized records division, a wing of CBS that was not only hugely successful, but was almost as old as its broadcasting business, and as much a part of the company's character and identity. After the sale of

CBS Records to Sony, CBS was quite literally a different enterprise—no longer a media conglomerate, but a relatively small broadcasting company with a lot of cash. People began to realize that besides the price that Tisch had paid for control of CBS, there was another difference between a Tisch and a Turner takeover: Had Ted Turner bought CBS, the network would at least have had the Cable News Network, Turner's two twenty-four-hour news services, an enterprise that not only was profitable but might have propelled CBS News into an enduring position of leadership in broadcast news.

Still, as far as news was concerned, Tisch had kept his word in those early-autumn weeks, and the news division remained largely sanguine about its new owner. Just days after taking control of CBS, Tisch paid a visit to the beleaguered *CBS Morning News,* shaking hands with one and all ("Call me Larry," he said) and expressing his admiration for everyone involved in the broadcast. It was a real tonic for the tormented news staffers, and it was the same way when Tisch met the *Evening News* troops in Washington, on that trip with Stringer. Correspondents and bureau managers elbowed one another aside to get a place at a supper that Tisch was hosting for the senior members of the Washington staff. They rented a private room at Il Giardino, a restaurant near the bureau, and it was basically a love feast, Tisch just tickled to be with the famous CBS News stars, and the famous CBS News stars just giddy over having an owner so impressed with and respectful of their work (sentiments that Tisch once again expressed).

At a lunch with the correspondents the next day, without Tisch present, Stringer mentioned that on the way down, Tisch had expressed keen interest in the news budget. In fact, he'd talked about hardly anything else. There would be restraints at CBS News, Stringer said, but he'd gotten Tisch's word that any reductions would come from attrition; there would be no more layoffs.

Toward the end of the year Tisch proposed to Stringer that the two of them take another trip together, this time to Europe, to get a look at the overseas operations of CBS News. It was a memorable journey. In London nearly the whole bureau turned out for an evening gathering; in Rome the bureau chief arranged for Tisch to have a private audience with the pope. In Moscow

Tisch and Stringer visited the one-man CBS bureau, and again Tisch was impressed.

Back home, Dan Rather asked Stringer how the trip had gone, and, Rather recalled, Stringer told him, "Personally it went well." But Stringer also had reservations about the trip. Tisch had begun to ask him a lot of questions. How much should a news division cost? Were all those people really necessary? "He thinks we're spending money we shouldn't," Stringer told Rather, "and it could be trouble."

On the second Wednesday in January 1987 the board of directors of CBS met, as it did every second Wednesday of the month, and voted to make Paley the permanent chairman and Tisch the permanent chief executive of CBS. Back in September, after Wyman's ouster, Tisch had said that he wasn't interested in the job on a permanent basis, that he wanted to serve the company only until a search committee of the board had found someone suitable for the job. But somehow, the board's executive search committee didn't get very far. In fact, it never even interviewed a single candidate for the job.

Over at CBS News, Howard Stringer was asked for comment on the board's move. "I think it's the signal everyone's been waiting for," Stringer said. "It means the company's instability is over and its future is in creative hands. That's very exciting. It's a very significant milestone. It seals off the turbulence of the past few years, and not a moment too soon."

But even as he said those words, Stringer had more than a clue that the turbulence was anything but over and that what was coming next might make what had come before seem like a Sunday drive.

Two days earlier, on Monday, Tisch had come to the broadcast center to help launch the *Morning Program,* the entertainment-information show that replaced the *Morning News.* Afterward he held a meeting with Stringer and his senior staff. Tisch talked about getting money out of the news division. It was simply spending too much for what it delivered. He'd seen the figures, the estimates that the CBS News budget would approach $300 million in 1987, up from $89 million in 1978. Even allowing for inflation, Tisch figured, the CBS News budget shouldn't be much more than $200 million and certainly not more than $250 million. What did all those people do? How did they spend so much money? Wasn't much of the cost, $90 mil-

lion to $100 million of it, spent on maintaining CBS News oper-
ations around the world solely to service the twenty-two-minute
Evening News broadcast?

The CBS News budget had swelled disproportionately to
other parts of the business in the preceding decade, but there
had been reason for it. The huge cost of new technologies, such
as satellites, had to be borne in order to remain competitive.
Also, there had been the talent raids of the early Arledge era at
ABC, in response to which the salary scales at all three network
news divisions had risen by huge leaps; the talent payroll at CBS
accounted for nearly one fourth of the news division's budget.

Still, it had been a sobering visit by Tisch, and what made it
difficult was that he had not specifically ordered any reductions.
He had only questioned, as was his way. But it was clear to
Stringer that he was being asked to reduce the already stream-
lined news division even more. And apparently it wasn't just
trimming that Tisch wanted. He had seemed to suggest a cut as
high as $100 million. Stringer found himself playing a terribly
risky game, trying to design a cutback in the news division that
would satisfy Tisch without committing political suicide.

In the next few weeks Stringer and his staff quietly considered
various cutback plans, measuring the potential damage to news
gathering and drawing up plans to restructure the news division.
The staffers, meanwhile, carried on in sweet ignorance of the
blade suspended overhead. Then, on February 6, the *New York
Times* carried a front-page story reporting that Tisch had asked
CBS News for substantial new cuts, up to $50 million, "prompt-
ing a drastic reassessment of the worldwide CBS News operations."

The story caused a panic at CBS News, and even Rather was
stunned. He'd been told the night before that the *Times* planned
a story, and since the European tour with Tisch Stringer had
been telling Rather that the chief executive wanted major
changes in the news division's spending. But no one expected
cuts of the dimensions that the *Times* reported. A $10 million or
even a $15 million reduction could be sustained without major
readjustment, but anything more than that would necessitate a
fundamental reassessment of the organization's purpose. The
staff was so shaken that Rather, feeling the weight of his role,
announced that he would be a reporter that day. He would go

to Black Rock himself to confront Jankowski and Tisch and get to the bottom of the story and would report back that afternoon.

So Rather went to Black Rock, and that afternoon he reported back. It was a big moment, the news staff gathered expectantly in the silent newsroom, as Rather gave his report. He'd gotten assurances from Tisch, Rather reported, that the *Times* story was "ludicrous." That was the same word used by George Schweitzer, Jankowski's public relations aide, who also denied the story. Denial was the official management position that day.

Significantly, though, Howard Stringer did not deny the story. He issued a memo to the staff saying that "there may be ways to do our work more efficiently." He added: "The economic times we live in demand that we look at that problem and we have been discussing it here for some time already. We will continue to do so and we will need the help of everyone in the division as we do. Be patient and continue as I know you will even under this latest cloud to put on the best broadcast in journalism."

One month later CBS News announced the biggest cutback in its history, affecting every broadcast, every bureau, and every level of the news division. Two hundred and fifteen people, including fourteen on-air reporters, lost their jobs. The news division budget was cut by nearly $33 million.

It was the third major cutback in sixteen months, and by far the biggest; this time CBS had cut past the fat and into muscle and bone. Staff had been cut by about 15 percent, as big a reduction as the first two cutbacks combined. Rather had been right about the fundamental changes that such a cut would require: CBS News closed its bureaus in Seattle, Warsaw, and Bangkok. Chicago was reduced to two correspondents; Paris, to one. Larry Pintak, the CBS correspondent who'd covered the Middle East, was fired. In all Germany there were no CBS News correspondents or producers, just a camera crew.

The retrenchments showed. Stringer and his staff developed an operating philosophy known as "intelligent risk," which was another way of saying that each day when they decided how CBS News would cover the world, they first decided which stories they could most likely get away with *not* covering. So, when the pope traveled to Latin America later in the year, the CBS Rome correspondent, Bert Quint, was in the pope's travel party by himself. ABC and NBC each had full crews along for the trip, as well as people on the ground in Chile, taking the temperature of the local scene and preparing advance stories. CBS had no one waiting in Chile; Mike O'Connor, the balls-out Latin America correspondent (and one of the few network correspondents who was fluent in Spanish), had been fired. And on the plane the pope did the worst thing he could have done, as far as CBS News was concerned: He made news. He made it clear that he intended to throw down the gauntlet to Chilean leader Augusto Pinochet on the matter of human rights, an action that was sure to have explosive effect in the oppressed, heavily Catholic country.

When the pope's party arrived, ABC and NBC hit the ground running, but CBS had to scramble for free-lance stringers even to get the story on the air and was badly beaten. Such incidents, once cause for deep humiliation and heated postmortem debate, increased disturbingly. When the Democratic candidates for president held their first debate in Houston, CBS had no reporter on the scene. When the West German government announced that it would yield on a defense matter, smoothing the way for arms talks between the United States and the Soviet Union, CBS had to report the story out of Washington.

"It is inevitable, and it is already here, that we are going to cover less news," said Richard Cohen, the *Evening News* senior producer in charge of foreign coverage. "We have fewer people, less resources, fewer options, which are spread thinner. We're not going to go to the places that we used to go. We'll do fewer discretionary stories. We had done a piece on the rising Arab fundamentalism movement; those are the analytical stories that really separate us from other news organizations. But we're so busy covering our ass on hard news, we have fewer and fewer people to send places to get those kinds of stories."

The previous two cutbacks, under Joyce and Sauter, had caused pain and angry outcries, but this time there was something else, something sorrowful and poignant about the cuts. For one thing the cuts came against the backdrop of a CBS newswriters' strike during a particularly cold and dreary March, and to get in and out of the Broadcast Center each day, CBS journalists had to walk through the picket lines manned by their friends and associates. As one CBS News correspondent put it, "It's the *Little Shop of Horrors*. It's the only place in journalism where you have to cross a picket line to get fired."

There were a hundred heartbreaking stories. Ike Pappas, who'd covered the globe for CBS since 1967, who'd done two tours in Vietnam for the network, was up in New York with family and friends on the day the cuts were announced. Pappas, who was based in Washington, was in town to be inducted into an honor society of the Greek Orthodox Church for his meritorious career in news, in a ceremony that was to be attended by Jimmy Carter. It was a big moment for Pappas and his family. As he was out at Adelphi University in Long Island picking up his son, he checked in at the office and found out he was fired.

On the night the dismissals were announced, Andy Rooney sat at home thinking about the state that CBS had come to and about the sudden invalidation of the career of Ike Pappas. Once again, he expressed the sentiments of many when he told a caller, "This guy Tisch put his money in this company, but I put my life into the company, and so did Ike Pappas, and so did a lot of other people. I own that company, Tisch does not own that company, that's the way I feel. It's Ike's company more than it is Tisch's company."

"I was in the United States infantry during the war," said Perry Wolff, "and the saying was, 'The bitching army is the fighting army.' It's when they turn sullen that you'd better pull them out of the lines. And now what you'll find is just sullenness. We don't want to talk about it, we're all battle-fatigued, shell-shocked."

Down in Washington, Bill Leonard was numb. "Something's happening there," he said. "They're destroying the fucking place. It is heartbreaking. It's not just the news division. The company, the company is destroyed. Its soul . . . never mind its soul, the *body* is gone out of it. My grand illusion in life was CBS. I had an illusion about it, not entirely based on nonsense. It was a place. A place worth wanting to be at. It isn't a place to want to be at anymore."

That weekend Richard Cohen went up to the Rhode Island home of his wife's parents (his wife is the CBS correspondent Meredith Vieira), and he couldn't get the trauma off his mind. He kept thinking about the crossroads CBS had come to and the path Tisch had taken. "Mr. Tisch," he wanted to say, "you have to decide what you want to preside over. If you want to preside over a homogenized, lowest-common-denominator news service that will give you pictures and somebody else's editorial judgment, it's your candy store. But the great CBS tradition was a reportorial tradition, people on the ground telling you what their eyes and ears tell them. . . ." Then he decided he would do it. On Sunday morning he got up out of bed and drafted an essay, a sort of open letter to Larry Tisch. He read over what he'd written and liked it, and he decided to take bold action. He'd send it to the editorial pages of the *New York Times*.

Stringer was convinced that the cutbacks had gone as well as they could; they'd been handled sensitively, he thought, the worst was over, and come Monday, CBS News would get back to work, leaner and meaner, but still intact. But something happened over the weekend to change that. The *New York Times* was preparing a story about the feelings of anger and betrayal rippling through the organization, feelings that were vaguely aimed at Stringer and, more specifically, at Tisch. The *Times* called Tisch at home on the day after the cuts, and the executive seemed disturbed at the suggestion that anyone thought he'd betrayed CBS News. He expressed some astonishing things that day, including his theory that "a lot of these people are lucky to be laid off right now because there are other jobs available in broadcasting." He had not betrayed CBS News at all, he said. Then he made a startling statement. He hadn't ordered the cuts at all; they'd been designed, in fact, by Howard Stringer, who, Tisch thought, was behaving responsibly by doing so.

"I never said to Howard, 'We have to cut the budget at the news division,' " Tisch said. "That's the truth. Howard called me a month ago and said, 'Larry, I've got some ideas on restructuring the news division. It'll take me about thirty days to put them together. I said, 'Fine, Howard, I'll be happy to go over them with you.' " Tisch said that he had gone so far as to remove the names of six correspondents from Stringer's original list.

Asked about the Tisch statements over the weekend, Stringer issued a blunt "No comment." In fact, he was furious at Tisch and in profound fear of the reaction that the *Times* story was likely to cause. He was right to worry. When the story appeared the next day, the organization went into shock. Whom should they hate more, Stringer or Tisch?

Stringer made a show of his own anger that day, as he covered the rounds, assuring people that he hadn't ordered the cuts himself. "Sure," he said, "what did I do, look up Coopers &

Lybrand in the phone book?" He also reminded people of
Tisch's creative treatment of facts in the past. But it was clear
that Stringer would have to do something, and all day long he
threatened to quit. There was a rush of the old, perverse excitement for a day, the hint of doom, half threat, half promise, that
had become a kind of narcotic at CBS News in the last two years.
Stringer went to Black Rock, accompanied by Mike Wallace and
Don Hewitt, themselves in a somewhat awkward position because of their public support of Tisch. ("I believed then, and I
believe now, that Larry cares very much about the news division," Wallace had said on Friday night. "Having said that, I'd
like to better understand from him what he has in mind. The
cuts have gone somewhat deeper than I had expected. And I
think that a few of us would like to better understand where he's
heading.")

   In fact, one *60 Minutes* staffer said that there had been discussion of sending Wallace and a crew to Black Rock to give the
60 Minutes treatment to Tisch; the idea was quickly dropped.

   Amid all the excitement of that day, Richard Cohen let it be
known around the *Evening News* that he planned to send his
piece to the op-ed page of the *New York Times,* and along the way,
Dan Rather decided that it was time for a gesture of his own. Not
quite his own actually. He joined with Cohen in Cohen's article,
and put his own name to it. The *Times* printed the article on
Tuesday, and it sounded loudly.

   The headline was FROM MURROW TO MEDIOCRITY, and from the
first word, the tone was particularly biting:

> More than two hundred CBS newspeople will not be com-
> ing to work this week. Or next week. Or whenever the grace
> period ends and the new lean, mean CBS News officially
> begins. Two hundred and fifteen people to be exact.
>
>   Ike Pappas won't be in the Washington bureau anymore.
> After two tours in Vietnam and two decades with CBS, Ike
> has put down his notebook. Actually, it has been taken from
> him. Mike O'Connor, who has slogged through every hell-
> hole in Central America trying to make sense of an impossi-
> ble story, now has to figure out why he's gone. Paris
> cameraman Alex Brauer, who brought war and politics—
> historic events from around the world—into America's liv-
> ing room, lost his job too. Fired. Half the people on the

traffic desk—who rush every piece of tape shot anywhere in the world to where the viewer can see it—are lost. And the list goes on.

Cohen was a convincing writer—he had written some of Rather's speeches—and his editorial was a damning indictment of the hard-line imperatives of Larry Tisch.

"Let's get one thing straight," the article continued. "CBS Inc. is not a chronically weak company fighting to survive. CBS Inc. is not on the skids. CBS Inc. is a profitable, valuable Fortune 500 corporation whose stock is setting new records. But 215 people lost their jobs so that the stockholders would have even more money in their pockets. More profits. That's what business is about."

CBS News would from that moment on cover less news, the article said, and then it went on to pose a direct challenge to Tisch: "We are determined that our new corporate management not lead us into a tragic transformation from Murrow to Mediocrity. We take our public trust very seriously. It is why we are journalists in the first place. Our new chief executive officer, Laurence Tisch, told us when he arrived that he wanted us to be the best. We want nothing more than to fulfill that mandate. Ironically, he has now made the task seem something between difficult and impossible."

Tisch was said to be incensed over the article, which, on top of the other stories of the last couple of days seemed to have completely reversed his public standing from savior to villain; his new nickname at the Broadcast Center, which stuck for months, was "Short, Bald and Greedy"—clumsy, but telling. Stringer, too, was angry over the Rather move, calling it a typical example of the institution's "Samson quality," but that was nothing next to the response of Tisch supporter Don Hewitt, who said of Rather's article: "Murrow to mediocrity made me puke. That's a scale, right? Murrow to mediocrity? Put Rather on the scale."

It had been something of a grandstand; but in fact, Rather and Cohen were right, and everyone, newsman and newswoman, in the organization knew it.

CBS News, as conceived by Salant and Cronkite, was dead. It had been mortally wounded by the abandonment of values and the absence of corporate will to maintain a serious and independent worldwide news-gathering organization no matter what the cost, to repay the public for the use of the airwaves, even at a loss. What had replaced it was a corporate view that began with Wyman and Jankowski, was exacerbated by the economic storms that buffeted network television, and culminated in the arrival of Larry Tisch. As Bill Moyers later said, the economic forces and the rounds of cutbacks hadn't killed CBS News, but the corruption of its vision had. "Even if he hadn't cut a single penny," Moyers said of Tisch, "CBS News would still not be CBS News."

There were, for a moment following the Rather article, faint hopes of a new revolt. The essay had the ring of the manifesto to it, as had Moyers's essay in *Newsweek,* and everyone remembered the effect that the Moyers piece had had. And like Moyers's article, the Rather editorial was published on the eve of a board meeting. The rumor quickly circulated that Walter Cronkite would quit the board in protest of the cuts, an action he had, in fact, seriously considered.

Cronkite had experienced disillusionment and alienation toward the news division even since Sauter's arrival and had been acutely aware of his own diminished presence there in the era of Dan Rather, but he still felt closely associated with the place. He was shocked by the cuts and worried that Tisch wanted to turn the news division into a wire service. He didn't think that Tisch understood the news business, and he feared that the financier-turned-broadcaster believed CBS could have a really fine news organization by being simply a packager of news, rather than a worldwide news-gathering organization—a "retailer," as Cronkite put it, rather than a "wholesaler."

Cronkite had been talked out of quitting the board by Bill Paley, who believed that such a protest really would tear things apart, although Cronkite told friends that he found himself harboring the morbid thought that if Paley weren't alive, he could get off the board and be done with it. But his friends inside CBS News were pressing him for action, and Cronkite felt obliged to do something. The board meeting was on Wednesday, and on Monday and Tuesday he tried frantically to convene another rump session of the board, like the one before the Paley-Tisch takeover. But this was a new era. Tisch didn't want an informal meeting of the board and scotched the idea. Instead, he promised Cronkite a full hour during the board meeting to vent his spleen. Cronkite took nearly two. He railed about news, how it wasn't a pencil-pushing business, and he pulled out an old newsman's analogy. "My God," he said, "you can go by any fire station in town and look in and see these guys playing checkers and say, 'God damn it, why do I have to pay to have ten guys in there to sit playing checkers all day?" But when the fire comes, you'll wish you had thirty in there, not ten. And you find out that you've gotten down to ten because that's all you think you can afford to pay. This is journalism. We're not a production line. It doesn't work that way."

Tisch and the rest of the board listened politely and then moved on to other business. They'd heard it before from Cronkite. He was a newsman; of course he would feel that way.

But Cronkite was determined not to let it go at that. He went home and stewed, and his friends continued to pressure him to do something. Then a possible way to save CBS News struck him. He wrote a long memorandum to Tisch, in which he proposed that CBS commission a study, a blueprint for news in the 1990s and beyond. There would be meetings and seminars, a chance for everyone to have a voice, and Larry Tisch would be asked to endorse publicly the master plan that resulted, so that any future cutbacks would have to fall within the parameters it established.

The memo also called for "council of elders" or "wise men," such as Bud Benjamin, Bill Leonard, Frank Stanton, and Dick Salant, whose duty it would be to monitor the situation and to hold Tisch to his commitment.

Cronkite presented his plan to Tisch. The chief executive said that it contained some nice ideas, some important thoughts. Then he rejected it.

In an unexpected way Larry Tisch and Howard Stringer made for a happy partnership. Stringer did not possess a kamikaze instinct, he wasn't likely to immolate himself in protest, and Tisch had come to trust him. Stringer happened to agree with Tisch that there had been a lot of deadwood around CBS News. He certainly wouldn't have initiated the cutbacks, but once he realized that reductions were what Tisch had in mind, he went about the matter with some vigor (too much vigor, detractors thought). Van Sauter had once said that the thing he'd be remembered for after he left CBS News was bringing financial stability to the place, and he'd been roundly criticized for the statement; it wasn't the sort of thing CBS News presidents were supposed to think, much less say. But this was a new age, and Stringer was determined not only to survive in it but to prevail.

He seized upon the cutbacks—suggested by Tisch, designed and implemented by Stringer—as an opportunity to zero-base CBS News and build from the ground an organization that he believed would last into the future. In blueprints, anyway, it was a vision that suited Larry Tisch just fine.

There had always been two kinds of people at CBS News: journalists who worked at television and television producers who worked at journalism. Stringer was a television producer who worked at journalism. He had never been a daily reporter, and his instincts were not those of a reporter but those of a producer. He was a gifted producer, probably the best at CBS News, and at the *Evening News* he'd adapted his skills nicely to the imperatives of daily reporting. Still, in his heart he was a producer, and his master plan as president of CBS News showed it.

Stringer's vision for CBS News was to make it a kind of company-held production house that would make television shows *based* on news. He'd said from the beginning of his tenure that CBS News would produce its way out of despair. "I'll spew so many things out it'll make your head spin," he'd said, and that was exactly what he set out to do. In the outside world the contemporaries of people like Stringer and Andy Lack were making millions of dollars by producing news-based programs for syndication (Susan Winston had a big Hollywood deal, and so did Steve Friedman, the former producer of NBC's *Today,* and the list went on).

Stringer believed that he could do the same thing inside CBS, and he was brimming with ideas. Besides *West 57th,* there was *Try to Remember,* the nostalgia show that he'd given to Shad Northshield to produce; *48 Hours,* a weekly series of instant documentaries; and *True Stories,* a new program that Andy Lack was developing and that made Bill Moyers wince—dramatizations of real events. There was precedent for such an enterprise at CBS News, a rather embarrassing series in the 1950s called *You Are There,* which had been hosted by no less a personage than Walter Cronkite. Still, the precedent did not allay concerns that *True Stories* represented the ultimate triumph of Hollywood values at CBS News.

As for the *Evening News,* Stringer had a plan for that, too, though it would be a little harder to pull off. When Sauter had become preoccupied with other matters in mid-1986, Rather and the Tom Bettag-Richard Cohen wing of the *Evening News* staff had hardened the broadcast considerably. They loathed the parody of moments television it had become and nearly brought the *Evening News* back to the no-nonsense hard newscast that it had been. They spoke of the "reformation" and of the public trust. Rather told interviewer Mary Hart, somewhat disingenuously, "We were hard news yesterday, we're hard news today, and we'll be hard news tomorrow."

The direction they'd taken mortified Sauter, who believed that the cadre that had seized the *Evening News* would run it into the ground. NBC and ABC were gaining, Sauter had warned, "And unless CBS gets marketing smart, product smart and is committed to winning, I think this can go right out the door on them. It can happen awfully quick." Stringer agreed ("If I hear the words *public trust* one more time, I think I'll shoot someone"). But the "reformation" had the weight of Dan Rather behind it, and nothing could shake it. "I think Dan, in his gut, really wants to be tough and serious and hard," Richard Cohen explained at the time. "He wants to be Walter Cronkite, frankly. I think Dan was willing to put a lot of that on ice with Sauter on the theory that if you could just buy some success and buy some security, someday he could get back to his agenda. I think Dan has decided to go back to that agenda regardless of security. I think Dan has shaken the sleep from his eyes."

After Stringer became president, he used the Tisch cutbacks and the restructuring of CBS News to try to temper Rather's power. The *Evening News,* which had once led a revolt against a president because it couldn't get enough A List correspondents on the air, was stripped of its producers, and all staffers were put into an organization-wide pool. Basically the organization was to return to the structure that had existed before Sauter and Joyce arrived, and the idea was that there would be no such thing as a *Morning News* producer or an *Evening News* producer, just CBS producers who worked for all broadcasts.

But the cutbacks had taken a heavy toll, the plan collapsed after just a couple of months, and Rather and his broadcast emerged stronger than ever. Stringer and the anchorman were cast into opposite camps over the direction of the broadcast, and everyone in the organization knew it. Stringer wanted to move the broadcast back in the direction it had been headed when he was producer—a softer, more entertaining newscast, something, in fact, in line with the Sauter vision. Stringer didn't pull out Sauter's old locker-room speech about how the *Evening News* wasn't the *New York Times* or the *Washington Post* or the *Los Angeles Times* but a mass-audience tabloid, but that was how he felt. "There's a certain joy in reaching out to the mass medium," Stringer explained. As for the idea that CBS News knew what was best for the audience, Stringer said, "That kind of elitism is what drove me out of Britain."

Tom Bettag resisted the plan, though, and he had the power of the anchor behind him. Bettag had proved an especially attentive and loyal Rather acolyte, their bond having been strengthened by yet another in the long series of strange incidents involving Rather. In October 1986 Rather had been walking down Park Avenue when two nicely dressed men jumped him and brutally beat him. Rather told police that he knew neither of the men, he had no idea why he had been attacked, and he could offer no clue except that the attackers had kept asking him, "Kenneth, what's the frequency?" It was a weird and, to some, darkly humorous episode that prompted more Johnny Carson monologue jokes and caused all manner of seamy speculation inside CBS News. But Rather was physically hurt by the incident, and embarrassed, and Bettag had been especially helpful throughout. Rather, who valued loyalty above all, was grateful.

As for going back to the sort of broadcast that Stringer had produced, Bettag said, the *Evening News* would have to be a broadcast that people in the organization could be proud of. Stringer took the comment as a personal insult. It was an open secret that Stringer desperately wanted to replace Bettag, but it was also known that he didn't dare try it. It became a test of power and will, and when Stringer and his wife, Jennifer, were out in Wyoming for summer vacation, Rather showed his spurs. Angry at the late filing of a report on the death of Fred Astaire from the Los Angeles bureau, Rather testily summoned the producer-reporter of the piece, David Browning, and the Los Angeles bureau chief, Jennifer Siebens, to New York for a very public dressing down. Siebens was a special favorite of Stringer's, and with Stringer out of town the action was seen as a direct slap at the news president.

On the matter of Bettag, Rather was emphatic. He told the *New York Times* that Tom Bettag was his producer, and if he hadn't made that clear enough by now, he'd gladly take out a billboard proclaiming the fact, and he told Kevin Goldman of *Newsday*, "Tom Bettag is my last executive producer."

To Stringer, that was an unnerving prospect; he believed (and he was by no means alone) that Bettag, for all his editorial strengths, was too much the anchorman's yes-man, a potentially dangerous relationship. The fear was that instead of acting as a check on Rather's worst instincts, which was part of the charge of the executive producer, Bettag too often confirmed and defended those instincts. And that fear was embarrassingly realized in an incident that occurred on the *Evening News* in the early summer of 1987.

The incident involved a story out of Beirut. A former ABC correspondent named Charles Glass, who'd distinguished himself with his coverage of a hijacked TWA jetliner in 1985, had disappeared in Beirut while researching a book. After several anxious weeks, Glass was released by his captors. He told a dramatic story of how he got away from his captors, but there was a great deal of skepticism about the "escape," and speculation that Syria, hoping to score points with the United States, had arranged for the journalist's release. For the networks, it was a competitive news story, and Glass took special pains to make himself readily available to his former employer, ABC; the other networks accused ABC of inappropriately staking proprietorship over a legitimate news story, even of deliberately blocking satellite access time to NBC and CBS. Rather, the relentless adversary, ill-advisedly allowed his competitive fervor to spill over onto the air. Instead of merely noting that Glass's "escape" had been questioned, Rather seemed to challenge whether Glass had been kidnapped at all. "A young American who says he was a hostage has turned up free and talking out of Beirut tonight," Rather told his *Evening News* viewers. "Journalist Charles Glass said he was kidnapped two months ago . . ."

If CBS News had reason to believe Glass had faked his kidnapping, it didn't report it; instead, Rather simply cast doubt upon Glass, and left it at that. Many journalists, including several of Rather's colleagues inside CBS, were appalled. ABC's Ted Koppel said that Rather's insinuation was "beneath contempt."

"If Rather is saying Glass in some way concocted his kidnapping," Koppel said, "I find that to be an outrage. Either Rather did not write that himself and did not read the script before he went on the air, or he has lost all sense of proportion." Predictably, Tom Bettag came to Rather's defense, explaining that the circumstances of Glass's case were "murky" and therefore justified Rather's characterization. Few inside or outside CBS agreed.

As doubts about Rather deepened, in the background there stood, beckoning, an immediate alternative in the person of Diane Sawyer, who had just come to a new agreement with CBS that raised her salary to $1.2 million. Her extravagant pay raise was beyond the limit that Stringer had set for the negotiation, but Tisch was so eager to keep her that he personally approved the final offer, which also was said to include the promise of an expanded role (such as an anchoring position) in the future. It happened that Rather's new hard-edged *Evening News* was becoming a ratings sieve, and around the Broadcast Center, Tisch was widely quoted as having asked Stringer, "Why do I have to pay the number-one salary to the number-two anchorman?" Tisch denied the quote (which was printed in *Washingtonian* magazine), but it had an impact; inevitably, the rumble at CBS News was that Rather might soon surrender part, or maybe all, of his anchor chores to Sawyer.

Stringer was not convinced that Sawyer was the answer, and he was said to be a little annoyed at her apparently open campaign for the job (which included, it was said, telephone calls from Sawyer's boyfriend, former under secretary of state Richard Holbrook, to Larry Tisch, suggesting that Stringer wasn't according Sawyer a proper amount of attention). However, Rather's ratings slip, which put the *Evening News* in third place for much of the summer of 1987, gave Stringer some leverage in dealing with his anchorman—and he did consider replacing Rather with Peter Jennings, whose ABC contract was up in 1987.

Stringer knew from research that a new system of measuring ratings, which was to take effect in September, favored Dan Rather. No one knew why, it was one of the mysteries of the quirky ratings universe, but Stringer wasn't about to question a break like that. He determined to wait until the switch in rating systems put Rather back in first place and then, acting from a position of supposed strength, he would recapture the broadcast from Rather and Bettag and put in a producer who would execute the Stringer vision.

The new ratings system—"people meters"—kicked in in September, and it did, in fact, have the predicted effect. Rather was back in first place. But in the interim something had happened that already gave Stringer the edge in his battle of wills with Rather. The infamous episode in Miami, when Rather had walked off the set and caused himself and the network huge embarrassment, was said to have chastened the anchorman. The slow, steady pace of the changes that Stringer was slipping into the broadcast suddenly quickened, and although Bettag remained producer for the time being, it was clear that Stringer had reclaimed the *Evening News.*

The broadcast became a new incarnation of the moments newscast that it had been under Stringer's hand. Rather's hair had been allowed to go nearly fully gray, softening his on-screen persona just as the sweaters once had; and the broadcast itself became just what Stringer—and Sauter, for that matter—would have it be. Suddenly, Rather was seldom alone on the *Evening News* set. He chatted via satellite with newsmakers and his correspondents on the air—"Bruce Morton, what do you make of all this?"—giving the broadcast a local *Eyewitness News* feel.

The NFL players' strike, for example, became a long-running and prominently played story throughout the fall of 1987. On the December night that Soviet leader Mikhail Gorbachev arrived in Washington for his summit meeting with President Reagan, the Rather broadcast found time in its twenty-three minutes to cut to the lighting of the national Christmas tree, *live.* And the reinvented *Evening News* reached its essence, perhaps, in the story of little Jessica McClure, the Texas girl who'd fallen into a well and whose plight had captured the nation's attention. On the first night of the drama the Jessica McClure story not only led the broadcast (giving it the weight and status of being the most important story in the world that night), but to illustrate it, Rather, pulled out a piece of pipe and held it before the camera, explaining to viewers that this was just the sort of pipe young Jennifer had fallen into. It was a truly telling scene, the heir to Murrow and Cronkite sitting at that hallowed desk with a piece of pipe in his hand, and it became more so in a moment. Putting the pipe down, Rather lifted his arms above his head and explained that young Jessica had been in just such a position when she fell down the well.

No tabloid could have done it better.

Chastened, Rather retreated—literally. Feeling too much at

the intersection of CBS News, Rather moved his office in the late autumn of 1987 from the edge of the newsroom up to the sumptuous office formerly occupied by Van Sauter—the "luxury box" overlooking the newsroom, which had been vacant since Sauter's ouster.

All these elements of Stringer's master plan for CBS News meshed nicely with Larry Tisch's sensibilities. Although Tisch himself was unsophisticated in matters of journalism (personally he probably would have preferred the harder-edged newscast), he was pleased with Stringer's program ideas, which, not coincidentally, provided a very inexpensive form of prime-time programming for a network that was failing in the entertainment competition.

Giving Stringer free rein to carry out his vision also granted Tisch some relatively easy PR to counter the bad press he'd received during the cutbacks earlier in the year. Tisch had been wounded by the criticism (especially Rather's "Murrow to Mediocrity" piece), and in an effort to improve his public relations, he had turned to John Scanlon, the public relations master—the same John Scanlon hired by CBS to help turn the tide of public opinion during the Westmoreland affair. The apparent effect of Scanlon's advice was soon evident, in another incident involving Jennifer Siebens, CBS's Los Angeles bureau chief.

After the cutbacks, when the loss of staff was putting a particular strain on the bureaus, Siebens was asked about morale in the news division. "The only thing I think can turn [the low morale] around is some believable signal from Mr. Tisch," she said, to show that "he really is not interested in dismantling the organization. My desire would be to have him state what his vision of a network news division is. He says it should make money. How much money? And when we know how much money we're supposed to make with whatever resources he will give us we can put two and two together and figure out whether that network news organization can continue to be the best, as Mr. Tisch has repeatedly said he wishes it to be. But he seems to be caught between a purported desire for excellence and a proven desire to make money."

Her views were published by *Broadcasting* magazine, and a couple of days later Siebens got a call at work in Los Angeles. It was Tisch. Had she really said those things? Yes, Siebens said, she had. As Siebens told the story to associates, Tisch then asked, "Where in the hell did I ever say that CBS News should make money?" She told him that an objective assessment of his history at other companies, as well as his brief history at CBS, seemed to speak for itself. Tisch said that he was sick of being quoted out of context and that his only concern was waste. And for several long minutes Tisch and Siebens engaged in a conversation about the "gilded cage" that Paley had built for CBS News, with Tisch trying to convince the young newswoman that he wasn't interested in dismantling it.

It was a stunning tactic, having the head of the company directly confront an employee who'd give a "damaging" quote, and the organization saw the fine hand of John Scanlon written all over it. Many noted its irony, too: The man who'd once been hired to sell the CBS News side of the Westmoreland case to the public was now selling the head of the company to CBS News. That was just the beginning. It was determined that part of Tisch's public relations problem stemmed from the perception (wholly accurate) that Tisch was a financier, not a broadcaster, so Tisch embarked on an active campaign to build his image into that of a broadcaster-statesman. He gave speeches (written by David Fuchs and a Tisch adviser) at national broadcasting conventions, and in one memorable week he addressed both a gathering of journalists at Columbia University and a committee of the United States Congress, essentially denying that the new managements at the networks constituted a threat to the public trust.

In the Columbia meeting Tisch, surrounded by a phalanx of public relations advisers, again offered his assurances that he intended CBS News to remain a vital and independent organization. But he focused on the seemingly irrational growth of the organization's budget through the 1970s and 1980s, from $80 million to $300 million. Such a leap couldn't be defended, Tisch said, but it could be explained: Every other year CBS News blithely increased its staff to cover elections, but when the election year was over, the organization lacked the will or discipline to let the new people go and instead absorbed them. Tisch did not mention that one of the men who'd accompanied him that day, Howard Stringer, had originally come to CBS News as part of an election-year buildup and been allowed to stay on.

Scanlon eventually faded from the scene, but Tisch's public relations effort continued, handled deftly by an extremely clever

longtime Tisch associate, Jay Kriegel, who'd helped bring Scanlon to Tisch. CBS News staffers began to notice Kriegel's increasing presence as he set about fashioning Tisch's new image,
which was particularly form-fitting as it pertained to CBS News.
When a reporter ran into Tisch on a flight from New York to
Washington and began to ask questions about his plans for CBS
News, Kriegel, who was seated next to Tisch, neatly intervened
every time the conversation strayed into potentially sensitive
territory. At CBS Kriegel became very involved, even attending
program meetings; it was a sign of where things had come to
that Howard Stringer would say of him, "Jay Kriegel is the best
friend that CBS News has at the moment."

And so it was a man immensely concerned about his image to
whom Howard Stringer presented his master plan in the fall of
1987. Tisch was amenable. He gave the go-ahead to Northshield's *Try to Remember* pilot, and over the objections of the CBS
Entertainment executives, he put Stringer's *48 Hours* instant
documentary series in the prime-time lineup beginning in early
1988 and gave his promise to let it live long enough to build an
audience. (The series was to be anchored by Dan Rather, which
was a clever Stringer tactic; with Rather as anchor, Stringer's
new show was guaranteed fairly free access to *Evening News* resources, rather than the opposition that new CBS News efforts
usually were accorded.) Personally Tisch was partial to news
programs—he loved the Northshield show—and CBS Entertainment was not exactly lining the network shelves with hit shows
that would warrant keeping Stringer's ideas off the air.

For Stringer, the commitment to his programs was a major
triumph. CBS News had, in January 1988, three hours of prime-
time programs; ABC News, in contrast, had one hour, and NBC
News had none. And in a major boost to morale, CBS News was
handed back its full two-hour morning time period after the
disastrous entertainment show *The Morning Program* was canceled. The new morning news show, called *CBS This Morning*,
presented Stringer with new headaches (including the fact that
his first two choices as male anchor refused him), but the return
to the news division of seven and a half hours of time each week
was a significant victory.

And Stringer made certain that his new ally received credit for
this development, going so far as to arrange interviews with
Tisch for television reporters. "I think our news division is of

such high quality and capable of turning out such high quality programming, it's incumbent upon us to deliver that to the American people," Tisch said. "That's part of the mission of CBS."

In late 1987 and early 1988, Stringer and Kriegel devised a major public relations campaign designed to convince the world that the biblical disasters of CBS News were over, that CBS News was back on top, that the tumult and controversy was an old story. Key to this strategy was Dan Rather, the "lightning rod," who had been the most visible symbol of CBS's turmoil, and who would have to be the symbol of the new age of calm and prosperity that Stringer and Kriegel were trying to sell.

The new instant-documentary series *48 Hours* provided a handy vehicle for this PR campaign. For one thing, it truly did represent a triumph for the news division—another hour of prime time—and it provided a chance for the rank and file to expand their energies, to get a chance to report for or help produce an hourlong documentary each week; it gave a genuine lift to morale. And Dan Rather was to be anchorman.

Rather had retreated into a shell of silence since the Miami incident, staying out of the papers, and out of controversy, for five months. Stringer, Kriegel, and the new publicist for news, Tom Goodman, knew that reporters would leap at the chance to talk to Rather if he made himself available, and in January, they set him loose, timing his "release" to coincide with the inauguration of *48 Hours*. The plan was for Rather to talk about the new program and to emphasize that the troubles and controversies were behind him and the organization. That is what he did, and that is what was written by TV columnists across the country. Tom Shales of the *Washington Post* wrote an adoring piece about Rather, friendly beyond the wildest dreams of even Stringer, in which Rather explained away virtually every controversy he'd ever been involved in. Things were looking up, Rather was better than ever, CBS News was back.

Two weeks later there came another Rather incident. The CBS News political team had been working for weeks on a report about Vice President Bush's inconsistencies on the subject of the Iran/contra affair, and Bush, leading other Republican presidential contenders in the polls, was eager to bury the issue. The CBS staffers put together a tough, lengthy report on the matter, making a strong case against Bush—too strong, they believed,

for him to dodge. Bush's camp refused to grant an interview for
the piece. However, they said that the vice president would
happily appear on Dan Rather's broadcast live—a tried-and-true
ploy used by politicians when they could get away with it, because it allows the politician control over what goes out over the
air.

At CBS, it seemed worth the gamble. A strategy was devised
that, on paper, seemed likely to counter whatever feints and
moves Bush's people had planned for the live encounter. The
Evening News would turn over up to half of one night's broadcast
to the Bush-Iran/contra matter, giving the story more weight
and significance than any story had been given on the *Evening
News* since Walter Cronkite did a special report on Watergate
fourteen years earlier. The segment would begin with a tough
five-minute taped report—a video indictment of Bush, really—
and then it would cut to Bush and Rather live. Let the vice
president try to get out of *that*.

But Bush turned the tables. Not only did he not answer
Rather's questions, he seized the opportunity to attack Rather—
even reminding him (and the millions of CBS viewers) of his
six-minute walkout in Miami. The more Bush danced and
dodged, the more flustered and angry Rather became. His voice
rose, he became fiercely combative, and at one point yelled at
the vice president: "You made us hypocrites in the eyes of the
world!"

The news staffers at the CBS Broadcast Center were stunned
by what they were seeing. They'd prepared an important and
compelling piece of journalism that was utterly obscured by the
fact that their anchorman had apparently lost control. Viewers
telephoned CBS and its affiliated stations by the thousands, so
many calls that the telephone company had to reroute many of
them. Affiliate station managers were outraged, and the newspapers had a field day. *Time* magazine put Rather on the cover next
week, with the caption "The Ambush That Failed." Once again,
Dan Rather was back on the front pages. Ironically, the incident
eventually had its intended effect—it focused attention on
Bush's involvement in the Iran/contra affair. But in the short
term, it had the effect of taking the bloom off the new PR campaign for CBS News. It was another Dan Rather incident.

What bothered some was not just the occurrence of one more
Rather "incident"—those, at CBS News, are as expected as

storms on the Texas plain—but the underlying philosophies
that caused it. The *Evening News* had a good, thorough piece on
Bush, but instead of simply airing that report, the broadcast
tried to create a television event, a "moment," so to speak, and
it backfired. That the Rather-Bush confrontation spun out of
control was, in retrospect, utterly predictable. "We put a stick
of dynamite to fire," said one *Evening News* producer, "and we're
surprised that it exploded?"

There was one individual, however, who thoroughly appreciated the Rather-Bush encounter for the television moment
that it was, so much so that he wrote an article about it for the
Los Angeles Times. "It was marvelous political theater," wrote Van
Sauter. "A classic barroom brawl with heavyweights had made
its way onto television. Finally."

In all, it had been a remarkable first year of the Howard Stringer
era at CBS News. The new news president had not only weath-
ered draconian cutbacks but had used them to begin to shape
the institution to his vision. It was not the vision of Cronkite and
people of Cronkite's thinking, who longed for a CBS News that
blanketed the world with first-rate newspeople and strove to be
the *New York Times* of broadcasting, but that CBS News had long
since vanished, forever.

Out in California, where he was now producing entertainment
shows for syndication, Van Sauter had to smile. Stringer's master plan to save CBS News, a scaled-back news-gathering operation with an emphasis on programs, had more than a familiar
ring, and one didn't have to scratch very hard to find the image
of Van Sauter just beneath the surface. The plan for the future
of CBS News was genuine reach-out-and-touch-someone Sauterism, the television of moments. Stringer's program slate—
West 57th, *48 Hours*, the Northshield program, Lack's *True
Stories*—consisted of commercial prime-time shows designed to
attract a wide audience. And the *Evening News* had finally become the broad-reaching video tabloid Sauter had wanted.
Sauter was gone, but Sauterism had endured.

In the end Van Sauter had won.

Index

PETER J. BOYER was born in Los Angeles and spent his youth on the Mississippi Gulf Coast. He attended the University of Mississippi and completed his undergraduate studies at UCLA. While doing graduate work at the University of Southern California, he joined the Associated Press, where he first began to write about television.

He worked for the *Los Angeles Times* from 1981 to 1985, writing about the entertainment industry and as a national correspondent in the South, and was also the television critic for National Public Radio's *Morning Edition.* He joined CBS News as a media critic before becoming the television correspondent of the *New York Times.*

Mr. Boyer lives in Tappan, New York, with his wife, Kari Granville Boyer, and their children, Samuel and Eleanor Jane.